The Temple of Solomon

The Temple of Solomon

"In His Temple doth every whit of it utter His glory"
(KJV Psalm 29:9)

"In His Temple everyone says 'Glory' " (NKJV Psalm 29:9)

"To behold the beauty of the Lord and to enquire in His Temple"
(KJV Psalm 27:4)

"One greater than the Temple" (Matthew 12:6)

"A greater than Solomon is here" (Matthew 12:42)

KEVIN J. CONNER

Published by City Bible Publishing
9200 NE Fremont
Portland, Oregon 97220

Printed in U.S.A.

City Bible Publishing is a ministry of City Bible Church (Formerly Bible Temple) and is dedicated to serving the local church and its leaders through the production and distribution of quality materials.

It is our prayer that these materials, proven in the context of the local church, will equip leaders in exalting the Lord and extending His kingdom.

For a free catalog of additional resources from City Bible Publishing please call 1-800-777-6057, or visit our web site at www.citybiblepublishing.com.

ISBN 0-914936-96-4
Australian ISBN 0-949829-18-8

Australian Distribution

Waverley Christian Fellowship
1248 High Street Road
Wantirna South
Victoria 3152
Phone: 613-9801-2155

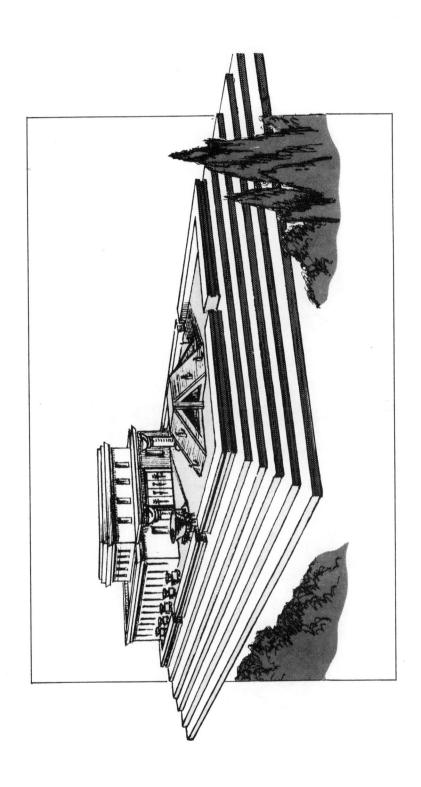

THE TEMPLE OF SOLOMON
TABLE OF CONTENTS

SUPPLEMENTAL CHAPTERS ON THE TEMPLE

FOREWORD

There are four special structures mentioned in Scripture which were given by inspiration as to their pattern to men of God.

Each of these structures were intended to be habitations of a temporary nature relative to the redeemed people of God. The pattern given of each was given by Divine sovereignty and all were built according to that pattern by human responsibility. The end result was the evident presence and glory of God coming to dwell with His people.

These four distinctive structures were (1) *The Ark of Noah,* (2) The Tabernacle of the Lord, generally spoken of as *The Tabernacle of Moses,* Moses being the builder, then (3) *The Tabernacle of David,* undoubtedly given to him by revelation and generally known by that name, and (4) The Temple of the Lord, generally spoken of as *The Temple of Solomon,* Solomon being the builder under God. It is especially with the last that our text is concerned.

Much has been written over the years on *The Tabernacle of Moses* and there are a number of good and sound textbooks dealing with this fascinating structure. Christians are much more familiar with this Divine habitation.

Very little has been written on *The Tabernacle of David.* This seems to have been overlooked as a truth in Scripture, even though there is great foreshadowing of the Gospel era therein. Also, the Commentaries have a divided opinion over the Tabernacle of David as to whether it speaks of the Davidic Kingdom and House of David and his dynasty or whether it speaks of the Davidic order of worship established by David on Zion. Some expositors see that both kingdom and worship orders were involved in the expression *"The Tabernacle of David".*

Again, when it comes to the structure of *The Temple of Solomon,* very little seems to have been written on this subject. This also has been a neglected area of truth.

Undoubtedly, one of the reasons for this neglect of this area of the Word of God is the following.

There are much fuller details given concerning the structure and furnishings of the Tabernacle of Moses than that of the Temple of Solomon. Much of the furniture follows the pattern of Moses Tabernacle and therefore exact details are not always repeated once the pattern of God has been given.

Also there are far fewer chapters given to the details of the Temple than that of the Tabernacle. The Temple embraces all that was in the Tabernacle and more. Perhaps because of these facts, the Temple being basically the same as the Tabernacle, only on a larger scale, study has been neglected on this tremendous subject.

However, even though these things be so, a study of the Temple yields rich and precious truths concerning Christ and His Church. After all, both Christ and the Church are spoken of as being "the temple of God" by the New Testament writers. Therefore, anything symbolic and prophetic of Christ and the Church is worthy of our attention.

This is the third textbook by the author relative to Divine habitations and it completes this triology of studies concerning God's dwelling places amongst His people. The first text is *"The Tabernacle of Moses".* The second is *"The Tabernacle of David".* This, the third text on *"The Temple of Solomon",* is sent forth with the prayer that it will be a great blessing to the reader as it has been to the writer over the years of research on this Divine dwelling place.

All believers look forward to the ultimate fulfilment of God dwelling with men as seen in the Book of Revelation. John saw "no temple" in the heavenly city, the heavenly Jerusalem, "for the Lord God and the Lamb are the temple thereof" and the redeemed shall dwell with God and the Lamb in the city of God for ever!

Perhaps one final word is necessary. For those who have studied the author's textbooks on *The Tabernacle of Moses* and *The Tabernacle of David*, the author asks some forbearance on some areas of repetition and overlapping of truths. Our study of *The Temple of Solomon* will show us that it actually becomes the embodiment of all that has gone before and includes in itself *The Tabernacle of Moses, The Tabernacle of David*, and even the concept of *Noah's Ark*, as well as having its own rich deposit of truth.

Kevin J. Conner
16 O'Brien Crescent
Blackburn South
Victoria, 3130
AUSTRALIA

March 1987

CHAPTER ONE

WHY STUDY THE TEMPLE

THE TEMPLE OF THE LORD, with its detailed description, its furnishings and measurements, sacrificial order, and priestly ministrations is a wonderfully rich and rewarding study for those who desire to enrich their spiritual life.

Men through history have endeavoured to erect beautiful buildings and structures, magnificent in architectural design, beauty and glory, in order to commemorate a name for themselves.

However, none can compare with the structures which God, the Wise Master Builder, designed. These He gave by revelation and inspiration to His servants who built according to the Divine pattern shown to them.

Heathen kings built temples for themselves or their people and priesthood, but all became idolatrous temples, and "the habitation of devils" in due time. But God's temple became the habitation of His glory, His presence, His Spirit. There He communicated with His people. God Himself dwelt in the structures which He Himself commanded to be built. God Himself is the Wise Master-Builder. He gave plans for His house, the house He wanted to live in amongst His redeemed.

Many believers have a reasonable knowledge and understanding of the Tabernacle in the Wilderness with its inexhaustible truths. Few seem to enquire into the same glorious truths as found in the Temple of the Lord, but in greater amplification, along with Divine additions.

Why study the Temple? Why study the Tabernacle of Moses? Why study the Tabernacle of David? Following we note a number of reasons as to why we should study this neglected portion of the Holy Scriptures.

1. BECAUSE the study of the Temple is a most neglected portion of Scripture, yet it is part of the "All Scripture is given by inspiration of God, and is profitable for doctrine, for reproof, for correction, for instruction in righteousness" (2 Timothy 3:16).

2. BECAUSE "whatsoever things were written aforetime were written for our learning" (Romans 15:4). The New Testament writers constantly made use of Old Testament language, passing all to and through the cross, from the natural to the spiritual, from the material to the spiritual and from the temporary to the eternal.

3. BECAUSE the things that happened in Israel were given as ensamples (Greek types), and are written for our admonition upon whom the ends of the age are come (1 Corinthians 10:6,11).

4. BECAUSE Scripture tells us, "In many separate revelations, each of which set forth a portion of the truth, God spoke to the forefathers in and by the prophets . . ." (Hebrews 1:1-2, Amplified New Testament).
   The Temple, as the Tabernacle, is a separate revelation. It sets forth its portion of truth by which God speaks to us also.

5. BECAUSE Christ opened the eyes of His disciples and their understanding as He expounded unto them the things concerning Himself in the Law, the Psalms and the Prophets. This undoubtedly included the temple and its services (Luke 24:26,27,44,45).

6. BECAUSE the writer to the Hebrews said, "In the volume of the book it is written of Me . . ." (Hebrews 10:7; Psalm 40:6-8). The temple and its services are part of that volume and speaks of Christ.

7. BECAUSE the law was a schoolmaster (a guardian) to bring us to Christ. A study of the temple brings us to Christ who is God's perfect temple and in whom all the fulness of the Godhead dwelt in bodily form (John 2:19-21; 1:14-18; Colossians 1:19; 2:9).

8. BECAUSE Jesus came to fulfil all that was shadowed forth and prophesied of in the law and the prophets (Matthew 5:17,18; 11:13). The temple and its whole sacrificial system shadowed forth and prophesied of the sufferings of Christ and the glory that should follow (1 Peter 1:10-12).

9. BECAUSE as we study the external form of the temple, we will discover the knowledge and truth hidden therein (Romans 2:20. Amplified New Testament). The external and the material has passed away, but the knowledge and the truth hidden therein remains. It is unveiled by New Testament truth and revelation.

10. BECAUSE what is spoken concerning the Tabernacle of Moses, the same is applicable to the Temple of Solomon.
    The Tabernacle was "a figure" (Hebrews 9:24), "an example" (Hebrews 8:5), "a parable" (Grk. Hebrews 9:9), and "a pattern" and "type" of heavenly things. So is the Temple of Solomon (Hebrews 9:23; Acts 7:44).

11. BECAUSE the Old Testament period was "the age of the shadow" and a shadow of good things to come. As we follow the shadow we eventually come to the person whose shadow it was, even the Lord Jesus Christ (Hebrews 8:5; 9:9,23,24; 10:1; Colossians 2:17; 1 Corinthians 10:11).
    The purpose of the shadow is to bring us to the substance. The purpose of prophecy is to bring us to the fulfilment. The purpose of a type is to bring us to the antitype. So the earthly temple, as a shadow, is to bring us to the heavenly temple, the substance and the reality of all things.
    The Temple, as the Tabernacle of Moses, was a pattern (Grk. type) of heavenly realities, of the heavenly temple (Revelation 11:19; 15:5).

12. BECAUSE a Divine principle is "First the natural, then afterwards that which is spiritual" (1 Corinthians 15:46,47). We look at the natural, the material, which is temporal, in order to discover by the Spirit that which is spiritual and eternal. The seen brings us to the unseen, the visible helps us to understand the invisible (2 Corinthians 4:18; Romans 1:20).

13. BECAUSE man himself was created to be the temple or dwelling place of God. Sin ruined the temple. God is now restoring man through redemption to be His temple, indwelt by the Holy Spirit of God (1 Corinthians 3:16,17; 6:16-20). Believers, both individually and corporately constitute the temple of God today.

14. BECAUSE the temple was a symbolic and typical representation first of Christ (John 2:19-21), and secondly of the Church (1 Corinthians 3:16,17; 6:16). Believers are spoken of as "living stones", being built into a "spiritual house" as the "temple of the Holy Spirit" (1 Peter 2:5-9). The temple was a prophetic structure. Immaterial truth was hidden in material form to help us understand. The material structure represented spiritual insights.

15. BECAUSE, as will be seen, the earthly temple was a shadow of the heavenly temple. Both the Tabernacle of Moses and the Tabernacle of David were earthly shadows of heavenly things. The same is true of the Temple of Solomon. The true temple is eternal and heavenly. John saw "the temple of the tabernacle of the testimony in heaven opened" (Revelation 15:5; 11:19). The things built on earth were built after the "patterns of things in the heavens" (Hebrews 9:23). Both Moses and David, who received the revelation of the tabernacle and temple in heaven actually saw the same truths.

These, we would say, are the major Scriptural reasons for a study of "The Temple".

Jesus Himself often spoke in parabolic form to the multitudes. However, the disciples knew that within and beyond the parable was eternal truth. Only those who had ears to hear and eyes to see would know the truth veiled within the parable.

So the temple has many hidden truths veiled in it and those truths are brought to light by the Holy Spirit who is the Spirit of Wisdom (Psalm 43:3).
The multitude may never see these truths for it is the glory of God to conceal a matter, but it is the honour of kings to search it out (Proverbs 25:2). The language of creation becomes the language of

redemption. Creation's language is actually God's secret code for either concealing or revealing truth according to the attitude of the hearers (Matthew 13:9-17). Symbolic language reveals eternal truths in the Bible.

Spiritual ignorance may pass the study of the temple as "merely a type", but to the hungry in Christ, the Holy Spirit will take the word line on line, here a little and there a little, precept upon precept and reveal the glory of Christ and His Church (John 14:6; 16:13-16). It is the ministry of the Holy Spirit to glorify Christ. He will do this in our study on the Temple of Solomon.

He Himself said, "In this place (i.e., the temple) is One greater than the temple". And again, "Behold, a greater than Solomon is here" (Matthew 12:6,42). The heavenly tabernacle was a greater and more perfect tabernacle than that Wilderness tabernacle. So the temple of heaven is a greater and more perfect temple than the earthly temple that Solomon built.
Christ is greater than Solomon and all his wisdom and glory because Christ is the wisdom and glory of God personified. He is greater than Solomon's temple in all its grandeur because He Himself is THE TEMPLE, and the wisdom and glory of God manifest in bodily form (John 1:14-18; 2:19-21; Colossians 1:19; 2:9).

Christ Himself is greater than the material building, greater than the articles of furniture, greater than the sacrifices and oblations, greater than the priesthood orders, greater than all. He Himself is THE TEMPLE personified. We come in worship now to Him as a person, not in worship to a building. "Gather My saints together unto Me", says the Psalmist. "Unto Him shall the gathering of the people be", says Jacob (Psalm 50:5; Genesis 49:10). He is the living temple. The living temple is greater than the material temple. The eternal temple is greater than the temporal temple.

Solomon's temple was local, geographical and especially designed for one nation, the chosen nation of Israel. Christ, as God's temple, is the universal temple to whom all nations may come for worship.

Another important truth to keep in mind is this. Even though God commanded the temple to be built and He dwelt therein by a visible manifestation of His glory-presence, Solomon recognized the truth of God's essential attributes.
He said, "Behold, heaven and the heaven of heavens cannot contain Thee; how much less this house which I have built!" (2 Chronicles 2:6; 6:18; Acts 7:49; 1 Kings 8:27).
Here Solomon recognized the attributes of God's Spirituality, immensity of being, omnipresence as well as omnipotence and omniscience. God cannot be limited to temples made with hands, for He inhabits eternity (Isaiah 57:15).

God who is Spirit cannot be confined to the material, yet in His mercy and grace He manifested Himself in the material temple. "The heaven is My throne, the earth is My footstool; where is the house that you build unto Me, and where is the place of My rest? For all those things has My hand made . . . says the Lord . . ." (Isaiah 66:1,2).

The tragic thing was, in the time of Messiah, as also in Jeremiah's time (Jeremiah 7:1-4), the Jews ended up worshipping *the temple of God* and missed *the God of the temple* (Matthew 23:16-22).

It is also noteworthy that God did not inspire men to give full and complete details in Scripture of the temple. God knows that man is a great duplicator and imitator of Divine things. Man would simply repeat the fatal mistake of the Jewish nation and worship a building and miss THE BUILDER of all things.

However, God did give enough details for us to understand the general design and construction of it. The diagrams and sketches provided in this text are simply to give some idea of the architectual skill manifested in the buildings, the decorations and furnishings of the house of the Lord.

In concluding this chapter, it is noteworthy that there are more specific references in the New Testament to the Church being "the temple of God" rather than "the tabernacle of God", although both are true (1 Corinthians 3:16,17; 6:16; Ephesians 2:20-22). The Church is now the habitation of God in the earth.

Thus Solomon's Temple was a type, a shadow and prophetic figure and structure of (1) Christ, (2) the Church, which is His Body made up of individual members, and (3) the heavenly temple and eternal realities, and ultimately of (4) the city of God, New Jerusalem, the eternal habitation of God and His redeemed.

It abounds with spiritual truth and precious gems. All of the glory of Solomon's Temple was but a faint revelation of all the glory revealed in THE TEMPLE, Christ and His Church!

CHAPTER TWO

PRINCIPLES OF INTERPRETATION

Any preacher, teacher or author who sets out to expound the sacred Scriptures must needs be governed, guided and controlled by certain basic principles of interpretation.
This is especially so when it comes to interpreting and expounding those portions of Scripture that have to do with historical and typical things. If these principles are not followed and used properly, then the Scriptures, and more particularly the types, can be made to say anything that the expositor may want them to say.

Many times, when exposition is given concerning typical things as under the Mosaic Covenant, such as the Tabernacle, the Priesthood and Offerings and the Feasts of the Lord, the hearer will ask, ''How does the speaker arrive at that conclusion?'' The same question may be asked concerning the interpretation of the Temple of Solomon.

Hence because of these honest inquiries and the author's strong convictions about having sound hermeneutics, we set forth some of the basic principles of interpretation which will be used throughout this text, and by which the author arrives at various conclusions.

(**Note**: For a fuller treatment of these Principles, the reader is directed to the published text, ''*Interpreting the Scriptures*'', by Kevin J. Conner and Ken Malmin, available from the publishers of this text).

1. **The Context Group of Principles**

    The Context Group of Principles involves the First, Comparative, Progressive and Complete Mention Principles.

    The Context Principle is that principle by which the interpretation of any verse of Scripture is determined upon a consideration of its context, either verse, passage, book or Testament context.
    In our study of the temple we will note the verses, passages and the book and Testament in which the temple is spoken of. All will be considered in the light of the whole Bible. We will consider the historical setting of the temple, where and what was the literal fulfilment of the same in the nation of Israel. Only by doing this can we then move to the typical and spiritual significances that are to be found in Christ and the Church, the people of God today.

    In using the First Mention Principle we will check and see what was meant in the first mention of anything pertaining to the temple. Generally the first mention, either in specific word or concept, gives the truth in seed form.

    In using the Comparative Mention Principle we will compare Scripture with Scripture and bring together the passages that may be contrasted or compared, in order to help our understanding of the temple. This will be so especially in the light of the Old Testament and the fulfilment in the New Testament. This is ''comparing spiritual things with spiritual'' (1 Corinthians 2:13). This is seeing ''First the natural, then afterwards that which is spiritual'' (1 Corinthians 15:45,46).

    In using the Progressive Mention Principle we will consider God's progressive revelation which God gave as pertaining to the temple. The revelation is given line upon line, here a little and there a little throughout the Scriptures.

    Then by use of the Complete Mention Principle we will have considered all the direct references to the temple of the Lord in the Bible. By putting together all of the fragments we will be able to see more fully the truth which God scattered throughout His Word in both Old and New Testaments.

2. **Theological Principles**

There are certain Principles which arise out of Theology and these principles may be grouped together because they have to do with the purposes of God. These Principles are the Election, Covenantal, Ethnic and Chronometrical Principles. They are especially seen in relation to the nation of Israel in Old Testament times, and then seen in the New Testament relative to Christ and His Church. In using these principles the interpreter works from part to the whole and whole to the part.

The Election Principle shows how God elected David, Solomon and the nation of Israel in His purposes in Old Testament times, and then Christ and His Church in New Testament times.

The Covenantal Principle is especially used as it pertains to the Old or Mosaic Covenant and the New Covenant in Christ. Moses and Jesus represent these two covenants. The temple relates also to promises in the Davidic Covenant. The Old Covenant economy under which the temple was given finds fulfilment spiritually and eternally in the New Covenant economy, in Christ and the Church. It is important to recognize that God takes nothing of the Old Covenant to place on the New Covenant but passes all through the cross of our Lord Jesus Christ.
The Davidic Covenant finds its ultimate fulfilment in David's greater Son, the Messianic King, Jesus Christ.

The Ethnic Principle is an important principle also. It has to do with God's purposes in the nations, whether Hebrew, Gentile or the new ethnic, the Church, made up of Jew and Gentile. This is now God's "holy nation" (1 Peter 2:5-9). A proper application of this principle will help us to understand that the temple of the Lord concerned Israel in the Old Covenant, but it pertained to the letter, to the external form. The temple of the Lord in the New Testament pertains to Christ and His Church, but it is after the Spirit, the spiritual and internal reality.

In using the Chronometrical Principle, which has to do with time, we find understanding to discern the "times and the seasons" as set forth in the temple of the Lord. This especially is seen in the month of the temple's dedication, in the Feast of Tabernacles, the Feast of the Seventh Month.

3. **The Christo-centric Principle**

The Scriptures show that Christ is the central person of the Bible. The written Word revolves around Him who is the living Word. He is the hub of the wheel of truth and all truths are as spokes relating to Him.
Therefore, we will see how the temple points first to Christ, the hub of Divine revelation, and then to the church. "In the volume of the book it is written of Me", Jesus said (Psalm 40:6-8). Thus in using the Christo-centric Principle we will see Christ in His temple.

4. **The Moral Principle**

The Moral Principle has to do with the practical lessons or principles which may be applied to a person's life, general conduct and behaviour. In our study of the temple there will be many practical lessons and principles which may be seen and applied to the believer in Christ, who enjoys these spiritual truths in Him.

5. **The Figures of Speech Group of Principles**

There are several specialized principles which may be grouped together because they have to do with figures of speech or extensions of them. Three of these principles are especially noted here, these being the Symbolic, Numerical and Typical Principles.

The temple abounds with things that are used in symbolic sense, and these symbolic elements can only be understood by using the Symbolic Principle. By use of the symbol God used one thing to represent another. In discerning the common link between the symbol and that which is symbolized we discover the truth that God desired to convey. In the temple we have symbolic objects, symbolic garments, vessels, colours, creatures, actions, measurements, etc. All these have to find proper interpretation.

In using the Numerical Principle we will discover the truth God has hidden in His use of certain numbers. Numbers belong to the symbolic grouping also. Thus the building of the temple of the Lord took place in a specific month, over specific days. Various measurements are specified for the temple building, as well as the furniture. All of these things set forth truth which, by the use of the Numerical Principle may be discovered.

The Typical Principle is also of great importance in helping us to arrive at the truth set forth in the temple of the Lord. The temple services were types. In fact, the whole of the temple institution is a typical and prophetic foreshadowing of great things to come. A type is an anticipative figure, a prophetic symbol. In the temple there are typical persons, offices, institutions and events. It is not that doctrines are built on these types, but types are used to illustrate doctrine. The Typical Principle may be used to interpret portions of the temple in the form of an extended analogy between the temple itself and the person and work of Christ. This will be seen in the course of this textbook.

These are the basic Principles of Interpretation applied in this text and the student will do well to keep such in mind as the study continues.

The author has endeavoured to follow these sound principles and thereby avoid extreme, fanciful or erroneous interpretations. The Old Testament Prophets and the New Testament Apostles link hands with the Lord Jesus Christ in the revelation of the temple and its Messianic truth. So may the believer in this great study on the Temple of the Lord.

RESTORATION OF TEMPLE OF SOLOMON BY FRISBEE

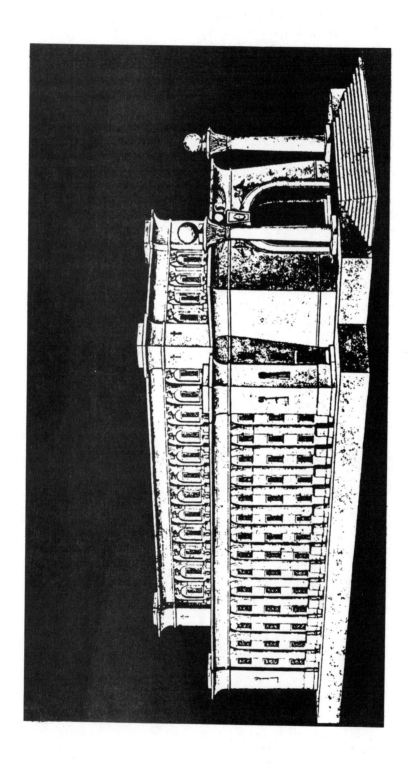

CHAPTER THREE

TEMPLES IN SCRIPTURE

There are a number of temples mentioned in the Scripture in both Old and New Testaments. However, there is basically one interpretation of them all. That is, the temple was meant to be the habitation of God among men.

The related truths of these will be interwoven throughout our study, using Solomon's Temple as our base.

An overview of the major references to temples will be beneficial at this point of our study.

1. **The Temple in Heaven**

   This is the heavenly reality, the archetype, the original and pattern temple. All earthly temples were a shadow on earth, whether the temple of God or counterfeit heathen temples (Psalm 11:4; Revelation 3:12; 7:15; 11:19; 15:5; 16:1, 17; Habakkuk 2:20; Isaiah 6:1-6).

2. **The Tabernacle in the Wilderness**

   Exodus 25-40 gives us the revelation of the Tabernacle in the Wilderness, the Tabernacle of the Lord. It was a temporary "temple" and is spoken of as such in 1 Samuel 1:9; 3:3. However, it was a tent habitation of God and pointed to the more permanent stone habitation of God in Solomon's temple. This dwelling place of God was with Israel over the 40 years wilderness wanderings and then for some years in the land of promise. This Tabernacle was patterned after things in the heavens.

3. **The Tabernacle of David**

   The Tabernacle of David was a tent pitched in Mt Zion for the ark of the Lord until the actual building of the temple of the Lord by Solomon. The details of the order of singers and musicians established there by David are dealt with in 1 Chronicles chapters 15,16,17 as well as 2 Samuel Chapter 6.

   Again, there was that established in this tabernacle which pertained to heavenly things.

4. **The Temple of Solomon**

   1 Kings chapters 5 to 9 and 2 Chronicles chapters 1 to 7 deal with the great portion of details of this temple of the Lord, which pattern had been given to king David. About 400 years later, this temple was destroyed by king Nebuchadnezzar, king of Babylon because of the abominations and idolatries Israel brought into it (Ezekiel chapters 8-10; Jeremiah 7:1-14; 2 Kings 25:8-17). The burden of this text deals with this temple.

5. **The Temple of Zerubbabel**

   This temple refers to the rebuilt temple of the restoration period at the close of the 70 years Babylonian Captivity. The Restoration Books, both Historical and Prophetical are centred around this restored temple (Ezra 1:3; 3:12,13; 4:1-24; Isaiah 44:28; Haggai 2:15-18; Zechariah 6:12-15; Malachi 3:1).

6. **The Temple of Herod**

   The rebuilt temple of the restoration period had been plundered and defiled from time to time under the wars of the kings of the north and kings of the south. Herod, the Idumean, had helped restore and beautify it to win the favour of the Jews during the Roman period of rule. It took about 46 years to build and beautify this temple (John 2:20).

This temple was larger than the temple of Solomon and had additional courts around as shown by diagram. (Note — The reader is referred to Thompson's Chain Reference Edition of the King James Bible for a diagram of this temple and its various courts.)

However, in spite of this fact, the Lord Jesus spoke of this temple as He ministered in it over His 3½ years ministry as "My Father's house". He still recognized the Old Covenant habitation of God in spite of the hypocritical condition of His times (John 2:16-20; 14:2; Matthew 21:12-15).

This temple was destroyed by the Roman armies under Prince Titus in A.D. 70 in fulfilment of Christ's prophetic word concerning its destruction (Matthew 23:38; 24:1-2; Daniel 9:24-27; Luke 19:41-48). The Father's house then became, "Your house is left unto you — desolate!"

7. The Temple of God in Christ

All material temples pointed to THE TEMPLE of God personified in the Lord Jesus Christ.
Even as He was the fulfilment of "The Tabernacle" (John 1:14-18), so He declares Himself to be the true "Temple of God" (John 2:19-21). There is no mistake here. The fulness of the Godhead bodily dwells in Him. He was God's habitation among men in the earth (Colossians 1:19; 2:9).
There was the material temple in Jerusalem on Mt Moriah, but where ever Christ walked, He was the bodily temple, the dwelling place of God in the earth.
In due time the disciples were to forget the Old Covenant material temple and worship God, through Christ, the New Covenant bodily temple, the habitation of God made flesh.

8. The Temple of the Holy Spirit

The Church, the Body of Christ with its members both individually and corporately is also spoken of as the temple of the Holy Spirit.
This is the New Covenant temple in the earth since Christ's ascension and the day of Pentecost with its attendant outpouring of the Spirit. God lives in the believer, in the church, by the indwelling Holy Spirit (Ephesians 2:19-22; 1 Corinthians 3:16,17; 6:16-20; 2 Corinthians 6:16-18).

9. The Temple of Antichrist

2 Thessalonians 2:1-12 speaks of the temple of the Man of Sin, the Antichrist, in which he sits declaring himself as God and demanding the worship due only to God. There is difference of opinion among expositors as to what this temple may be. Whether it is a rebuilt material temple, or whether it is that which pertains to the church is the question. At the appropriate section of this text comments will be written concerning this temple.

10. The Temple of Ezekiel's Vision

The prophet Ezekiel was given a vision of a temple and many details of it are given in his book, chapters 40-48. There is much similarity between it and the temple of Solomon.
Again, much difference of opinion exists among the commentaries as to whether this is a literal rebuilt temple or a symbolic vision only.
Comments will also be made concerning this temple at the appropriate section of this book.

11. The Temple of Revelation

In Revelation 11:1-2 John is given a vision of a temple. He is given a measuring rod and told to use it to measure the temple of God, the altar and the worshippers. Difference of opinion exists over this passage also. Is this a rebuilt material temple or is it a vision of the church?
This will be considered in due time also.

12. The Temple of the New Jerusalem City

The last specific reference to a temple is found in John's vision of the holy city, the new and heavenly city of Jerusalem (Revelation 21-22 chapters).

The city of God has no material temple for ''the Lord God and the Lamb are the temple thereof'' (Revelation 21-23). What need is there for the material, temporal or earthly temple when we have the spiritual, eternal and heavenly temple in God, the Father, and the Lamb, His Son?

13. **The Temples of Idolatry**

There is hardly need to mention these temples but in the light of the New Testament revelation it is helpful to remember these counterfeit temples.

The cities of Asia Minor, as well as the Greek and Roman peoples, followed the path of all idolatrous nations. All generally had a temple or temples to their various deities.

These temples were places of corruption, idolatry and immorality of a corrupted priesthood and people. They became the habitation of demons and perverted religion (Revelation 18:1-2). Such were in stark contrast to the church, the holy temple of the Lord, the habitation of the Holy Spirit.

Babylon had the great Temple of Bel (Daniel 5; 2 Chronicles 36:7).

Ephesus had the great Temple of the Goddess Diana (Acts 19:27).

The Philistines had their House of Dagon, the fish-god (1 Samuel 5:2-3). Practically all cities had their temple to false gods, all being a counterfeit of the temple of God.

Out study on the temple of the Lord will help us to understand the truth that God set forth in His habitation. His desire is that believers everywhere be His holy temple. He desires all to be filled with His glory and His Spirit, and not to become habitation of devils.

DIAGRAM CLASSIFICATION OF TEMPLES IN SCRIPTURE

Heavenly Temple
Heavenly Tabernacle
The Prototype

Tabernacle of Moses	Tabernacle of David	Temple of Solomon	Temple of Ezekiel	Temple of Zerubbabel	Temple of Herod

Earthly material Temples

CHRIST

The Temple of God
Tabernacle of God
Living Temple

THE CHURCH

The Temple of God   Believers
Individually
Corporately
Physical Temples

CHAPTER FOUR

TITLE EXPLANATION AND STUDY APPROACH

A. A Word of Explanation Concerning the Title

It is clearly recognized that the expression "The Temple of Solomon" is not found in the Scripture as such, even as "The Tabernacle of Moses" is not found. The proper designation would be "The Temple of the Lord" or "The House of the Lord".

However, it is also clearly recognized that "The Temple of Solomon" simply means that Solomon built it for the Lord (1 Kings 7:51; 2 Chronicles 5:1; Acts 7:47). "The Tabernacle of Moses" also speaks of the fact that it was the tabernacle built by Moses, i.e., "The Tabernacle of the Lord" (2 Chronicles 1:3).

"The Temple of the Lord", or "The Temple of Solomon", will be used throughout the text interchangeably, as being synonymous.

Whatever other temples are subsequently spoken of Scripture, whether the restored temple built by Zerubbabel, or Ezekiel's visionary temple, or Herod's rebuilt and restored temple, all have their origins, their roots, their foundations in the original temple built by Solomon. There may have been alterations, additions, differences and variations in these temple structures and orders, but all can be traced back to the first temple built for God and that by king Solomon and his workers.

Therefore "The Temple of Solomon" will be used interchangeably with "The Temple of the Lord" simply for the purpose of identification of the human builder of God's house, namely, king Solomon. Solomon's temple is the original and the "foundation temple" for all others.

B. Our Study Approach

The student should familiarize himself with the Scriptures which deal with the lives of David and Solomon, especially those chapters pertaining to the revelation and construction of the temple. The major portions of the Scripture recommended for reading are 2 Samuel chapters 6, 7, 24; and 1 Kings chapters 1 to 10 along with 1 Chronicles chapters 13 to 17, 21 to 29 and 2 Chronicles chapters 1 to 9.

Additional Scripture references will be given in connection with the details of the construction of the temple as the study proceeds.

In the study of the Tabernacle of Moses the approach could be twofold; inward to God, from the outer court to the holiest of all. This would represent man coming to God. Or, the alternate approach would be outward to man, from the holiest of all to the outer court. This would represent God coming to man. The former speaks of faith — man coming to God. The latter speaks of grace — God coming to man.

The same approach is true of the temple. In our study of the temple, we find that the placing of the ark of God and the withdrawal of its staves is the final act in the completion and dedication of the building. This act was sealed by the descending glory-fire of the Lord.

Therefore, our study approach will be as follows:

1. The revelation and pattern of the temple given to king David.
2. The temple structure, site and building.
3. The outer courts and furnishings.
4. The holy place and furnishings.
5. The most holy place and furnishings.
6. The dedication of the temple and the glory of God.
7. The temple priestly courses and ministrations.

For convenience of study, our approach therefore will be man coming to God.

However, it should not be forgotten that it was GOD who took the initial approach. It was God who came to man, not man who came to God. It was God who came to David. It was God who gave him the revelation of both the Tabernacle of David and the Temple of the Lord. It was God who appeared to Solomon and gave him wisdom, understanding, knowledge and insight as well as the skill to build the temple. It was God who gave the pattern of the temple order. Grace is God coming to man, not man coming to God.

The total temple structure is a revelation of the grace, government and glory of God dwelling among His redeemed people, on His terms and in Divine order.

SUPPOSED POSITION OF SOLOMON'S TEMPLE

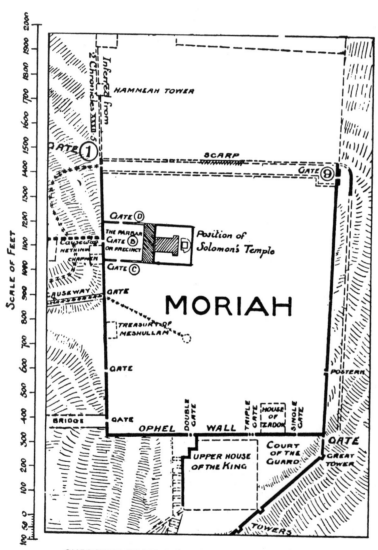

SUPPOSED POSITION OF SOLOMON'S TEMPLE
(SOME LATER CONSTRUCTIONS ARE ALSO SHOWN)

CHAPTER FIVE

DIVINELY INSPIRED HABITATIONS AND MOUNTAINS

When it comes to the overall revelation of God's habitations in Scripture we discover that there are five great structures that God gave by revelation to His people. Four of these are found in Old Testament times, in which God, the Wise Master Builder involved man in the building thereof. One is in the New Testament in which God Himself is the Architect and Builder. These five structures are (1) The Ark of Noah, (2) The Tabernacle of Moses, (3) The Tabernacle of David, (4) The Temple of Solomon and (5) The New Jerusalem, the city of God.

That there is a significant link between these five is evident in the following overview.

A. The Divine Structures

1. **The Ark of Noah** — Genesis 6:14-16

   In these verses we have the brief description of the Ark of safety in Noah's time. It was given by revelation as to its pattern and purpose to Noah. It did not originate with Noah but in the heart and mind of God. It was an ark of salvation for man and beast who entered by the door of that three-storied Ark.

   It symbolized the salvation made available by the Godhead.

	1) The Foundation — symbolic of the Father
ONE ARK YET THREE STORIES	2) The Door — symbolic of the Son (John 10:9)
ONE GOD YET THREE PERSONS	3) The Window — symbolic of the Holy Spirit

   God was with Noah and his family and the animals in that Ark.

   It is significant that there is that in Solomon's temple which corresponds with the Ark that God told Noah to build. This will be discovered in time.

2. **The Tabernacle of Moses** — Exodus 25-40

   There is no doubt about the fact that all that is in the tabernacle — and more — is to be found in the temple of Solomon.

   The Tabernacle of Moses with its outer court and furnishings of the brazen altar and brazen laver finds a vaster fulfilment in the temple courts. The holy place with its furnishings of the golden candlestick, table of shewbread and golden altar of incense finds greater fulfilment in Solomon's temple, in the holy place.

   The same is true of the most holy place with its lone piece of furniture, the ark of the covenant. This finds its richest and ultimate fulfilment in the holiest of all in the temple of the Lord also.

3. **The Tabernacle of David** — 1 Chronicles 15-17; 2 Samuel 6

   The order of singing of praise, the order of the musicians around the ark of God and the worship established in the Tabernacle of David finds its ultimate fulfilment in the temple built by Solomon.

   It was David who received the revelation of both the Tabernacle of David and the Temple of God, and Solomon built the latter accordingly.

   As will be seen, that which was established in David's Tabernacle follows right on and is incorporated in the house of the Lord, Solomon's temple. This tabernacle or tent was undoubtedly pitched in Zion by David by revelation as he served his own generation by the will of God (Acts 7:45-50; 13:22,36).

4. **The Temple of Solomon**

    The greatest significance of this final Old Testament structure is that Solomon's temple is the embodiment in one structure of all that has gone before. It involves the Ark of Noah, the Tabernacle of Moses and the Tabernacle of David in its temple order.

    The details of this will be unfolded in the course of our meditations. Sufficient lesson for us at the present is to see that God, in moving on in ''present truth'' never forsakes previously recovered truth but brings all truth to its fulness in Christ the head, and then in the church, which is His Body.

5. **The New Jerusalem City of God**

    The previous four structures were all designed by God the Wise Master Builder. It was God who took the initiative in each case. However, God did involve His man and His people in the actual building of these material structures. Divine sovereignty and human responsibility flow together in these buildings. But when it comes to the city of God, the new and heavenly Jerusalem, this ultimate structure, it is God Himself alone who is the Architect and Builder — not man (Hebrews 11:10-16; 12:22-24; 13:14; Revelation 3:12; 21-22 chapters). Abraham looked for a city whose builder and maker is God, along with Isaac and Jacob, heirs with him of the same promises.

    When we come to the details of this city of God we find that it is the embodiment of all earthly structures as to their symbolism and truth typified therein.

This city is the city of salvation. It is the tabernacle of God with men. God and the Lamb are the temple thereof. And the interesting details of Solomon's temple will be found to be symbolic and prophetic of the city of God, the city foursquare. Here God will dwell with His redeemed forever in eternal praise and worship.

B. **The Holy Mountains**

    This chapter would be incomplete without speaking of the significance of ''the mountains'' with which each of these structures or Divine patterns were associated.

    ''Mountains'' become very important symbols in the history of the nation of Israel. The Lord God always seemed to be doing something special relative to His people in the mountains.
    The Psalmist says, ''As the mountains are round about Jerusalem, so the Lord is round about them that fear Him . . .'' (Psalm 125:1-2).
    And again, ''His foundation is in THE HOLY MOUNTAINS . . .'' (Psalm 87:1-2). We may think of Mt Sinai, Mt Gerizim, Mt Ebal, Mt Pisgah, and Mt Hermon. But here we speak of the special mountains relative to these Divinely inspired structures.

    1. **Mt Ararat** — Genesis 8:1-5

        When the Flood had ceased, having fulfilment its judgmental purpose and work on the wicked world, the Ark of Noah rested on the mountains of Ararat. Here we have the ark and the mountain! From here the ''new world'' began.

    2. **Mt Sinai** — Exodus 20; Hebrews 12:18-21

        When the revelation of the Tabernacle of the Lord was given to Moses, it came from a mountain, Mt Sinai. We cannot think of the Tabernacle of Moses and the Law Covenant without thinking of a mountain — Mt Sinai.

        Thus we have the Tabernacle of the Lord and the mountain. From here the ''new nation'' of Israel began its national history under the Law Covenant.

    3. **Mt Zion** — 1 Chronicles 15-17; 2 Samuel 6:1-19

        Again, the revelation of the Tabernacle of David cannot be separated from a mountain — Mt Zion. Mt Zion took on special significance from the days of David and onwards because of

the order of praise and worship established there in David's Tabernacle.
Thus we have the Tabernacle of David and the mountain! From here the "new kingdom" of David was established in its Davidic Covenant and glory.

4. **Mt Moriah** — 2 Chronicles 3:1

    Here in the building of the temple of the Lord we are again struck by the significance of its site. The Temple of the Lord was built on a mountain — Mt Moriah.
    Here again we see the temple and the mountain! The significance of this must be taken up in a subsequent chapter.

5. **Mt of God** — Revelation 21:9-10; Revelation 21-22 chapters

    It would be incomplete and inconsistent if we did not see the ultimate structure of God associated with a mountain. John was taken in the Spirit to an exceeding great and high mountain. There he saw the bride city, the holy and heavenly Jerusalem.
    Once more we the city of God and the mountain!

Who can fail to see that God has some great significance in the association of both the structures and the mountains?
The prophets often link these habitations of God with mountains in prophetic significance.
Isaiah the prophet says, "In the last days THE MOUNTAIN of the LORD'S HOUSE will be established in the top of the mountains and exalted above the hills. And many people shall say, Come and let us go up to THE MOUNTAIN of the Lord and to THE HOUSE of the God of Jacob . . ." Isaiah 2:2,3).

Ezekiel, the prophet says, "This is the law of THE HOUSE; upon the top of THE MOUNTAIN the whole limit thereof round about shall be most holy. Behold, this is the law of THE HOUSE" (Ezekiel 43:12).

Haggai the prophet also says, "Go up to THE MOUNTAIN, and bring wood, and build THE HOUSE and I will take pleasure in it, and I will be glorified, says the Lord" (Haggai 1:8).

Here these prophets note "the mountain" and "the house".

The significance and interpretation of these symbols must be left to the appropriate chapters.
Here in this overview we see the association in the mind of God and His people, Israel, of structures and mountains. The pattern, the measurements and details originated with the heart and mind of God. Nothing was left to the mind or imagination of man. Salvation and all of its associated redemptive truths originated in the heart of God, the one and only Saviour of all who believe.

STRUCTURES AND MOUNTAINS

Old Testament				New Testament
Mt Ararat Ark of Noah	Mt Sinai Tabernacle of Moses	Mt Zion Tabernacle of David	Mt Moriah Temple of Solomon	Mt of God City of God Tabernacle of God

CHAPTER SIX

KING DAVID AND KING SOLOMON AND GOD'S HABITATIONS

Before launching expressly into the more detailed study of the Temple of the Lord, it is important to note the relationship of the two kings, David and Solomon, to the three Divinely given habitations of God. These are the Tabernacle of Moses, the Tabernacle of David and then the Temple of God. Here we see them moving with God from tabernacle to temple.

A. King David

1. The Tabernacle of Moses

David, as king, knew the Divine order as set forth in the Tabernacle of the Lord and as established by the prophet Moses from Mt Sinai.

The Psalms of David have numerous references and allusions to things pertaining to this Tabernacle.

The Tabernacle of Moses was the one and only ordained place by God for the sacrifices of sin and trespass to be offered. Here was the functioning priesthood of Aaron and the tribe of Levi. Here redemptive truths were shadowed forth.

However, after the judgment of the Lord on this Tabernacle at Shiloh, in Canaan land, the ark of God was taken into captivity into enemy hands (Psalm 78:55-64; Jeremiah 7:1-15; 1 Samuel 2-3-4-5-6-7 chapters). From then on the full service never seemed to function as before. Judgment fell on the house of Eli the priest and his two sons, Hophni and Phinehas. The ark of God never ever returned to the Tabernacle of Moses. Under Saul's reign, the nation was in a very low spiritual state and little was spoken of concerning the services of the Tabernacle of God.

In David's reign we discovered the Tabernacle of the Lord was functioning on Mt Gibeon with a company of priests and even some singers and musicians as appointed by David (1 Chronicles 16:39-42; 21:28-30; 2 Chronicles 1:1-6).

David knew the Lord and maintained a good relationship with the priesthood and the Tabernacle of the Lord even in those days of great transition.

2. The Tabernacle of David

A study of 1 Chronicles 13-14-16 chapters, along with 2 Samuel 6 reveals the fact that David set the ark of the Lord in a tent (or tabernacle) on Mt Zion. Along with the ark of God there was an order of singers and musicians to praise and thank the Lord continually in sacrifices of praise.

After David offered the initial and dedicatory voluntary offerings (the burnt, meal, and peace offerings — NOT the compulsory trespass and sin offerings which had to be offered at the brazen altar at Moses Tabernacle), only sacrifices of praise and thanksgiving were offered before the ark of the Lord.

2 Chronicles 1:1-6 clearly shows the existence of two tabernacles at the same time; one on Mt Gibeon, the other on Mt Zion. The Tabernacle of Moses and the Tabernacle of David were both functioning on two distinct mountains in the same period of time. The tabernacle at Gibeon had the functioning priesthood order in relation to the brazen altar, and laver in the outer court, as also the golden altar and table and lampstand in the holy place. However, they had no ark of the covenant, only an empty holiest of all!

The tabernacle at Zion had a functioning priesthood in relation to the ark of God, but had no outer court or holy place. In type, it was the transfer of the holiest of all, symbolizing worship "within-the-veil" kind of access and worship before the presence of the Lord.

The details of these things are dealt with in *"The Tabernacle of David"* by the author.

Thus David also worshipped before the Lord here (2 Samuel 6:1-23), after he had brought the ark into the tent according to Divine order.

It was in connection with this tent, or tabernacle, that David became burdened in his heart for a more permanent habitation for the ark of God.

The Lord had given David rest from all his enemies. As David sat in his house of cedar, he expressed to the prophet Nathan his burden for the ark or throne of God. He himself dwelt in a house of cedar while the ark of God was within curtains. Nathan encouraged the king to do what was in his heart. However, God spoke to Nathan to tell David that he would not be able to build God a house. The Lord had moved as a pilgrim from tent to tent and from one place to another. He had never asked any of the tribes of Israel to build Him a permanent house of cedars to dwell in.

Because David was concerned for the house of God, God said that He would build him a house, and would establish his seed and throne and kingdom for ever. All these words were part of the vision to Nathan and given to David involving the Davidic Covenant, which ultimately pointed to the Messiah, the greater Son of David.

The Lord clearly promised that David's son would build A HOUSE for the name of the Lord. These chapters of 2 Samuel 7-8 along with 1 Chronicles should be read and studied in connection with these things.

The lesson for believers is clear. If believers will be concerned for the house of God, the Lord will build them a house also.

3. The Temple of Solomon

Out of the burden of David and the prophetic word of promise through the prophet Nathan, the revelation was given to David for the building of the temple, the house of the Lord. 1 Chronicles chapters 22,23,24,25,26,27,28,29 provide much of the detail concerning the temple order as given to David in writing by the Spirit upon him.

The details of the temple were given to Solomon to build according to the pattern given to David, which is the substance of our study.

Solomon did not originate the temple plans or design. It originated with the Lord, it was given to David and then presented to king Solomon to build to the Divine pattern.

Sufficient it is to say that king David in his experience before the Lord touched something relative to these three Divine habitations. He knew the redemptive truths of the Tabernacle of Moses. He knew the worship truths of the Tabernacle of David. He saw in vision the embodiment of redemption and worship in the order that would be established in the days of Solomon, his son, the builder of the temple, the house of God.

B. King Solomon

1. The Tabernacle of Moses

As it was with David, so it was for Solomon. Solomon also experienced the truths relative to each of these Divine structures, even more so than David. When Solomon became king over all Israel, he and all the congregation with him went to Gibeon, to the tabernacle of the Lord which Moses had made in the days of the wilderness wanderings.

There he and the congregation sought the Lord at the brazen altar, and offered a thousand burnt offerings on it.

It was in Gibeon, relative to this visit, that the Lord appeared to Solomon in a dream and told him to ask whatever he would. Here Solomon asked the Lord for wisdom, knowledge, understanding and discernment to govern the people of God. Here at Gibeon God granted him his request along with riches, wealth, and honour such as none other ever had (2 Chronicles 1:1-7; 1 Kings 3:3-14).

Thus Solomon experienced redemptive truths at the Tabernacle of Moses.

2. **The Tabernacle of David**

    Solomon also knew something of the experience of worship at the tent of David where the ark of God was set in Mt Zion.

    After his experience with the Lord at Gibeon at the Tabernacle of Moses and the brazen altar, Solomon came to Jerusalem, to Zion, to the Tabernacle of David where the ark of the Lord was placed. Here again he offered burnt offerings and peace offerings, voluntarily unto the Lord (2 Chronicles 1:4,13; 1 Chronicles 21:25-30).

    Symbolically Solomon touches the BRAZEN ALTAR (the first article of furniture in the outer court of Moses tabernacle), and the ARK OF THE COVENANT (the ultimate article of furniture in "the holiest of all" in David's tabernacle).

    Surely there is Divine revelation here for all believers too. For we must know the cleansing blood of atonement at the cross (the brazen altar), before we can know the glory and presence of God at the throne (the ark of the covenant).

3. **The Temple of Solomon**

    Little needs to be written at this point. It is clear that, after the Tabernacle of Moses, and the Tabernacle of David experiences, Solomon sets about to build God's temple. He sees both tabernacles combined and brought together in one structure in the building of the temple.

    The details of the temple are given to him by his father, David, and he builds according to the Divine blueprint. Nothing is left to his mind or imagination or ingenuity. He must build according to the architectual plan and drawings David received of the Lord by the Spirit in writing.

The Books of Kings and Chronicles supply the various details of the temple of the Lord.

The climax of experience for Solomon is the bringing in of the ark of the Lord from David's Tabernacle and setting it in the holiest of all in the finished temple. Here the Lord crowned all this with His fire and glory, the Divine seal on that which was built according to His pattern (1 Kings 8; 2 Chronicles 5:11-14; 7:1-4).

Thus Solomon, as David, but more fully, experiences those truths symbolized in the Tabernacle of Moses, the Tabernacle of David and the Temple of the Lord.

For the believer, there is progressive truth. All believers must know and experience the REDEMPTIVE TRUTHS of the Tabernacle of Moses. All believers should know and experience the WORSHIP TRUTHS of the Tabernacle of David. And all should ultimately come into the GOVERNMENTAL TRUTHS of the Temple of Solomon. In Solomon's temple, redemption, worship and government truths are combined.

Here we go from glory to glory, grace to grace, strength to strength, truth to truth, faith to faith in the dealings of God with His people.

The truths of Solomon's temple hidden in symbolic manner will be discovered in the unfolding of this text. It is the glory of God to conceal a matter, but it is the honour of kings to search it out (Proverbs 25:2).

As the Lord moved from tent to tent and one tabernacle to another into His final resting place in the temple, so must believers who follow Him (1 Chronicles 17:5; 2 Samuel 7:6).

"Let us go on unto perfection" is the exhortation the writer to the Hebrews gives to all believers (Hebrews 6:1-2).

SUMMARY DIAGRAM

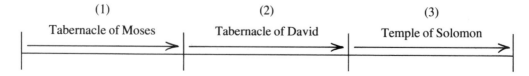

(1)	(2)	(3)
Tabernacle of Moses	Tabernacle of David	Temple of Solomon

GENERAL GROUND PLAN OF THE TEMPLE AND COURTS

Great or Outer Court. 1Kgs7:12.

Upper or Inner Court.
1Kgs6:36.

Steps.

Steps.
2Chr4:8.

The Brazen Altar.
20x20x10.
2Chron4:1.

Altar Ascent.

Pillar
Jachin.

1Kgs7:21.

Pillar
Boaz.

The
Molten Sea.
1Kgs 7:23.

30 cubits

Folding Doors.

Porch.

The Lavers and Bases. 1Kgs7.

The Priests Chambers. 1Kgs6:5-8.

Candlesticks.

Tables of Showbread -
1Kgs 7:48-49.

The Priests Chambers.

The Lavers and Bases. 4cubits square base, Round Laver.

Incense
Altar.

Holy
Place.

Holy
Place.

Folding Doors.

Cherubims
Veil.

Ark.

Two Great Cherubim.

The Holy Oracle.

N.B. Not to Scale. Temple Measurements : 1Kgs6:2. Length 60 cu. Width 30 cu. Height 30 cu.
Most Holy Place - 20x20x20. vs16. Upper Treasure Chamber above.
The Holy Place - 40x20x30. vs17.

Kevin J. Conner.

Diagram Adapted — I.S.B.E.

CHAPTER SEVEN

KING DAVID AND THE REVELATION AND PATTERN OF THE TEMPLE

In this chapter we consider the events that preceded and led up to the revelation of the pattern of the temple as given to king David.

A. **The Tabernacle of David**

We have already referred to the setting up of the Tabernacle of David. In 2 Samuel 6 and 1 Chronicles chapters 15-16 we have the record of David placing the ark of the Lord in a tent and establishing the order of singers and musicians not previously known in Israel's history, especially as pertaining to the worship of the Lord.

This order of worship and praise was established about 30 years or more before the building of the temple of the Lord. This order was also incorporated into the temple order in due time. The ark of God would one day be taken out of this tabernacle and set in the temple. The tent was a temporary habitation of the ark of the Lord. Sufficient it is to remember that this order of worship was in function in the Tabernacle of David in Mt Zion at this period of time.

B. **Rest from all Enemies** — 2 Samuel 7:1

David was a man of war and the Lord used him to smite the enemies of Israel. There came a time when the Scripture says that "the Lord had given him rest round about from all his enemies." David was a worshipper of the Lord but also a conqueror of the Lord's enemies. It was for this latter reason that God would not permit David to build His house, "because you have been a man of war, and have shed much blood" (1 Chronicles 28:3; 22:6-8).

The house of the Lord must be built by a man of peace, not by a man of war. The Lord used king David to put his and Israel's enemies under his feet. This was in fulfilment of the promises God gave to Abraham that his seed would possess the gate of his enemies (Genesis 22:17; Exodus 23:22,27; Leviticus 26:7,8; 2 Samuel 7:9,11; 22:1,4,38,41,49; Psalm 3:7; 110:1-2).

C. **David's Desire to Build a House for the Ark of God**

Again, as noted previously, David desired to build a house for the ark of the Lord. One day, as king David sat in his house and God had given him rest from all his enemies, there came into the heart of David a great desire. This desire is expressed in 2 Samuel 7:1-2 and 1 Chronicles 17:1-2 and 1 Chronicles 17:1-2 along with Psalm 132. David said to the prophet Nathan, "I dwell in a house of cedars, but the ark of the covenant of the Lord dwells within curtains."

He expressed his desire to Nathan to build God a house, a place more worthy of the ark of God. Israel had lived in tents in the wilderness journeys. Now they were dwelling in houses and cities. The ark of God had been in the Tabernacle and under tents for the wilderness journeys also. But now that Israel was in the land of promise, in houses, and enemies had been subdued, why should the ark of God still be in a tent and not in a house?

The prophet Nathan told David to do all that was in his heart (2 Samuel 7:3; 1 Chronicles 17:2).

D. **The Davidic Covenant** — 2 Samuel 7:4-29; 1 Chronicles 17:3-27

During the night, the Word of the Lord came to the prophet Nathan. It was opposite to the word of Nathan the day before. The Lord sent Nathan to David and gave him what is now spoken of as being "The Davidic Covenant".

Among the promises given in this covenant was the fact that David would not build God a house. David's son, Solomon would do that.

However, because David desired to build God a house, God promised that He would build David a house.

The evident lesson is seen. If God's people are concerned for "the house of the Lord", then the Lord will build them a house, a household of faith.

We outline the promises of the Davidic Covenant, especially noting those pertaining to "the house" or the temple of the Lord.

1. The promise of an appointed place, another land (2 Samuel 7:10; 1 Chronicles 17:9).

2. The promise of victory over enemies (2 Samuel 7:11; 1 Chronicles 17:10).

3. The promise of kingship (2 Samuel 7:11-16; 1 Chronicles 17:11-15).
    This involved a Davidic seed, house, throne and kingdom (Genesis 17:6,16; 49:8-12; Psalm 78:67-72; 89:3-4).

4. The promise of sure mercies (2 Samuel 7:15; 1 Chronicles 17:13; Psalm 89:1-34; Acts 13:34).

5. The promise of the Messianic seed (2 Samuel 7:11-16; 1 Chronicles 17:11-15; Hebrews 1:5; Isaiah 7:13-14; Matthew 1:1; Revelation 22:16).

6. The promise of the temple, the house of the Lord (2 Samuel 7:13; 1 Chronicles 17:11-15; 22:6-11).

7. The promise of David's own seed, Solomon, to build the house of the Lord (2 Samuel 7:12-15; 2 Chronicles 17:11-15).

The covenant was ratified by blood sacrifices and confirmed with an oath as to being an irrevocable covenant.
(NOTE — The student is referred to the textbook, *"The Covenants"*, by the author for a fuller exposition of the Davidic Covenant.)

E. **David's Prayer and Thanksgiving** — 2 Samuel 7:18-29; 1 Chronicles 17:16-27

With the establishment of the covenant to David, through the prophet Nathan, David's heart is filled with prayer and praise.
He went and sat before the Lord. His whole prayer and thanksgiving concerns the name of the Lord, and the two houses that would be built. God would build David a house, because David desired to build God a house. God would not permit David to build His house, but David's son, Solomon, would (2 Samuel 12:24,25; 1 Chronicles 22:6-13).
David "found in his heart to pray this prayer unto the Lord" (2 Samuel 7:27; 1 Chronicles 17:25).

F. **The Revelation and Pattern of the Temple**

In 1 Chronicles chapters 28-29 we have the account of king David's word to the leadership of the nation, as well as to the congregation.
David explained the desire he had to build the house for the Lord. However, because he had been a man of war, he was not permitted to build it. A man of peace must be the builder. This, of course, would be Solomon, David's son (2 Samuel 12:24,25; 1 Chronicles 22:6-13).
David told Solomon and the leaders how he had been given the vision of the temple of the Lord by revelation and that he had received the pattern of it all by the Holy Spirit. Under inspiration of the Spirit he wrote it down for Solomon and those who would be involved in the building of it. Note the emphasis on the word *"pattern"* in the following brief quotations.

". . . the pattern . . ." (1 Chronicles 28:11).
". . . the pattern of all that he had by the Spirit . . ." (1 Chronicles 28:12).
". . . the pattern of the chariot of the cherubims . . ." (1 Chronicles 28:18).
"All this, said David, the Lord made me understand in writing by His hand upon me, even all the work of this pattern." (1 Chronicles 28:19).

God was the Architect, the Designer of the temple. Nothing was left to man's mind, or imagination or creativity. It was all of God's wisdom. In 1 Chronicles 28, verses 11-19 we have the following description of the pattern given to David.

". . . the pattern of the *porch,*
and the *houses* thereof,
and the *treasuries* thereof,
and the upper *chambers* thereof,
and of the inner *parlours* thereof,
and of the *place* of the *mercyseat,*
and the pattern of all he had by the Spirit,
of the *courts* of the house of the Lord,
and of all the *chambers* round about,
and of the *treasuries* of the house of God,
and of the *treasuries* of the dedicated things,
also for the *courses* of the priests and Levites,
and for all the *work of the service* of the house of the Lord,
and for all the *vessels of service* in the house of the Lord,
with the pattern for the chariot of the cherubims.
All this, said David, the Lord made me understand by writing by His hand upon me, even all the work of this pattern.''

Thus, the porch, the houses, the treasuries, the chambers, the holy oracle, the courts, the priestly courses, the work of the house, the vessels, the chariot of the olive cherubim — all were given to David in vision, and he was inspired to write it down as he had seen the vision.

David had a vision of the house of the Lord. He received the Divine pattern. He was able to ''write the vision and make it plain'' so that Solomon and his workers could build accordingly. Without a vision the people would perish (Proverbs 29:18; Habukkuk 2:1-3). All leaders need to have a clear vision that the people of God can see and understand and follow out to fulfilment.

1. **The Tabernacle of Moses** was built according to Divine pattern, not being left to the mind of Moses or his co-builders (Exodus 25:9,40; Numbers 8:4; Hebrews 8:5; 9:23).

2. **The Tabernacle of David** undoubtedly followed the Divine pattern in the order of singers and musicians and the order of praise and worship to the Lord. This order of courses was continued on into the temple order.

3. **The Temple of Solomon** was to be built according to the pattern revealed to David by the Spirit in writing. It is important to remember that David received both orders for the Tabernacle by his name and the Temple of the Lord (1 Chronicles 28:11,12,18,19).

4. **The Temple of Ezekiel** is also according to the Divine pattern (Ezekiel 43:10)

Why was God so particular about the pattern in these various structures? The answer is twofold. FIRST, the earthly temple was but a shadow on earth of the heavenly temple. The heavenly temple order is the prototype, the original, the real, the eternal, while that on earth is the shadow, the temporary, the type.
The Scriptures definitely speak of a heavenly temple (Isaiah 6:1; 66:6; Revelation 11:19; 14:15-17; 15:5).
David in spirit saw the heavenly temple, even as Moses in spirit saw the heavenly tabernacle.
All that is heaven's order is perfect and complete. It is according to the Divine blueprint, the pattern of God, the Architect of the universe. Therefore the earthly temple, the earthly dwelling place of God must be according to the pattern of the heavenly dwelling place (Isaiah 57:15).

SECONDLY, the temple on earth was to be God's earthly dwelling place where He could dwell among His people by His Spirit. Here He could reveal His glory, speak with voice to His appointed and anointed high priest on the ground of redemption.

This pointed to Christ who is THE TEMPLE of God bodily in the earth (John 2:19-21). God was in Christ, His Temple. His Spirit, His glory, and His voice was heard in and through Him. He was God's dwelling place everywhere He walked. He was sinless and perfect. He was "*the pattern Man*".

Therefore, the earthly material temple which was prophetic of the Christ of God must be "according to the pattern".

Christ measured up to the Divine standards and pattern of God as THE Temple of God.

The same is true of the Church, the Body of Christ. The Church, God's New Covenant temple, must be built according to the pattern laid out in the Word of God, the Holy Bible.

God can only bless in His people that which is wholly of Himself. God can only dwell amongst His people in the fulness of glory as all measure up to the Divine measurements, by the Spirit. God can only seal with His glory-fire that which is according to the heavenly pattern.

Christ and His Church are one in the mind of the Father. All of this is in the writings of the Scriptures, given by the Spirit. It is the ministry of the church and its leadership to build according to the pattern (1 Timothy 3:16; 1 Peter 1:11-12; 2 Peter 1:20-21).

Paul, as a wise master-builder, received the Divine pattern and order for the New Testament church, the temple of God, and admonished all other builders to "take heed how you build" (1 Corinthians 3:9-17; 6:19; Ephesians 2:20-22).

If God was particular about the material temple being built to His pattern, He will be so concerning both Christ (the head), and the Church (His Body), together constituting THE TEMPLE of God! Surely this should challenge all ministry in the Body of Christ!

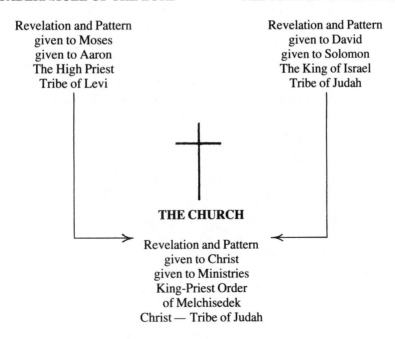

THE TABERNACLE OF THE LORD

Revelation and Pattern
given to Moses
given to Aaron
The High Priest
Tribe of Levi

THE TEMPLE OF THE LORD

Revelation and Pattern
given to David
given to Solomon
The King of Israel
Tribe of Judah

THE CHURCH

Revelation and Pattern
given to Christ
given to Ministries
King-Priest Order
of Melchisedek
Christ — Tribe of Judah

G. **King David and King Solomon**

Undoubtedly one of the most significant things relative to the temple building is in the fact that the Lord God gave the revelation and pattern of it to A KING — king David!

Then from king David it was given to KING SOLOMON! Both David and Solomon were of the tribe of Judah, the royal tribe.

In contrast, we see the revelation and pattern of the Tabernacle of the Lord, the Tabernacle in the Wilderness, was given to A PRIEST, to Moses of the tribe of Levi, the priestly tribe.

Though Moses is called a king and lawgiver, yet his major office was PRIEST and Mediator of the Old Covenant (Deuteronomy 33:4,5; Hebrews 3:1-5).

David, however, is KING of the royal tribe of Judah, yet he touches things pertaining to priestly ministrations, especially in the setting up of the Tabernacle of David.

In the Tabernacle of Moses, Aaron also figures predominantly in ministry as HIGH PRIEST. However, in the Temple of the Lord, it is Solomon as KING who figures predominantly. The high priest is not mentioned in all of the building or the dedication and the glory-fire that came to the temple on that day. This is certainly an unusual thing.

Surely there is something significant in the emphasis on these two separate offices and persons, at two separate habitations.

However, this is not to say that the office of high priest was not in function, for it was, but we have both the offices of KING and PRIEST manifested relative to God's temple.

For sharper focus we set this out in contrast.

The significance of the matter is seen in the fact that, under the Old Covenant these two offices were basically separated to two persons and two different tribes. There was the priestly office of the tribe of Levi, and the kingly office of the tribe of Judah.

Several men only touched something in measure of these two offices, and each were involved in the building of a habitation for the Lord.

MOSES was a PRIEST-King and built the Tabernacle of the Lord. DAVID was a KING and also touched something of priestly ministry and built the Tabernacle of David. SOLOMON also touches something of both even though he is a king, the king of Israel.

The fulfilment of these things and these offices is seen in the Lord Jesus Christ, who is our Moses, our David, and our Solomon in one person. He fulfilled and abolished the Levitical and Aaronic priesthood and sacrifices. He is of the tribe of Judah, the greater Son of David. He is the Builder of the New Testament temple, the church, God's greater house. He combines in His humanity and divinity the two offices of king and priest after the order of Melchisedek.

In concluding this chapter we bring these things into sharp focus and see how they point to David's greater Son, Jesus Christ.

KING DAVID	—	**KING JESUS**
1. Built the Tabernalce of David for worship	—	Builds the Church for worshippers
2. Conquered all his enemies	—	Conquers all His enemies
3. Brings in rest	—	Brings rest to the people of God
4. Desires to house the ark of God	—	Desires to establish God's throne
5. Receives Davidic Covenant	—	Establishes the New Covenant
6. A Man of prayer and thanksgiving	—	A Man of prayer and thanksgiving
7. Receives revelation and pattern of the temple	—	Receives revelation and pattern of the church
8. Is a king, touching priesthood	—	Is a king-priest after the order of Melchisedek

CHAPTER EIGHT

KING DAVID'S CHARGE CONCERNING THE TEMPLE

With the revelation of the temple given to David, we find David calling Solomon, the princes and captains of the nation of Israel together for a great assembly. Here he gives charge concerning the building of God's temple.

A. **David's Preparation for the Temple**

The true heart of David is seen in his preparation for the building of the temple. Even though David himself would not be allowed to build it, and even though he would not live to see its dedication and glory, yet he prepared abundantly for it before his death.
Solomon, his son, would receive the praise of its construction. But there was no jealousy, no resentment in David's heart, no withholding from God for His house.

How often God gives vision to leaders who never live to see it fulfilled, but it finds fulfilment in another generation. Wise men, who have a heart after God's purposes will prepare for the fulfilment of the vision even though they never live to see it. One generation should prepare for another generation (Psalm 78:1-8).

David prepared in abundance the material for the temple before his death, because he had set his affection to the house of God. The spoils from his victories in battle were dedicated to the house of the Lord (1 Chronicles 22:1-5,14-16; 18:7,8,11; 29:1-5; 1 Kings 7:51; 2 Samuel 8:10-11).

David also gathered the strangers in the land of Israel and set them to work on the stones to build God's house.
David himself prepared in abundance iron, brass, and timber and stone for the temple. He told the people that the house to be built was to be exceeding magnificent for it was a house for the Lord to dwell in.

The list of materials given will be noted in a subsequent chapter.

B. **David's Charge to Solomon** — 1 Chronicles 22:6-16

After calling his son, Solomon, David gave him a charge to build the house for the Lord God of Israel. He reminded him how it had been in his own heart but because he was a man of war he was not permitted to build it. He reminded Solomon also of the word of the Lord that came to him concerning his son. Solomon would be a man of peace, and rest would be given him from all his enemies. The house of the Lord can only be built in a time of peace, not a time of war with enemies. God would be a father to him and he would be His son. His throne would be established forever.

David challenged him to take heed to the law of the Lord through Moses, encouraging him to seek the Lord in wisdom and understanding to fulfil this charge laid on him. He would build the vision of his father David.

Solomon was also reminded of the gold, silver, brass and iron, the timber and stone that David had prepared for the house of the Lord.
David told his son of the abundance of workers available to help in the work of stone and timber as well as the other metals prepared for God's house.

C. **David's Charge to the Princes** — 1 Chronicles 22:17-19

So that Solomon would not feel alone in the great charge laid on him, David commanded the princes of Israel to help him. God was with them. Rest was theirs. The enemies had been subdued. Therefore they were to seek the Lord with heart and soul and build the sanctuary of the Lord. The ark of the covenant, the holy vessels of God had to be brought into the house built for the name of the Lord. So the charge was laid upon the princes to support Solomon in the building.

D. **David's Charge to the Levites** — 1 Chronicles 23:3-32

David also set the Levites in their various courses. They are commanded to keep the charge of the Lord as given to them by Moses in the priestly ministrations.

David reminded them to keep "the charge of the tabernacle of the congregation, the charge of the holy place, and the charge of the sons of Aaron their brethren, in the service of the house of the Lord"

In this chapter we see king David laying the charge to build God's house on Solomon and the leaders of the nation, the princes and the Levites.

The people could not rise above or go beyond the leadership. If the princes and the Levites had no heart for the building of the house of God, neither would the people of Israel.
The same is true today. No congregation can rise above or go beyond its leadership.

Moses charged Joshua before his death to take Israel into the promised land and to divide their inheritances to them. Joshua would complete the vision that Moses had been given, yet never lived to see it fulfilled. This charge was done before Eleazer the high priest and by the laying on of hands before all the congregation (Numbers 27:15-23).

Paul charged the elders of the church at Ephesus to care for the flock of God, to watch against themselves rising up and drawing disciples after them, and to watch against wolves that would come in from outside (Acts 20:28-29).

Paul also laid charges on his sons, Timothy and Titus, to keep the faith once delivered to the saints, to guard the deposit God had given, and hold fast to sound doctrine in the midst of apostasy and tribulation (1 Timothy, 2 Timothy, Titus Epistles).

And here David gives Solomon, his son, before his death, along with the princes of Israel, and the Levites, the charge to build the temple, and keep the charge of the Lord. The charge of David was in reality the charge of the Lord (1 Chronicles 22:17; 23:2,32).

All ministers of the Gospel and believers have a charge to keep in the New Testament house of the Lord, His church.

KING SOLOMON ON THE BRAZEN SCAFFOLD

CHAPTER NINE

KING SOLOMON IN ALL HIS GLORY

The Lord Jesus spoke of "Solomon in all his glory" not being arrayed even as one of the lilies of the field (Matthew 6:29).

In this chapter we consider the glory of Solomon and his kingdom before taking up the temple which he built for the name of the Lord. We consider the builder before the building.

In any character study of Bible men or women, we have to remember that none were perfect. All were born in sin, shapen in iniquity, all were imperfect. However, it pleased the Lord to use imperfect people to typify His perfect Son, Jesus Christ.

In using various persons as types of Christ, we see that it is generally the OFFICE and the FUNCTION of that person more than the CHARACTER that speaks of Christ.

There is that in Solomon, as a person, in his office and function as temple-builder that shadows forth Christ. These are the things of which we speak here — not the failings of Solomon. His failures speak of the failures of sinful men, of imperfect believers also. His office as KING, and his function as TEMPLE-BUILDER speak of Christ, as do other things pertaining to his person.

Some expositors see in David a type of Christ, as the Warrior, the Man of War, who shed blood and conquered all our enemies, making preparation for the building of the church, God's temple.

They also see Solomon as a type of the Holy Spirit, as the Man of Peace, the Man of Wisdom, who builds the church, God's temple.

Others suggest that David is a type of Christ in His death, after suffering and rejection, and Solomon as type of Christ in His resurrection and the glory of His kingdom, building His church.

Realizing that there is no such thing as "a perfect type", by reason of the imperfection of human beings used as types, either application may be used. The author here presents Solomon as Christ in His resurrection and kingdom glory, building the church by the wisdom and Spirit of God. But "a greater than Solomon is here" (Matthew 12:42). We note some major points of comparison and contrast in our use of the typical principle.

A. Solomon — His Name

Solomon had two names given to him and both were given by the Lord before his birth (1 Chronicles 22:9,10; 2 Samuel 12:24,25).

1. **Solomon** = "Peaceable, peaceful, perfect, one who recompenses".

2. **Jedidiah** = "Beloved of the Lord, Beloved of God"; named so by the prophet Nathan (2 Samuel 12:25).

These two names were prophetic. Solomon was a man of peace, his kingdom was peaceable. Solomon was also beloved of the Lord.

The Lord Jesus Christ was also named before His birth by his heavenly Father (Luke 1:30-33). He is the king of peace, and of the increase of His government and peace there shall be no end (Isaiah 9:6,7; Zechariah 9:10). His heavenly Father spoke to Him from heaven saying, "This is My beloved Son, in whom I am well pleased" (Matthew 3:16,17).

Truly "a greater than Solomon is here".

B. Solomon — His Anointing

Solomon also had two anointings as king before he was established in the Davidic throne, the throne of covenant.

1. **First Anointing** — 1 Kings 1:28-40; 1 Chronicles 23:1
   This first anointing took place before David's death. Solomon was anointed with the holy horn of oil out of the tabernacle of the Lord. The trumpet was blown, and all shouted, "God save the king!"

   Zadok the PRIEST, Nathan the PROPHET, and David the KING were there at this anointing of Solomon to the throne in the midst of great joy. This anointing took place in the midst of rebellion and an attempted usurpation of the throne without anointing by David's rebel son, Adonijah.

2. **Second Anointing** — 1 Chronicles 29:22-25
   The second anointing took place at David's message to all the assembled princes and captains of Israel as he announced that the Lord had chosen Solomon to build the temple of the Lord (Read 1 Chronicles 28-29 chapters).
   This anointing was a great public anointing and inauguration as king over all Israel.

   It is worthy to remember that David also had two anointings as king. The first was an anointing before his family (1 Samuel 16:13). The second was a public anointing to office before the nation (2 Samuel 5:1-3).

The Lord Jesus became "the anointed", as the Father poured upon Him the oil of the Holy Spirit. Jesus received this anointing of the Spirit in His earthly ministry at the river Jordan as He rose out of the waters of baptism (Matthew 3:13-17). Old Testament prophets, priests and kings were anointed and called "the Lord's anointed" also (1 Samuel 2:10).

When Jesus ascended on high, He received the promise of the Father which could be outpoured · on the church, the Christians (Acts 2:29-36).

The title "Messiah" means "The Anointed" in Hebrew. The title "Christ" in the Greek is the same, and means "The Anointed". Jesus Christ is the Lord's anointed, set on the holy hill of Zion (Psalm 2:6, Margin). He is the Christ, the Son of the living God (John 1:41; Matthew 16:16).

Truly again, "a greater than Solomon is here."

C. **Solomon — His Kingship**

Ecclesiastes 1:1,12 tell us that Solomon, the son of David, was king over all Israel in Jerusalem. Jerusalem is the city of righteousness, the city of peace. Jerusalem is the city of the great king.

Jesus Christ, David and Solomon's greater Son, is king of righteousness and king of peace, after the order of Melchisedek (Hebrews 7:1-4; Isaiah 32:1,17; Jeremiah 23:5; Psalm 45:7; 85:10; Matthew 6:33; 3:15). He reigns from the heavenly Zion, the heavenly Jerusalem which is above the earthly Zion and Jerusalem.

Again, "a greater than Solomon is here".

It is significant to note throughout the whole of the building of the Temple that the high priest is not the one in focus (although he does function), but it is THE KING, king Solomon, who is the major office. This is prophetic of Christ, who is both priest and king, but in the final glory He is seen as THE KING OF KINGS and LORD OF LORDS (Revelation 19:16).

D. **Solomon — His Throne**

Scripture tells us that Solomon sat upon the throne of the kingdom of his father David. He sat upon the throne of the kingdom of the Lord. He sat on the throne of the Lord. All Israel obeyed him. The leaders of Israel submitted themselves unto him. The Lord bestowed such royal majesty on him as no other king ever had and so the kingdom was established in the hand of Solomon (1 Chronicles 28:5; 29:23-25; 22:9; Psalm 72:11; 1 Kings 2:45,46).

1 King 10:18-20 and 2 Chronicles 9:17-19 give a description of the throne of Solomon. W.W. Patterson, a noted Bible Teacher has set out a beautiful study of the throne of Solomon, which we adapt here. Solomon's throne points to a greater throne, even Christ's throne, especially at His second coming as King of Kings, Lord of Lords, and Prince of Peace (Isaiah 9:6-9; Psalm 72).

1. **It was a Great Throne**

   There was no throne greater. The Lord Jesus sits in the greatest throne of the universe, even His Father's throne (Revelation 3:21).

2. **It was a Unique Throne**

   There was no other throne like it. Earthly thrones will pass away. The throne of God and the· Lamb is a unique throne, eternal, unchanging, redemptive (Revelation 22:1-2). It is a heavenly throne, ruling the whole universe.

3. **It was a Throne of Ivory**

   Ivory from the elephant suggests strength. Ivory whiteness suggests purity and holiness. Christ came forth from the "ivory palaces" (Psalm 45:8) to earth to redeem us. The throne of God and the Lamb is a throne of holiness and purity.

4. **It was a Throne with Six Steps**

   Six steps of ascent to the throne were made. This can speak of the 6000 years of the Lord (6 Days of the Lord, Psalm 90:4; 2 Peter 3:8), which brings us to the throne of the Lord when He rules over the whole earth in the Millennial Kingdom.

5. **It was a Throne with a Footstool of Gold**

   Heaven is God's throne, earth is His footstool (Isaiah 66:1; Psalm 132:7; 99:5; Matthew 5:34,35; 1 Chronicles 28:2). The temple was His footstool in the Old Testament days. In the Kingdom Age, earth will be His footstool, covered with His glory (symbolized by the gold). The Lord will dwell among His people. This footstool was fastened to the throne. Heaven and earth will indeed be connected.

6. **It was a Throne with two Lions by its Stays**

   Two lions were by the stays of the throne, one on the right hand, the other on the left. These can speak of the two witnesses, Moses and Elijah on the Mt of Transfiguration. Christ, the Lion of the tribe of Judah sits upon the throne, and there is a place on the right hand and left hand reserved for these two men (Matthew 20:22-23; Revelation 11:4; Zechariah 4:14).

7. **It was a Throne with Twelve Lions, Two on each Step**

   Twelve is the number of Divine government. In New Testament truth twelve speaks of apostolic government. The twelve lions here, two on each of the six steps, can speak of the twelve apostles, sent out by Jesus, two by two into every city into which He Himself would come. (Matthew 19:28,29). The twelve were to reign with Him in the regeneration when He sits upon His throne of glory. Christ, the greater Solomon sits in the throne of His Father and reigns in Mt Zion, from the heavenly Jerusalem, over His people, the church, spiritual Israel. His people submit to Him in such royal majesty as His kingdom is established in peace.

E. **Solomon — His Enemies**

   In order for Solomon to reign in peace and his kingdom to be established in peace, there were some final enemies that had to be subdued. David had subdued the enemies without, external and national enemies of the kingdom. But David left some enemies within, internal in the kingdom for Solomon to subdue. All enemies had to be put under the soles of his feet before he could build the temple of the Lord (1 Kings 5:4; 4:24,25).

   Four particular enemies had to be dealt with, these being Adonijah, Joab, Abiathar and Shimei. We note the dealings of Solomon with each of these enemies of David.

1. **Adonijah** — "The Lord is Jehovah"

   Sad to say, Adonijah had a godly name, but certainly did not live up to his name. He would find that the Lord would be Jehovah in judgment upon him. He was David's fourth son (2 Samuel 3:4). 1 Kings chapter 1 gives the account of his self-exaltation, making himself king and usurping the throne of David that was to be for Solomon. When Solomon had been anointed king, Adonijah fled to the Tabernacle of Moses and caught hold of the horns of the altar, seeking mercy and refuge from Solomon. Solomon did grant him the desired mercy on the condition that he would remain in his house, in asylum. However, later on he left his "house of refuge" and was put to death by the word of the king. Who knows whether he would rise in rebellion and usurpation again?

2. **Joab** — "God his Father"
    Joab was General-in-Chief of David's army (2 Samuel 2:18-32, etc). He had a very brilliant career. However, in the closing days of David's life Joab got caught in the usurpation of Adonijah and tried to help him seize David's throne by force. Again, he forgot the message in the interpretation of his own name. Joab, following the death of Adonijah, fled to the Tabernacle of Moses also and caught hold of the horns of the altar of brass, pleading for mercy from Solomon. However, no place of mercy was found. He was slain by the altar. Joab was buried in his own house in the wilderness (1 Kings 2:34).

3. **Abiathar** — "Father of Abundance"
    Abiathar was the eleventh high priest in the line of succession from Aaron. He was the priest who escaped under Saul and fled to David in the wilderness. He was a joint-priest with Zadok. However, he also became involved in the usurpation of Adonijah, along with Joab. Solomon sent a word to him that he would not be put to death because he bare the Ark of the Lord in David's time. However, he was sent back to his own house in Anathoth and was disposed from priestly ministration to the day of his death (1 Samuel 22:19,20; 23:9; 1 Kings 2:26,27,35). Zadok was placed in the room of Abiathar for priestly ministry.

4. **Shimei** — "My Reputation, Famed"
    In 2 Samuel 16:5-13 we have the account of Shimei who cursed king David. David allowed him to do so not knowing whether the Lord had bidden him to do it or not. When Solomon ascended the throne, he called Shimei before him. He found mercy because of David's oath (1 Kings 2:8). Solomon told Shimei to go and dwell in his house and never to leave it. If he did, then his blood would be upon his own head. This was a test of submission and obedience. However, Shimei, in time, disobeyed the word of the king and his promise and so was slain (1 Kings 2:36-46). Thus Solomon dealt with internal foes, characterized by disobedience, rebellion, and usurpation against the throne of David.
    1 Kings chapters 1-2 deal with these four internal enemies of the throne. Before the temple could be built, rest, peace and harmony in the kingdom has to be established.
    So for Christ Jesus. All enemies are to be put under His feet as He rules and reigns in the kingdom of His Father God (Psalm 110:1-2).

    Truly, "a greater than Solomon is here".

F. Solomon — His Kingdom

Psalm 72 is a prayer of David for his son Solomon as he takes the throne. It is a prayer for righteousness, justice and judgment and peace. It is a prayer that all enemies would be under his feet and his dominion would be universal in scope. It is a prayer that his name would continue for ever and all nations would be blessed through his reign. It is a prayer that the whole world would be filled with the glory of the Lord.

Who can fail to see that the ultimate fulfilment is seen to be in the Lord Jesus Christ and His kingdom? As Solomon's kingdom was to be characterized by righteousness, peace, wisdom and propriety, so the kingdom of God and His Christ, His king, would be characterized by these same attributes, for ever.

Truly, "a greater than Solomon is here".

G. Solomon — His Government

Solomon's kingdom was stamped with the number twelve, or multiples of the same. Twelve is the number of Divine government. In the New Testament it speaks of apostolic government, perfect government.

In 1 Kings 4:7-19 we have the TWELVE OFFICERS over all Israel. Solomon divided his realm into twelve districts, each having an officer over it and each provided for Solomon's household over the twelve months of the year.

The number twelve and its multiples will be noted later on in the chapter dealing with the temple courses. However, we note for the present several twelves. There were twelve lions on the six steps of the throne of Solomon. There were twelve officers over twelve districts of Israel. These ministered to the house of the king over twelve months of the year, taking a month each. There were twelve brazen oxen under the molten sea in the outer court.

The Lord Jesus Christ chose twelve apostles to be over the twelve tribes of Israel in the regeneration. These twelve are especially called the twelve apostles of the Lamb. These twelve men are apostolic ministries, in apostolic government, who rule over Christ's kingdom with Him in kingdom glory (Matthew 10:1-4; 19:28; Revelation 21:14).

Again, "a greater than Solomon is here".

H. Solomon — His Wisdom

Solomon's kingdom was established and known world-wide for his wisdom. "All the kings of the earth sought to hear his wisdom which God had put in his heart" (1 Kings 10:23; 4:29-34; 4:31).

The Gentile kings of the earth came to hear the wisdom that God had given him, wisdom which excelled all the wisdom of man and nations about him. All nations had their "wise men", their astrologers, magicians, necromancers, etc., but none knew the wisdom of God. God often confounded their wisdom and brought in His own "wise men" as seen in Joseph before Pharoah, and Daniel before Nebuchadnezzar.

The queen of Sheba came from the uttermost parts of the earth to see and hear the wisdom of Solomon (1 Kings 10; 2 Chronicles 9).

Jesus said, "a greater than Solomon is here" (Matthew 12:42). He was the wisdom of God personified, yet the Jews failed to hear such wisdom. They failed to hear the One in whom are hid all the treasures of wisdom and knowledge (Colossians 2:3).

The church is also called upon to manifest the wisdom of God to the world, and to principalities and powers in heavenly places (Ephesians 3:10,11).

The Tabernacle of Moses was built through wisdom (Exodus 35-36 chapters). The Temple of Solomon was built through the wisdom of God. Christ Himself is the wisdom of God personified. And the church has to be built by the wisdom of God also (1 Corinthians 1-2 chapters).

In bringing this chapter to a conclusion, again we would bring these things into focus as they point to Solomon's greater Son, the Lord Jesus Christ.

KING SOLOMON	KING JESUS

1. **His Name**   — **His Name**
    Solomon — Peace, Perfect   Prince of Perfect Peace
    Jedidiah — Beloved of the Lord   My Beloved Son

2. **His Anointing as King**   — **His Anointing as Christ**
    Before David   Before John the Baptist
    Before Israel   Before all heaven

3. **His Kingship**   — **His Kingship**
    King over Israel in Jerusalem   King of the Jews, King of Israel,
                                                    King of Saints, King of Kings

4. **His Throne**   — **His Throne**
    None to compare with it   The throne of God and the Lamb

5. **His Enemies**   — **His Enemies**
    Conquered — under his feet   Reign over enemies — under His feet

6. **His Kingdom**   — **His Kingdom**
    Greatest kingdom in earth   Greatest kingdom in the universe

7. **His Government**   — **His Government**
    Twelve officers   Twelve apostles of the Lamb

8. **His Wisdom**   — **His Wisdom**
    Unsurpassed in earth   The wisdom of God personified

Indeed and indeed, ''A greater than Solomon is here'' (Matthew 12:42).

FLOOR PLAN OF SOLOMON'S TEMPLE

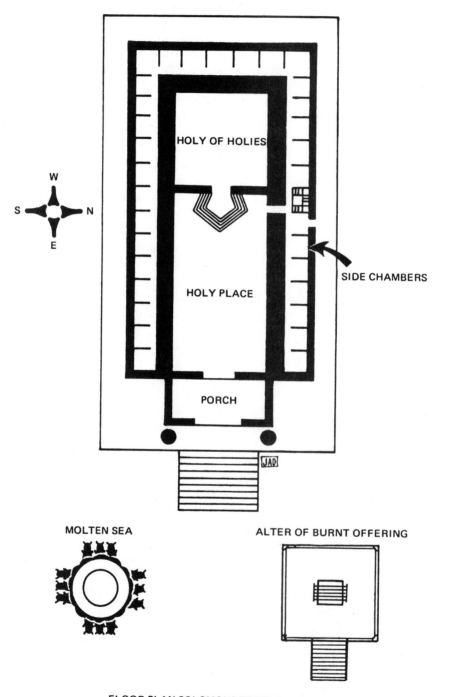

FLOOR PLAN SOLOMONS TEMPLE BY R. CAPT

CHAPTER TEN

GENERAL DESCRIPTION OF THE TEMPLE

1. **The Temple Site**

The site of the temple was the threshing floor of Araunah the Jebusite. Here David erected an altar to the Lord at His command at the cessation of the plague after numbering the people. Here the Lord answered by fire from heaven on the burnt and peace offerings David gave. In due time Solomon would build the house of the Lord in Mt Moriah, in Jerusalem on this very site of the threshing floor.

The temple was on the boundary line between Judah and Benjamin, and so formed a link between the northern and southern tribes, almost in the centre of the nation.

2. **The Temple Structure**

The general plan of the temple was the same as that of the Tabernacle of the Lord built by Moses, but on a larger and much grander scale. Actually its measurements were a little more than double that of the wilderness Tabernacle.

The temple proper was built of hewn stones. These stones were made ready in the quarries before being brought to the temple site so that neither sound of hammer nor axe nor any tool was heard in the building. The temple measured 60 cubits long, 20 cubits wide, and 30 cubits in height.

The temple or Sanctuary was divided into two places, respectively called "the Holy Place" and "the Oracle", or "the Most Holy Place".

These two places were divided by folding doors made of olive wood and ornamented with carvings of cherubim, palms, and open flowers. They were hung on hinges of gold.

These doors into the Holiest of All also had a veil associated with them similar in material and ornamentation to the veil in the Tabernacle of Moses.

The entrance into the Holy Place also had folding doors made of fir wood with door-posts of olive wood and ornamented in the same manner as the doors into the Holy of Holies.

The Holiest of All was a cube, 20 cubits square, and the 10 cubits above it in the remaining height of the temple proper was used as a treasury, forming "the upper chambers".

The Holy Place or Sanctuary was 40 cubits long, 20 cubits wide and 30 cubits high. The walls inside the temple were lined with timber so as to cover the stones; the walls and roof being covered with cedar, and the floors with fir timber. The side walls were covered over with carved works of cherubim, palm trees and open flowers.

At the top of the walls there were latticed windows, probably for ventilation, to admit light and allow the smoke of incense and burning lamps to ascend.

Everything within the temple was overlaid with thin plates of gold. The floor as well as the ceiling and walls was also overlaid with gold.

3. **The Porch and Pillars**

In front of the temple and joined to it was the porch 20 cubits wide, 10 cubits deep and 30 cubits high, the height of the temple itself (rather than 120 cubits which would make it a tower and not a porch. Unger's Bible Dictionary).

In front of the porch also stood two great brass, or bronze, pillars called "Jachin" and "Boaz", richly ornamented, standing as monuments, not for support.

4. **The Priest's Chambers**

Around the sides and rear of the temple walls was built a three-storied building, containing rooms for the priests. These were used as priests chambers, temple stores for furniture and other things for temple services.

This three-storied building was not part of the temple proper but actually leaned against the walls. Each story was 5 cubits high, thus totalling half the height of the temple, and each story was 5 cubits, 6 cubits and 7 cubits wide, respectively. These chambers were entered by means of a door into the passage and by winding stairs.

The whole house was overlaid with gold plates and the temple glittered in the sunlight, dazzling the eyes of all who approached it.

5. The Temple Courts

Surrounding the Sanctuary as a whole were two great courts called "the inner court" and "great court". The inner court running round the temple was reserved exclusively for the priests. It was formed by a boundary wall made of three layers of hewn stones and a row of cedar beams apparently laid on top of the stones for protection and beautification.

Outside of this was the outer or "great court" intended for the use of the people, the Israelites, apparently surrounded by a stone wall with gates. In Jeremiah 36:10, the court of the priests is called "the higher court". This would indicate that it was on a higher level than the outer or great court. Several Bible Dictionaries suggest that the temple and its courts would have a terraced setting and aspect to anyone who would approach it.

6. The Temple Furniture

In the Holy of Holies or the Holy Oracle, was placed the ark of the Covenant with its mercy seat, which was taken from the Tabernacle of David on Mt Zion.

The ark was placed between the two great cherubim, each 10 cubits high, made of olive wood and overlaid with gold. Their wings were outstretched, each being 5 cubits long, touching each other overshadowing the ark of God, while the outer wings touched the side walls of the Holy Oracle. They stood on their feet with their faces toward the Holy Place.

In the Holy Place was the golden altar of incense, made of cedar wood, overlaid with gold. It stood before the Holy of Holies for the daily burning of incense and for use on the great Day of Atonement.

Then there were ten golden candlesticks with their seven lamps. These were placed, five on each side, on the right hand and the left of the Holy Place.

Then there were ten tables of shewbread, again, five being placed on each side of the Holy Place.

In the outer court was the great altar of brass, the altar of burnt offering. Its measurements were 20 cubits square, and 10 cubits high, made after the pattern of the brass altar in the Tabernacle of Moses. The various vessels belonging to this altar were of brass also.

Between the altar and the porch stood the great molten or brazen sea, a huge round basin of water, replacing the brazen laver of the Tabernacle of the Lord. This was for the priests to wash there before entering the services of the Lord in the temple proper.

Then on each side of the altar of brass, on the right side and left side of the temple, were 10 smaller brazen lavers on wheels, these being for the washing of the sacrifices for the altar.

7. The Temple Dedication

The temple was dedicated in the Feast of the seventh month, the Feast of Tabernacles, amidst much prayer and dedicatory offerings.

The Lord sealed the dedication of His house with the descent of the Shekinah Glory-Fire and dwelt among His redeemed people.

For a fuller and more detailed description of the temple, as well as archeological evidences, the student is referred to "*The Temple*" in the following Dictionaries.

* Unger's Bible Dictionary   * International Standard Bible Encyclopaedia
* Fausett's Bible Dictionary   * Westminster Dictionary

CHAPTER ELEVEN

GENERAL COMPARISON AND CONTRAST OF TABERNACLE AND TEMPLE

It is to be recognized that the real understanding of the temple and its furnishings is founded upon a working knowledge of the Tabernacle of Moses. The temple is identified with this tabernacle and replaces it on a much larger and grander scale.

The truths, as found in the tabernacle, its furnishings and measurements with their details will be amplified into fuller light and glory, beauty and harmony, in the study of the temple.

As our study unfolds, tabernacle and temple will be compared and contrasted as both were of heavenly order and pattern. The earthly tabernacle and temple were but shadows of the heavenly tabernacle and temple, but there is only ONE pattern. God had ONE purpose in mind.

The more intricate details will unfold in their respective chapters. However, it will be profitable, for this present chapter, to note some general comparisons and contrasts of both tabernacle and temple.

A. The Temporary and The Permanent

1. The Tabernacle

The tabernacle speaks of that which is temporary and transitional. Israel as a nation wandered in the wilderness for 40 years. They were pilgrims and strangers in the earth. In due time they possessed the land of promise and the tribes were allotted their inheritances. The tabernacle functioned over many years during the formation of the young nation under theocracy prior to the monarchy.

2. The Temple

The temple speaks of the permanent. The land had been won. Journeys were over. Battles had been fought and victories won. All enemies were under their feet. With the rise of the monarchy, the tribes being established as a united kingdom under the Davidic covenant, the temple would become the centre of the nation's religious life and their worship of Jehovah. The Lord had gone from tent to tent, and one tabernacle to another, but now He would dwell in a house in a more permanent dwelling place amongst His own.

B. Christ and Christ in His Church

1. The Tabernacle

The tabernacle primarily speaks of Christ, and secondarily points to the church. In the tabernacle there was one ark of the Lord, one golden altar of incense, one golden lampstand, one table of shewbread, one brazen altar and one brazen laver.

The whole emphasis is in the number ONE, all of which points to Christ. He is the ONE and ONLY way to the Father (John 14:1,6; Hebrews 7:25; 1 Timothy 2:5). There is only ONE Mediator between God and man; Christ is the ONE and ONLY Saviour.

There was ever one and only tabernacle in the wilderness and all testified, there was only one way to God. There was one high priest who functioned in this Sanctuary, this being Aaron. All other Levitical priests were lesser priests. So Christ is the one and only high priest and all other believers are lesser priests of that body, of which Christ is the head.

2. The Temple

The temple also spoke of Christ but more especially of Christ in His church. There are things in the temple, as in the tabernacle, that speak of the one Christ, the one and only Saviour. They could not be duplicated.

But there are things in the temple that speak of the church and Christ's ministrations as multiplied in the church, which is His holy temple.

In the temple there was the one and same ark of the Lord, one golden altar of incense, and one brazen altar and molten sea. All again spoke of Christ as the one way to God, the one Saviour and Mediator and sacrifice in His redemptive work.

But there were TEN tables of shewbread, and TEN brazen lavers in the Holy Place and Outer Court, respectively. There were also TEN golden lampstands in the Holy Place.

Then there was the court for the priests and the court for the Israelites allowing for a greater company of worshippers.

And again, the temple measurements were twice the size of those of the Tabernacle of the Lord. The temple, therefore, spoke of a double portion. The double portion points to Christ and His church, the head and the body brought together in one.

In the temple order the 24 courses of the priesthood were established, day and night in their orders. The temple was stamped with the significant number 24. The contrast is seen in the fact that the Tabernacle of Moses was stamped with the number twelve and its significance. Again, $2 \times 2 = 24$ and speaks of the double portion ministry of Christ and His church in priestly function.

C.   The Tabernacle and Temple Materials

1.   The Tabernacle

The tabernacle in the wilderness was characterized by timber, acacia wood, overlaid with gold or brass. Other materials involved were silver, fine linen and precious stones.
The priests ministered on the "desert floor". All spoke of pilgrimage and wilderness wanderings on the way to the promised land of rest. All spoke of that which was transitional and temporary.

2.   The Temple

In great contrast the temple was characterized by stone, timbers of fir, cedar and olive wood, overlaid with gold and beautified by ornamentation. Gold, silver, brass and iron, as well as precious stones were involved also. Here the priests ministered on a "gold floor"

Surely this points to the foursquare city of God where the streets are paved with transparent gold. The temple speaks of both time and eternity. The city of God is garnished with twelve precious stones.

D.   Pentecost and Tabernacles

1.   The Tabernacle

Another significant thing is seen in the fact that the revelation of the Tabernacle of the Lord was given to Moses by revelation at Mt Sinai. This was relative to the Feast of Pentecost, the feast of the third month after Passover feast.
At the dedication of the Tabernacle of the Lord at Mt Sinai the Shekinah-Glory came down and filled the tabernacle so that none could minister in the Sanctuary (Exodus 40).

2.   The Temple

In contrast and comparison the dedication of the Temple of Solomon took place in the Feast of Tabernacles, the feast of the seventh month, not the Feast of Passover nor the Feast of Pentecost.

Again, the glory of God came down and filled the house so that none could enter in or minister in the Sanctuary.
The significance of this is to be found in the chapter on the dedication of the temple.

E. **Prayer-Worship and Praise-Worship**

  1. **The Tabernacle**

     In the Tabernacle of Moses, the ascending daily ministrations were the ascending sacrificial offerings on the brazen altar, the ascending incense from the golden altar and the burning lamps of the lampstands. Otherwise all was quiet in the Sanctuary services.

  2. **The Temple**

     In the temple of the Lord, we have the same daily ministrations of the ascending sacrifices, the incense and the burning lamps. But here we have the order of the Levitical singers and musicians and their ascending sacrifices of praise and worship.

     The tabernacle was prayer-worship. The temple was prayer and praise-worship in the priestly courses.

F. **The Priest and The King**

  1. **The Tabernacle**

     As has already been noted in a previous chapter, the Tabernacle of Moses is emphatically associated with the office of the high priest and the Levitical priests.

     None could approach the Lord in His tabernacle in the wilderness apart from priestly ministrations.

  2. **The Temple**

     In contrast, we cannot think of the temple of the Lord without first thinking of KING Solomon, then of the PRIESTLY courses. The offices of king and priest are brought together into sharper focus in a very real way in the administration of the temple services.

     Godly kings and Godly priests worked together in the maintenance of the spiritual life of the nation over the years. All kings were judged by the Lord by their relationship to the house of the Lord and the priests. The king represented the kingdom. The priest represented the temple. The governmental and ecclesiastical were seen to run parallel in the offices of king and priest.

IN CONCLUSION we note these contrasts and comparison in two columns.

THE TABERNACLE OF MOSES	THE TEMPLE OF SOLOMON
1. The Wilderness habitation The temporary	— The Promised Land habitation The permanent
2. Three places, Holiest of All, Holy Place, Outer Court	— Three places, Holiest of All, Holy Place, Outer Courts
3. Acacia wood, gold, silver, brass, fine linen, precious stones, spices	— Cedar, fir, olive timber, gold, silver, brass, iron, linen, precious stones, spices
4. One ark of the Covenant One Altar of Incense One Table of Shewbread One Golden Lampstand One Brazen Altar One Brazen Laver	— The same ark of the Covenant One Altar of Incense Ten Tables of Shewbread Ten Golden Lampstands One Brazen Altar Ten Brazen Lavers One Molten Sea
5. One High Priest and household Levitical Tribe of priests	— One High Priest and household Twentyfour Courses of priesthood
6. Quiet order of worship	— Singers and musicians order of worship

7.	The desert floor	—	The gold floor
8.	The Shekinah Glory-Fire Dedicated at Mt Sinai Feast of Pentecost	—	The Shekinah Glory-Fire Dedicated at Mt Moriah Feast of Tabernacles
9.	Moses, the wise masterbuilder along with others	—	Solomon, the wise masterbuilder along with others

Other points of contrast and comparison will be seen in the various chapters. Enough of the major ones have been provided to show that God was not merely duplicating the Tabernacle of Moses, but actually amplifying all that was there with greater, richer, fuller and more significant administration of Divine truths.

The Tabernacle of the Lord speaks of Christ in His earth walk, His earthly ministry and glory. The Temple of the Lord speaks of Christ in His heavenly ministry, His heavenly glory.

CHAPTER TWELVE

THE BUILDERS AND WORKERS IN THE TEMPLE

In this chapter we consider the lessons which may be learnt from the temple builders and the workers in the Lord's house.

The builders and workers in the temple become typical people also, even as in the building of the Tabernacle of Moses.

Moses received the heavenly pattern as the wise master-builder, but he had men and women of Israel involved in the building as joint labourers (Exodus 31:1-6; 35:4-35; 36:1-4).

The same is true of the temple here. David received the pattern of the temple by the Spirit. He gave the revelation to Solomon. Solomon built according to the pattern by the ministry of other builders and workers.

Let us consider these builders and workers in more details for they become typical of those builders involved in building the New Covenant temple, the church, which is God's house.

1. David — The Pattern of God

As previously noted, David in many aspects of his life and character is a remarkable type of Christ, the greater Son of David.

David's name means "Beloved of the Lord" and points to God's "Beloved Son", Jesus, in whom the Father was well pleased (Matthew 3:17).

David was first a shepherd, then a king. Between these two functions, David experienced much suffering and rejection. After his anointing as king in the midst of his brethren, and the Spirit of the Lord had descended on him (1 Samuel 16), David suffered a period of rejection, humiliation, hatred and betrayal. He was persecuted from place to place by Saul who had lost the anointing of the Spirit of God. In his rejection David gathered to himself a great company of people, welding them into a mighty army. These shared in his sufferings.

In due time David was exalted to the throne as king (Study 1 Samuel chapters 16-31; 2 Samuel chapters 1-5).

The analogy is evident. Christ, the Son of David, after His anointing, experienced rejection and humiliation. He was betrayed and suffered under the hands of the "Saul system" of His day. In due time He was exalted to the throne of His Father God and built His church out of the disciples who came to Him. Those that suffer with Him shall also reign with Him, says the Scripture.

As already seen, David was also a man of war and shed blood abundantly before his death. In these battles he gained great spoils from the victories over his enemies. From these spoils he provided materials to build the temple.

David also established the Tabernacle of David with its order of singers and musicians and worship and praise in Zion. All of this order would, in due time, be incorporated into the temple order in Mt Moriah (1 Chronicles chapters 15-16).

Before his death, David received the revelation of the temple, the house of the Lord to be built, and gave the same to his son, Solomon, the man of peace.

Who can fail to see the many similarities in the life of David and Christ? Christ is the good shepherd. Christ is now king. Christ suffered for us greatly. He is the Man of War, conquering Satan and the enemies of God for us. He is the leader of our praise and worship. He received the revelation of the church which He said He would build (Matthew 16:15-19). He will build this temple by the power of the Holy Spirit.

Christ, David's Son by humanity, and David's Lord by Divinity, has the pattern of the New Testament church, God's temple. So we follow Him!

2. **Solomon — The Wisdom of God**

At the risk of repetition we note again some of the most pertinent things concerning Solomon.

Solomon's name interpreted means "Peace, peaceable, peaceful, perfect, one who recompenses."

David was a "man of war". Solomon was a "man of peace". David is noted for the shedding of much blood and the man who made great preparation for the temple, the pattern of which he received by the Spirit.

Solomon is noted for peace and wisdom. He was the one chosen of the Lord to build the temple of God according to the pattern given to David.

David precedes Solomon. Solomon completes David. One is incomplete without the other. David received the pattern. Solomon builds to that pattern. David represents the revelation and pattern. Solomon represents the wisdom and peace to build that pattern. One ministry made way for the other ministry. One king made way for the next king.

It is clearly recognized that all men are imperfect. Yet God Himself used imperfect men to typify His perfect Son, the Christ to come, and His redemptive plans and ministry. David and Solomon were both imperfect, as all men are. However, it is evident by God's choice of these men that there is something significant and typical in their offices and ministries with regard to the temple of the Lord. It is this that we discover here.

Solomon, in relation to the house of the Lord, may be viewed in a twofold manner. FIRSTLY, Solomon may represent Christ in His resurrection ministry. Jesus Himself alluded to this when He said, "The queen of the south shall rise up in the judgment with this generation, and shall condemn it: for she came from the uttermost parts of the earth to hear THE WISDOM OF SOLOMON; and behold, a greater than Solomon is here" (Matthew 12:42).

He also said "that in this place (i.e., the temple) is one greater than the temple" (Matthew 12:6).

Surely Christ speaks of Himself as the "one greater than the temple", for He Himself is the true temple of God. Surely Christ speaks of Himself as the "one greater than Solomon", for He Himself is the wisdom of God, the peace of God, personified (1 Corinthians 1:30; 12:8; Proverbs 8:22-36; James 3:17-18; Ephesians 3:9-10; Proverbs 9:1).

In this type we may view David as Christ in HIS DEATH, as the shedder of blood and the conqueror of all enemies. Christ in His victory over our enemies is the "Man of War".

Solomon may be viewed as Christ in HIS RESURRECTION, as the "Man of Peace and Wisdom". The house of the Lord can only be built in a time of rest and quietness, in a time of peace, not in a time of war. Christ as the King-priest and the Branch is the builder of the temple of the Lord (Zechariah 6:12-13; Hebrews 3:2-4; 1 Chronicles 22:9-10; Psalm 72:1-4; Isaiah 9:6; Micah 5:2-4).

On the other hand, some expositors liken Solomon's ministry in relation to the temple building to the ministry of the Holy Spirit.

With Bible characters, it is not always what they were but often what they did that God used to typify His purposes in relation to Christ and the church.

The work of Solomon was to build the temple by the Spirit of wisdom. The temple was built by wisdom, knowledge, understanding and insight in a time of peace (1 Kings 3:5-28; 4:29-34; 2 Chronicles 1). Solomon prayed for these things.

As Solomon (Wisdom and Peace) built according to the pattern given to David (War and Victory), so the Holy Spirit builds the church, the New Covenant temple, according to the pattern that the Father gave to His Son.

The Father works through the Son. The Son works through the Holy Spirit. So Christ builds His church by the ministry of the Holy Spirit.

Paul was a wise master-builder. Paul depended on the Holy Spirit to build the church. He prayed that the Spirit of Wisdom, understanding and knowledge would be upon all believers in this habitation of God (Ephesians 1:15-18). It is by the church that the manifold wisdom of God is to be manifested unto principalities and powers in heavenly places (Ephesians 3:9-10).

All the kings of the earth sought to hear the wisdom of Solomon (1 Kings 10). All the nations are to see God's manifested wisdom in the church. This can only be as the Holy Spirit, the Spirit of wisdom, rests upon the builders of this temple.

The Tabernacle of Moses was built by the Spirit of wisdom in Bezaleel and Aholiab (Exodus 31:1-6; 36:1-8; 35:10,25,30-35).

The Temple of Solomon would be built by the Spirit of wisdom in the builders also (1 Kings 3:12-13).

Likewise the New Covenant temple will be built by the wisdom of God (Proverbs 1:1-6; 9:1; 24:3-4; 1 Corinthians 3:9-11; Ephesians 1:14-18). It will not be by might, nor by power, but by My Spirit, saith the Lord (Zechariah 4:6).

3. Hiram, the Gentile King of Tyre

The third most important person in connection with the building of the temple was Hiram. Hiram had been a long time friend of king David (2 Samuel 5:11; 1 Kings 5:1; 1 Chronicles 14:1). He was a Gentile, a Syrian king, and supplied materials for David's house.

Hiram's name means "whiteness, noble, exaltation of life".

Solomon, the king of Israel, sent to Hiram, the king of Tyre to communicate with him about the house of the Lord he was to build. He requested from him various materials to build the Lord's house for payment in material goods from Israel (1 Kings 5:2-12; 9:11-14,27; 10:11,22; 2 Chronicles 2:3-16; 9:10,21).

It is significant that Hiram was a Gentile, yet God used this man to supply materials for His house. Hiram also had his skilful men working alongside the skilful men of Israel (2 Chronicles 2:14). Thus Israelites and Gentiles worked together, side by side, in the building of the Lord's house.

Solomon, the Israelite king specialized in the vessels of gold. Hiram, the Gentile king, specialized in vessels of brass.

Surely this shadows forth the coming in of the Gentiles along with Israel into the New Covenant church, the temple of the Lord, the Body of Christ (Ephesians 2:11-22). The Gentiles would no longer be strangers and foreigners but fellow-citizens in the household of faith. Jew and Gentile would become God's material in His spiritual house after calvary and Pentecost.

4. Hiram, the Skilful Worker

The fourth man particularly noted is another man by the name of Hiram (2 Chronicles 2:7,13,14; 1 Kings 7:13-14).

As seen in the above, Hiram's name interpreted means "whiteness, noble, exaltation of life".

This Hiram was part Hebrew, part Gentile, or so it seems. Hiram's mother was of the tribe of Dan ("Judge"), her husband being of the tribe of Naphtali ("Wrestling or Striving").

His mother became widowed and she married a man of Tyre. Jamieson, Fausett and Brown comment on 2 Chronicles 2:14 concerning an apparent discrepancy. "Hiram's mother, though belonging to the tribe of Dan, had been married to a Napthalite, so when married afterwards to a Tyrian, she might be described as a widow of Naphtali. Or, if she was a native of the city of Dan (Laish), she might be said to be of the daughters of Dan, as born in that place; and of the tribe of Naphtali, as really belonging to it."

He was filled with wisdom and understanding to work all works of gold, silver, brass, iron, stone, timber and material as well as the work of engraving. He was sent in response to Solomon's request of Hiram the king of Tyre to help in the temple building along with Solomon's skilled workers. He specialized in the making of the vessels of brass, the pillars of brass, the molten sea, the lavers and other works of brass also (1 Kings 7:13,14). Hiram, a Gentile king, majored in vessels of brass formed and fashioned in clay ground. Solomon, a Hebrew king majored in vessels of gold. The main point to note is that ISRAEL and GENTILE people were involved in the temple of the Lord. What a contrast to that of the building of the Tabernacle of Moses.

5. **The Multitude of Temple Workers**

    In the Tabernacle of Moses there were specialized builders, but there were many Israelites who did their part by the wisdom of God also. All submitted their work to Moses in the final before its construction. Both men and women were involved in the building of that habitation (Exodus 31:1-11; 35:1-35).

    So here in the building of the temple there was a multitude of workers also who had a part in the house of the Lord. This multitude of workers supported the specialized builders of God's house.

    From the following references we note this great multitude of workers for the habitation of God (1 Kings 5:15; 9:1-2,20-21; 2 Chronicles 7:17,18).

    A. **Strangers in Israel**

        Strangers in Israel numbered 153,600.
        70,000 became "bearers of burdens", or burden bearers.
        80,000 became "hewers in the mountains", or timber fellers.
         3,600 were "overseers" to set the people to their work.

        It seems that 3,300 were chief officers, rulers over the people in the work. Possibly the other 300 of these chief officers were chief overseers.

    B. **Men of Israel**

        The chosen men of Israel levied out of the tribes numbered 30,000 in all. Of these, 10,000 were sent by course each month to Lebanon. The man Adoniram was set over these 30,000 in their courses (1 Kings 5:13-16). Adoniram means "My Lord is most high", or, "The Lord of might and elevation".

        Out Lord Jesus Christ is "The Lord most high", and "The Lord of might and elevation" since He was made LORD by the Father in His exaltation (Acts 2:34-37; Philippians 2:5-11; Psalm 110:1; Hebrews 1:3).

        In this multitude of temple workers we have:

        1. Hewers of timber
        2. Stonesquarers or stone masons
        3. Builders of the house
        4. Carpenters
        5. Labourers

        All manner of workmanship and willing and skilful workers were there (1 Chronicles 22:14-16; 28:21).
        All these thousands of labourers worked together for one purpose — to build the house of the Lord. Regardless of their varied and differing abilities and skills, talents and gifts and offices, all functioned harmoniously for the building of God's temple.

SPIRITUAL LESSONS

The spiritual lessons for the church, God's people are manifest. Christ, by the Spirit, is building His church. He has set in the church wise master-builders, gifted and equipped by the Spirit of wisdom, knowledge and understanding (1 Corinthians 3:9-17; Ephesians 2:19-22; 1 Corinthians 12:1-13; Romans 12:1-8).

The fivefold ascension-gift ministries of apostles, prophets, evangelists, pastors and teachers are the specialized overseers in the house of the Lord (Ephesians 4:9-16).

1. **The apostles and prophets** together lay the foundation of the house, building according to the pattern shown to them (Ephesians 2:19-22; 3:1-9; Luke 11:49,52; 1 Corinthians 12:27,28).

2. **The evangelists**, as quarry-men and hewers of trees also, obtain the materials to be prepared and beautified to fit into the house of the Lord.

3. **The shepherds and teachers**, as stone-masons, and stone-squarers, fulfil their ministry in shaping and polishing the stones and timber for God's holy temple.

4. **The elders and deacons** are involved as overseers and servants in the temple of the Lord, taking the oversight and care of the people of God, serving them in every way they can (Acts 20:17-35; 1 Peter 5:1-5; 1 Timothy 3; Titus 1; Philippians 1:1).

5. **The multitude of believers** in the Body of Christ, as living material in a spiritual house, all work together in the building of God's habitation by the Spirit (Ephesians 2:19-22; 1 Peter 2:5-9; 1 Corinthians 12).

The various members in the Body of Christ have been given gifts, talents, offices and various abilities to build His church according to the Divine pattern. Paul says, "I as a wise master-builder (or an architect) have laid the foundation and others build there upon. Let every man take heed how he builds." (1 Corinthians 3:9-17).

The builders in the tabernacle and temple were appointed of God and they appointed others.
The tabernacle and temple were built by the wisdom of God, by the Spirit of God, and according to the pattern of God through human instrumentality (Exodus 31:1-6; 35:30-35; 36:1-3; 2 Chronicles 1:3-12; 2:13-14).

The Tabernacle of Moses was wholly built by Israelites of the various tribes. All spoke of Christ's coming of the chosen nation of Israel.
By way of contrast, the temple of Solomon was built by Israelites and Gentile strangers, which speaks of the New Covenant church being built of Jews and Gentiles, set in one Body, one temple in Christ. Though the temple revelation was committed to the Hebrew nation, yet Gentiles partook of the blessing in the construction of the temple.

There are numerous prophecies of blessing on both Jew and Gentile in the one Body of Christ. Jews and Gentiles, fitly framed together, grow together into a holy temple for the Lord, a habitation of God by the Spirit (Ephesians 2:11-22; Romans chapters 9-11; Acts chapters 10-11, 15; 1 Corinthians 12:13; Isaiah 56:3-8).

It is worthy to compare the specialized builders and other workers in relation to both tabernacle and temple.

THE TABERNACLE		THE TEMPLE
1. Moses — The pattern receiver Of the tribe of Levi A shepherd, a priest, a king	—	1. David — The pattern receiver Of the tribe of Judah A shepherd, a king, touched priesthood
2. Built the Tabernacle of the Lord	—	2. Built the Tabernacle of David
3. Bezaleel — wise builder Of tribe of Judah	—	3. Solomon — wise master-builder Of tribe of Judah
4. Aholiab — skilful worker Of tribe of Dan A teacher in wisdom	—	4. Hiram — skilful worker Of Dan (by mother) Wise and skilful worker
5. Many men and women helpers	—	5. Many thousands help in building
6. Built by the wisdom of God	—	6. Built by the wisdom of God
7. Built by the Spirit of God	—	7. Built by the Spirit of God
8. Built according to pattern of God	—	8. Built according to pattern of God

9. Materials of gold, silver, brass,   —   9. Built by materials of gold, silver,
   acacia wood, precious stones, and   brass, iron, timber, precious stones
   from spoils of the Egyptians   and spoils of Israel's enemies

10. Built only by Israelites   —   10. Built by Israelites and Gentiles

Zechariah the prophet foretold the building of the New Covenant temple by Christ and the involvement of both Jew and Gentile. ''Behold the Man whose name is THE BRANCH; and He shall grow up out of His place, and He shall build the temple of the Lord: Even He shall build the temple of the Lord; and He shall bear the glory, and shall sit and rule upon His throne; and He shall be a priest upon His throne; and the counsel of peace shall be between them both (i.e., the two offices of king and priest).

And they that are far off (i.e., the Gentiles) shall come and build in the temple of the Lord, and you (Judah) shall know that the Lord of hosts hath sent me unto you'' (Zechariah 6:12,13,15).

THE VESSELS OF THE HOUSE OF THE LORD

The Vessels of the House of the Lord

There were many thousands of them (see Ezra 1)

1. Spoons of Brass
2. Knives of Brass
3. Open Flowers
4. Golden Snuffers
5. Golden Snuffdishes
6. Golden covers for bowls
7. Golden Hinges
8. Golden Censers

9. Gold, Silver and Brazen Pots
10. Basins of Gold and Silver
11. Chargers of Gold and Silver
12. Brazen Fleshhooks
13. Nails of Gold
14. Iron Hammer
15. Brazen Shovels

CHAPTER THIRTEEN

THE OFFERINGS AND MATERIALS FOR THE TEMPLE

A. **The Freewill Offerings** — 1 Chronicles 29:5-22

The materials for the Temple, as also for the Tabernacle, were given by the freewill offerings of the people; not from the tithes which were set aside for the priesthood ministry. The Holy Spirit moved upon the people to give of their substance.

The emphasis in these Scriptures, concerning the Tabernacle of Moses, is upon those "whose heart stirred him up" and "every one whom his spirit made willing" (Exodus 25:1-9; 35:4-29). The people actually brought more than enough to Moses for the Tabernacle of the Lord and had to be restrained from giving (Exodus 36:5-7). What a spirit of giving was upon the people, and this under the era of the Law!

The same spirit of giving was manifested in the building of the Temple. "The people rejoiced for that they offered willingly" (1 Chronicles 29:5-22). This was of the Lord for this is unnatural for the natural man.

David prayed to the Lord: "For all things come of Thee, and of Thine own have we given Thee" (1 Chronicles 29:14). The people gave back to God what He had given to them.

God Himself is the great giver and when He gave His only begotten Son, He gave us all things freely with Him. The Father gave His Son. The Son gave Himself. He also gave the Holy Spirit. The Holy Spirit also gives spiritual gifts to the church. God loves. Love gives. And God willingly gave to His people (John 3:16; Romans 8:31-32; Ephesians 4:11-16; 1 Corinthians 12:1-13).

This same spirit of giving is to be manifested in the redeemed. All that we have already belongs to God, who is the supreme owner of all things. We are only giving back to the Lord what is already His (Psalm 24:1). The Spirit of Christ will cause God's people to give freely, willingly, generously, hilariously both that which is natural and spiritual as the material for the building of His Temple, which is the church.

Anything that is truly built by God will be built by the Spirit and not by force or compulsion. God only can cause people to give as He does and He can only bless that which is of Himself. He gave Himself and all things in Himself. We give ourselves and all we have to Him. The believer brings tithes and offerings to Him, as well as presenting himself a living sacrifice to the Lord (2 Corinthians 8:9-15; Luke 21:2-4; Romans 12:1-2; Acts 2:45; 4:37; Malachi 3:8-10).

When God spoke to Abraham concerning his seed coming forth out of bondage with "great substance" from Egypt (Genesis 15:14), which word was fulfilled later on in the Exodus, God had in mind the Tabernacle (Exodus 3:21-22; 11:1-3; 12:35-36; Psalm 105:37-38). The Israelites received the riches and spoils of the Egyptians as payment for the hundreds of years slave labour of the chosen nation. They received riches of gold, silver, precious stones and other materials. They gave back to God what He had given them for the building of the Tabernacle. That which they had received from the Egyptians was not only to make them rich but to give to God for His service.

The same was true concerning the Temple of the Lord. When Israel received the wealth of the promised land and the disinherited nations, a land of gold, silver, brass, iron and precious stones, as well as other spoils from their enemies, God had in mind the building of His Temple (Deuteronomy 8:7-20).

The people returned to the Lord the substance He had blessed them with. The Temple was worth millions — it was priceless, yet so costly!

In subsequent years, even under King Hezekiah, there was a great spirit of willingness in giving to the Lord for His house and the temple service (2 Chronicles 31:8).

God's people are to be a willing offering in the day of His power (Psalm 110:3). God's people have to be stirred to give to the Lord and His house (Isaiah 64:7).

The Church, God's new covenant temple, has been bought with a great price. It is priceless, yet costly! (1 Corinthians 6:16-21.) However, it is built entirely out of people who are "freewill offerings" unto the Lord, first of themselves, and then of all that they have.

B. Materials and Gifts for the Temple

There were basically three major groupings of materials brought for the temple of the Lord, these being, metals, stones and timbers. Other materials involved various cloth for curtains and hangings.

We note here some of the vast amount of materials given for the house of the Lord from King David, the Princes and the congregation.

Again we note, as in the Tabernacle of Moses, that God took the materials of *creation* to set forth truths of *redemption*. The materials listed here come from the mineral kingdom, the plant kingdom and the animal kingdom. All the kingdoms of this world belong to Him who is the King of kings and Lord of lords. He may use all things from all lower kingdoms for the glory of His house and His kingdom.

1. King David's Gifts for the Temple

* David's Preparation of Materials for the Temple (1 Chronicles 22:1-5,14-16; 28:11-21; 29:1-3).

* David's own personal gift (1 Chronicles 29:3-5).
  3,000 talents of the *gold* of Ophir.
  7,000 talents of refined *silver*.

* David's gift from the Treasury (1 Chronicles 22:14).
  100,000 talents of *gold*.
  1,000,000 talents of *silver*.

2. The Chief Rulers and Offerings of the people (1 Chronicles 29:5-9)

5,000 talents of *gold,* and 10,000 drams of *gold*.
10,000 talents of *silver*.
18,000 talents of *brass*.
100,000 talents of *iron* (for the tools and nails; 1 Kings 6:7; 1 Chronicles 22:3).
Precious stones.

3. King Solomon's Gifts of Exchange (1 Kings 5; 2 Chronicles 2).

20,000 measures of beaten *wheat*.)	
20,000 measures of *barley*.)	Corn, Wine and Oil
20,000 measures or baths of *wine*.)	
20,000 baths of *oil*.)	

All this was given in exchange for *timbers* for the hewers and builders.

How David, Solomon and the people loved the house of the Lord (1 Chronicles 29:3; Psalm 26:8). They were motivated by love for the Lord's house to give of their God-given wealth, the wealth of the nations.

Much of the material given for the Temple was similar to the gifts given for the Tabernacle of Moses, with some differences which are seen in the following comparison.

Materials of Moses Tabernacle	—	**Materials for Solomon's Temple**
(Exodus 25:1-9; 35:4-9)		(1 Chronicles 22:2-16; 28:14-18; 29:1-8; 2 Chronicles 2:8-10)

1. *Metals* — Gold, silver, brass   —   Gold, silver, brass, iron
2. *Stones* — Precious gem stones   —   Precious gem stones, quarried stones
3. *Timber* — Shittim or acacia wood   —   Cedar, fir, algum, and olive woods
4. *Cloths* — Linen, blue, purple and scarlet   —   Linen, blue, purple and scarlet
5. *Food* — Manna, Water   —   Corn, wine and oil

All of these materials have some aspect of truth and therefore some spiritual significance of the glories of Christ and His church. Indeed, as the Psalmist says, "every part of it utters His glory" (Psalm 29:9).

We, as new covenant believers, become "the material" for God's temple. God is building His church, a spiritual house. The material involves that which is both physical and spiritual, as well as material. We bring all that we are, spirit, soul and body and all that we have and such becomes the kind of material with which God builds His holy house (Romans 12:1-2; 1 Thessalonians 5:23-24).

C. The Vessels of the Temple

The vessels of the Lord's house were made predominantly out of the gold, silver and brass. There were other tools and instruments made from the iron and there were the curtains and hangings made from cloth material.

Before noting some of the spiritual significance of the temple materials, we set out the list of the vessels and utensils of the Lord's house.

1. Golden flowers — 1 Kings 6:35. Open flowers, fully developed.
2. Golden Tongs — 1 Kings 7:49 with Isaiah 6:6.
3. Golden Bowls — 1 Kings 7:50; 2 Chronicles 4:8. One hundred bowls, used for the sprinkling of the sacrificial blood.
4. Golden Snuffers — 1 Kings 7:50. These were for the trimming of the lamps.
5. Golden Snuffdishes — Used for the ashes of the burnt wicks of the lamps (Exodus 25:38).
6. Golden Spoons — 1 Kings 7:50 with Jeremiah 52:19; Numbers 7:86.
7. Golden Censers — 1 Kings 7:50. Used for the incense.
8. Golden Fleshhooks — 1 Chronicles 28:17. Used for the sacrifices.
9. Golden Cups — 1 Chronicles 28:17. Used for covers. (Hebrew = "to cover").
10. Golden Basins — 1 Kings 7:45 with Ezra 1:10.
11. Golden Chargers — Ezra 1:9. Used to carry the offering parts.
12. Golden Shields — 1 Kings 14:26.
13. Silver Basins — 1 Kings 7:45; Ezra 1:10.
14. Silver Chargers — Ezra 1:9.
15. Brazen Vessels — 2 Chronicles 4:16; 1 Kings 7:45; Jeremiah 52:18,20. Bright brass, kept bright by scouring.
16. Brazen Pots — Leviticus 6:28.
17. Brazen Shovels — 1 Kings 7:45. Used for ashes from the sacrificial altar.
18. Knives — Ezra 1:9; Genesis 22:6. Used for sacrifices.

19. Iron Tools and Nails — 1 Kings 6:7; 1 Chronicles 22:3. Used for the doors and gates of the Temple.

20. Silver Lampstands — 1 Chronicles 28:14-17. Used for priests chambers.

21. Silver Tables — 1 Chronicles 28:14-17. Used in the priests chambers also.

Numerous vessels were used in the house of the Lord. The charge of the Lord to His people, and the temple priesthood is given in Isaiah 52:11, "Be ye clean, that bear the vessels of the Lord."
The Lord wants His own, those in His great house, to be "vessels unto honour, sanctified and suitable for the Master's use, and prepared unto every good work" (2 Timothy 2:19-21).
The Lord chooses those who will be vessels unto Him for His house and His people (Acts 9:15).
He wants to have vessels of mercy, vessels unto honour, rather than vessels of wrath, vessels unto dishonour (Romans 9:20-24). He is the great potter and desires that vessels not be marred in His hand (Jeremiah 18:1-6).

We note some of the spiritual significances of the various materials used in the Temple of the Lord.

1. **GOLD —**   In both Old and New Testament, we find that gold speaks to us of Deity, Divine nature, the glory of God in His holiness. Gold has always symbolized deity, even in heathen idolatrous feasts which corrupted the truth God gave to Israel.
This metal was especially used in the Holiest of All, as well as in the utensils listed above.

2. **SILVER —**   Silver is ever used as symbolic of redemption, the atonement, the ransom money. It points to the Son, even as the gold points to the Father God. Silver was used for the ransom money, the atonement for the soul in the nation of Israel (Exodus 30:11-16). Jesus, like Joseph was sold by His brethren for silver pieces (Zechariah 11:12-13; Matthew 26:15).
Silver was used for silver lampstands in the Temple also (Note — no doubt in the priest's chambers only, 1 Chronicles 28:14-17).
Refer also to silver in Exodus 38:26-27; 26:19-32; 27:10-17; 36:24-36; 38:10-27. Believers are redeemed, not with silver or gold, but with the precious blood of Christ (1 Peter 1:18-20).

3. **BRASS —**   Brass is found to be symbolic of judgment against sin, against self. The Holy Spirit is titled "The Spirit of Judgment and the Spirit of Burning" (Isaiah 4:4). The heavens were to become as brass (and iron) against Israel if they sinned against the Lord and His Word (Deuteronomy 28:13-23). The feet of Christ walking in His Church are as brass burning in a furnace (Revelation 1:12-15). The serpent of brass was used to deal with Israel's sin (Numbers 21:5-9). Brass is especially noted in both Tabernacle and Temple in their respective Outer Courts.

4. **IRON —**   Iron is often linked with brass. It is symbolic of strength and endurance. Also of judgment and inflexibility. David prepared iron in abundance for the nails for the doors and gates of the temple (1 Chronicles 22:3).
The heavens would be as iron and brass, or brass and iron against Israel if they sinned against the Lord (Deuteronomy 28:23,48 with Leviticus 26:19).

5. **GEMSTONES** — Precious stones were used in the temple in the walls, as well as in the garments of the High Priest, in particular, the breastplate of judgment. They speak of the various gifts of the Spirit, the glories of the saints, and the preciousness of God's people and their righteous acts. Revelation 21:18-20; 1 Corinthians 3:9-17.

6. **STONES** — Quarried stones used for the building of the temple speak of believers taken from the quarries of this world, prepared by the various ministries to be placed in the house of the Lord (1 Kings 5:17-18; 1 Peter 2:5). This will be noted more fully in the chapter on the Temple Structure.

7. **TIMBER** — In contrast to the wood used in the Tabernacle of Moses, which was acacia wood, the Temple used timber from the cedar, the fir and olive trees more especially.
    Trees in Scripture point also to Christ and His church. The believer is likened to a tree planted by the rivers of water (Psalm 1:1-3). Many Scriptures speak of trees and use such in symbolic manner. Further details of such will be noted in the appropriate sections (Psalm 92:12-13).

Other details of materials and their significances will be seen in the succeeding chapters. However, enough insight has been given here to see that God, in specifying the particular materials to be used in His house, had some truth in mind to be discovered in the symbolics used.

In bringing our chapter to a conclusion we note the main lessons learnt. As Israel gave freewill offerings to the Lord of their material substance, so the believer is to give freely to the Lord. He is to present himself and all that he has to the Lord as a freewill, a voluntary offering. There the Lord used actual materials to build His house. The material He uses today is people. God's people are the material He uses to build a spiritual house, His new covenant temple. The various materials from the various kingdoms all symbolized some redemptive truth in His house, all showed forth some aspect of His glory. So all believers today, out of every kindred, tongue, tribe and nation, who are built into God's house, manifest some aspect of His glory in covenantal and redemptive truth.

The Psalmist writes, "Because of thy Temple at Jerusalem kings shall bring presents unto Thee" (Psalm 68:29; Isaiah 56:3-8). So Jew and Gentile, out of all nations, bring themselves as presents to the Lord for His spiritual house, the church.

CHAPTER FOURTEEN

THE DIVINE PURPOSE FOR THE TEMPLE

The Divine purpose for the existence of the Temple is very specific. God wanted to have a place in which to record His Name, a place in which He could dwell among His people in His glory and presence.

"The Name" in Scripture always speaks of "the nature" of God, the character of God, who He is in His own essential Being.

God has always wanted a place — indeed A PERSON — in which He could set His Name and all that is represented in that expression.

Let us note the progression, especially in relation to God's dwelling places with Israel, of THE NAME OF THE LORD!

1. **The Name in Shiloh**

Shiloh became a central city in the time of Joshua, and until the time of Samuel the prophet, it was the place where the Tabernacle of the Lord was settled. The student should read these Scriptures. Joshua 18:1-10; 22:9-13; Judges 18:31. The house of God was at this time at Shiloh. Judges 21:12-21; 1 Samuel 1:1-24; 3:21. Here the word of the Lord appeared to Samuel.

It was at Shiloh where the ark of the Covenant of the Lord was taken captive by the Philistines after the presumptuous act of Eli's priestly sons (1 Samuel 4:1-12; 14:1-3). It was at Shiloh that the prophet Ahijah dwelt, bringing to God's people the word of the Lord.

Because sin, iniquity and various abominations abounded, the nation of Israel lapsed into the idolatry and apostasy of other heathen nations. God "forsook the tabernacle that was in Shiloh", where His Name had been recorded. Thus Shiloh was desolated by the departure of the presence of God. He forsook the tabernacle in Shiloh (Psalm 78:60).

The prophet Jeremiah lamented this fact of Israel polluting the Name of the Lord by the way they lived among the heathen. God forsook His people for "His Name's sake".

In Jeremiah 7:1-16;30 God speaks to Judah saying to them, "Go back to Shiloh where I set MY NAME at the first, and see what I did to it for the wickedness of My people Israel. . .".

It seems that the name "Shiloh" had prophetic significance also and pointed to the Messiah, who would bring "rest" to the people of God. Christ Jesus is indeed "the place of rest" for all who would come to God through Him (Matthew 11:28-30).

Jacob prophesied, "The sceptre shall not depart from Judah until Shiloh come, and unto Him shall the gathering of the people be" (Genesis 49:10).

There is therefore a twofold application of "The Name" in Shiloh. First in Christ, who is God's Shiloh, there is the rest of God and God's Name is in Him. He is God's Word, God's prophet, God's Tabernacle, God's Ark and God's Name dwells in Him in fulness (Colossians 1:19; 2:9). God rests in Christ's finished work at Calvary. To Him all true believers gather, in His Name and to His word and work.

The other aspect is applicable to the Church, and it is seen in the fact that as God forsook Israel because of iniquity, so God will forsake any church that become idolatrous. When sin and corruption manifests itself in Israel, or the people of God, upon whom the Name is called, then God permits the Ark of His presence to be taken away. They are judged even by God forsaking them as He forsook Shiloh.

Here at Shiloh, the glory of God departed, it became desolate without His presence and this is seen in the symbolic name "Ichabod" — "the glory is departed", or "where is the glory?".

Any company of God's people who "pollute the Name of the Lord" by sin and apostacy will lose the presence of the Lord. God has to remove the Ark of His presence and judge His people and do to them what He did to Shiloh. He does this ".for His Name's sake".

Paul states in Timothy, "Let every one who names the name of Christ depart from iniquity" (2 Timothy 2:19). They must depart from iniquity or God will depart from them, even as from Shiloh.

This is exemplified in the Church of Laodicea where the Lord is on the outside of His church, desirous of entering in. They are so wrapped up in the externals of religion on the inside, they do not hear His gentle knock outside.

Thus Shiloh was a place where the Lord recorded His Name, at the first.

2. **The Name in the Tabernacle**

Much Scripture is given to the place of God's dwelling, the Tabernacle of the Lord. Generally it is spoken of as the Tabernacle of Moses.

Concerning the creation of this vast universe, the Author passes over it in a matter of verses only, for this earth is man's dwelling place (Genesis chapters 1-2). But concerning the Tabernacle, which occupied a small part of this earth, in the wilderness, God gives many chapters and verses, both in Old and New Testaments, as to its details and construction.

The distinctive purpose for its existence was that God might have a place wherein His Name could dwell. This is seen in the Scripture relative to the Tabernacle.

"In all places where I record MY NAME, I will come unto thee and bless thee" (Exodus 20:24).

"Let them make Me sanctuary that I may dwell among them . . ." (Exodus 25:8).

"The Lord thy God shall choose a place to put HIS NAME there . . . choose to cause HIS NAME to dwell there . . ." (Deuteronomy 12:5-12; 10:8; 14:23-24; 16:1-12; 26:2).

The Tabernacle, which was God's very dwelling place on earth, the very place of His throne in Israel, in all of its furnishings and details was a prophetic structure. It pointed to Christ and His church. It was the one and only place where God recorded His Name, and all Israel had to gather to the Tabernacle, where His Name was for all worship, prayer and other set occasions for the Lord. No other place was acceptable to God, but where His Name was recorded. His Name meant His presence. His Name dwelt in the Tabernacle. His Name is Himself.

Here to the Tabernacle, where His Name was recorded, Israel brought their tithes and offerings, their sacrifices, vows and freewill offerings. There they gathered to bless and worship the Lord. It was because His Name was recorded in that place (Ezra 6:12). His Name meant His presence. We are told that God SET His Name there. He PLACED it there. He caused it to DWELL there. There He RECORDED His Name. The Feasts of the Lord took place relative to that place. Everything in Israel centered around the Name and this place.

In the New Testament we are told "The WORD was made flesh and dwelt (lit. tabernacled) among us, full of grace and truth, and the glory as of the only begotten of the Father" (John 1:1-3,14-18).

Jesus Christ is the express and complete fulfilment of all that was typified in the Tabernacle of the Lord. God dwelt in Christ in His fulness. All the fulness of the Godhead was in Him, in bodily form (Colossians 1:19; 2:9). Therefore the Name of God is recorded in Him in fulness. He is the true Tabernacle of which the old was but the type and shadow.

It is to HIM that all New Testament believers gather. The church gathers to HIS NAME!

In Matthew 18:20, Jesus Himself declares, "Where two or three are gathered together IN MY NAME, there I AM in the midst" (Amplified New Testament).

It is to Him all our tithes and offerings, our worship, prayer, praise and spiritual (and material) sacrifices must be brought. The church, as the New Covenant people of God, experience festivals in Him. God has set, placed, and recorded His Name in the Lord Jesus Christ. He is the only one in whom God dwells in absolute fulness. All must come to God by Him.

The Tabernacle was positioned "in the midst" of Israel's camp. God has set His Christ "in the midst" of His church, the camp of the saints and it is to Him and around Him we gather.

No tribe dare place their name on His Tabernacle. Thus believers do not gather in their denominational names, which divide God's people, but all gather in the God-revealed Name of the Lord Jesus Christ, the uniter of His people and the guarantee of God's presence (1 Corinthians 1:10).

3. The Name in the Temple

The Temple of Solomon now confirms the same truth as in the Tabernacle and Shiloh.

The Temple replaced the Tabernacle only on a more glorious scale. However, the very purpose of its existence was that God might record HIS NAME.

David desired to build a house for the Name of the Lord (2 Samuel 7:1-26). God had dwelt in a tent up to this time. However, the prophet Nathan told David that it would be his son, Solomon, who would build a house to the Name of the Lord. 1 Kings 5:3-5; 8:16-29,33-44,48. Solomon purposed to build this house to the Name of the Lord.

In the dedication of the Temple "the Name" is mentioned in numerous verses. God declares, "Concerning this house MY NAME SHALL BE THERE . . . I have hallowed this house . . . to put My Name there . . ." (1 Kings 9:1-7).

Read also these Scriptures (1 Kings 10:1; 11:36; 2 Kings 21:7; 23:27; 1 Chronicles 22:7-19; 28:3; 29:16; 2 Chronicles 2:1-4; 6:1-28; 7:14-16,20; 12:13; 20:8-9; 33:4-7).

However, the same tragic thing would happen to the Temple as happened to the Tabernacle at Shiloh. God forewarned Israel that this house would become desolate because of their abominations (Nehemiah 9:28-37; Jeremiah 7:10-14,30; 32:34).

It was for this very reason God allowed the king of Babylon to destroy the Temple of God. Once the presence of God departed, then the Temple had no protector. It was the presence of God in His Name in the Temple that made it the glory of the whole earth.

Again we see a twofold application of the truth relative to the Temple and the Name of the Lord.

Its primary fulfilment is first in God's temple, the Lord Jesus Christ. In John 2:20-21 He declares Himself to be THE TEMPLE of God, the one and only temple. His body was the temple of God. God's glory dwelt in Him. The Name of God was also in Christ. All that applied to the Tabernacle also applies to the Temple. Christ is God's true Tabernacle and true Temple. He taught us to pray "Our Father who art in heaven . . . hallowed by THY NAME . . ." (Matthew 6:6-9).

If the Name of God was in the Temple of Solomon, how much more should we find it in the true Temple of God, in Christ Jesus our Lord. This is what the New Testament teaches. God was in Christ. The Name of God is in Christ (Philippians 2:9; Colossians 1:19; 2:9; Acts 2:36-38).

The second application is to the church, which is also spoken of as the Temple of God (2 Corinthians 6:16; 3:16; 2 Corinthians 6:16). God has His Temple now in the church. God has recorded His Name in the church. It is spoken of as the Name of the Father, and of the Son and of the Holy Spirit (Matthew 28:19). This triune Name is revealed in the interpretation of the triune Name of the Lord Jesus Christ. It is not to be found in denominational or sectarian church names.

If individual believers, as temples of God, temples of the Holy Spirit, dare to live in sin and iniquity, then God shall do to them — as temples — what He did to the Temple at Jerusalem, for "His Name's sake".

He permitted the Temple, after all the glory it had witnessed, to be desolated, forsaken and destroyed by fire. So the apostle Paul warns, "if any man defile the temple of God, him shall God destroy". God's Name is in the believer, both individually and also corporately. As surely as God forsook the temple at Jerusalem because they brought in abominations, as Ezekiel chapters 1-14 reveal, so surely will He forsake those who bring in abominations in their temple-bodies, and defile His Name by not departing from iniquity. The Temple of the Lord must be kept clean for His Name is recorded there (2 Timothy 2:19; James 2:7, Amplified New Testament; Matthew 23:38,39).

4.   The Name in the ark of the Covenant

The central point and place of God's Name in the Tabernacle and Temple was the article of furniture called THE ARK OF THE COVENANT!
This was the actual piece of furniture on which God chose to dwell and record His Name and His manifest presence.
The ark of the Covenant was the most prominent and most important piece of furniture of all the Tabernacle furnishings. In fact, the whole of the Tabernacle structure, with its furnishings, stood in relationship to this article. Without this article and all that it symbolically fore-shadowed, the Tabernacle was just a mere tent. This article gave meaning and life to all the structure and its furniture. ,
It was the first piece of furniture to be made and rightly so, for it was the very throne of God in the earth. God's very presence dwelt there. Upon the blood-stained mercy seat the Shekinah Glory of God dwelt, between the wings of the Cherubim (Psalm 80:1; 99:1). From this place of glory and atonement, the audible voice of God was heard. God spoke out of "the glory" through a blood-stained mercy seat (Numbers 7:89).

The ark itself was made of acacia wood, overlaid within and without with gold. Then upon the ark was the pure gold mercy seat with the Cherubim. The majestic beauty and truth of this was in the fact that the mercy seat and the Cherubim were all beaten out of one piece of pure gold. The two Cherubs faced each other, yet gazed toward the blood-stained mercy seat. Between this tri-unity (the union of three in one) the very Shekinah Glory of God dwelt in brightness, yet in the cloud, and here the audible voice of God was heard.

It cannot but be recognized that the truth veiled in the symbol and type here finds its rich fulfilment in the Lord Jesus Christ.
Jesus Christ is now THE ARK OF GOD'S COVENANT — the New and Everlasting Covenant as revealed in His Son (Matthew 26:26-28; Hebrews 13:20). The incorruptible blood speaks to God. The incorruptible wood speaks of the perfect, sinless and incorruptible humanity of Jesus Christ. Overlaid within and without with gold speaks of Christ's Divinity. He is the God-Man, the union of God in Man is seen in Him.

In the mercy seat is the blood of atonement which brings us nigh to God (Romans 5:1; Colossians 1:20).

But the glorious truth of His union with the Father and with the Holy Spirit is revealed in the three-in-one Cherubimed mercy seat. The triunity of God, the fulness of the Godhead bodily in Jesus is symbolically seen in the ark of the Tabernacle. One Cherub points to the Father God. The other Cherub speaks of the blessed Holy Spirit. The mercy seat speaks of the Son of God. Three parts, yet one piece of gold. Three Divine persons, yet one God, the eternal Godhead. The Godhead is involved in the atonement. As the Cherubs gazed upon the blood-stained mercy seat, so the Father and Spirit gaze with satisfaction upon the blood-stained Son of God. These three are one (1 John 5:8-10); three Divine persons, yet one in redemptive plan and ministry. Jesus Christ, as the mercy seat, is very part of the Godhead, as seen in the mercy seat being absolutely one with the two Cherubs.
This forever settles the Divinity of the Son, and His co-equality with the Father and the Holy Spirit in the work of redemption. This also declares that the Cherubum are not angelic creatures for they are not one with, nor part of, the mercy seat, that is, Jesus Christ, in redemptive plan. In Jesus Christ we behold the express brightness of the Father's glory (John 1:14-18; Hebrews 1:1-3; Matthew 17:1-9). He Tabernacled with us. We beheld His glory, the glory as of the only begotten of the Father (John 17:1-4). It is eternal glory. It is glory greater than the sun (Revelation 1:12-20; John 14:11; Colossians 2:9; 2 Corinthians 4:6).

And yet again, in Him we see the Name of God as seen dwelling in and upon the ark of the Lord.

In 2 Samuel 6:2 (Margin), and 1 Chronicles 13:6 we are told, ''The ark of God, whose name is called by THE NAME of Jehovah of Hosts, that dwelleth between the Cherubim''.

Also, ''The ark of God, at which THE NAME, even THE NAME of the Lord of Hosts was called (invoked) upon it.'' (Marginal reading).

And yet again, ''To bring up thence the ark of God the Lord, that dwelleth between the Cherubims, whose NAME is called upon it''.

These Scriptures plainly show that it was actually the ARK of the Covenant upon which the unutterable Name of YAHWEH (or Jehovah) was called. This was without doubt in Exodus 40 when the Shekinah Glory filled the Tabernacle after the ark had been placed in the Holiest of All, in its appointed place.

The Tabernacle, in this type, becomes a wonderful shadow of the church, the body of Christ, the habitation of God by the Spirit (Ephesians 2:20-22). The ark becomes a magnificent representation of the Lord Jesus Christ, the head of the church, ''in the midst'' of His redeemed people.

And then again, the Name in and upon this ark becomes a marvellous prophecy of Him who is THE ARK of the New Covenant, and in whom, the Name of God — the redemptive Name of Deity — dwells. This Name dwells in a triune form in Him. It is the one and only triune Name revealed in the whole Bible, even the Name of the Lord Jesus Christ; truly symbolized in the triune piece of gold.

His Name is surely the mercy seat through which we come to the Father. He shed His own blood. To call upon His Name is to trust in His redeeming blood.

The Name of the Father, and of the Son and of the Holy Spirit, the Name of Elohim (God in three persons in the Old Testament) is found in the Name of the Lord Jesus Christ. The triune Name of the triune God thus fulfills some of the rich symbolism found in the triune Cherubim and mercy seat. It is the Name in unity and triunity.

The fulness of the Godhead Name dwells bodily in the Son, who dwells in the midst of His church, now God's Tabernacle and Temple. The glory and presence of God is seen in the face of Jesus Christ (2 Corinthians 4:4-6).

This revelation of God's Name in the ark of the Covenant is the very same revelation as seen in the revelation of the Name declared in the burning bush to Moses. In the bush it was a burning blaze of Divine glory-fire. The voice of Elohim spoke from out of that bush. God in tri-unity spoke. Then the Name of God was revealed, even the redemptive Name ''I AM WHO I AM''. This became JEHOVAH (the LORD) and became spoken of by the Jews as the unutterable and incomprehensible Name. This was the foundation of Moses ministry.

Here in the Tabernacle, or more particularly the Temple, the deliverance for Israel from Egypt and from the Wilderness is complete. The glory that had been on Mt Sinai, and then in the Tabernacle of the Lord, would soon re-enter into the Temple of God; no longer in the burning bush, nor Mt Sinai, nor a Tabernacle but a Temple. However, it would still be manifested in the ark of God. The voice would speak, not now from the bush, nor from Mt Sinai, but from the mercy seat sprinkled with sacrificial and atoning blood.

The revelation is the same. It is God and His Name!

Thus Jesus Christ, the ark of the New Covenant, is the I AM, part of the Elohim (the Godhead) and thus bears the Name of God in and upon Him, in the midst of His church.

The church also is to bear ''His Name'' as a witness in the earth, even as He did (Acts 9:14-16; 15:14-17; Ephesians 3:15; James 2:7). We are one with the Father, one with the Son and one with the Holy Spirit (1 Corinthians 1:10).

5.   **The Name in the City of Jerusalem**

The Name of God was also vitally linked with the city of God, Jerusalem. God dwelt in the

Tabernacle at Gilgal in the original entrance to the land of promise. Then later on the Tabernacle was taken to Shiloh (Joshua 18:1; 8-10).

When the Temple replaced the Tabernacle, it was built in the city of Jerusalem, the city of peace, the holy city.

It can readily be seen what joy and glory was in the city of Jerusalem, because THE TEMPLE of God was in that city. It became the joy of the whole earth. The Temple made the city the glory of all the kingdoms of this earth.

It is in this city that God says His Name was recorded. It was recorded not only in the Temple but also in the city. The city and the temple were therefore united on the one Name of Jehovah.
2 Chronicles 33:4 says, "In Jerusalem will I put My Name . . ."
Daniel 9:18-19 speaks of "The city which is called by Thy Name (whereupon Thy Name is called) . . . for Thy city and thy people are called by Thy Name . . ."

God finally had to judge the city with destruction along with the Temple because of the corruptions and iniquity of the chosen nation.
The visions of the prophet Ezekiel reveal how various abominations were brought into the Temple of God and caused the glory of God to depart from the Temple and from the city (Ezekiel chapters 8-10).

However, in the closing chapters of Ezekiel (Ezekiel 40-48), God gave Ezekiel a vision of a new Temple, and a new city. Here the Shekinah Glory returns and His Name is placed there in that city — for ever!

It is in the Temple and the city as described in the closing chapters of Ezekiel that we have a final note concerning God's Name. The redemptive Name revealed therein is "Jehovah Shammah — The LORD is there, the LORD ever-present.

All of this finds its ultimate fulfilment in Revelation chapters 21-22 and Hebrews 11:10-6; Galatians 4:26 and Psalm 46:4-5. The city here is NEW Jerusalem. The OLD city is past (Revelation 11:8). The New Jerusalem is the city of the living God. It is a heavenly city, with foundations in it, whose builder and maker is God. The old Jerusalem was corrupted by the people who had the Name of God called upon them (2 Chronicles 7:14). They had failed through iniquity. The heavenly city of Jerusalem is the holy city, the righteous city, the city of God.

In this city there is THE TEMPLE. "The Lord God (the Father), and the Lamb (the Son, the sacrifice) are THE TEMPLE thereof." And His Name is there — in the Temple, in the Lamb, in the city. His Name is also in the foreheads of all who enter into the city of God. His Name is His nature.

"His Name shall be in their foreheads" (Revelation 22:4; 14:1-4). "I will write upon him the Name of the city of My God which is New Jerusalem, and I will write upon him My new Name . . ." (Revelation 3:12). This is the promise to the overcomer.

This city and Temple in Ezekiel is named JEHOVAH SHAMMAH, the Lord is there, the Lord ever-present. The light and the glory of God fills the city of the redeemed. This city will never be polluted by sin or corrupted by iniquity, for in it shall reign everlasting righteousness.

Thus we have the Divine purpose for the building of the Temple. God wanted to have a place in which He could dwell, a place for His presence, a place for His Name. All the glory of His redemptive Name would be made manifest amongst His redeemed as they honoured and hallowed it among the nations.

The Scripture says, "And Solomon determined to build an house for THE NAME of the Lord . . ." (2 Chronicles 2:1).
The church is now God's house. It is to be built for the Name of the Lord in the Name of the Lord Jesus Christ. All the redemptive Names of the Lord are comprehended in this all-inclusive redemptive Name. The church must live and minister to the lost in the power of that Name unto the glory of the Father.

The progressive unfolding of the Name of the Lord in regard to dwelling places shows that the Lord set His Name in a place, on an article of furniture, in a habitation and in a city, as well as upon His people.

The ultimate revelation is that God sets His Name no longer in A PLACE but in A PERSON, even the Lord Jesus Christ. And from Him His Name is placed upon His people. It is of Him ''the whole family in heaven and earth is named'' (Ephesians 3:14,15). The church is God's Temple in which the Name of the Lord dwells — forever!

CHAPTER FIFTEEN

THE FOUNDATION SITE OF THE TEMPLE

"Then Solomon began to build the house of the Lord at Jerusalem, in mount Moriah, where the Lord appeared unto David his father, in the place that David had prepared, in the threshing floor of Ornan the Jebusite" (2 Chronicles 3:1).

This verse sets forth the truth concerning the site of the Temple of the Lord. In this same verse are rich seeds of truth which must be considered in this chapter concerning the site which the Lord chose for the building of His house. Such is rich in its prophetic implications for the New Testament church also.

We break open the verse in its related parts to gain insight into the truths therein.

A. The Temple City — Jerusalem

It has already been seen in our previous chapter that the Lord chose the city of Jerusalem to place His Name therein.

Jerusalem is the central city, in the Old Testament, relative to the redemptive purposes of God. It was the holy city, the righteous city, the city where the word of the Lord went out to the chosen nation and from there to all others. Jerusalem is the city to which the Saviour would come in the appointed time. All other cities in Israel and Judah, as well as the heathen cities, were judged by their response to that which took place in this city of Jerusalem.

Jerusalm is variously interpreted to mean "City of Righteousness, City of Peace". Salem is especially interpreted to mean "Peace" (Hebrews 7:1-2).

Jerusalem was the city of God, the city of the great king.

When Melchisedek appeared to father Abraham, it seems evident that he revealed to Abraham about the city of God, whose maker and builder is God. Abraham, along with Isaac and Jacob, looked for this city with foundations (Hebrews 11:10-16).

Melchisedek's name interpreted means, "King of RIGHTEOUSNESS and King of PEACE". He was a King-Priest, Priest of the Most High God. Most expositors see him to be the King of Jeru-Salem. However, most seem to think it was the earthly city of Jerusalem.

However, a study of the Book of Hebrews shows that there was both the earthly city of Jerusalem, and there is the heavenly city of Jerusalem, the Jerusalem that is above (Hebrews 12:22-24; Galatians 4:26).

The apostle John saw this glorious city in Revelation chapters 21-22. This, without doubt, is the city that the patriarchs, along with all believers, look for, not the earthly city.

Melchisedek is King of Righteousness and King of Peace. The kingdom of God is as the king, a kingdom which is righteousness, peace and joy in the Holy Spirit (Romans 14:17). Whatever the king is, so will be the kingdom (Genesis 14:17,18).

Solomon himself was seen to be a king of peace, executing righteousness in Jerusalem, the city of righteousness and peace. Thus he becomes a suitable type of the reign of Christ Jesus, who is THE King of Righteousness and THE King of Peace ruling in His kingdom and in His church.

The Temple city was chosen to be Jerusalem, the earthly Jerusalem. It was meant to be the earthly manifestation of the heavenly Jerusalem, manifesting the nature, character, function and ministry of that heavenly city.

The ultimate truth of this is seen in the heavenly and holy city, New Jerusalem, in which God and the Lamb are the Temple. The earthly city with its Temple was the shadow in earth of the heavenly city and the true Temple and sacrifice in the Father and the Son, the Lamb of God. This is the eternal city of eternal righteousness and eternal peace. It is free. It is above. It is built by God.

B. **The Temple Mount — Mt Moriah**

The next significant part of the verse tells us that the house of the Lord was built, not only in Jerusalem, the city of God, but in mount Moriah. The tremendous significance of this can only be seen by considering the Biblical account of that which took place in this mount.

In Genesis chapter 22 we have the account of God calling upon Abraham, the father of all who believe, to offer up his only son, Isaac, as a burnt offering in a mountain that He Himself would specify.

God the Father spoke to Abraham the father. He asked him to take his only begotten son, whom he loved, and offer him for a burnt offering on one of the mountains that he would tell him of. Abraham took his only beloved son, Isaac, the son in whom the promises of God were bound, and proceeded to travel three days journey to the mount of sacrifice.

In the course of the journey, Isaac asked his father, ''Behold the fire, and the wood, but where is the lamb for the sacrifice?'' Abraham told his only son that God Himself would provide the lamb in the appointed place and time. After three days journey, father and son came to Mt Moriah, the appointed mount. Abraham told the two witnesses, the two young men, to wait as he and his only son would go and worship and then come again to them. What faith! What faith in the God of the resurrection.

Abraham believed that God would somehow raise his only son from the dead after the sacrifice, for in him were the promises of God to bless the nations of the earth.

As Abraham was about to sacrifice his son, on the prepared sacrificial altar and wood, the Angel of the Lord called to him out of heaven to spare his son. Abraham was to offer in the stead of his son the ram he saw caught in the bush.

Upon the absolute and unquestioning obedience of Abraham, God confirmed the covenant promises to him of the land, the seed and the victory over enemies as well as the blessing upon all nations.

Abraham received revelation and called that place of sacrifice in Mt Moriah, ''JEHOVAH JIREH, the Lord will provide''. And again, ''In the mount of the Lord, it shall be seen''.

We would ask, What shall be seen? Undoubtedly, with the revelation of this redemptive Name of Jehovah, God saw that in due time, THE TEMPLE OF THE LORD would be built in this Mt Moriah. This is undoubtedly that which would be seen!

Moriah means ''Seen of JAH'', or ''Seen of the Lord''. The Lord saw Abraham's willingness to sacrifice his only son. The Lord saw Abraham's faith in the resurrection of this son. The Lord saw Abraham's unquestioning obedience to His word. The Lord saw the unity between Abraham and Isaac, the father and the son. All of this shadowed forth on earth that which would take place in the appointed time between the Father God and His only begotten Son, Jesus Christ. This time it would be on Mt Calvary, not Mt Moriah, but certainly in the sight of Mt Moriah.

The Father also saw that in time the Temple, the house of the Lord, would be built in Mt Moriah. Mt Moriah was the place of the sacrificed only begotten son, and his typical resurrection. Mt Moriah would be the place where the house of the Lord would be built. The foundation of the Lord's house would be an only begotten son, and his typical death and resurrection after three days journey (Note Hebrews 11:17-19 with John 8:56-58).

Who can fail to see the tremendous significance in the choice of Mt Moriah for the place on which to build the Temple of the Lord?

The Bible shows that there are only two ''only begotten'' sons, Isaac in the Old Testament and Jesus in the New Testament. It was upon the basis of the sacrificed and resurrected Old Testament only son that the promises of covenantal blessing of seed, possession of enemy gates, and salvation to the nations were renewed. So it is upon the basis of the New Testament ''only begotten Son'' of God that covenantal blessings are available for all nations.

Jesus, after His three days and three nights atoning work relative to Mt Calvary rose from the dead and makes available to all nations the blessings of the New Covenant. An animal sacrifice was offered in the stead of Isaac in the Old Testament. In the New Testament, Jesus was offered in the stead of animal sacrifices. Jesus is THE Lamb of God taking away the sin of the world (John 1:29,36; 3:16; Matthew 12:39-40; Galatians 3:16,29; 1 Peter 1:18-20). Animal sacrifices were unwilling sacrifices. Jesus was willing to lay down His life for us doing the Father's will.

Now it is upon the foundation of His sacrifice at Mt Calvary that the church, the New Covenant house of the Lord can be and is being built.

Mt Calvary replaces Mt Moriah. The church replaces the Temple. Jesus replaces Isaac. Earthly Jerusalem is replaced by Heavenly Jerusalem. He taketh away the first that He may establish the second. He takes away the Old Covenant economy to establish the New Covenant economy (Hebrews 10:9-14).

C. The Temple Place — The Threshing floor

The exact site of the Temple was the threshing floor of Ornan the Jebusite as noted in 2 Chronicles 3:1. Solomon began to build the house of the Lord at Jerusalem, in Mt Moriah, "where the Lord had appeared to David his father, in the place that David had prepared, in the threshing floor of Ornan the Jebusite".

2 Samuel chapter 24 and 1 Chronicles chapter 21 provide the account for us of that which pertains to this threshing floor.

Satan motivated king David, out of pride, to number the people of Israel. From Satan's viewpoint, he hates the people of God. From David's viewpoint, it was national pride, pride of numbers. This is why the Scripture says that the king's word was abominable to Joab. God had promised that Abraham's seed would be innumerable, as the sand and as the stars. However, beyond that and more importantly, God had commanded Moses that whenever the people were to be numbered, all had to bring the ransom money, the atonement money, the half shekel of redemption money, the price of a soul (Exodus 30:11-16).

Again, from Satan's point of view, he hates the atonement and the whole plan of redemption and so caused David to by-pass the ransom money and number the people. God had promised that no plague would come near the nation as long as they took the redemption price. Without the atonement money, Israel was open to the plague and judgements of the Lord.

Rich and poor were to give alike, according to the standard of the sanctuary (Exodus 30:11-16).

Without the ransom money the plague struck (1 Chronicles 21:7). Because the king's word was abominable to Joab, both records vary in their accounts of the numbering of the people, because David was disobeying the word of God (2 Samuel 24-1-9); 1 Chronicles 21:1-7; Genesis 15:5; 32:12; Exodus 15:5; Psalm 147:4). Abraham's seed was to be numberless as the sand and the stars.

David was given a choice of three things as Divine punishments for his sin:

1) Seven years of famine in the land, which would be three more years beside the present years (2 Samuel 21:1).

2) Three months of defeat before their enemies; loss of victory in battle.

3) Three days of pestilence in the land.

David's choice was that of the merciful hand of the Lord rather than the hand of merciless man. The pestilence strikes and 70,000 people die in the plague (2 Samuel 24:15-16; 1 Chronicles 21:14-15).

The Lord sends the destroying angel to destroy Jerusalem. David laments for his sin, and shows his shepherd heart. He says, "What have these sheep done that they should be judged for my sin?"

The Angel of the Lord came to Jerusalem, right to the place of Ornan's threshing floor, with his drawn sword. With David's prayer, the Lord restrains the plague and commands him to build an

altar on this very site (2 Samuel 24:16-18; 1 Chronicles 21:15-20).
Ornan was threshing wheat, getting rid of the chaff (1 Chronicles 21:20).

David now purchased the threshing floor and the oxen for sacrifice from Ornan for the price of fifty shekels of silver. Here we have redemption money, the price of a soul (2 Samuel 24:20-25; 1 Chronicles 22:1). David built an altar, offered sacrifices of blood there, as king-priest, and the plague was stayed on the basis of sacrificial blood. It was the price of blood, the price of the atonement (Leviticus 17:11).

David then purchased the whole area or site of the Temple for six hundred shekels of gold (1 Chronicles 21:21-27). It was *silver* for the place for the altar of sacrifice. It was *gold* for the place for the Temple! The Temple could be built upon the foundation of sacrifice. God's glory can only dwell upon redemption ground.

The Lord sealed this act by answering from heaven with Divine fire (1 Chronicles 21:28-30). Fire had come from heaven at the dedication of the Tabernacle of Moses; now here again at David's sacrifice. Later on fire would come from heaven at the offerings of Solomon's Temple dedicatory service (2 Chronicles 7:3).

David recognized the Divine seal. He said, "THIS is THE HOUSE OF THE LORD GOD, and THIS is the altar of burnt offering for Israel" (1 Chronicles 22:1).

It was God who commanded David to build an altar upon the site of the threshing floor at Jerusalem. What did God have in mind? What a price to pay for this site. Why did God choose the threshing floor of Ornan the Jebusite? Because here was the mountain of the Lord's house.

Ornan's name interpreted means "That which rejoices, their bow or ark". He is also called by the name Araunah, which means "Ark" or "Song" according to some writers.

Undoubtedly his name has prophetic significance. It was in this place that the "Ark" of God would rest. Here in the Temple there would be the "Song" of the Lord and "that which rejoices" as the people rejoiced in the presence of God.

The threshing floor was a place for getting rid of the chaff and bringing out the wheat for food. Surely it is significant that Mt Moriah was the place of sacrifice and Ornan's place is for threshing of wheat. From this foundation would arise the holy house of the Lord.
John the Baptist spoke of the Lord's ministry of "threshing out the chaff", gathering the wheat into His barn and burning the chaff with unquenchable fire (Matthew 3:11-12). This was through the baptism of the Holy Spirit and fire. Our God is a consuming fire (Hebrews 12:29).

D. The Temple Site

Thus we have explored the riches of 2 Chronicles 3:1. Jerusalem became the Temple city. Mt Moriah became the Temple mount. The threshing floor became the Temple place, and now we come to the total truth that this is the Temple site.

All of this becomes wonderfully prophetic of Christ and His church.

1) **Mt Moriah** — The place of a sacrificed and resurrected only begotten son, Isaac.

2) **Jerusalem** — The place where God would record His name, in His city.

3) **Threshing floor**— The place of purging the chaff from the wheat.

4) **The Temple**— The place of the Lord's house, His presence, His Name, His glory and habitation, the ark of God.

For the New Testament church we have the following antitypical fulfilment.

1) **Mt Calvary** — The place where Jesus, the only begotten Son was crucified, and 3 days later resurrected from the dead.

2) **Jerusalem** — The heavenly city of God, the city the patriarchs looked for.

3) **Threshing floor** — The place of God's dealings in the lives of His people to take away the chaff and purge His wheat.

4) **The Church** — The New Covenant house or temple of the Lord, the place of His glory and presence and His Name.

Type and antitype meet in glorious union as evidenced by the above. The atoning work of Christ stays the plague of God's wrath for all who accept God in Christ.

For Abraham, Mt Moriah was the Mount of Sacrifice.
For David, Mt Moriah was the Mount of Visitation.
For Solomon, Mt Moriah was the Mount of God's Glory and Habitation.

In relation to the building of the Tabernacle in Israel's first generation we see the following, in contrast to the generation who saw the Temple of the Lord.

Moses' Generation	—	Solomon's Generation
The Passover Lamb	—	Sacrifice of Substitution
Three days journey	—	Three days plague
Mt Sinai	—	Mt Moriah
The Wilderness	—	The Promised Land
Wanderings	—	Rest
The Tabernacle	—	The Temple

In conclusion, we note the type of the Old Testament and antitype of the New Testament as to the scene set before us in this chapter.

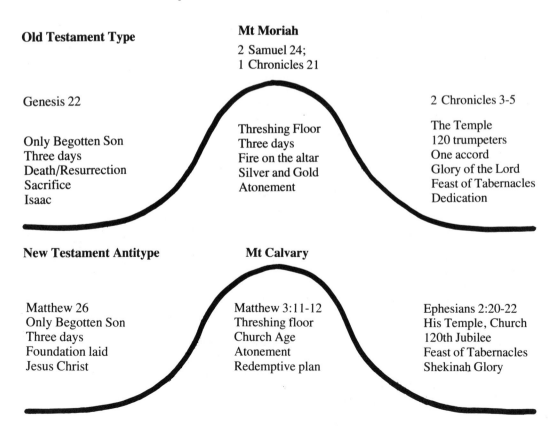

Old Testament Type

Mt Moriah
2 Samuel 24;
1 Chronicles 21

Genesis 22

Only Begotten Son
Three days
Death/Resurrection
Sacrifice
Isaac

Threshing Floor
Three days
Fire on the altar
Silver and Gold
Atonement

2 Chronicles 3-5

The Temple
120 trumpeters
One accord
Glory of the Lord
Feast of Tabernacles
Dedication

New Testament Antitype

Mt Calvary

Matthew 26
Only Begotten Son
Three days
Foundation laid
Jesus Christ

Matthew 3:11-12
Threshing floor
Church Age
Atonement
Redemptive plan

Ephesians 2:20-22
His Temple, Church
120th Jubilee
Feast of Tabernacles
Shekinah Glory

CHAPTER SIXTEEN

BUILDING THE TEMPLE OF THE LORD

INTRODUCTORY:

We come now to the actual building of the Temple of the Lord, the Temple structure itself. The Temple structure consisted of the same basic sections as in the Tabernacle of Moses. It had the Holiest of All, called the Most Holy Place or the Holy oracle. In this stood the ark of the Covenant. Then immediately in front of this was the second department called the Holy Place, or the Sanctuary. Then surrounding this, the Temple proper, were the Outer Courts, at least two Courts in which were the respective articles of furniture as the Lord commanded David.

The whole structure was built after the pattern of the Tabernacle in the wilderness but was twice as large in measurements. The house also was surrounded by various chambers for the priests and other sacred utensils, except of course the entrance to the Holy Place. The whole structure was wonderfully made, richly prophetic and abounding in spiritual gems of truth.

We consider its names, its foundation, its walls, its boards and the ornamentation of the house.

A. The Names of the Temple

The Temple of the Lord was known by various names as listed out here.

1. The Palace (1 Chronicles 29:1,19; Psalm 45:8,15).

2. The Temple (1 Kings 7:50; 2 Chronicles 3:17; 4:7-8).

3. The Temple of God (Matthew 21:12; Revelation 11:1).

4. The Temple of the Lord (2 Chronicles 27:2; Ezra 3:6; Jeremiah 7:4).

5. The Lord's Temple (Haggai 2:18).

6. The Holy Temple (Psalm 5:7; 11:4).

7. The House (1 Kings 6:7).

8. His Temple (Malachi 3:1).

9. The House of God (2 Chronicles 3:3; 4:11).

10. The House of the Lord (1 Kings 6:1; 2 Chronicles 3:1).

11. The House of Prayer for all nations (Isaiah 56:7; Matthew 21:13).

12. My Father's House (John 2:16,17; 14:2).

13. Your House (Matthew 23:38). To become desolate after Christ's rejection.

14. The Sanctuary (1 Chronicles 28:10; Daniel 8:14).

15. The Temple and The Oracle (1 Kings 6:5). i.e., The Holy Place and The Holiest of All.

So Christ and His Church are known by various names, each having their own distinct facet of truth. No one designation is able to express the fulness of the glory of Christ in His church.

B. The Foundation of the House

The first and most important thing in a structure is the foundation, upon which the whole structure stands or falls. The foundation site of the Temple was chosen by the Lord and the significance of that site has been seen in our previous chapter.

Here we see the significance of the material chosen to be the foundation of the Lord's house, these being great, costly and hewn stones.

We note some of the Scriptures which speak of the importance of foundations.

"If the foundations be destroyed, what can the righteous do?" (Psalm 11:3).

"Behold, I lay in Zion for a foundation, a stone, a tried stone, a precious cornerstone, a sure foundation . . ." (Isaiah 28:16).

"His foundation is in the holy mountains . . ." (Psalm 87:1).

Abraham looked for "a city with foundations, whose builder and maker is God" (Hebrews 11:10 with Revelation 21:14-19).

Paul said, "Other foundation can no man lay than that is laid, which is Jesus Christ" (1 Corinthians 3:9-12).

Note also these Scriptures — Luke 6:48,49; 2 Chronicles 8:16; Psalm 104:5; Isaiah 48:13; 51:13,16; Zechariah 12:1; Luke 14:29; Romans 15:20.

For the Temple to be built according to the pattern, a solid foundation, foundation stones, had to be laid.

There are several aspects that may be considered when we look at the truth of the foundation stones of the Temple of the Lord.

1. Christ THE Foundation

There is absolutely no mistake in the fact that the Lord Jesus Christ is THE foundation of the church, His holy temple. He is THE Rock, THE Stone, THE foundation Stone, in all He is, all He said, and all He did.

Paul says that other foundation can no man lay than that is laid, Jesus Christ. It is the *person* of Christ — Who He is. It is the *work* of Christ — What He has done. It is the *words* of Christ — What He has said. These together constitute Christ as THE foundation of the house of the Lord, which is the church (1 Corinthians 3:9-15; 1 Peter 2:4-9).

The prophet Isaiah said, "I lay in Zion for a foundation stone, a tried stone, a precious cornerstone" (Isaiah 28:16). Christ is this tried stone, tried by the Gentile rulers the priests and scribes of the Sanhedrin of the Jewish nation. He is the proven stone. He is the sure foundation.

The theme of the Rock/Stone is evident throughout the Scripture. It is the life story of Christ.

* Christ is the Anointed Stone of Jacob's ladder (Genesis 28:11-14).

* Christ is the Shepherd-Stone of Israel in Joseph (Genesis 49:24).

* Christ is the Smitten Rock providing the waters of the Holy Spirit for the people of God (Exodus 17:6; Isaiah 53:4-5; Psalm 78:15-16; 1 Corinthians 10:4).

* Christ is the Rock of our salvation (Psalm 18:1-2; 62:2; 40:2-3).

* Christ is the Rock of redemption and revelation (Exodus 33:21-23).

* Christ is the Rock into which we enter and find safety (Isaiah 2:10; Deuteronomy 32:4,15).

* Christ is the Rock that begets lively stones (Deuteronomy 32:18).

* Christ is the Smiting Rock that becomes the Stone Kingdom (Daniel 2:44-45; Luke 20:17-18; Matthew 21:44).

* Christ is the Rock upon which His church is built (Matthew 16:16-19).

* Christ is the foundation for the wise man who built His house upon a Rock (Matthew 7:24-29). Solomon was a "wise man" who built the house of the Lord on the rock foundation.

* Christ is the living stone by reason of His resurrection (1 Peter 2:5-9).

* Christ the rejected Stone becomes the headstone and cornerstone (Psalm 118:22-23; Matthew 21:42).

* Christ is the Stone with the saving name in it (Acts 4:8-11).

When we look at Scripture, Christ is seen in all His glory as the Rock of Ages, the Rock of our salvation, the foundation stone upon which the church will be built. When all around is sinking sand, on Christ the solid Rock we stand!

He who laid and is the foundation of this house will complete it (Zechariah 4:9; 6:12-13).

The Tabernacle of Moses had its foundation in the silver sockets of redemption. The Temple of Solomon had its foundation in Moriah and the foundation stones. The church of Jesus Christ has its foundation in Him, His person, His word and His work.

To those who rejected Him, He is the stone of stumbling and rock of offence (Romans 9:30-33; 1 Peter 2:6-7). To those who believe, He is the stone with the seven eyes of the Lord (perfect insight) in it (Zechariah 4:7,10). To Him we sing (Psalm 95:1).

2. **The Foundation of Apostles and Prophets**

    The next aspect of foundations is that which pertains to the apostles and prophets both in the Old Testament and New Testament.

    Paul tells us that the church is built upon the foundation of the apostles and prophets, Jesus Christ Himself being the chief cornerstone (Ephesians 2:19-22). It is from here that the church grows into a holy temple, a habitation of God by the Spirit.

    The apostle Peter reminds us of the words spoken before by the holy prophets (i.e., the Old Testament prophets), and the commandments of the apostles (i.e., the New Testament apostles) of the Lord Jesus Christ (2 Peter 3:1-2).

    In John's vision of the city of God he saw the city with its twelve foundations and in the names of the twelve foundations were the names of the twelve apostles of the Lamb (Revelation 21:12-14).

    The early believers continued stedfastly in the apostles doctrine, in fellowship, breaking of bread and prayers (Acts 2:42).

Thus we have this aspect of the foundation also. Christ is THE foundation but the Scriptures and ministries of the Old Testament prophets and New Testament apostles are also foundational to the building of the church, God's holy temple. It may be said that Christ is THE foundation, personally and redemptively, as no other. Apostles are the foundation, doctrinally and ministerially.

Jesus said of Peter that he was a rock, a stone. His name Peter or Cephas means "A stone" (John 1:41-42). However, he is not THE Rock, or THE Stone. Christ is that. But as an apostle of the Lamb he is a foundation stone in the church, in the city of God, along with the other apostles of the Lamb.

Paul, an apostle, laid the foundation. He himself was a foundation ministry in the church and spoke much of the revelation of the church being the temple of the Lord.

3. **Foundation Doctrines of Christ**

    In Hebrews 6:1-2 we also have another aspect of that which pertains to foundations. The writer lists out the foundation principles of the doctrine of Christ.
    These are:—

    * Repentance from dead works

    * Faith towards God

    * Doctrine of Baptisms

    * Laying on of Hands

    * Resurrection from the Dead

    * Eternal Judgment

If these foundational doctrines are not properly laid, then God, as the building inspector cannot give "the permit" to go on unto perfection, or the completion of the building.

Many Christians (and churches) do not have these foundational doctrines, yet seek to build "a New Testament Church". This cannot be accomplished without a proper foundation of these apostolic principles of the doctrines of Christ.

The Lord knows those who have a proper foundation (2 Timothy 2:19; 1 Timothy 6:19; Job 38:6; Luke 14:27-30).

It is significant that Luke's account of the two builders states that the "wise man" laid the foundation on a rock. There is a twofold thought here. Christ is THE Rock, and the foundation doctrines of Hebrews 6:1-2 arise out of and are built upon Him. That is, Who He is, What He has done and What He said — His person, His work and His words. All doctrine must be related to Him, otherwise all falls into a philosophical system of historical facts unrelated to the person of Christ Himself.

4.   The Believers as Living Stones

The final aspect of both foundation and building stones is that which relates to all believers, both "foundational" members of the church, and all subsequent believers in the house of the Lord.

In Solomon's Temple, the stones had to be blasted and shaken out of the quarries of king Solomon by his quarry-men. They were removed from their natural surroundings. They were originally rough stones, unhewn stones, unshapen stones and without purpose.

The Scripture says that these stones for the Temple were made ready before brought to the Temple site to be placed. There no sound of hammer, nor axe, nor any tool of iron in the house while it was in building (1 Kings 6:7).

We note some things about the stones, not only for the house of the Lord, but also for Solomon's house, which was also made of stones.

The spiritual truths evident therein may be applied to believers who are now the "living stones" for a spiritual house. Undoubtedly the apostle Peter had these things in mind when he wrote this to the believers (1 Peter 2:5-9).

A study of 1 Kings 5:17-18; 6:37; 7:11 and 1 Chronicles 22:2; 22:14-15; provide the information noted here.

The stones for the Lord's Temple were:—

* Costly stones
* Great stones
* Hewn stones
* White stones
* Prepared stones
* Wrought stones, sawed within and without
* Measured stones, for Solomon's house they were 8 by 10 cubits (i.e., number of resurrection and law and order)
* Foundation stones
* Covered stones, covered with cedar wood (1 Kings 6:18)
* Garnished stones, with precious gems for beauty (2 Chronicles 3:6).

All these stones were "sawed within and without" (1 Kings 7:9). After being quarried, these stones were hewn, sawn, squared, measured and shapen in order to find their place in the house of the Lord. Everything was to fit perfectly in His house by the builders. Israel had been "hewn by the word of the prophets" (Hosea 12:10; 2 Kings 17:13).

The stone-squarers had to work on these stones, chiselling, shaping, polishing and beautifying them to fit into God's house. The stone-masons knew what they were doing to the various stones.

All of this preparation speaks of the dealings of God and the disciplines of God in the life of a believer. There it was material stones, worked on externally. Here it is spiritual stones, worked on internally, being built up a spiritual house (1 Peter 2:5-9). There was much noise in the quarries and forests but when the Temple came together there was not the sound of hammer or tool (1 Kings 6:7).

God has set in the church spiritual stone-squarers, stone-masons; these being the apostles, prophets, evangelists, pastors and teachers, along with elders, deacons and other believers. God uses all to shape us to measure up to His will and pattern.

The *evangelists* represent God's quarry-men used to obtain stones from out of the quarries of sin, the quarries of this world. They are used as soul-winners also.

The *pastors* and *teachers* are used to shape, hew, saw, square, fashion and polish with hammer and saw and chisel of the Word, the lively stones brought before them. They are to work on these stones, and see that they measure up to God's standard and pattern for their lives in order to find their place in His Body, His Church, His Temple.

The *apostles* and *prophets* are like the "wise master-builders", who position the stones in their appointed place in the temple of the Lord. God knows where the stones are to be placed. Placement in God's house is the work of these ministries. Paul was a "wise master-builder" who found and gave placement to lively stones in the house of the Lord.

The Lord Jesus, who is also the Divine Architect, knows where people are to be placed, where they fit in His house, His temple (Ephesians 2:19-22; John 2:19-21; 1 Corinthians 12:1-28; 3:16-17).

How sad it must be when the Master-builder finds stones who are "misfits", and do not want to fit into His house, but want to be individual stones, alone and find no placement.

Judas became a "rejected stone", cast away, refusing to be measured within and without by the Master-builder, Jesus Christ Himself. He rejected THE Stone and became a rejected stone himself.

Peter allowed the Master-builder to work on him, and thus Peter, "a stone", found his place and name in the foundations of the city of God.

As the Master Himself was a tried stone, a tested stone, so will all stones be that find their place in the house of the Lord. He calls us to be like Him (1 John 3:1-2). The work of conviction, regeneration and sanctification are all part of the process to make us the lively stones He wants us to be. The church is a spiritual house, a holy temple, a habitation of God by the Spirit.

* The Temple is fulfilled in Christ Himself first.

* The Temple finds fulfilment in the Church universal also.

* The Temple finds fulfilment in believers individually.

* The Temple also finds expression in the Church locally.

C. The Walls of the House

The walls of the house, as also the foundation, were made of white marble stone, or simply "white stones" (1 Chronicles 29:2).

Walls speak of safety, protection, enclosure and security. The city of God in John's vision has its walls (Revelation 21:12-19). It keeps out those who are unclean and unfit to enter the presence of the Lord. It also protects those who are within, the priests of the Lord.

Isaiah speaks of "the walls of salvation" (Isaiah 60:18; 62:6; Jeremiah 1:18; 15:20; Zechariah 2:5; Isaiah 26:1). The Lord promised to be a "wall of fire" around His people in time of trouble.

God has a place for all in His Temple. Not all believers are foundation stones. Many are stones prepared to fit into the walls of God's house. However, the walls are dependant upon the foundation stones (Song of Solomon 8:9-10).

All the stones fitted together when brought in from the quarries. Today, God has millions of believers in various "quarries", being shapen, hewn, chiselled and polished, being measured and prepared to fit together on the ultimate day of His building. Today is the day of salvation. Now is the accepted time to get ready and prepared for the ultimate coming together of God's Temple, His church. Sometimes God uses other stones to polish other stones, even as He uses other believers to polish other believers.

God is the great Architect. Christ, by His Spirit, is the wise Master-builder. Each stone must submit to the workings of the Lord. It is the grace of God that shapes the rough and unhewn stones, the unlovely stones, and thereby makes us beautiful for His house, His dwelling place. There will be no unhewn, unsquared or unpolished stones in His house.

D. **Walls Overlaid with Silver**

According to 1 Chronicles 29:4 in KJV (as also other translations), it seems that the walls of the Temple were overlaid with silver. The thought here is "to plaister the walls" or "to daub" the stone walls with silver.

Seven thousand talents of refined silver were given for that purpose, as well as three thousand talents of gold. We note the amount of gold and silver that was provided for the Temple.

Gold		**Silver**
1. Prepared — 100,000 talents of gold	—	1,000,000 talents of silver (1 Chronicles 22:14,16)
2. David's gifts — 3,000 talents of gold	—	7,000 talents of silver (1 Chronicles 29:4)
3. Princes gifts — 5,000 talents of gold	—	10,000 talents of silver (1 Chronicles 29:7)
4. Extra — 10,000 drams of gold		
Total = 108,000 talents of gold 10,000 drams of gold	—	Total = 1,017,000 talents of silver

Thus the silver was over ten times the amount of gold. All of this was for use in the Temple. This is an amazing amount and all was placed at Solomon's disposal by his father David.

The Scripture says that silver was in an *abundance* in Solomon's day, it was nothing to be accounted for (1 Kings 10:21-22,25,27; 2 Chronicles 1:15).
What was all this silver used for?

1. Silver vessels and instruments — 1 Chronicles 28:14; 2 Chronicles 5:1; 1 Chronicles 29:2.

    a) Candlesticks of silver — 1 Chronicles 28:15.

    b) Tables of silver — 1 Chronicles 28:16.

    c) Basons of silver — 1 Chronicles 28:17. Silver ware.

2. Silver overlay — 1 Chronicles 29:4.
    Silver overlay or plaister for the Temple walls.

What would all this vast amount of silver be used for apart from overlaying the walls of stone, for there is nothing in the Temple itself of silver, as all in the Holy Place and Holiest of All was all of GOLD!

Even after the building was finished, the silver had not all been used and the remainder of it was placed in the treasuries in the Lord's house (1 Kings 7:51; 2 Chronicles 5:1).

In the light of this abundance of silver, it seems evident that the stones were plastered over with silver, as well as the stones covered with silver. Thus no stone would be seen. All would be encased, joined together, and overlaid with silver. What a magnificent sight!

Silver, as noted, speaks of redemption, the atonement money, the ransom, the price of a soul.
Joseph was sold for 20 pieces of silver by his brethren (Genesis 37:28).
Samson was also sold by his brethren for 1,100 pieces of silver (Judges 16:5; 17:2-3).
Jesus was sold by Judas for 30 pieces of silver, the price of a slave (Matthew 26:15).
Israelites could only be numbered amongst the redeemed if they brought the half shekel of silver, the ransom money, the price of a soul, to the sanctuary (Exodus 30:11-16).
David bought the threshingfloor of Ornan for 50 shekels of silver (2 Samuel 24:24).

The first commandment of the Lord for soul atonement was silver! The final commandment of the Lord for soul atonement is blood! Leviticus 17:11. Thus we have silver and blood.
No doubt much of the silver given came also from numbering of the children of Israel and the half shekel of the ransom money. Silver represents the thousands of the redeemed Israelites (Exodus 30:12; Job 33:24, Margin; Psalm 49:7; Mark 10:45; Isaiah 35:10; 1 Timothy 2:5-6).

Peter interprets the symbolic truth for us in his epistle. He tells us that we are "not redeemed with corruptible things as silver or gold, but with the precious blood of Christ as of a lamb slain from the foundation of the world" but manifested in these last times for us (1 Peter 1:18-21).
We are not redeemed with corruptible things as silver and gold, which were used in the Tabernacle and Temple, but with the incorruptible blood of Christ. We are bought with a price (1 Corinthians 6:19-20).

As the stones were encased in silver, so God sees the "lively stones" — the believers "in Christ", redeemed, in this world, yet not of it (John 17; Ephesians 1:6; 2 Corinthians 5:17). The stone within the silver symbolizes the believer in Christ.

God sees our Saviour, then He sees us, accepted in the beloved (Ephesians 1:6). All that the stone was by nature is covered by silver, as all that we were by nature is covered by Christ's redemption. Stones overlaid with silver speak of believers overlaid by Christ's redemption. Bought from the quarries of sin and this earth, shaped to the Divine standard and measurements, by the Word of God and His ministries, and given a place in the house of the Lord, believers, as living stones may rejoice!

The stones were related together, by the silver. So believers are related together through the redemptive work of Christ, set in their place in the house of the Lord (Ephesians 2:19-22).
To find a place in the Lord's house all must know the silvery truth of redemption.

E. **Walls Covered with Boards**

A study of 1 Kings 6:9, 14-16, 18 show that the stones, the silver-covered stones, are now covered with boards, boards of cedar. There was no stone seen. The walls and the ceiling of the house were covered with timbers. The main beams and planks were of cedar tree.
The floor and ceiling were lined or covered by boards from the fir tree, and the walls with timber from the cedar trees.

By comparing 1 Kings 6:14-16 with 2 Chronicles 3:5 it suggests that the main beams of the floor were cedar, as well as the walls of the house being lined with cedar, but the floor boards and the ceiling planks were of fir tree timber.

These trees came from Huram (or, Hiram), King of Tyre, in exchange for gifts from king Solomon (1 Kings 5:1-10; 2 Chronicles 2:1-16).

Note the timbers used in the Temple of the Lord and their spiritual and symbolic significance.
Trees in Scripture are often used in symbolic sense, of people, whether saints or sinners, or, of Christ and His Church. Because these trees are used in the house of the Lord, they become symbolic of believers in their various beauties in God's house.
Nebuchadnezzar was likened in his kingdom of Babylon to a tree (Daniel 4). The royal house of Judah is likened to a cedar tree (Ezekiel 17).
The kingdom of heaven is likened to a mustard seed which grows into a great tree (Matthew 13:31-32).
The righteous are likened to a tree planted by the rivers of water which bring forth fruit in their season (Psalm 1:3; Jeremiah 17:5-8).

The Psalmist says "the trees of the Lord are full of sap" (Psalm 104:16). The righteous are like the cedars of Lebanon (Psalm 92:12-14; Numbers 24:5-6; Hosea 14:5-6).

Jesus said, I am the vine and you are the branches (John 15:1-16).

Solomon spoke parables of the trees, from the cedar down to the lowly hyssop, from the greatest to the humblest (1 Kings 4:33).

Trees, therefore, in the Temple represent believers in Christ, different in nature to stones, yet all shaped to be part of His habitation. Variety of trees speak of variety of God's people, yet all one in Christ become part of the house of the Lord.

We consider the symbolic truth in the various trees used in the Temple.

1. **The Cedar Tree**

    It is the first tree wood to be mentioned in connection with the Temple (1 Kings 5:6).

    In Scripture the cedar tree is symbolic of royalty, of kingship. It is symbolic of incorruptibility. It is like imperishable wood. It kills worms which would seek to invade it.

    In relation to Christ, it speaks of His kingship, His royal kingdom and His incorruptible humanity (Psalm 16:10; 1 Corinthians 15:33; 1 Peter 1:23)

    Christ was THE BRANCH, who was cut down in death but came to life in resurrection glory and power as the king eternal, immortal and invisible. He is no longer death-doomed. He is the tender branch (Isaiah 11:1-4; Zechariah 6:12-14; Isaiah 53:1-2; Romans 6:9; 1 Timothy 6:13-16).

    David the king dwelt in a house of cedars. The house of the King of Kings is also a house of cedar (2 Samuel 7:7; Psalm 29:5; 80:10; 92:12-14; 148:9; Song of Solomon 1:17; 5:15; 8:9).

    Cedar wood was used relative to the cleansing of the leper and for purification of the Israelites (Leviticus 14:4-6,49-52; Numbers 19:6; 2 Samuel 7:2).

    Cedar is especially used to speak of the royal house of Judah, of which Christ came (Ezekiel 17).

    The believer in Christ is also a king and a priest (Revelation 5:9-10; 1 Peter 2:5-9). The character of royalty is upon them.

    As the tree was cut down and trimmed of its natural beauty and shaped to fit into the Lord's house, so the believer is cut off from the former natural life of the soil, sawn and shaped to be covered with the beauty of the Lord in His house.

    The characteristics of cedar are incorruptibility, fragrance, strength, imperishableness, able to resist decay and rot, and durability. These are the characteristics of Christ in His people.

    Other Scriptures on cedar trees are Isaiah 41:19; Jeremiah 22:7,14,15,23; Isaiah 9:10; Ezekiel 31:1-11.

2. **The Fir Tree**

    The fir (or cyprus) tree was used in the house of the Lord also. The fir tree provided planks of foundation for the floor of God's house. Also the doors of Temple were of fir tree (1 Kings 6:9). The vaultbeams were of fir.

    The prophet says, "I am like a green fir tree" (Hosea 14:8). Note these Scriptures which speak of the fir tree (2 Chronicles 3:5; 1 Kings 5:8-10; 6:15,34; 9:11; Song of Solomon 1:17; Psalm 104:17; Isaiah 41:19; 14:8;·55:13; 60:13; Zechariah 11:2; Nahum 2:3).

    The fir tree is symbolic of strength, support, power to uphold. Christ is our strength, our support, and He has the power to uphold His house.

    This same strength, support and power should be revealed in His people also.

3. **The Algum or Almug Tree**

    According to Bible Dictionaries this tree was a tree of *red* sandal wood. It was a very heavy, hard and fine grained wood, and of a beautiful red colour. A red vein ran throughout the timber. J.N. Darby translates it "red sandalwood".

In the Temple and its surroundings it was used for steps and stairs, for handrails, and for pillars. It was also used for musical instruments such as harps, psalteries and other instruments for the Temple singers and choir. There were none such as this in the land with which to compare. It was a fragrant wood.

Solomon requested Hiram to send him timbers from the cedar, the fir and the algum trees for the Temple. It was a very costly wood (2 Chronicles 2:8).

In relation to Christ Jesus, this tree speaks of the atoning work of Calvary. It speaks of the *blood* of Jesus. He was crucified on "the tree" (Galatians 3:13). He became a curse on the tree for us. The theme of blood-atonement runs through the total Bible as a "red vein" connecting all 66 books together as one.

This tree was used also for making of musical instruments whereby the priests could sing and minister to the Lord. It is because of Calvary's tree that all believers, as priests unto the Lord, can sing and make melody in their hearts unto the Lord. The believers heart is the true "instrument" unto the Lord (Ephesians 5:18-19; Colossians 3:16; 1 Chronicles 15:16; 2 Chronicles 5:11-14; 7:6; 1 Chronicles 16:42; 23:5).

Believers are also to uphold the truth of blood-atonement in the house of the Lord, for this is the price and cost of our redemption. Christ's death was vicarious.

4. The Palm Tree

The palm tree was also seen in the Temple timbers. The palm tree was actually *carved* into the cedar wood wherever it was used in the Temple.

The palm tree is significant and symbolic of righteousness, uprightness, and fruitfulness, peace and rejoicing as seen in the following Scripture references. The truth is, as always, first applicable to Christ and then finds fulfilment in the church, the believers in His house.

The righteous shall flourish like the palm tree, for those who are planted in the house of the Lord (Psalm 92:12-13).

At Elim there were 12 wells of water and 70 palm trees (Exodus 15:27). This finds fulfilment in the New Testament 12 apostles and 70 others which Jesus sent forth in healing ministry (Luke 9:1; 10:1-2).

Palm branches were used in the rejoicing in the Feast of Tabernacles (Nehemiah 8:15; Leviticus 23:40).

The triumphant redeemed wave palms of victory before the throne of God and the Lamb (Revelation 7:9).

Note also these Scriptures — Song of Solomon 7:7-8; Jeremiah 10:5; John 12:13.

The ornamentation of the palm tree was used very much in the Temple. It was carved on the lavers in the Temple courts. It was carved upon the walls of the Temple, in the Holy Place and the Holiest of All. Also the doors of the Sanctuary were ornamented with the palm tree. This tree was most prominent in the Temple of the Lord (1 Kings 6:29-36; 7:36; 2 Chronicles 3:5).

All point to Christ the Righteous One, the Victorious One, the Fruitful One both in His own person and that which is manifested in His saints.

The early church used the palm tree as a symbol of Christ's triumph over death through resurrection, as also the Christians who were martyred. The bride of Christ is likened in stature to the palm tree (Song of Solomon 7:7).

5. The Olive Tree

The olive tree is actually "the oil tree". It was used for the posts of the doors of the sanctuary (1 Kings 6:23-33). It was also used for the two great winged Cherubim in the Holiest of All and for the posts of the doors of this place.

The "oil tree" is the Hebrew word "shemen", and this word is also translated "anointing", "ointment" and "oil". It is the word used for the holy anointing oil and the pure olive oil used in the golden lampstand in the Tabernacle of Moses.

The olive tree is therefore symbolic of the anointing of the Holy Spirit in the house of the Lord, first upon Jesus the Christ, THE ANOINTED, and then upon the believers, the Christians, the anointed ones, the Body of Christ.

The olive tree is mentioned in the parable of Judges 9:8-9, when the trees went forth to anoint a king over them. It is the first mentioned tree after the Flood (Génesis 8:11). The dove had the olive branch in its mouth. The two witnesses in the vision of Zechariah and John are likened to olive trees by reason of the anointing upon them (Zechariah 4 with Revelation 11:4).

Olive oil from the berry of this tree was used in all the anointing of the Tabernacle of Moses, on furniture and priesthood (Exodus 27:20; Leviticus 24:2).

The olive tree was also used of the true Israel of God, the spiritual nation in which Jew and Gentile are one and partakers of the anointing and fatness of the tree (Romans 11:17-24). Christ after the flesh came out of the "olive tree" nation of Israel.
Christ also suffered in Gethsemane which means "Oil" or "Olive press". He will return to the Mt of Olives even as He ascended from this mount (Acts 1:12; Zechariah 14:4). He is the anointed prophet, priest and king.
Read also these Scriptures — (Acts 10:38; Luke 4:18; Psalm 52:8; Jeremiah 11:16; Hosea 14:6; Isaiah 41:19).

Each of these trees speak of Christ and the believers. The trees were cut off from their natural surroundings, the former source of life in the earth. All their natural beauty was stripped from them. Then they were sawn up, shaped and planed. They all experienced death to their "old life".
After this they go through the process of preparation by the hands of the carpenters in order to find their place in the house of the Lord, to partake of His glory. They were clothed with unnatural beauty and fitly framed together (Ephesians 2:19-22). Christ, as the Branch, was cut off out of the land of the living. There was no natural beauty that we should desire Him. In His death He suffered for us. But He was raised to resurrection glory and beauty to God's Temple in heaven. He is the perfect One, the royal One, the righteous One, the incorruptible One (Isaiah 11:1-4; Jeremiah 23:6; Isaiah 53:1-2; 1 Corinthians 1:30).

He is the Master Carpenter when it comes to His work in the believers. He shapes us for His building. Every part of the Temple speaks of His glory or His glory in the saints. The preparation speaks of the dealings of the Lord in the lives of His people.

In contrast to the Tabernacle of Moses, the main wood used there was the shittim or acacia wood. This was a desert wood and timber. It flourished in the desert by means of a tap root deep down beneath the surface of the sand, yet also had a profuse amount of dry roots on the desert surface.

It speaks of Christ's humanity, the root out of dry ground, in whom there was no form or comeliness. His humanity was incorruptible.

It is significant that the only piece of acacia wood that was placed in the Temple was the ark of the Covenant, which came from the wilderness wanderings and journeyings. All this was a reminder of the journey to the land of rest, the land of promise.

So Christ as THE ARK OF GOD has taken the "acacia wood of His incorruptible humanity" into heaven's Temple, and there He is in His glorified humanity, as a reminder of His pilgrimage days on earth when He came to redeem us.
Acacia wood was used in the Tabernacle for the Tabernacle pillars, for the door, for the walls, and also in the articles of furniture. All was prophetic of His incarnation, the Word made flesh, His sinless and incorruptible humanity (John 1:14-18; Hebrews 10:5).
It spoke of His EARTHLY ministry first of all, then His heavenly ministry.

The Temple, however, had the cedar wood, along with the fir, the almug, the palm and olive trees. The Temple was overlined with cedar as well as other beautifications and ornamentations.
This spoke more of Christ in His HEAVENLY ministry, though it involved that which took place in earth. He came from heaven to earth to atone, and then returned from earth to heaven to intercede.

Heaven and earth are brought together in His ministry.

In summary of the use of the Temple timbers we may say:

* **The Cedar** — speaks of Christ's incorruptible humanity and Christ as king.

* **The Fir** — speaks of Christ's power and strength to uphold.

* **The Almug** — speaks of Christ's work on the cross, His atoning death, His blood.

* **The Palm** — speaks of Christ the upright One, the righteous One, the victorious One.

* **The Olive** — speaks of Christ as the anointed One, the Messiah of God.

In relation to believers then we may say that, when the character qualities and attributes of Christ are inwrought and outworked in the believer, then these trees speak of the believers place in the house of the Lord. Christ in you, the hope of glory is the revelation (Colossians 1:27-29).

Surely Isaiah 55:12-13 would be true in the Temple; *"All the trees of the field shall clap their hands . . ."*

"Then shall the trees of the wood sing out at the presence of the Lord" (1 Chronicles 16:33). Surely the trees in the Temple clapped their hands and sung out at the presence of the Lord in His Temple — not the literal trees, but the believers in Christ!

The Ornamentation of the Boards

"And he carved all the walls of the house round about with carved figures of cherubims and palm trees and open flowers, within and without" (1 Kings 7:29; 6:14-18. 2 Chronicles 3:5,7).

The cedar boards are now carved, according to the Divine command, carved and wrought and outworked in them ornamentations and beautifications. They had lost their natural beauty but now would have the beauty of the Lord upon them (Isaiah 61:3). These were trees of righteousness, of the Lord's planting and they were given "beauty for ashes" of mourning.

It speaks of Christ and His people who lose the beauty of the natural man and receive a God-given, or spiritual beauty upon them, precious to the Lord. This outworked and inwrought beauty was carved upon them by the hand of another, not of themselves. It was unnatural to them but God-given and ordained.

So God would carve in and upon the believer by the carving instruments of His Word and Spirit the beauty of the Lord Jesus Christ. This is to be inworked and outwrought in us. The same beauty in the door of the Sanctuary is to be upon the walls. The same beauty that is in Christ is to be in His saints. What He is in this world, so are we to be.

Let the beauty of the Lord God be upon us (1 John 4:17; 3:1-2; Psalm 90:17). His Word is to ornament and beautify us for His palace. The carvings in the cedar walls were as follows, and we take them in the following order.

1. **The Knops** — 1 Kings 6:29

   The word has the thought of gourds, a cucumber like food, round shaped. It is the same ornamentation as on the brazen sea in the outer court (1 Kings 7:24).
   It speaks of the fruit of the Spirit of Christ (Galatians 5:22; 1 Corinthians 13). The fruit of love encompasses each of the nine listed fruit of the Spirit. So the fruit of the Spirit is to be inwrought and outworked in the life of the believer as it was manifested in Christ.

2. **The Open Flowers** — 1 Kings 6:29,14-18

   An open flower speaks of maturity manifested. Christ is the lily of the valley, and the rose of Sharon. It speaks of beauty and the fragrance of the life of Christ. He was fully matured and blossomed to reveal His Father (John 1:14-18). This maturity of the beauty of Christ is also to be inwrought and outworked in the believer, carved into his experience by the Spirit and the Word.

3. **The Palm Trees** — 1 Kings 6:29

   Palm trees, as already noted, speak of uprightness, righteousness, victory and rejoicing. It is the most frequent ornamentation of the trees in the cedar wood (Psalm 92:12-14).

   These character qualities need to be carved into the believers life as each were in Christ's life.

4. **The Set Chains** — 2 Chronicles 3:5

   It seems that the knops, open flowers and palms were linked together by the chains set in the cedar wood also.

   Chains are made up of so many links. These chains speak of the numerous "links" in the covenantal promises of God throughout the Bible. We are to bind the Word of God as chains about our neck so that we may fulfil them (Proverbs 1:9; Song of Solomon 1:10; Ezekiel 16:8-11). Chains about the neck were given as a token of greatness and honour to Daniel (Daniel 5:7,16,29). The Temple doors had chains upon them also.

   All truths in the Word of God are linked together in progressive revelation and thus form one chain of Divine truth, covenantal theology.

5. **The Cherubims** — 1 Kings 6:29; 2 Chronicles 3:7

   The word "Cherubim" means "those grasped, held fast". There is a progressive revelation of the Cherubim in Scripture.

   A fuller treatment of this will be noted in the chapter on the Oracle and the two great olive Cherubim overshadowing the Cherubim on the ark of the Covenant.

   However, we note a brief overview of the Cherubim here.

   The Cherubim are seen in Eden guarding the tree of eternal life with the flaming sword (Genesis 3:24).

   The Cherubim are seen in the veil of the Tabernacle of Moses guarding the entrance to the Holiest of All (Exodus 26:31-34).

   The Cherubim are seen overshadowing the blood-stained mercy seat of the ark of the Covenant (Exodus 25:10-22).

   The Cherubim are always associated with the throne of God and His holiness. The vision of Ezekiel shows the Cherubim there with the four faces, as does John's in Revelation 4 (Ezekiel chapters 1 and 10).

   Their predominant revelation is the holiness of God relative to the atonement.

   Note these references to Cherubim also — 1 Samuel 4:4; 2 Kings 19:15; 1 Chronicles 13:6; Psalm 80:1; Isaiah 37:16. The Lord dwells between the Cherubims.

   So the holiness of the Godhead was manifested in Christ and is to be inwrought and spiritually carved into the lives of His saints in His house.

G. **Walls Overlaid with Gold** — 2 Chronicles 3:4-9

   With the completion of the beautification and ornamentation of the cedar boards on the walls, the WHOLE HOUSE is then overlaid with gold, fine gold (1 Kings 6:11-22).

   All the walls of the house, the Holy Place and the Holiest of All were covered or overlaid with gold. The ceiling and the floor were also overlaid with gold (1 Kings 6:20). The gold glorified all the carvings in the cedar boards and walls.

   Gold always speak of God, of the Divine nature, either in Christ or the believer. It also speaks of the glory of God. The bride-city in Revelation is like transparent gold (Revelation 21-22 chapters). It is filled with the glory of God.

   The gold was the gold of Parvaim, the most precious gold known. Even the nails were of gold (2 Chronicles 3:6-9).

   In the Tabernacle of Moses, the walls and boards were overlaid with gold also, but the boards stood in sockets of silver. There all the furniture stood upon the earth floor, so to speak. The priests ministered on the earth floor, the sand of the desert. The Tabernacle pointed to Christ in His earth walk.

In the Temple the stones of the wall are overlaid with silver, then cedar boards ornamented, and now all is overlaid with gold, standing on the stone foundation. Here the furniture is all standing on a gold floor, so to speak. The priests walked on the gold covered floor in ministry here. The Temple speaks of the glory of Christ in His heavenly sanctuary, as well as to His ministry in the church.

The ultimate revelation, consummation and combination of both Tabernacle and Temple is seen in the city of God where the city of gold is seen. There the redeemed of earth, as kings and priests, walk on streets of gold. The city is filled with the glory of God and the Lamb (Revelation 21:21). The Divine nature shall be fully manifested in redeemed humanity, even the character of Jesus Christ, the eternal God-Man, glorified by the Father.

H. **Garnished with Precious Stones** — 2 Chronicles 3:6-7

Here we discover that they "garnished the house with precious stones for beauty".

The final beautification of the walls of the house was the garnishing with precious stones. The stones would dazzle with brilliance, glittering with all the colours of the rainbow as the lamps of the candlesticks illuminated the Holy Place and the Glory of God illuminated the Holiest of All.

These precious stones were gifts from the princes for the Temple as they offered willingly to the Lord (1 Chronicles 29:2).

The Book of Proverbs says that "A gift (or grace) is as a precious stone in the eyes of him who has it, wherever it turns it prospers" (Proverbs 17:8). Note also Proverbs 3:15; Ezekiel 28:13; Isaiah 28:16; 1 Corinthians 3:12-15; 1 Peter 1:7,19; 2 Peter 1:1-4; Psalm 49:8; and Matthew 26:7.

These precious stones each had their particular beauty, glory and light reflected. They would shine with the various light and colours of the rainbow.

We see the use of precious stones in both Tabernacle and Temple ministrations.

The High Priest's foursquare breastplate had 12 precious stones with the names of the twelve tribes of Israel engraven in them.

Then there were the two onyx stones on his shoulderpieces with the tribal names engraven in them (Exodus 28).

In the breastplate were the two mysterious stones called "Urim" and "Thummin", or "Lights" and "Perfections". By these stones the High Priest received the mind of the Lord and the will of God for the people.

The Bridegroom and his bride are decked with jewels and ornaments (Isaiah 61:10). The Bride city is also garnished with twelve manner of precious stones in her foundation (Revelation chapters 21-22). The city, like the breastplate of the High Priest, is foursquare. The streets are of gold, and the Shekinah-Glory light of God shines in the city.

The precious stones become symbolic of the gifts of the Spirit in the saints, as well as their good works which glorify God. Each gift and God-inspired work glorifies God and shows aspect of His glory in the saints.

The works of the believers are likened to (a) Gold, (b) Silver and (c) Precious stones, the same materials that were used in the building of Tabernacle and Temple (1 Corinthians 3:9-15).

These stones were "*precious* stones" (1 Kings 10:2,10-11; 1 Chronicles 20:2; 29:2; 2 Chronicles 3:6).

God's thoughts to us are precious (Psalm 139:17).

He has given to us precious promises (2 Peter 1:4).

The city of God has light like unto a stone most precious (Revelation 21:11,19). Read also 1 Peter 1:7,19; 2 Peter 1:1.

Hence these precious stones in the Temple walls may represent the gifts of the Spirit, the good works of the saints, works of love and faith done according to the Word and the Spirit of God.

In contrast we view Tabernacle and Temple.

The Tabernacle		**The Temple**
Sockets of silver	—	Stones for foundation of the house silver lined
Boards of acacia wood	—	Boards of cedar, fir, almug, olive, palm tree
Overlaid with gold	—	Ornamented with knops, open flowers, chains, palms, all overlaid with gold
Cherubim in linen curtains	—	Cherubim carved into cedar walls
No boards seen, only gold	—	No stones seen, only gold covered boards
Light of lampstand	—	Light of lampstands
Pertains to "earth floor"	—	Pertains to "gold floor"
Christ in earthly ministry	—	Christ in heavenly ministry in His church

IN SUMMARY:

1. The stones from the quarries, shaped and prepared,
2. Overlaid with silver,
3. Covered with cedar wood,
4. Ornamented with knops, open flowers, chains, palms and Cherubims,
5. Overlaid with gold,
6. Garnished with all manner of precious stones.

So the believer, in the house of the Lord, experiences redemptively all the truths symbolized in the above preparation, ornamentation and beautification of the materials for the Temple of God. He goes from "glory to glory". We behold the work of grace in the process of God's dealings with His people.

The believer is taken as a stone from the quarries of this world, redeemed with the blood of Christ, made a king and priest unto God, experiencing the inwrought beauty of Christ's character, graces and gifts and the Divine nature, and is garnished with gifts and good works unto the glory of His church.

Truly the Psalmist says "And in His Temple does every bit of it cry 'Glory' " (Psalm 29:9). The glory of Moses Tabernacle was internal; the glory of the Temple was internal and external. What magnificent splendour and glory in the material house of the Lord. However, it is nothing compared to the magnificent splendour and glory of Christ in His church. It is nothing compared to the glory that shall be revealed in His saints, the habitation of God through the Spirit, and this, for all eternity!

With the Psalmist we may say, "Except the Lord build *the house* they labour in vain that build it, except the Lord keep *the city,* the watchman watch in vain" (Psalm 127-1). Undoubtedly this spoke of the Temple and of Jerusalem. The Lord built His house and watched over His city and their labour and watchfulness was not in vain.

God's house on earth is now the church. He dwells in it. God's house in heaven is seen to be the city. We dwell in it. The house and the city are brought together in the ultimate revelation of God with His people.

THE FOLDING DOORS OF THE TEMPLE

The Folding Doors (1 Kings 6:35)

The two-leaved, gold-covered doors made the entrance
to the Temple and also to the Holy of Holies.

CHAPTER SEVENTEEN

THE DOORS OF THE SANCTUARY AND THE ORACLE

By a careful reading of 1 Kings 6:31-35 with 2 Chronicles 3:7 we find that the entrance into the Sanctuary or the Holy Place and the Holiest of All, called the Holy Oracle, was by means of doors and curtains.

In this chapter we consider the entrances to the Sanctuary and to the Holy Oracle, the Holy Place and the Most Holy Place.

A. **The Doors into the Sanctuary, the Holy Place** — 1 Kings 6:33-35

A door is always significant of access, of entrance into something. So the doors of the Sanctuary here speak of access into the house of the Lord, into the presence of God, and that which gives one access to the articles of furniture in the Holy Place.

Any priest who entered this Holy Place must come by way of the doors. To seek to enter any other way would be as a thief and a robber.

Jesus said "I AM THE DOOR, by Me if any man enter in he shall be saved . . ." (John 10:9). It is through Him we have access unto the Father by the Spirit (Ephesians 2:18).

We note the design and ornamentation of the doors of the Sanctuary, and the spiritual lessons we gain from the symbolic elements therein.

1. **Made of Fir Tree**

   The fir tree speaks of Christ as the Strong One, mighty to save. It is a sweet and fragrant tree, pleasant to the smell.

   Wood speaks of Christ's sinless humanity. Mankind, as already seen in a previous chapter, is spoken of under the symbol of various trees, including the fir tree (Isaiah 41:19; 55:13; 60:16; 14:8; Hosea 14:8; Psalm 104:17). It is Christ the Man, as to His humanity.

2. **Two Side Posts of Olive Tree**

   Speaks of Christ as the Anointed One, the Messiah. The two side posts which supported the door may speak of the two persons in the Godhead who supported Christ in His total ministry, even the Father and the Holy Spirit. The Father and the Spirit witnessed to the fact that Christ is THE DOOR of access into the presence of God.

3. **A Fourth Part of the Wall**

   The doors measured a fourth part of the wall. Four is the number of the earth. The four Gospels present Christ is His earthly ministry. His Gospel of salvation also is to go to the four corners of the earth, to all creatures, all mankind (Acts 1:8; Matthew 28:18-20; Mark 16:15-20).

   It is out of every kindred, tongue, tribe and nation the redeemed will come to the Father, through Christ the Door to God.

4. **Folding Two-Leaved Doors**

   There were two two-leaved or two folding doors (Similar to old telephone booths, or some stores), thus making four doors in all.

   The same truth is here as above. We have the four Gospels, the Gospels of Matthew, Mark, Luke and John.

   Each present Christ's Sonship in a unique way. Matthew presents Christ as the Son of David. Mark presents Him as the Son of Man. Luke presents Him as the Son of Adam. John presents Him as the Son of God.

   And again, Christ is King in Matthew; the Prophet in Mark; the Priest in Luke, and the Judge in John; four offices together in Him which can be used in the symbolic sense of the four doors into the Holy Place.

5. **Ornamentation of the Doors**

   The ornamentation and beautification of the doors of the Sanctuary was the same as that of the Holy Oracle and the cedar walls.

   * **Open Flowers** — The beauty of Christ in His perfect humanity and maturity.

   * **Palm Trees** — The righteousness of Christ as the perfect and upright One.

   * **Cherubims** — The One in whom the fulness of the Godhead dwelt bodily.

6. **Doors overlaid with Gold**

   These doors, as the walls of the house, were also overlaid with gold. Gold always speaks of Deity, the Divine nature, the glory of God in his attributes. So Christ the door was the Word made flesh, the fulness of the Divine nature and attributes were manifested in Him, in all perfection.

7. **Gold Hinges** — 1 Kings 7:50

   These doors, both in the Holy Place and the Holiest of All were hung upon gold hinges. Doors depend upon their hinges for opening and shutting, for allowing the priests entrance or closing them outside.
   We may say that the whole plan of redemption hinges upon covenantal revelation involving the Father, Son and Holy Spirit.
   Gold again speaks of that which is Divine. Redemption's plan hinges upon the revelation and ministry of the Godhead. Without such there is absolutely no access to the glories of God and His church.

B. **The Doors into the Oracle, the Holiest of All** — 1 Kings 6:31-32

   Again we have another two sets of folding doors for the entrance into the Holiest of All, or the Holy Oracle.
   They present the same truth of access and entrance into the presence of God. However, as the doors into the Holy Place gave access to the priests to the Tables of Shewbread, the Lampstand lights, and the ministry of the Golden Altar of Incense, here, these doors give access into the very Shekinah — Glory of God, to the ark of the Covenant. In other words, these doors give one access "within the veil".
   We note the same truths as in the doors into the Sanctuary.

1. **Made of Olive Tree**

   In contrast to the doors of the Holy Place which were of fir tree, these doors here are made of olive tree, or the "oil tree".
   There was no mention of the olive tree in the Tabernacle of Moses, the desert dwelling place of the Lord.
   The olive timber speaks of Christ as the Anointed One, in whom the fulness of the Divine unction and oil was manifested (John 3:33-34; Matthew 16:15-19). In Him was the priestly, prophetical and kingly anointing in fulness. His life was of the Spirit, who is the "chrisma", or the holy oil.

2. **The Lintel and Two Side Posts of Olive**

   These doors had a lintel and two side posts which were of olive timber also. In the Feast of Passover God commanded that the blood of the Passover Lamb be sprinkled in triune application on the lintel and the two side posts of the door, as the family fed upon the body of this sacrificed Lamb (Exodus 12:21-22).
   All Egypt faced the door, a blood sprinkled door, and either accepted it or rejected it, to their gain of life or loss in death.
   The olive posts speak of the oil of the Spirit, and then the blood back in Egypt speaks of the blood of Christ. The shed blood of Christ provides the oil of the Holy Spirit.
   (Note also Ezekiel 41:23,24 here).

3. **Lintel and Side Posts — A Fifth Part of the Wall**

The doors of the Sanctuary took a fourth part of the wall. These doors here take a fifth part of the wall.

Undoubtedly God had in mind every facet of truth He wanted symbolized. But the Scripture reveals that five is the number of grace, the number of the atonement, the number of life. Jesus, as the door, received five wounds on Calvary in His body for us to provide access into the glory of God, into that which is "within the veil".

4. **Folding Two-Leaved Doors**

Again we have the two folding doors, each with two leaves in them. Thus we have double folding doors, or four doors altogether here, as in the Holy Place doors.

As noted, four is the number of earth, the number of that which is worldwide. The Gospel of Christ and the message of access goes to all the world, every kindred, tongue, tribe and nation (Acts 1:8; Matthew 28:18-20; Mark 16:15-20). Christ must be presented as the way of access to God to the four corners of earth, to all mankind.

The Scripture provides many aspects of the number four. There are four descriptions of God in the Bible: (1) God is Light, 1 John 1:5; (2) God is Love, 1 John 4:16; (3) God is Spirit, John 4:24; (4) God is a Consuming Fire, Hebrews 12:29.

The four doors providing access into the presence of God, "within the veil", must be entered with the understanding that God is Light, Love, Spirit and Holy Fire. These are four eternal attributes of God's very nature and being.

5. **Ornamentation of the Doors**

The ornamentation of these doors is the same as the doors of the Sanctuary and the walls of the house. Christ is the same whichever way we view Him. He is the same yesterday, today and for ever (Hebrews 13:8).

* **Open Flowers** — The beauty and fragrance of Christ in His perfect and mature humanity, revealing God the Father (John 1:14-18).

* **Palm Trees** — Christ the upright and righteous One, the victorious One who brings rejoicing to His people (John 12:13; Revelation 7:9).

* **Cherubims** — Christ the One in whom all the fulness of the Godhead dwells in bodily form (Colossians 1:19; 2:9).

All of these beautifications were carved and inwrought by the knife, by the instruments of suffering. Thus Christ suffered for us in His perfect and sinless humanity. But His perfect beauty of His manhood is seen.

6. **Doors overlaid with Gold**

Symbolic of His absolute Deity, His Divine nature, His union with the Father and the Holy Spirit. He is GOD Made flesh. His work, His words, His person were Divine. Gold = His Divinity. Wood = His Humanity. Two materials here, as two natures in the one person of Christ. The gold never becomes the wood, the wood never becomes the gold, yet these two were as one. Christ in His Deity and Humanity, two natures, yet is one person.

7. **Hinges of Gold** — 1 Kings 7:50

The hinges upon which the doors were upheld were of gold. The doors depend on the hinges for opening and shutting, for letting the priests in or keeping them out.

The Father and the Spirit uphold the person of Christ in all He is, all He does, and all He says.

8. **Golden Nails for the Temple**

According to 2 Chronicles 3:9 we see that there were golden nails to be used in the Sanctuary.

In 1 Chronicles 22:3 we have iron nails for the courts, but for the Sanctuary proper there were the golden nails, with the same symbolic truth therein of that which is Divine.

Nails in Scripture also point to Christ as "the nail" fastened in a sure place. Nails hold things together, they keep structures in place, they are fastened in the walls upon which to hang things. So Christ is all that to His church.

He is the nail fastened in a sure place, when the antichrist nail is cut down (Isaiah 22:22-25). Upon Him all the Father's glory is to be hung (Revelation 5:9,12).

He is the nail out of the tribe of Judah (Zechariah 10:4)
He is the nail in a sure place (Ezra 9:8; The nail in the Amen place, margin).
He is the nail with the words of God. His words are as goads to prod us on in His ways, and as nails fastened by the collectors of sayings, given from the one shepherd (Ecclesiastes 12:11). We may hang things upon all His words which are sure and stedfast.

9. **Chains of Gold before the Oracle** — 1 Kings 6:21; 2 Chronicles 3:16
    There were golden chains placed before the Oracle as a partition. Probably these chains were used to open the doors of the Oracle.
    As seen previously, chains are made up numerous links. In Proverbs 1:9 and Song of Solomon chains are used as ornaments around the neck of the people of God.
    Symbolically we may say that there are numerous truths that flow through the Scripture, from Genesis through to Revelation, and all are "linked" together, forming a chain of revelation from God to man.
    No one link on its own forms a chain. Scripture has numerous "chain-references" in its numerous themes.
    In the volume of the book it is written of Christ (Hebrews 10:5-10). Perhaps the greatest chain of truth is covenantal revelation. The student can study the word of God and pick up the numerous links in this major chain of Divine truth.

In bringing our chapter to a conclusion, we note in these entrances to the Holy Place and the Oracle that there were eight doors in all, two sets of two-leaved folding doors.
Eight is the number of resurrection. There is therefore no mistake in identifying the door. Christ is THE DOOR and the Scripture presents Him as "the door" in a number of different ways (John 10:9).

Through Him we have access (the door) to the Father by the Spirit (the golden hinges), (Ephesians 2:18).
The priests could go "in and out" through these doors according to ministry. So we believers enter in by Christ the door, and may go "in and out" and find pastures.

Christ is THE DOOR, not A door, as if there were many other doors to God. The truth of a door is that there are two sides, inside and outside. An old children's song went this way:

"One door and only one, and yet the sides are two,
   Inside and outside, and which side are you?"

Note these doors in Scripture:
*   Christ is the door into Noah's Ark of salvation (Genesis 6:16).
*   Christ is the blood-sprinkled door of Passover (Exodus 12:22-23).
*   Christ is the door of the Tabernacle, God's dwelling place (Exodus 26:36; 29:4,32).
*   Christ is the door that shut out the Sodomites and blinded them (Genesis 19:6-12).
*   Christ is the door of the sheepfold (John 10:1-9).
*   Christ is the door into the marriage (Matthew 25:1-13).
*   Christ is the door into the gospel field (1 Corinthians 16:9; 2 Corinthians 2:12; Colossians 4:3; Revelation 3:8).
*   Christ is the door into heaven and the throne of God (Revelation 4:1-2).

Wherever we look, Christ is the door. In the Temple, Christ is the door into the courts of the Lord; Christ is the door into the porch of God's house; He is the door into the Holy Place, and the Holiest of All. Christ is the door to the Father and all eternal glories. Christ is the door into His church.

Note these other Scriptures also (Exodus 33:9-10; 38:8; 40:12; Leviticus 1:3-4; 8:3-4,31; 15:14; Numbers 6:13,18; 10:3; 20:6; 27:2; 1 Samuel 2:22.

Israel continually had to face the door of the Tabernacle with their sacrificial offerings, or the door of the Temple. It pointed to the fact that no access was available to them except through sacrificial blood and the ministry of the High Priest. What lament there was when the carved work in the doors of the Sanctuary was destroyed by the enemy (Psalm 74:1-10).
So for the believer. All access to God is through the sacrificial blood of Christ and His High Priestly ministrations.

Perhaps the Psalmist was alluding to these doors when he said: "Lift up your heads, O ye gates; and be ye lift up, ye everlasting doors; and the King of glory shall come in . . ." (Psalm 24:7).

THE VEIL OF THE TEMPLE

The Veil of the Temple

CHAPTER EIGHTEEN

THE VEIL OF THE TEMPLE

In 2 Chronicles 3:14 we have the one and only reference to the veil in the Temple.

"And he made the vail of blue, and purple, and crimson, and fine linen, and wrought cherubims thereon."

Because of the significance of this veil (or "vail" in Old Testament), we find it necessary to devote a chapter to this special entrance associated with the Holiest of All, or the Holy Oracle. Only the Chronicles records the making of the veil. It is not mentioned in Kings.

There are a number of various veils mentioned in Scripture, each of them having their own unique and distinctive truths.
We have the following veils:

1. The veil upon Moses face which veiled the glory on his face and which the children of Israel could not behold (Exodus 34:33-35).

2. The veil of the Tabernacle of Moses (Exodus 26:31-35). This was basically the same veil as in the Temple here, as will be seen.

3. The veil of blindness upon the heart of the Jewish nation (2 Corinthians 3:13-16). It can only be rent when the heart turns to their Messiah.

4. The veil of death upon all nations (Isaiah 25:6-9).

5. The veil of Christ's flesh, of which all veils were symbolic and prophetic (Hebrews 10:19-20).

6. The veil of Solomon's Temple, here under consideration (2 Chronicles 3:14).

The veil was associated with the two folding doors of the Oracle. Whether it was placed immediately in front of the doors or behind the doors is hard to say. However, it seems more likely that the veil was in front and the priests could see that veil as the priests in the Tabernacle of Moses did.

We consider in fuller details the making of the veil and its pattern. It follows the same truths as in the Tabernacle of Moses.

A. The Material of the Veil

The material was of fine linen. Fine linen again points to the Lord our Righteousness (Jeremiah 23:6; 1 Corinthians 1:30; 2 Corinthians 5:21).
Fine linen is spoken also of the righteousness, or the righteous acts of the saints (Revelation 19:7-8).
Christ is the Righteous One. This is set forth more especially in the Gospel of Luke.

B. The Colours of the Veil

There were three special colours woven in and inwrought in the veil.

1) **Blue** — The colour of heaven. Jesus is the "Second Man" . . . the Lord from heaven. He is the heavenly Man as revealed in the Gospel of John (1 Corinthians 15:47; John 3:13,31). He originated from heaven. He is the heavenly High Priest (Hebrews 7:26).

2) **Purple** — The colour of royalty, kingship, rulership. Kings were clothed in purple often. Purple is a blending of blue (heavenly) and scarlet (blood sacrifice). Christ is the King of Kings and Lord of Lords. He is the Royal Man to whom the Gospel of Matthew witnesses and He takes the throne of David (Luke 1:30-33).

3) **Scarlet** — The colour of sacrifice, sacrificial blood. Jesus is the Lamb of God, our sacrifice. He came to shed His blood and redeem mankind. Mark's Gospel presents Him as the sacrificial servant. Note also John 1:29,36; Matthew 20:28.

Each of these colours were to be inwrought in the veil. The veil was of cunning and skilful workmanship. It was according to the Divine pattern. As the veil in the Tabernacle of Moses, it was done by the ability of the Spirit and the wisdom of God. So the marvellous design and intricate details in the life of Christ were inwrought and outworked by the wisdom and Spirit of God. Christ was THE WORD made flesh, by the power of the Spirit (John 1:1-3,14-18).

Son of Man and Son of God (blue and scarlet) united together in His one person is seen in the veil.

The four colours may again be likened to the four Gospels which present Christ in His earth walk. Luke presents Christ as the fine linen. Matthew presents Christ as the purple. Mark presents Him as the scarlet. John presents Him as the blue.

C. The Ornamentation of the Veil

The design inwrought in the veil was the same as in the veil of Moses Tabernacle, which was the Cherubim.

At the risk of repetition we note again the emphasis on the Cherubim in the Scriptures. Cherubim are always seen in Scripture in relation to the Godhead. In Genesis 3:24 they guarded the way to the tree of eternal life with the flaming sword. In the Tabernacle of Moses veil, as in the Temple veil, they are inwrought in the material of fine linen with its colours. Over the ark of the Covenant were the two Cherubs each end of the mercy-seat, part of that one piece of gold (Exodus 25:10-22).

The Cherubim inwrought within the veil speak of the Father and the Holy Spirit and the Divine attributes of the Godhead inwrought into the person, life and ministry of Christ. In Him dwells all the fulness of the Godhead in bodily form (Colossians 1:19; 2:9).

The veil therefore taught the same truth as the veil in Moses Tabernacle, or as the doors into the Holy Place and the Holiest of All in the Temple. There is only way of access into the Shekinah-Glory presence of God, that is, through the veil. It seems the veil hung on wreathen chainwork (2 Chronicles 3:16).

The writer to the Hebrews seems to especially interpret this veil for us. He says: "Having therefore, brethren, boldness to enter into the holiest of all by the blood of Jesus, by a new and living way which He has consecrated for us, *through the veil, that is to say, His flesh* . . . let us draw near . . ." (Hebrews 10:19-22).

We note some of the important lessons to be learnt from a study of the veil in Scripture.

* **The veil was a divider**, a separator from the presence of God. This is the message it spelt out to man. Thus far and no further. The word veil actually means "that which hides", or "a separation, a curtain".
So sin brought separation between God and man. There is a veil between God and man that has to be broken down, that has to be rent. It is sin which dwells in man's flesh, in which is no good thing.

* **The veil hid God from man's view**. God's glory could not be seen because of the veil. There could be no face to face communion with that veil there. Even as the children of Israel could not have face to face communion with Moses because of the veil that hid his face of glory, so man could not have face to face communion with God, or behold His glory.

* **The veil was "Rent in the midst"** when Christ died on Calvary. It was rent in two, torn apart by the supernatural power of God, thus declaring that access into His presence was available through Christ (Luke 23:45).

* **The veil was "Rent from top to bottom"** when Christ died (Matthew 27:51). It was an act of God, not of man. It was rent from top to bottom, not bottom to top. God's grace comes to man. He takes the initiative. Grace is God coming to man, not man coming to God.

* **The veil was rent in connection with Christ's death**, with the rending of the "veil of His flesh" (Hebrews 9:8; 10:19-20). Christ was God's Temple in flesh, and when the veil of His flesh was rent in crucifixion, so the veil of the material Temple was rent. Christ crucified is the rent veil making access to God for all who come to God by and through Him.

* **The rent veil signified the truth that "the way" was now open.** It signified the fulfilment and abolishment of the Old Covenant, the Mosaic covenant with all its economy and ceremonials pertaining to animal sacrifices and ritualism.

So many precious truths are hidden in the truth of the veil. Now all believers have access to the very presence of God "within the veil". There is nothing between from God's viewpoint.

The *inwrought veil* spoke of the beauty and perfections of Christ's life. As long as He lived, and the veil of His flesh stood, there was no access to God. His perfect, sinless life condemned us.

The *rent veil* spoke of His vicarious death, making access available to God the Father. It spoke of His broken body and shed blood. The veil must be rent. Christ must die. He is THE WAY to the Father.

In the rent veil we have the closing off of the Old Covenant and the opening of the New Covenant. The "middle wall" of partition has been broken down never to be re-instituted again. All that we lost in Adam is restored in Christ. Man lost the way, the truth and the life in Adam. Christ restored and became the way, the truth and the life (John 14:6).

He also, in another aspect, relative to the heavenly Sanctuary has gone "within the veil" and ministers there as our High Priest (Hebrews 6:20; Acts 1:8-11; 1 John 2:1). No wonder a great company of Aaronic and Levitical priests accepted "the faith" when they saw the truth of the "rent veil" (Acts 6:7).

One day, heaven's veil will be rent, and Jesus will come from "within the veil", but this time in flaming fire and judgment on all who do not believe in Him. Read 1 Peter 3:22; Hebrews 5:1-5; Mark 16:19; Hebrews 10:19-22; Revelation 19:11-16. Though we here on earth cannot see Him, yet we know He ministers in heaven's Sanctuary in behalf of His people as our great High Priest.

In concluding our chapter we bring into sharper focus, by way of contrast, the entrances in the Tabernacle of Moses and the Temple of Solomon.

Tabernacle of Moses		Temple of Solomon
The Court Gate, Tabernacle Door, and Veil	—	**The Temple Doors, and Veil**
1. Of fine twined linen	—	Fine linen
2. Blue	—	Blue
3. Purple	—	Purple
4. Scarlet	—	Crimson
5. Cherubims inwrought in veil only	—	Cherubims inwrought in veil
6. Pillars of acacia wood, or brass	—	Doors of Cedar, ornamented with knops,
7. Veil pillars, acacia overlaid with gold	—	flowers, palms, cherubims. Overlaid with gold. Veil hung by chains of gold.

Christ is both the door (John 10:9), and the rent veil (Hebrews 10:19-20). This is seen in His life and His death.

When the veil was rent in the Temple at Jerusalem it repudiated Jerusalem as a holy place where all worship must be directed to the Father (John 4:20-22). Now we have access "within the veil" into the heavenly temple through the heavenly Zion and heavenly Jerusalem (Hebrews 12:22-24).

The colours as in this veil were in the garments of the High Priest also, thus linking High Priest with the veil.

Christ is our rent veil and our High Priest. The Day of Atonement (Leviticus 16), on which day alone the High Priest entered within the veil finds its fulfilment in Christ who "rent the veil in two" as our High Priest, giving us access to God through His broken body and shed blood.

The song-writer says:

"O behold the Man of Sorrows,
O behold Him in plain view,
Lo! He is the mighty conqueror,
Since He rent the veil in two."

INTERIOR OF THE HOLY PLACE

Interior of the Holy Place

CHAPTER NINETEEN

THE MEASUREMENTS OF THE TEMPLE

Having considered in detail the site, the foundation and the building of the Temple in previous chapters we note the measurements of the Lord's house as given by inspiration of the Spirit in the pattern to king David. This is the pattern to which Solomon builds the Temple.

The details of the overall measurements of the Temple are found in 1 Kings 6:1-2 and 2 Chronicles 3:1-3 along with more specified measurements for the holy place and the holy oracle, as will be seen in due time.

The measurements of the Temple, as for the Tabernacle of Moses, must have some Divine significance to be discovered in the use of its numbers. We contrast the measurements of the Tabernacle of Moses and the Temple of Solomon. The latter is found to be twice the size of the former.

A. **Tabernacle Measurements**

The overall measurements of the Tabernacle were: Length = 30 cubits

: Breadth = 10 cubits

: Height = 10 cubits

The Temple was twice the size of the Tabernacle in these measurements and also a little higher as to its height. It is the same truth, but doubled.

In the study on the Tabernacle of Moses, we found these measurements to be prophetic of the dispensations of time relative to God's "Week of Redemption".

The outer court measurements, as to lineal curtain area, equalled 1500 lineal cubits. This was prophetic of the 1500 years of the Law age, from Moses to Jesus.

The holy place measurements were $10 \times 10 \times 20 = 2000$ cubical content, and were prophetic of the 2000 years of the Church age, from Christ's first to His second coming in the time known to the Lord.

The most holy place measured $10 \times 10 \times 10 = 1000$ cubical content, prophetic of the 1000 year Millennial age of the kingdom in its fulness of glory.

In all we cover the dispensations of time over 4,500 years. Dispensationally the Tabernacle's prophetic measurements bring us through the Law age, through the Church age and to the close of the 1000 year Kingdom age, unto the beginning of the new heavens and new earth, or eternity.

The "Wilderness" period of time of 2,500 years may be covered in the time period from Adam to Moses. The total would cover the 7,000 years of God's redemptive week in His dealings with man pertaining to earth.

B. **Temple Measurements** — 1 Kings 6:1-2; 2 Chronicles 3:1-3

The Temple measurements were: Length = 60 cubits

: Breadth = 20 cubits

: Height = 30 cubits.

These measurements were for the whole house, inclusive of the oracle and the holy place. If the measurements of the Tabernacle of Moses were prophetic of time relative to redemption's plan, then without doubt the same would be true of the Temple measurements.

1. **The Holy Place** — 1 Kings 6:17,20

The measurements of the holy place were 40 cubits long, 20 cubits broad, and 30 cubits high. These were the measurements over all. It depends on whether or not there was an "upper chamber" over the holy place as there was over the most holy place. Scripture does not specifically state whether this was so or not. The inclusive area would therefore equal

40 × 20 × 30 = 24,000 cubical content. The number 12 or 24 is therefore prominent in its triplicate of thousands. The number 24 is also symbolic of God's order and government. It is especially seen in the priestly courses established by David for the temple order. A study of 1 Chronicles 23-28 chapters reveals this and this will be considered in the appropriate chapter.

The number 24 is the number of priestly administrations. In the "daily ministrations" there were 24 priests on duty 24 hours of day, representing the 24,000 priestly courses, who represented the thousands of Israel before the Lord in His Temple. It is the ultimate number in the city of God, the new Jerusalem (Revelation 21-22).

Therefore the holy place of the Temple is stamped with the significance of the number 24 in its multiples.

2. The Holiest of All — 1 Kings 6:16,20; 2 Chronicles 3:8

The measurements of the holiest of all, or, the holy oracle, the very throne room of the glory of God Himself, also add to this truth and point ultimately to the city of God, where the throne of God and the Lamb is found.

The measurements of the holiest of all were: Length = 20 cubits
                                           : Breadth = 20 cubits
                                           : Height = 20 cubits.

In other words, it was a foursquare, or a perfect cube. This is exactly as the most holy place of the Tabernacle of Moses, which was foursquare also. There the ark of the Covenant stood on the "earth floor". All pertained prophetically to the redemptive plan of God relative to this earth. The glory of God will cover the earth.

However, all that pertains to the Temple has to do with the "gold floor" and points ultimately to the city of God with its streets of gold, the city foursquare.

C. The Tabernacle and The Temple — Dispensationally

In considering the Divinely given revelation and measurements of the Tabernacle of Moses in the wilderness and the Temple of God in the land of promise, it would seem that the major truth, dispensationally, is that which pertains to time and eternity.

1. The Tabernacle

The Tabernacle in its revelation seems definitely to pertain to earth and time in the plan of redemption. As mentioned, all has to do with the "earth floor" in the wilderness wanderings. The ark of God, as all the other furniture stood on the desert floor.

The prophetic measurements of the outer court curtains, the cubical content of both holy place and most holy place point to the plan of redemption relative to time from the Law to the Kingdom age. Once again, the student is referred to this textbook for fuller details of this.

2. The Temple

The Temple in its revelation, that is, the Temple proper, not the outer courts or furnishings, pertains more to that which is of heaven and eternity in the plan of redemption. All here has to do with the "gold floor" and the walls garnished with precious stones. The house does not have that which is of brass in it. There is also that which is foursquare in the Temple. The emphasis in the Temple proper is upon gold, God's holiness and glory being revealed.

We note some of the features of the Temple proper that seem to point ultimately to the heavenly city, the city of God foursquare, with its golden streets.

The Temple of God (O.T. Type)	The City of God (N.T. Antitype)
1. The Temple, the habitation of God	— The City, the Tabernacle of God
2. The Ark of God sat in the Holiest of All, which was foursquare	— The City of God is foursquare
3. The Glory of God was the only light	— The Glory of God is the light thereof
4. The Presence of God in the midst of His people	— The Presence of God and the Lamb in the midst of the redeemed
5. The staves removed from the Ark, journeyings ended	— The throne of God and the Lamb journeyings are over
6. No Manna in the Ark	— Christ, the hidden Manna (Revelation 2:17).
7. No fruitful Rod in tha Ark	— Christ and the Church have the Rod of God (Revelation 2:26-27)
8. The Tables of the Law only remain in the Ark	— The Law of God now written in the fleshy tables of the heart of the redeemed (Jeremiah 31:31-34)
9. Mt. Zion and Mt. Moriah vitally linked in David's Tabernacle and Solomon's Temple as God's habitation	— The City of God seen in an exceeding great and high mountain as God's eternal habitation
11. The walls are studded with all manner of precious stones	— The foundation walls are garnished with twelve precious stones
12. Dedicated in the Feast of Rest and Glory; Feast of Tabernacles	— Saints will experience eternal Rest and Glory in Tabernacle of God
13. The Feast of the Seventh Month was called the Feast of Tabernacles	— Revelation is a Book of Sevens, and closes with the Tabernacle of God being with men forever
14. Rest, peace, and permanency characterize the Temple	— Eternal rest, peace, and permanence characterize the City of God
15. The Priests minister with sacrifices and incense to the Lord	— The redeemed are Kings and Priests to God and the Lamb, offering spiritual sacrifices and incense of prayer and praise eternally
16. The Priests minister in their twenty-four courses day and night	— The redeemed will minister day and night eternally in their courses
17. David's order of worship with singers and musicians was incorporated into the Temple order	— The Son of David's order of worship with singing and music will be established forever in the Tabernacle of God

A consideration of this comparison certainly points to the ultimate revelation of God in the Bible, the city foursquare, and eternal dwelling place of the redeemed. There they rule and reign and worship as kings and priests unto God and the Lamb. The student can see that an understanding of the Tabernacles of Moses and David, and the Temple of Solomon is a key to understand Hebrews and Revelation.

D. Significance of Numbers

Undoubtedly the most dominant link between the Temple of God and the city of God has to do with the Divinely given measurements. A comparison of both Tabernacle, Temple and the city of God reveals the multiples of the number twelve, the number twentyfour and the number 144, or actually multiples of 12,000.

1. In the Tabernacle

We can only speak of a few examples of these numbers in the prophetic structures.

* **Twelve** — There were 12 loaves on the table of shewbread.
  There were twelve stones in the breastplate of the high priest.
  The shaft of the golden lampstand had twelve in its ornamentation and unity.

* **Twentyfour** — The 12 loaves of shewbread were each of two-tenths deal of fine flour, hence 24 tenths.
  The 4 silver sockets of the veil for the holiest of all represented $4 \times 6,000 = 24,000$ redeemed Israelites.
  The same is true of the 96 silver sockets for the Tabernacle boards. These 96 sockets represented 576,000 redeemed souls, or $4 \times 12 = 48 \times 12,000$ ransomed souls.
  Each board stood on two silver sockets. Each socket represented 6,000 souls, thus we have 12,000 souls represented in one board of the Tabernacle.

* **One-hundred and fortyfour** — This has already been referred to in the multiples of twelve. In the sockets under the boards we see $4 \times 144,000$ redeemed Israelites (or $48 \times 12,000$). In the curtain of goat's hair covering, the first set of six curtains over the holy place only were $30 \times 4 \times 6$ cubital area, or 5×144 cubital area over the holy place.

2. In the Temple

Again we can only speak of some prominent twelves and multiples.

* **Twelve** — There were 12 loaves on the ten tables of shewbread, or, 120 loaves of bread.
  The high priest still had the 12 stones on the breastplate of judgment.
  He also had the 12 names of the 12 tribes of Israel on the two onyx stones on his shoulders.

* **Twentyfour** — The Temple is prominent with its twentyfours.
  There were 24 courses of priests on duty 24 hours a day.
  The courses of the captains, princes, priests and Levitical singers were in their twenty-fours.
  These were also in their 24,000's in their responsibilities for Israel and the Temple of God.

* **One-hundred and fortyfour** — This may be seen in the measurements of the Temple proper.
  The Temple measured $60 \times 20 \times 30$, or $144 \times 5 \times 10$.
  The holiest, including the upper chamber was $20 \times 20 \times 30$ or 12,000 cubical content.

3. In the City of God

The ultimate of each of these numbers, as well as their multiples, is seen in the Book of Revelation, and finally in the city of God. Again, we note but some of them.

* **Twelve** — There are 12 stars on the woman's crown in Revelation 12:1.
  In the city of God there are 12 gates of 12 pearls, 12 unnamed messengers standing in these gates, 12 manner of fruit on the 12 trees of life for the 12 months of the year.

There are 12 names of the 12 tribes of Israel.
There are 12 names of the 12 apostles of the Lamb in the 12 foundations.

* **Twentyfour** — There are 24 elders seen worshipping God and the Lamb in Revelation 4-5 chapters.
There are many twelves in the city, which are combined in their truth making the number twentyfour as to significance.

* **One-hundred and fortyfour** — The wall of the city of God measures 144 cubits high. There are 12,000 chosen out of each of the 12 tribes of Israel, making 144,000 who follow the Lamb where ever He goes. This, no doubt, was symbolized in the 12,000 souls represented in the 96 silver sockets of the Tabernacle of Moses.
The city of God is 12,000 cubits and foursquare, or, $4 \times 12,000$.

Who can fail to see the significance of the numbers 12, 24, 144 or 12,000 as seen in Tabernacle, Temple and finally the eternal city of God in the Book of Revelation, the Book of Ultimates. It is the glory of these numbers carried to their triplicate in their thousands.

The prophet Isaiah prophesied of the Bride city in all her glory and all is confirmed by the apostle John in Revelation (Isaiah 54:1-7; 60:10-22; 61:10-11; 62:1-5,10-12 with Revelation 21-22 chapters).

As has been noted in earlier chapters of this text, the Temple may be considered in several ways:

1. The Temple as a type of the Lord Jesus Christ. He is THE Temple of God (John 2:19-21).

2. The Temple as a type of the Church, the Body of Christ (1 Corinthians 3:16; 6:19; 2 Corinthians 6:16).

3. The Temple as a type of the individual believer who is spoken of as being God's holy Temple (1 Corinthians 3:16; 6:19-20).

4. The Temple may also be seen as a type of the eternal kingdom of God as seen in the city of God which is called the Tabernacle of God with men (Revelation 21:3).

It is this that is seen in the symbolic measurements and the gold floor of the Temple, and its walls garnished with precious stones, as the house is filled with the glory and presence of God. This is the facet of truth which is emphasized in this chapter.

God has always desired to dwell with and amongst His redeemed people. The Old Testament typical dwellings show the progressive revelation of this redemptive theme.

He dwelt with man in the Garden of Eden (Genesis 3:8,24).
He dwelt among His people Israel in the Tabernacle of Moses (Exodus 25:8,22).
He dwelt with Israel in the Tabernacle of David (1 Chronicles 17:1-3).
He dwelt with His people in the Temple of Solomon (2 Chronicles 5).

The full revelation was in the Lord Jesus Christ, who was God's Tabernacle and Temple personified (John 1:14; 2:19-21; Colossians 1:19; 2:9). His eternal dwelling place is the City of God, the new and heavenly Jerusalem (Revelation 21-22).

"And I John saw **the holy city,** new Jerusalem, coming down from God out of heaven, prepared as a bride adorned for her husband. And I heard a great voice out of heaven saying, Behold **the Tabernacle of God is with men,** and He will dwell with them, and they shall be His people, and God Himself will be with them, and be their God. And God shall wipe away all tears from their eyes; and there shall be no more death, neither sorrow, nor crying, neither shall there be any more pain; for the former things are passed away" (Revelation 21:2-4).

CHAPTER TWENTY

THE COURTS OF THE TEMPLE

Surrounding the Temple were two great courts (2 Kings 23:12). These were spoken of as:

1. **The Inner Court** for the priests (2 Chronicles 4:9; 1 Kings 6:36; 7:12);

2. **The Outer Court** for Israel, called the great court (2 Chronicles 4:9; 2 Kings 23:12).

We consider the significance of these courts for Israel and for the church both personally and spiritually as well as dispensationally.

A. The Inner Court for the Priests

The inner court was strictly for the priests and their ministrations at the brazen altar, the molten sea and the lavers.

In this inner court was the Temple porch and the Temple proper with its holy place and most holy place.
Ezekiel speaks of it also as the inner court (Ezekiel 46:1). Here also, according to Ezekiel, the priests boiled the trespass offerings and prepared the sin offerings for the cleansing of the Israelites (Ezekiel 46:20).

The emphasis in this court is upon *sacrifice* (the brazen altar), and *cleansing* (the molten sea and the ten lavers). This is the message of the inner court. Before any priest could enter into the house of the Lord, they must know the cleansing by sacrificial blood and washing by the cleansing water. The same is true for New Testament believer-priests. Before we come into the house of the Lord we must know the cleansing by blood and water which flowed from the side of Jesus on Calvary (John 19:33-34; 1 John 5:6-8).

B. The Outer Court for the Israelites

The outer court, especially called the great court, was for the people of Israel. Ezekiel called it the outward court (Ezekiel 40:17; 46:21; 2 Chronicles 7:3;4:9). In Ezekiel's vision there seemed to be several gates into this court. The people could come in one gate but had to leave by another gate, the gate opposite (Ezekiel 46:9). If they came in by the north gate they must leave by the way of the south gate, or if by the south gate, then they would leave by way of the north gate. None would leave the same way they entered.

The emphasis in this court with its gates is *thanksgiving and praise*. The fact that there were two courts point to distinctions in the approach to God. The Israelites could enter the great court. The priests only could enter the inner court. Later on, in Herod's Temple, there were several courts. There was the Court of the Women, the Priests Court, and the Court of the Gentiles and a Court of Israel.
All such pointed in national sense to the racial and ethnic divisions of Jew and Gentile, the circumcised and uncircumcised peoples. In Christ, the divisions between these ethnic groups would be broken down at the cross and both Jew and Gentile could come into the courts of the Lord and become one in His house, His church.

C. Measurements of the Courts

No measurements are given for these courts of the Lord (1 Chronicles 28:12,19). They were all part of the pattern given to David by the Spirit in writing. In Revelation 11:1-2 John is given a vision of the house of the Lord, and he is told to measure the Temple and the altar. However, the outer court was not to be measured but to be "trodden under foot" forty and two months. Surely this vision points to that which pertains to the time of the end and to that which does not measure up to Divine standard.

In contrast, the court in the Tabernacle of Moses measured 100 by 50 cubits in length and breadth. The court there was measured (Exodus 27:9-19; 38:9-20). No measurements are given here.

D. Materials of the Court

The materials of the courts are mentioned, each of them having some Divine significance.

1. **Built of three rows of stones** (1 Kings 6:36; 7:12)

   Three, as always, is the number of the Godhead, the number of perfect witness, complete testimony.
   Under the Law there had to be the word confirmed in the mouth of two or three witnesses (Deuteronomy 17:6; 19:15). This was also confirmed under the New Testament. (Matthew 18:16; 2 Corinthians 13:1; 1 John 5:7-8). God is three, yet one. The Old Testament was built of the Law, Psalms and Prophets (Luke 24:27, 44-45).

2. **Built of Stones**

   The whole emphasis in the courts was that of stone. The Old Covenant or Law age was the age of "stone". The ten commandments were written on two tables of stone (Exodus 31:18; 34:1-4; Deuteronomy 4:13). Violation of the Law meant that people were put to death by stoning (Deuteronomy 13:10; 17:5; Joshua 7:25; Leviticus 24:14-23; John 8:1-7). The Law written on tables of stone was a ministration of death (2 Corinthians 3:7; John 10:31-33).

   The Temple proper was built of stones, but these were silver-encased, and then covered with boards and gold overlay.
   In the court of the Tabernacle of Moses, all was made of fine linen, hung on pillars of brass or acacia wood. The Tabernacle court emphasized linen (righteousness), and brass (judgment on sin). The court of the Temple emphasized stone (the law of stone). Also, the Scripture speaks of the "stony heart" that He would take away and give them an heart of flesh under New Covenant times (Ezekiel 36:25-29). Christ alone kept the law perfectly.

3. **Cedar Beams**

   Cedar beams were placed on top of the three rows of stone for both the inner and outer court (1 Kings 7:12).
   Cedar speaks of the incorruptible humanity of Christ. It also speaks of royalty. Christ is the incorruptible King of kings and Lord of lords. These rows of cedar beams would speak of the "royal line", the Messianic line of Christ from Adam through to Christ. This Messianic hope of Israel runs through the Law, the Psalms and the Prophets.
   It also pointed to the house of the Lord, the house of cedar, the royal house of the Lord who is the King of the universe (Ezekiel 17; 2 Samuel 7:2-7).

   Ceremonially, under the law, cedar wood was used in the cleansing of leprosy and bringing the leper back into fellowship and communion with the camp of the saints (Leviticus 14:4,6,49,51,52; Numbers 19:6).

4. **The Doors of the Court** (2 Chronicles 4:9)

   There is no mention of how many doors in the court. There must have been at least two, for the word is in the plural. There were doors for the court of the priests and the court of the Israelites.
   Doors, as always, speak of entrance into something. They speak of Christ. Christ is the entrance into all the blessings and benefits of redemption and things pertaining to His house. It is through Him we must enter in. No doubt the doors were of cedar wood also (John 10:9; Genesis 49:9-10). He is of the tribe of Judah, the royal house of David (Matthew 1:1-17).

5. **Overlaid with Brass**

   The doors were overlaid with brass. Brass is the symbol of strength and judgment against sin (Deuteronomy 28:23; Numbers 21:6-9). They would appear like "gates of brass" in the sunlight to all who would approach them or to the Lord in His Temple.

The Psalmist speaks of the ''gates (Doors. Hebrew) of brass'' (Psalm 107:16; Isaiah 45:2). Thus all who would even enter the courts of the Lord would enter through these gates of brass. All must face the judgment of God against sin to enter His courts and His house.

The outer court of the Tabernacle and the courts of the Temple all declare the same truth. Sin must be judged. Then we can enter His courts with praise, thanksgiving and find cleansing and washing by blood and water.

In the Tabernacle of Moses there was but one entrance, the gate of the court. This gate was of fine linen with its colours of blue, purple and scarlet as well as its respective measurements. Four pillars upheld this gate and each stood in sockets of brass. These pillars were silver-capped and the linen hung on silver connecting rods.

No matter what part of the camp, near or far, and no matter which tribe any Israelite belonged to, all must enter the gate to come near to God. All must face the righteousness of God in Christ. All must face judgment against sin and redemption through the sacrificial blood of Christ.

In the Temple, no measurements are given for the courts, no number of doors are mentioned, nor measurements. Only the material of stones, cedar wood and brass for the courts and doors.

However, the same truth is set forth here in different material. All was prophetic of the ministry of the Law age, the type and shadow being fulfilled in Christ.

The doors of the courts are overlaid with brass. The doors of the Temple are overlaid with gold and ornamented. Both the doors of the courts and Temple are of cedar wood, fir and olive woods. Christ is the door; royal, strong and anointed, as symbolized in these three timbers used.

We contrast these courts.

Tabernacle Court		Temple Courts
Linen curtain walls	—	White marble stone walls
Five cubits height	—	Three rows of stone high
Sixty pillars in the court	—	No measurements of the court
100 × 50 cubits measurements	—	No measurements
One court	—	Inner and outer courts
Sockets of brass	—	Doors overlaid with brass
Silver rods and crowns	—	No silver (only in Temple walls)
One gate of fine linen	—	Doors of cedar wood
Blue, purple and scarlet		

The courts of the Temple were stone, cedar and doors overlaid with brass. The walls of the Temple were stone, silver encased, cedar covered and ornamented and overlaid with gold.

The courts speak of judgment on sin by the law and death. The Temple speaks of redemption and glory through Christ Jesus.

E. **Significance of the Courts**

Courts in Scripture and in the nation of Israel took on special significance which are considered in a threefold manner here.

1. **Spiritually**

The Psalmist speaks of his desire after the courts of the Lord. He longed to dwell in the courts of the Lord (Psalm 65:4). He fainted for the courts of the Lord (Psalm 84:2). He felt a day in the courts of the Lord was better than a thousand other days (Psalm 84:10).

The Psalmist spoke of those who were planted in the house of the Lord and how they would flourish in the courts of the Lord (Psalm 92:12). We are to enter into His gates with thanksgiving in our heart and enter His courts with praise (Psalm 100:4; 116:19; 135:2; 96:8).

The Psalmist also speaks of the gates of the Lord, the gates of righteousness. The tribes looked forward to standing in the courts of the Lord and within the gates of the city of God (Psalm 9:13,14; 24:7,9; 87:2; 100:4; 118:19; 122:2).

For Israel the courts were a place of cleansing and sacrifice (Psalm 96:8; 2 Chronicles 7:7; 6:13). For Israel there was separation of priests and Israelites in their respective courts (Psalm 134:1-3; 135:1-2; 1 Chronicles 23:28; Zechariah 3:7-9).

In the New Testament all believers are priests and may enter in and minister in the priestly office (Revelation 1:6; 5:9-10; 1 Peter 2:5-9).

2. Prophetically

Prophetically the court speaks of the ultimate period of tribulation when that innumerable company of Revelation 7:9-17; 13:7,10; 15:1-3, stand on the sea of glass (i.e., Molten Sea) after having come out of great tribulation. It seems to be symbolized in the unmeasured court of Revelation 11:1-2. It speaks of the treading down and casting under foot of all who are in that court, for the period of 3½ years, the period of wrath and tribulation.

The souls under the altar (Revelation 6:9-11) and the martyrs of the tribulation period find their respective places under the altar or on the sea of glass. Both these articles are in the outer court — that unmeasured portion of the Temple area. The emphasis is on the brass here. Surely there is that which is prophetic in this fact of being unmeasured by the rod!

3. Dispensationally

Dispensationally, the courts speak of the age of the Law, even as did the outer court of Moses Tabernacle. The brass furnishings, the ceremonial cleansings by blood and water, all speak of the Law age consummating in the death of Christ, and the blood and water that flowed from His side.

The two separated courts point to Jew and Gentile. There they pointed to Israelites and Levites. The Lord has broken down any middle wall of partition and made Jew and Gentile one in priestly ministrations.

Dispensationally then the court covers Time through to the city of God, to Eternity, and the "streets of gold" as symbolized in the gold floor of the Temple. This was noted under our previous chapter and the measurements of the Temple proper.

THE GREAT BRAZEN ALTAR

CHAPTER TWENTYONE

THE BRAZEN ALTAR

INTRODUCTORY:

We come now in these chapters to a consideration of the Temple furniture. The Temple furniture basically follows that which is set forth in the Tabernacle of Moses, only on a much grander scale. However, there are some important and significant things to notice in the Temple furniture. This is seen especially in the Temple "ones" and the Temple "tens". There was but one altar of brass in the outer court, as in Moses Tabernacle. There was but one molten sea of brass in the court. There was but one golden altar of incense in the holy place, also one lampstand. There was but one ark of the Covenant in the holiest of all.

However, there were ten lavers of water in the Temple court, the inner court. There were ten golden lampstands in the holy place in the Temple. There were ten tables of shewbread in the holy place also.

The spiritual truths signified in these articles of furniture will be seen in our following chapters. Our order of consideration will be, first the furniture in the court, then the holy place and finally the most holy place, or the holy oracle.

A. The Brazen Altar

"Moreover he made an altar of brass, 20 cubits the length thereof, and 20 cubits the breadth thereof, and 10 cubits the height thereof" (2 Chronicles 4:1).

The Holy Spirit devotes about 15 verses to the revelation and details of the brazen altar in the Tabernacle of Moses. Significantly there is but one verse of Scripture given to the revelation and details of the altar in Solomon's Temple (Refer Exodus 27:1-8; 38:1-7).

In this one verse we have the material and the measurements. No doubt the reason for the limited details is that the truth of the brazen altar had already been firmly established in the national spiritual life and in the ministry of the house of the Lord. However, there are significant truths to be seen in the construction of this article.

We note the altars that are specifically mentioned in Scripture:

1. The altar of earth (Exodus 20:24; 2 Kings 5:17).

2. The altar of stone (Exodus 20:25-26 with Joshua 8:30-31; 1 Kings 18:30-39).

3. The altar of brass (or copper), (Exodus 27:1-8; 38:1-7).

    * In the Tabernacle of Moses.

    * In the Temple of Solomon (2 Chronicles 4:1).

    * In the Temple of Ezekiel (Ezekiel 43:13-18), material not mentioned.

All altars pointed to the cross of Calvary. Altars were the place of sacrifice. Their grates upheld the sacrificial victim as the body and blood of the offerings were presented to the Lord.

The writer to the Hebrews says, "We have an altar . . ." (Hebrews 13:10). The cross was the altar where Jesus Christ's body and blood sacrifice was offered to the Father God. The "cross-altar" brought a cessation to all previous altars. Calvary fulfilled and abolished all these Old Testament symbolic altars.

All men of faith built their altar of sacrifice and worship to the Lord as they called on His Name. Noah (Genesis 8:20); Abraham, Isaac and Jacob all built their altars to the Lord (Genesis 12:7-8; 26:25; 35:1).

"Altar" itself has two primary meanings. It means "lifted up", "high" or "ascending". Jesus Christ was lifted up on the cross, His altar. Since then He has ascended on high and is far above all (John 3:14; 8:28; 12:32-34; Acts 2:30-36).

It also has the Hebrew thought of "slaughter place". Calvary was the place where Jesus was slaughtered as the lamb of God for our sins (Acts 8:32; Isaiah 53:1-12). The altar therefore pointed to Calvary's cross and sacrifice.

The altar in Israel was the one and only place of blood-shedding. It was the place of substitutionary death. There was no blood shed, no death in the holy place. The court was the only place of sacrificial death. However, the blood of that finished sacrifice was taken from the court into the Temple and sprinkled there before the Lord.

B. **The Five Offerings** — 1 Kings 9:25; 8:64

In Leviticus chapters 1-7 we have the intricate details of the five offerings that were to be offered on this altar. These same sacrifices, both compulsory and voluntary or freewill offerings, remain the same on God's altar through to Calvary's sacrifice.

1. The details of the burnt offering are seen in Leviticus 1.

2. The details of the meal offering are given in Leviticus 2.

3. The details of the peace offering are found in Leviticus 3.

4. The details of the sin offering are in Leviticus 4.

5. The details of the trespass offering are to be found in Leviticus 5.

On the Temple dedication day, Solomon, as king-priest offered thousands of sacrifices on this altar under the blessings of the Lord. These same sacrifices were sealed by the consuming fire of God (2 Chronicles 7:5-8). He had already offered thousands of burnt offerings (freewill offerings) on the brazen altar in Moses Tabernacle some time before at Mt Gibeon (2 Chronicles 1:3-13).

The intricate details of these offerings are a textbook in themselves.

C. **The Altar of Brass**

This great altar was made of brass (copper or bronze). The brazen altar in the Tabernacle of Moses was an altar of acacia wood, overlaid with brass. No doubt this Temple altar was built after the general pattern of the brazen altar in Moses Tabernacle.

The most prominent metal in the court of the Tabernacle and the Temple courts was brass (2 Chronicles 4:16-18; 1 Kings 7:45-47). It was bright brass, made bright by scouring.

In the Tabernacle court there was the altar of brass, the brass laver, the brass pillars and their sockets.

In the Temple court, the inner court of the priests, there was the brazen altar, the brazen or molten sea, the brazen lavers and the doors overlaid with brass. Also there were the two great pillars of brass at the Temple porch.

Brass, as already noted, is ever the symbol of judgment against sin and selfishness. The heavens over Israel would be as brass upon Israel's sin of disobedience to the laws of the Lord (Leviticus 26:19; Deuteronomy 28:23). Christ was lifted up as the serpent of brass on the cross. There He was judged for our sin, and the disobedience and death that Adam brought on his unborn race (Romans 5:12-21; John 3:14-18; 2 Corinthians 5:21; Numbers 21:1-6).

Death is God's judgment against sin.

His feet are as burning brass when He judges sin in His church (Revelation 1:15; Ezekiel 40:3). Brass is Divine righteousness applied to man in judgment. William Kelly says that "GOLD is the righteousness of God for drawing near to where God is. BRASS is the righteousness of God for dealing with man's evil where man is."

The Holy Spirit comes to convict of sin, righteousness and judgment. He comes as the Spirit of Judgment and the Spirit of Burning (John 16:8-11; Isaiah 4:4).

The blood was taken from the BRASS ALTAR (the judgment seat), to the GOLD ARK of the covenant (the mercy seat).

D. The Measurements of the Altar

The Temple altar was about four times larger than the brazen altar in the Tabernacle. Its size was tremendous. There was no other vessel comparable in size with it. Surely also its measurements are symbolic and prophetic, as were those of the Tabernacle altar.

The measurements of the altar were 10 cubits high, 20 cubits broad and 20 cubits wide.

The number ten is the number of law, the number of human responsibility. Man has violated the ten commandments. Sin is transgression of the law of God (1 John 3:4). Death is the wages of sin (Romans 6:23). So Christ was crucified for our sin and our transgression of God's law.

In the Tabernacle of Moses, the grate of the brass altar in the outer court was 1½ cubits high, the same height as the mercy seat of the cherubimed ark of the Covenant in the holiest of all.

In the Temple of Solomon, the brazen altar was 10 cubits high, the same height as the two great cherubim in the holiest of all overshadowing the ark of the Covenant.

Therefore, both altars were related to the cherubim.

The significant truth is seen in the Psalms. The Psalmist spoke of the Shepherd of Israel who dwelt between the cherubim shining forth (Psalm 80:1). And again, he spoke of the Lord who reigns, sitting between the cherubim (Psalm 99:1).

Surely these Psalms are prophetic of Christ, the Son of God, the Shepherd of Israel, who dwelt in the eternal Godhead, between the Father and the Holy Spirit. He came into this world, by way of the incarnation, to die on the cross (the altar), and shed His blood there as the Good, Great and Chief Shepherd (John 10:1-10; Hebrews 13:20; 1 Peter 5:1-5).

He has returned to the throne of God "between the cherubims" and sits enthroned there having obtained eternal redemption for us by the blood of atonement. He is greater than all angels, who are but ministering spirits sent forth to the heirs of salvation (Hebrews 1:1-14; John 16:27-28).

His blood was spilt on the earth but taken to heaven. From Calvary's cross to heaven's throne; from earth's outer court to heaven's holiest of all is the path of Jesus. The Lamb on the altar in the court (the cross on earth) becomes the Lamb on the ark in the holy oracle (the throne of God in heaven).

In prophetic significance, the $20 \times 20 \times 10$ cubical content of the altar equals 4000 cubical capacity in the altar of brass ($20 \times 20 \times 10 = 4000$). From Adam to Christ we have an estimated 4000 years of time in which all animal blood sacrifices took place, all sacrificial blood was shed.

It began with the substitute victim in Genesis 3:21 and ended with the covenant blood of Jesus on Calvary's cross and altar (John 19:34-35; 1 John 5:7-8; Luke 22:20).

His blood is the blood of the cross, the altar of sacrifice for sin. All sin and sins, from Adam to Christ, were judged by God in Christ, against Christ, on Calvary.

This 4000 cubical content also corresponds to the four days in which the Passover Lamb was kept aside, foreordained to die (Exodus 12:1-6). A day unto the Lord is as a thousand years and a thousand years as one day (Psalm 90:4; 2 Peter 3:8). His once-for-all sacrifice brought an end to animal sacrifices, and caused "the sacrifice and oblation to cease" (Daniel 9:24-27).

As noted in the measurements of the Temple proper, the oracle or holiest of all measured $20 \times 20 \times 20$ or foursquare (1 Kings 6:20). The brazen altar here measured $20 \times 20 \times 10$ cubits (2 Chronicles 4:1). The upper room treasury above the holiest of all measured $20 \times 20 \times 10$, or, the very same measurements as the brazen altar.

How applicable would be the command of Jesus be to the rich young ruler to "take up your cross (the symbol of the altar), and follow Me and you will find treasure in heaven (the symbol of the treasure chamber)". Mark 10:21.

E. The Altar Foursquare

The altar was foursquare, 20×20 cubits square. The altar in the Tabernacle of Moses was also foursquare.

There were a number of "foursquares" in both Tabernacle and Temple.

* The breastplate of the high priest was foursquare.

* The holiest of all was foursquare in both Tabernacle and Temple.

* The golden altar was foursquare.

* The brazen altar was foursquare for both Tabernacle and Temple.

* The blood was taken from the foursquare sacrificial altar into the foursquare holiest of holies.

All pointed to the fact that the blood of Jesus, available to the four corners of the earth, is the only means of access to the ultimate revelation of that which is foursquare, the city of God (Revelation 21-22).

F.   The Horns of the Altar

Although not specifically mentioned in 2 Chronicles 4:1, other Scriptures confirm the fact that this Temple altar had horns attached to it, even as did the brazen altar in Moses Tabernacle.

The horns have several significant lessons and truths in Scripture.

1.   HORNS were used to bind the unwilling sacrifice to the altar (Psalm 118:27). ''Bind the sacrifice with cords, even to the horns of the altar''. However, Christ was not an unwilling sacrifice, but He delighted to do the Father's will, even unto the death of the cross (Hebrews 10:1-10; 9:28; Romans 5:3; Philippians 2:5-8).

2.   HORNS speak of power and strength. Animals use their horns to defend themselves. Horns are the power and strength of the animal (Daniel 7; Daniel 8; Revelation 13). The Lamb of God is seen with seven horns, symbolic of the power of His sacrifice, His body and blood, and omnipotence of the gospel to all the world (Revelation 5:6; Matthew 28:18-20).

3.   HORNS speaks of the four corners of the earth. No doubt there were four horns to this altar, even as on the altar in Moses Tabernacle (Exodus 27:1-8).
     Four is the number of the earth. It speaks of that which is worldwide, universal. So the power of the Gospel, as presented in Matthew, Mark, Luke and John is to go to the whole world, to every creature (Mark 16:15-20; Acts 1:5-8).
     The altar in Ezekiel's vison had four horns on it (Ezekiel 43:13-17).

4.   HORNS of the altar were also a place of refuge, a place of life or death.
     In 1 Kings 1:50-53, rebel Adonijah fled to the altar and took hold of the horns pleading for mercy. King Solomon granted him mercy upon fulfilling his conditions of obedience.

     In contrast, in 1 Kings 2:28-34, Joab, who had followed Adonijah, fled to the horns of the altar seeking mercy. However, because of his great light, and greater sins, he was slain at the altar.

     This same altar meant life to the one, and death to the other. At Golgotha, one repentant thief found life in Christ, the other found death (Luke 23:39-43; Matthew 27:44).
     Paul says that the gospel is a savour of death to some and a savour of life to others (2 Corinthians 2:14-16). The same sacrifice of Christ will be life to all who repent and believe and death to those who refuse to do so.
     Note the use of horns in Genesis 22:13; 1 Samuel 16:13 and Joshua 6.

G.   The Steps to the Altar

An altar this size undoubtedly would have steps or else a sloping ascent to it. Concerning the brazen altar in the Tabernacle of Moses, steps were forbidden so that nakedness would not be seen, as in heathen altars (Exodus 20:24-26; 28:40-43).
The priests garments included linen breeches to cover nakedness. Ezekiel's vison of the altar showed it had steps to it (Ezekiel 43:17).
God did not want anything that was heathenish associated with His sacred altar of atonement.

H. The Position of the Altar

The altar was placed in the inner court, between the court gate and the molten sea (Joel 2:17). It seems that its position was on the north side of the court. In the Tabernacle of Moses the altar was positioned between the court gate and the Tabernacle door (Exodus 40:6,29).

The burnt offering was killed on the north side of the altar in the Tabernacle of Moses. Therefore it would be the same for the Temple altar (Leviticus 1:11).

The north in Scripture distinctly points to Lucifer's fall, his sin and rebellion and uprising in the heavens with the fallen angels. The north was the place where the Assyrians and Babylonians came in judgment upon the Israel of God. Sin began in the north. The blood of Christ must deal with the origin of sin; hence the blood of the sacrifice was shed on the north side of the altar. Note — Isaiah 14:13; Job 26:7; Jeremiah 46:6; Psalm 48:1-2; Ezekiel 1:4; Numbers 2:25; Song of Solomon 4:16.

The brazen altar would be the FIRST article of furniture the priests and any Israelites would face in their approach to God. Sacrificial blood by substitutionary offerings would be the only way of approach to God. None dare by-pass the altar of God. Blood must precede worship. So none dare by-pass the cross of Jesus and His sacrifice to approach God (John 14:1,6; Hebrews 7:25-26). Christ is both priest (in His divinity), and sacrifice (in His humanity). The cross is the altar. The cross is the only place of redemption (1 Peter 3:18-20; Hebrews 9:14; 10:1-12; Galatians 1:4; 2:20).

The altar of the cross must always be first and foremost in all preaching and teaching and ministry to the Lord. Paul said, God forbid that I should glory save in the cross of our Lord Jesus Christ by whom the world is crucified unto me and I to the world (Galatians 6:14).

Elijah the prophet restored the altar of God at Mt Carmel, an altar of 12 stones. God consumed the sacrifice by heavenly fire (1 Kings 18).

Hezekiah the king restored the altar of brass in the cleansing of the Temple in the time of reformation under his reign (2 Chronicles 29-30).

I. The Cleansing Altar — Isaiah 6:1-8

Isaiah the prophet saw the glory of the thrice-holy God, the holiness of the Father, Son and Holy Spirit. He sensed the consciousness of his own uncleanness and his dwelling in the midst of a people of unclean lips. His cry was that of the leper who had to cry "unclean, unclean" (Leviticus 13:44-46).

The Seraphim, "the burning ones", took a live coal from off the altar and touched his lips, purging them of all uncleanness. Upon that basis, Isaiah was called by the Lord to minister as a prophet to his nation. He responded to the call of the Lord and was commissioned to speak for God to a hypocritical people.

No doubt the coal was taken from the brazen altar for this was the altar that was ever to be burning, never to go out, and this was the altar that dealt with sin (Leviticus 6:12-13).

J. The Counterfeit Altar — 2 Kings 16:1-16

In this chapter we have recorded the terrible deeds of king Ahaz of Judah. He walked not in the ways of David but became idolatrous and heathenish in his practices.

He took the silver and gold in the house of the Lord and sent it to the king of Assyria. In his compromising visit to the king of Assyria, Ahaz saw a heathen altar. He had Urijah the priest get the pattern of it and fashion one exactly like that for himself. He then presumptuously moved the great altar of the Lord from its rightful position and placed his substitute Assyrian altar in the court of the Lord. As a king, he assumed the role of a priest and offered sacrifices on his altar while the priest offered on God's altar.

So church history reveals the counterfeit altars and counterfeit sacrifices by priestly presumptions. There is ever only one cross-altar, one sacrifice for sins, one great high priest. Anything else is counterfeit, substitute and heathenish and does despite to the work of Calvary.

Israel's relationship to God was always dependant upon their attitude and relationship to the altar of God. Rebellious and wicked kings always sought to get rid of this altar and place numerous substitute altars around every high hill and grove as they worshipped false gods. Jeroboam is an example of this (1 Kings 12:25-33; 13:1-5).

Godly kings always restored the altar of the Lord and the appointed sacrifices in times of national restoration and awakening.

Ezra restored the altar of God first in the restoration of Judah from Babylon (Ezra 3:1-3). In the restoration of the church to New Testament order, justification by faith in the blood of Jesus must take its proper place.

Any other altars are simply "altars to the unknown God" (Acts 17:23).

K. The Altar in Revelation

The final references to the altar of God are to be found in the Book of Revelation. In Revelation 6:9-11 John sees the blood of the martyrs under the brazen altar. Here the blood of the sacrificial victim was poured out as an offering to the Lord. The blood is the soul life. These were souls under the altar. Their blood spoke and cried for vengeance. At the present the blood of Jesus speaks for mercy, but then at His coming all innocent blood of the saints will be avenged (Hebrews 12:24).

IN SUMMARY:—

We conclude our chapter with a sharper focus and brief comparison of the brazen altar in the Tabernacle and the Temple.

Tabernacle Brazen Altar	—	Temple Brazen Altar
Altar of acacia wood	—	Altar of brass
Overlaid with brass within and without		
Measured $5 \times 5 \times 3 = 75$ cubical contents	—	Measured $20 \times 20 \times 10 = 4000$ cubical contents
Foursquare	—	Foursquare
Five offerings on it	—	Five offerings for it
First article of approach	—	First article of approach
Only one altar of sacrifice	—	One place of redemption
Staves for the altar in transit for wildernesswanderings	—	No staves, Israel in promised land Permanency, rest, peace and order

All of that which pertains to the altar speaks to God of Christ and His redemptive work. There is only ONE altar, ONE place of redemption and salvation. There is and ever will be only ONE Christ, ONE Saviour, ONE Mediator between God and man, the Man Christ Jesus (John 14:1,6; Hebrews 7:26; 1 Timothy 2:5-6).

The student is referred to the Tabernacle of Moses for additional truths of the altar.

THE MOLTEN SEA AND TWELVE OXEN

CHAPTER TWENTYTWO

THE MOLTEN SEA

The Scriptures which deal with the revelation, pattern and construction of the molten sea are to be found in 2 Chronicles 4:2-6,15 with 1 Kings 7:23-26,44; 1 Chronicles 18:8. These Scriptures provide the details of the molten sea, its measurements and ornamentation.

A. General Description of the Molten Sea

The molten sea (or bronze) resembled a great basin or bowl containing a vast sea of water. Unger's Bible Dictionary says: "This was a huge round basin, 5 cubits high and 10 cubits in diameter at the brim, and a line of 30 cubits did compass it about. It was made of strong bronze, a hand breadth in thickness. Its brim was bent outward in a cuplike form, and made to resemble the flower of the lily, while underneath two rows of 'knops' (i.e., wild cucumbers of apples), ten to every cubit (300 altogether) ran around the sea for ornament. The capacity of this huge basin was 2,000 baths. This laver was supported by 12 bronze oxen, three looking towards each point of the compass . . ."

B. Construction of the Molten Sea

1. Made of Brass

The material of the molten sea was of brass. The molten sea in the Temple court actually took the place of the brazen laver in the Tabernacle, although there were additional lavers in the Temple court. These will be considered in a subsequent chapter. The molten sea was a vessel fashioned by fire.

Brass, as always, speaks of judgment against sin. Righteousness is the holiness of God in action against sin. The brazen altar dealt with sin. The molten sea dealt with self. It is self-judgment.

The brazen laver in Moses Tabernacle was made of the bronze looking mirrors of the women (Exodus 38:8). Here the molten sea was made of brass from the spoils of David's battles against the enemies of the Lord and His people (1 Chronicles 18:8).

Brass then is symbolic of strength, firmness, endurance and judgment against sin and self. We see brass in connection with the following:

* Gates of brass (Psalm 107:16).

* Bars of brass (1 Kings 4:13).

* Fetters of brass (Judges 16:21).

* Christ's feet as polished brass (Daniel 10:6; Revelation 1:15).

* The serpent of brass (Numbers 21:8-9).

* The censers of brass (Numbers 16:36-40).

* The heavens as brass against Israel's sin (Deuteronomy 28:23).

2. Measurements of the Sea

The measurements of this sea were Divinely specified in contrast with the laver in Moses Tabernacle where no measurements are specifically recorded.

God gave the measurements. Man must build it according to the Divine pattern, according to God's specification.

The molten sea measured 5 cubits high, 10 cubits in diameter at its brim, and 30 cubits in circumference. The spiritual truths are to be found in the use of these symbolic numbers.

a) **Round in Shape**

In contrast to the brazen altar, which was foursquare, the molten sea is round in shape. It is circular. A circle has no beginning or ending. It speaks of eternal things. Eternity is time without beginning or ending. So the cleansing of the washing of water by the Word will be eternally sufficient for the saints.

b) **Five Cubits High**

The molten sea was five cubits high. Five is the number of grace, the number of life, the number of the atonement. Jesus received five wounds on the cross, to bring life, to bring about the atonement or the reconciliation between God and man.

There are numerous fives mentioned in the Scripture of which we note only a few.

Jacob sents five droves of animals to effect reconciliation with his brother Esau (Genesis 32:13-16).

The Israelites came out of Egypt in ranks of five (Exodus 13:18, Margin).

The Tabernacle of Moses was replete with fives. The brazen altar was five cubits square. The court pillars were five cubits high. The anointing oil had five ingredients in it.

The Lord has set five ministries in the church to bring the church to maturity; the apostle, prophet, evangelist, shepherd and teacher (Ephesians 4:9-11).

Christ is the grace of God personified. He brings life through His atoning work.

c) **Ten Cubits Diameter**

The molten sea was 10 cubits in diameter, from brim to brim.

Ten is the number of law, order, government and responsibility. God gave Israel ten commandments which they were responsible to keep.

Five is the number of grace. Ten is the number of law. Christ who is the grace of God personified, was born under the law, to redeem those under the law. He alone kept the law perfectly (Galatians 4:1-4; Psalm 40:7-8). He died because we had broken the law of God.

The 10 cubits of brass diameter speak of the law that condemned sin but was fulfilled perfectly in Christ and is now, by the Spirit, kept by the believer who walks after the Spirit (Romans 8:1-4; 10:1-5).

Again the Scripture is replete with the number ten, of which we mention but a few.

In Genesis 1 "God said" is mentioned 10 times, bringing order out of chaos.

The tithe is a tenth of our income which we give to the Lord as our responsibility (Numbers 18).

Ten virgins were responsible to have oil and be watchful for the bridegroom's coming (Matthew 25:1-13).

In the Tabernacle of Moses, the most holy place measured $10 \times 10 \times 10 = 1000$ cubical content. In the Temple we have ten tables of shewbread, ten golden lampstands in the holy place, and ten lavers in the court of the priests.

The two great olive cherubim had wings that were ten cubits outstretched.

The two tables of stone had the ten commandments written on them by the finger of God.

d) **Thirty Cubits Circumference**

The molten sea was 30 cubits in compass, or circumference, being round shaped.

Thirty is the number of consecration to service, to ministry before the Lord.

Joseph was 30 years of age when he became next to Pharoah in the throne of Egypt (Genesis 41:46).

David was 30 years of age when he was anointed to take the throne over Israel (2 Samuel 5:4).

The ark of Noah was 30 cubits high for the saving of his house (Genesis 6:15).
The priests were 30 years of age when they began priestly ministrations (Numbers 4:3).
The Temple was 30 cubits high also.

The fulfilment of this is found in Christ Jesus who was 30 years of age when He began His ministry as prophet, priest and king after water baptism in Jordan, and His anointing with the Holy Spirit (Luke 3:23). The molten sea held water for cleansing, its circumference being 30 cubits. So Jesus was about 30 years of age when baptized in water!

In summary we may say that the numbers 5,10 and 30 find fulfilment in Jesus Himself. He is the grace of God personified, the only man who kept the law perfectly, and was the Father's consecrated Son (Hebrews 7:26-28).

e.) Handbreadth Thickness

The thickness of the molten sea was "a handbreadth" (2 Chronicles 4:5). The "hand" in Scripture is significant of service and is used in a great variety of ways and ministry.
The laver in the Tabernacle of Moses was for the priests to wash their hands and feet before their ministry in the holy places.
We speak of the doctrine of laying on of hands (Hebrews 6:1-2).
The hand of the Lord was with the early church as they preached the Gospel (Acts 4:28-30; 11:21).
Elijah saw the little cloud the size of a man's hand before the abundance of rain (1 Kings 18:41-46).
Christ laid His hand on John as he fell at His feet as one dead (Revelation 1:17).
The ministry of hands is essential in the vessels and house of the Lord.

C. The Foundation of the Molten Sea

There were twelve brazen oxen underneath the sea, upholding it. Therefore these were the foundation of the molten sea. These twelve faced the north, south, east and west. The significance of these things are seen in the following comments.

1. The Molten Sea

The molten sea, first of all, speaks of the Lord Jesus Christ, who provides cleansing for His priestly people, by the washing of water by the Word (Titus 3:5; Ephesians 5:25-32). There was only one great molten sea. There is only one saving Christ, one cleanser from sin and self.

2. The Twelve Brazen Oxen

These twelve brazen oxen speak of the 12 apostles chosen by Christ (Matthew 10; Luke 6:13). The twelve oxen were made to uphold the molten sea and its cleansing ministry for the priests. The 12 apostles uphold Christ in His cleansing ministry to the church, the new covenant priesthood. Their names are in the foundation of the city of God (Revelation 21:14).

Twelve is the number of government, especially apostolic government, government in the Israel of God. This is seen in the numerous twelves mentioned in Scripture, some of which we list here.

The sun and moon govern the 12 hours of both night and day (Genesis 1:14-19).
Twelve months in a year govern man's time (John 11:9).
Jacob had 12 sons which became the 12 names for the 12 tribes of Israel, natural and spiritual (Exodus 1).
Twelve wells of water quenched Israel's thirst at Elim (Exodus 15:27).
Twelve pillars stood at the foot of Mt Sinai (Exodus 24:4).

Twelve stones were taken into Jordan and 12 stones were taken out as a memorial when Israel entered Canaan land (Joshua 4:3-9).

Twelve stones with the 12 names of the 12 tribes were in the breastplate of the high priest (Exodus 28).

Solomon had 12 officers over Israel and 12,000 horsemen (1 Kings 4:7,26).

Solomon's throne had 12 lions upon its six steps, two on each step (1 Kings 10).

The bride of Christ has a diadem of 12 stars on her head (Revelation 12:1).

The 12 apostles of the Lamb will sit on 12 thrones judging the 12 tribes of Israel (Luke 22:30).

The Book of Revelation abounds with the number twelve and its multiples. Think of the 144,000 redeemed ones (12,000 from each tribe), (Revelation 7:1-8; 14:1-5).

Think of the many twelves in the city of God in Revelation 21-22, the New Jerusalem. It has 12 gates of 12 pearls, 12 names of 12 tribes, 12 foundations and 12 names of 12 apostles therein, and 12 manner of fruit for the 12 months of the year, and its wall with multiples of twelve.

In Revelation 4 we have 24 elders as king-priests.

The Tabernacle of Moses had its table of shewbread with 12 loaves of bread on it. The 12 princes brought 6 wagons with 12 oxen on the dedication day of the brazen altar (Numbers 7).

Oxen speak of Christ the servant, as well as apostolic ministries, who tread out the corn of the Word for God's people (1 Corinthians 9:9; 1 Timothy 5:18; 1 Kings 19:19-21).

Jesus sent out the 12 apostles two by two as His servants. They were yoked with His yoke (Matthew 11:28-30; Luke 10:1; Mark 6:7).

The living creatures have the face of an ox among their four faces (Ezekiel 1:10).

So the twelve oxen speak of the 12 apostles of Christ, apostolic rule and government, with a servant spirit, upholding the Lord Jesus Christ in the fulness of His cleansing ministry for believer priests.

3. The Four Corners of the Earth

These 12 oxen faced the four directions of the compass; three to the north, three to the south, three to the east and the west.

Four is the number of earth, that which is universal, worldwide, or the four points of the compass. Their faces were out and their hinder parts in.

It speaks of the fact that the Gospel of Christ was to go forth into the four corners of the earth, to every creature, tongue, tribe and nation. The power of the Gospel is universal (Matthew 28:18-20; Mark 16:15-20; Acts 1:8; Revelation 5:9-10).

Israel in the wilderness had the 12 tribes positioned in four groups of three; north, south, east and west.

We note some of the numerous references to the number four in Scripture.

There were four kinds of ground in which the seed of the Word fell (Matthew 13:1-8).

There are four Gospels which speak of Christ's ministry on earth.

There were four rivers which ran from Eden to water the earth (Genesis 2:10). There were four living creatures, each having four faces, and four wheels were in Ezekiel's vision (Ezekiel 1).

We have four horns on the altars, both brass and gold, in the Tabernacle of Moses which speak a worldwide message (Exodus 27:12; 30:1-10).

Four geographical places are mentioned to which the Gospel would go (Acts 1:8).

So Christ's Gospel, from the first 12 apostles, has gone into the four corners of the globe. The redeemed of earth will gather around the throne of God and the Lamb out of every "kindred, tongue, tribe and nation" (Revelation 5:9-10).

D. **Ornamentation of the Molten Sea**

The ornamentation of the molten sea consisted of flowers of lilies and knops upon its brim, the significance of such is seen here.

1. **Flowers of Lilies on the Rim**

On the top of the rim flowers of lilies were ornamented. The same lily work was upon the two great brazen pillars in the porch of the Temple (1 Kings 7:19; 2 Chronicles 4:5).
The lily speaks of the purity, beauty and fragrance of the Lord Jesus Christ. The Song of Solomon speaks of the lily in a number of verses, probably alluding to the ornamentation of the Temple vessels and pillars (Song of Solomon 2:1,2,16; 6:2-3; 7:2 with Hosea 14:5).
Christ told us to consider the lilies of the field, that Solomon in all his glory was not arrayed like one of these (Matthew 6:28; Luke 12:27). Christ blossomed to reveal the beauty of the Father.

2. **Lines of Knops under the Rim**

As there were flowers of lilies on the brim of the molten sea, so there were lines of ornamented knops under the rim (1 Kings 7:24).

a) **The Knops**

The Hebrew thought of "knops" seems to be "wild cucumbers of apples", similar to "gourds" which were round in shape as a cucumber.
Knops were also carved into the cedar wood of the Temple walls as well as on the brazen sea (1 Kings 6:18). Thus we have the same ornamentation on the molten sea and the two porch pillars (1 Kings 6:14-18,29).
"Knops" here speak of the fruit of the Spirit in which is the seed of the Word (Galatians 5:22; 1 Corinthians 13).
Christ Jesus is the Word made flesh. He is the incorruptible seed. In Him is the fruit of the Holy Spirit manifested in perfection. The perfection of beauty was upon Him (John 1:1-3,14-18; 1 Peter 1:23; Psalm 16:10).

b.) **The Two Rows of Knops**

There were two rows of these knops, speaking of a double portion. So in Christ was the double portion, or the fulness of the Spirit's operation; both FRUIT and GIFT (John 3:33-34; Isaiah 11:1-4; Acts 10:38; Luke 4:18).

c.) **The Ten Knops in a Cubit**

Also the Divine pattern shows that there were ten knops in the cubit. If the sea was 30 cubits around, then ten knops to a cubits would equal 300 knops in all.

Three hundred in Scripture is the number of God's faithful remnant. The ark of Noah was 300 cubits long preserving a remnant from the antediluvian world in the time of the Flood (Genesis 6:14-16). Gideon's army of 300 men was a remnant of Israel's armies, used to defeat the Midianities after the water test (Judges 7).
Samson used 300 foxes to destroy the Philistines harvest (Judges 15:4-5).
Enoch was walking with God 300 years and then experienced translation (Genesis 5:21-24).
And here we have 300 knops relative to the vessel of cleansing by water in Solomon's Temple.

Ten, as already noted, is the number of law and order. Thirty is the number of consecration. Three hundred is the number of the faithful remnant.
Together we can say, 300 is the number of that remnant, consecrated to the Lord and in Divine order. Such indeed was Gideon's army, and so will be the church as the army of the Lord.

E. **Position of the Molten Sea**

In 2 Chronicles along with 1 Kings 7:39 we discover the Divinely appointed position of the molten sea. It was set on the right hand side of the house eastward over against the south. Surely the significance of this position speaks of Christ's position before God. Christ has been set down at the right hand of the throne of God on high, in His Father's house (Hebrews 1:3; Colossians 3:1).

The "east" is always significant of His glory in both the first and second comings. His star was seen in the east in the first coming and He will come as lightning shines from east to west in His second coming (Matthew 2:2; 24:27).

F. **The Purpose of the Molten Sea**

The very purpose of this vessel of the molten sea was for the priests to wash thereat (2 Chronicles 4:6). Just as in the Tabernacle of Moses the priests had to wash hands and feet at the brazen laver, so that they die not as they entered into the Tabernacle of the Lord, so was the purpose of the molten sea (Refer to Exodus 30:17-21.)

Only those who have clean hands (externally) and a pure heart (internally) can ascend into the hill of the Lord (Psalm 24:4).

The molten sea was for the PRIESTS to wash thereat. The ten lavers around the Temple were for the SACRIFICES to be washed in.

The whole thought of the purpose of the molten sea is that of washing, cleansing for service, freedom from defilements. Water in Scripture has many symbolic usages. It is used to speak of:

1. Salvation — Isaiah 12:3; John 4:13-14.

2. Water Baptism — Acts 8:36-39; Mark 16:15-20; Matthew 28:18-20; Acts 2:34-47.

3. Holy Spirit Baptism — John 7:37-39. It has been suggested that the molten sea was like a great reservoir of water and that there was some kind of a pipe and tap that flowed out of the mouths of the twelve oxen. If so, this is how the priests were cleansed. Perhaps Jesus may have been alluding to this when He spoke of "rivers of living water" flowing forth from the belly. This He spake of the Spirit that believers should receive.

4. Washing of Water by the Word — Titus 3:5; Ephesians 5:26-27; Ezekiel 36:25. In Titus and Ephesians the Greek word for "washing" is "laver". It is the laver of regeneration (John 3:1-5), and the laver cleansing for priestly service (Exodus 38:8).

There are many Scriptures which speak of the need of washing in order to be able to serve the Lord in His Tabernacle, in His Temple (Exodus 30:18-21; 2 Corinthians 7:1-2; 6:11; Hebrews 10:22; John 13:10; Psalm 26:6; Ephesians 5:26; Titus 3:5; Psalm 24:4; Leviticus 8:6; John 3:1-5; 2 Corinthians 5:17).

All believers are called to be priests, but we must be clean priests to minister to the Lord in His house (Revelation 1:6; 5:9-10; 20:6, 1 Peter 2:5-9).

The water is the water of the Word. It is available, but it is only the application of the water of the Word that makes one clean. There must be the daily washing for service.

In another symbolic picture we may see the Lord Jesus Christ as the molten sea, the fulness of the Holy Spirit as the water, and the 12 apostles or the 12 oxen taking the Gospel of Christ to the whole world.

G. **Relationship of Brazen Altar and Molten Sea**

It is significant to see the relationship of these first two articles of furniture in the court. These would be the first two that any Israelite would see in their approach to God, as also for the priests. First the brazen altar, and then secondly it would be the molten sea, or blood and water, and always in the order, not water and blood (1 John 5:6-8).

The same truth is seen in the Tabernacle of Moses. It was the brazen altar, or the blood first, then the brazen laver, or the water. These two were the only two agents for cleansing from sin and self-defilement in the redemptive history of the nation of Israel and it was always in that order.

BLOOD is seen continually in Israel's history before the Lord.

1. The Blood of the Passover Lamb — Exodus 12.
2. The Blood of the Day of Atonement — Leviticus 16.
3. The Blood of the Offerings of the Feasts of the Lord — Leviticus 23.
4. The Blood of the Levitical Offerings — Leviticus 1-7.
5. The Blood atonement for the soul — Leviticus 17:11-14.
6. The Blood speaks to God — Hebrews 12:22-24.

WATER is seen continually in Israel's redemptive history.

1. The Waters of Separation and the Ashes of the Red Heifer — Numbers 19.
2. Water in Priestly Consecration — Leviticus 8:6.
3. Water in the cleansing of the Leper — Leviticus 14:1-8.
4. The Divers Washings of the Law — Hebrews 9:10.
5. Israel baptized in the Cloud and the Sea — Exodus 13-14; 1 Corinthians 10:1-2.
6. Israel and the Waters of Jordan — Joshua 4-5.

The spiritual significance of this is seen fulfilled at Calvary. When Jesus died on the cross, the soldier pierced His side and forthwith came blood and water (John 19:34-35). John, in his Epistle speaks of Him who came by water and blood and the Spirit bears witness (1 John 5:7-8). When the blood and water flowed from His side, it forever fulfilled and abolished the shedding of animal blood and ceremonially religious washings of water as of the outer court.

All new covenant believers may daily be cleansed by the BLOOD of Jesus and the washing of WATER by the Word (Zechariah 13:1; John 13:1-13; Matthew 26:26-28; Ephesians 5:26; Titus 3:5).

No priest could enter the Temple for ministry without first touching these two articles.

The smitten animals in Israel speak of the brazen altar, and its sacrificial blood. The smitten rock in Israel speaks of the brazen laver or molten sea, the water.

In the altar and the sea we have (1) Judgment for and against sin, which is death. The evidence of death is bloodshed, presented and accepted for our forgiveness, and (2) Judgment against self and the applications of the cleansing Word daily.

None dare touch the tables of shewbread, the lampstands, or the altar of incense unless they had experienced the cleansing of blood and water first. All must go to Calvary first, before the church, or heaven, can be entered into in priestly ministry.

The blood cleanses from sin. The water cleanses from self-defilement.

H. **Symbolic and Prophetic Measurements of Water**

Undoubtedly there is not only the actual measurements of water given by the Lord, but surely behind the actual there is that which is symbolical and prophetical.

In 1 Kings 7:26 we are told that the sea "contained 2000 baths" of water. In 2 Chronicles 4:5 we are told that the sea "received and held 3000 baths of water". The apparent contradiction is understood by a proper reading of the words used. The simple explanation is that it contained 2000 baths of water when in use, but it received and held 3000 baths of water when it was filled to the brim.

The significance again is seen in the use of the numbers 2000 and 3000 baths. In the Tabernacle of Moses and its measurements we saw prophetic truth relative to the dispensations of time in

God's plan and the "Week of Redemption". There were 2000 cubical contents of the holy place, plus the 1000 cubical contents of the holiest of all, making a total of 3000 cubical contents. No doubt the 2000 plus 1000 baths equalling 3000 baths corresponds to the Tabernacle of Moses measurements.

The student is referred again to the textbook *"The Tabernacle of Moses"* by the author.

In the Temple of God and its measurements we also see prophetic and symbolic significance relative to redemption. This may be seen in the measurements pertaining to the brazen altar and molten sea.

1. In the brazen altar the measurements equalled $20 \times 20 \times 10 = 4000$ cubical content. It was the place of bloodshed. It speaks to us of the 4000 years (4 Days of the Lord; Psalm 90:4; 2 Peter 3:8) from Adam to Christ, from the first Adam to the last Adam.

    In these 4000 years we have all the Divinely ordained animal blood sacrifices. They consummate in the sinlessly perfect and once-for-all sacrifice of the body and blood of Jesus.

2. The molten sea contained 2000 baths of water when in use. This speaks to us of the 2000 years from Christ's first coming to His second coming. This is the 2000 years of the dispensation of the Holy Spirit or the two days of the Lord.

    Then the molten sea received and held 3000 baths of water in its fulness. This is another 1000 baths in Chronicles beyond that spoken of in the King's account. This speaks to us of the dispensation of the fulness of times, bringing us to the 1000 year reign of Christ, the millennial kingdom.

Therefore we have 4000 cubits of the brazen altar,

 2000 baths of the molten sea when in use,

 1000 baths additional in its fulness, which becomes symbolical of the

 7000 years in the Week of Redemption from Adam to Christ's first advent,

His second advent and to the close of the millennial age (Hosea 6:1-2; Job 24:1; 2 Peter 3:8; Psalm 90:4; Revelation 20:1-10).

The distinctive truths, however, are those that speak of the cleansings by blood and water. The brazen altar and brazen sea both speak of judgment. From Adam to the close of the 1000 year kingdom age, we see God executing judgments on sin and Satan.

When Christ's blood and water flowed from His side at Calvary, that was the antitypical fulfilment of the brazen altar (blood) and molten sea (water).

I. Desecration and Destruction of the Molten Sea

Two kings in Israel's history stand out when it comes to the desecration and final destruction of the molten sea, these being king Ahaz of Judah and Nebuchadnezzar, king of Babylon.

1. King Ahaz of Judah

In 2 Kings 16:10-16 we have already seen how wicked king Ahaz pushed aside the altar of God and set his own counterfeit Assyrian altar in the court in priestly presumptions.

In 2 Kings 16:17 this same wicked king Ahaz proceeds to desecrate the great molten sea. He took down the sea from off the 12 brazen oxen that were under it and set it upon a pavement of stones. He also cut off the boarders of the 10 lavers and removed the lavers. He was a wicked, presumptuous and destructive king.

In placing the molten sea on a pavement of stones, he removed the 12 oxen and all that was significant in that foundation. A pavement of stones is not the foundation of the church. The 12 apostles of the Lamb are the foundation of the true Church for they lay THE FOUNDATION which is Christ.

Thus wicked king Ahaz despises God's altar (the blood) and despises God's sea (the water) as to its foundation. So have wicked rulers in church history who have despised the blood and water cleansings from sin in the house of the Lord.

2. **King Nebuchadnezzar of Babylon**

    It is evil enough when ungodly kings of Judah desecrate the vessels of God. But this makes
    way for heathen and Gentile kings to destroy these same vessels. What the church leaders
    despise, worldly leaders will destroy.

    In 2 Kings 25:13,16 we see the king of Babylon destroying the molten sea as well as other
    vessels of God's house. They were broken to pieces and the brass was taken to Babylon. It
    meant nothing to Babylon that the revelation of these things were God-given and their use
    God-ordained. Babylon despises and destroys the things of God's house. Jeremiah had
    prophesied of the coming Babylonian captivity and the destruction of these vessels because
    of the sins of Judah (Jeremiah 27:19-22).

J. **The Book of Revelation**

    The Book of Revelation, the "Book of Ultimates", shows us the antitypical fulfilment of both
    the brazen altar and molten sea relative to the people of God.

    There seems to be something prophetical and especially that which pertains to the period of time
    relative to the second coming of Christ in these two articles of furniture.

    1. **The Altar** — Revelation 6:9-11

        The martyrs of the ages (or end-times) find their place under the altar where the sacrificial
        blood was poured out as an offering to God. The blood is the soul life. These souls had made
        the supreme sacrifice. They were under the altar and their blood cried to God for vengeance.
        The blood speaks to God of outpoured life, as Abel's blood cried to God.

        The blood of Jesus cries for mercy at present (Hebrews 12:24). It speaks better things than
        that of Abel's blood. However, there comes a time when the Lord Jesus Christ comes as
        "the avenger of blood" and will avenge the blood of His saints, the blood of the innocents
        (Numbers 35:19-21,33; Revelation 17:6; 18:20,24).

    2. **The Molten Sea** — Revelation 4:6; 15:1-2

        The martyrs of the final tribulation period in the final 3½ years of antichristal reign find their
        place on the sea of glass. The brazen laver in Moses Tabernacle was made of the glasses of
        the women.(Exodus 38:8). Israel conquered Pharoah at the Red Sea. Here in Revelation we
        have a sea of glass. It is clear in chapter four. In chapter fifteen it is occupied and it mingled
        with fire. We think of the molten sea fashioned by fire and fires of tribulation that these
        saints have been through. Pharoah represents the beastly antichrist who hates the saints of
        God (Revelation 7:9-17; 12:17; 13:7-10; 15:2).

    Both these articles are brass. Both were in the court of the priests. So these saints have taken their
    respective positions on these two articles of furniture and receive their rewards accordingly. In
    John's vision the outer court was left unmeasured. These two articles were in the court
    (Revelation 11:1-2).

IN SUMMARY — we contrast the laver in Moses Tabernacle and the sea in Solomon's Temple.

Tabernacle of Moses	—	Temple of Solomon
The brazen laver	—	The molten sea
Made of brass glasses	—	Made of brass
No measurements specified	—	Measurements detailed
No adornment mentioned	—	Ornamented with lilies and knops
Foundation of the base	—	Foundation of 12 oxen facing compass
Position between altar and door	—	Positioned between altar and porch
For priests washing hands and feet	—	For priests before Temple service
Cleansing water	—	Cleansing water

What tremendous truths are seen in the significances relative to this great molten sea.

THE BRAZEN LAVER AND ITS BASE

CHAPTER TWENTYTHREE

THE BRAZEN LAVERS & BASES

For the description of the brazen altar, there is but one verse given. For the description of the molten sea there are about eight verses given in Kings and Chronicles. But for the description of the lavers and bases there are about sixteen verses given in both Kings and Chronicles accounts.

Therefore, in order to clarify the design of these brazen lavers we quote the greater portion of the Scripture given with some explanation of the Hebrew words used.

The particular passages are found in 1 Kings 7:27-40,43-47 and 2 Chronicles 4:6, 14-18. It is the passage from Kings which we quote here, especially verses 27-36. The Holy Spirit has seen fit to give a lot more detail to the revelation, design and use of the lavers in the Temple courts than other articles of furniture.

A. **Scripture Passage with Explanations** — 1 Kings 7:27-36

Vs 27 "And he made ten bases (stands, or pedestals) of brass.

Vs 28 And the work of the bases (stands, or pedestals) was on this manner. They had borders (panels, or sidewalls) and these were between the ledges (joining ridges or ledges).

Vs 29 And on the borders (panels, or sidewalls) were lions, oxen and cherubim: and upon the ledges there was a base above: and beneath the lions and oxen were certain additions made of thin work (wreathen work).

Vs 30 And every base (stand or pedestal) had four brazen wheels, and plates (axles) of brass. And the four corners thereof had undersetters (shoulder-pieces). Under the laver were undersetters molten, at the side of every addition (wreath or garland).

Vs 31 And the mouth of it within the chapter (crown, capitol or head of) and above was a cubit, and the mouth thereof was round (rounded), after the work of the (bottom) base, a cubit and a half; and also upon the mouth were gravings (sculpture) but their borders (panels or sidewalls) were foursquare, not round.

Vs 32 And under the borders (sidewalls or panels) were four wheels; and the axletrees (supports) of the wheels were joined to the (bottom) base (stand). The height of a wheel was a cubit and a half.

Vs 33 And the work of the wheels was like the work of a chariot wheel; their axletrees (supports, bearers on which the wheel turned), and their naves (hubs, from which the spokes radiate), and their felloes (exterior rim of the wheel), and their spokes (bars of the wheel) were all molten.

Vs 34 And there were four undersetters to the four corners of one base (shoulder-pieces to the stand or pedestal) and the undersetters were of the very base itself.

Vs 35 And in the top of the base (stand, pedestal), there was a round compass (circular piece or elevation) of half a cubit high: and on the top of the base (stand, pedestal) the ledges thereof and the borders thereof were of the same.

Vs 36 For on the plates of the ledges (stays or tenons), and on the borders (panels) thereof, he graved cherubim, lions and palm trees, according to the proportion (space) of every one, and additions (wreaths) round about."

The ten lavers were of one casting, one measure and one size. In contrast to the Tabernacle of Moses, which had one laver on its stand, the Temple has ten lavers with much more intricate details given to them all on their stands and wheels.

B. **General Description of Lavers and Bases**

From the above portion of Scripture we gather that the general description of the lavers would be something like the following.

* There was a bottom base, or stand. vs 28.

* There was also a top base or stand. vs 29. Both had ledges of their four sides.

* There were also panels foursquare, or sidewalls, that fitted into these ledges. vs 28.

* These sidewalls were ornamented, graved according to vs 29 and vs 36.

* The bottom base had four supports beneath it in which the axles of the wheels were thus acting as bearers for axles and the four wheels. vs 30.

* The bottom base also had four supports for the support of the laver as well as props to stay it. vs 30, 32.

* The mouth of the top base was rounded, also sculptured, and was one cubit within and above being braced or supported by a circular piece acting as seat for the laver which was circular also.
No doubt this circular support was half a cubit above the top base in which the laver rested, like a copper bath-tub for washing. (vs 31, 35). It had stays or supports also against it, holding up the laver, even as the bottom base had supports also against the bottom of the laver.
This circular piece would actually be the mouth of it, being half a cubit above and half a cubit below the top. In this the laver would be seated. The mouth was one and a half cubits diameter and was ornamented also. (vs 31). The top and bottom base-plates were four cubits square.

Thus the lavers and bases actually looked like trucks or four-wheeled carriages which could be transported around the Temple courts to and fro for the washing of the sacrifices. They stood on four rests attached to the axles so that the ornamented side panels were considerably higher or raised above the wheels. From the heavenly viewpoint, the lavers were seen to be foursquare with a circular laver, or washing vessel, set in this foursquareness.

As mentioned, in Moses Tabernacle there was but one laver and very few verses are given over to its description (Exodus 30:17-21; 38:8). Here we have some sixteen verses given by the Holy Spirit in the description of these lavers in the Temple court, and more especially to the bases.
The Tabernacle laver has no recorded measurements. The Temple lavers have very specific measurements.
We proceed now to a more detailed study of the symbolic and spiritual significances in these lavers and their bases.

C. The Brazen Lavers

1. Ten Lavers

There were ten brazen lavers in the court of the priests. Ten is the number of law and order. It is also a number that is prominent in the close of this age. We may think of the ten talents, the ten virgins, the ten commandments, the ten horns on the antichristal beast. Then we have the ten tables of shewbread, the ten golden lampstands, five on each side of the holy place. Ten is also the number of responsibility before the Lord. The ten lavers spoke of the responsibility of the priests to wash the sacrifices therein before offering them to the Lord.

2. Lavers of Brass

Brass has been seen as strength and judgment on sin. Everything in the court pertained to brass; the brazen altar, the brazen sea, the brazen lavers, the brazen pillars and doors. Read again Dueteronomy 28:23; 1 Chronicles 15:19; Numbers 21:6-9 with John 3:14. The court is the place of death. Death is judgment on sin. Christ was judged for our sins by death (2 Corinthians 5:21).

3. Height of the Lavers

It seems that the lavers were seated upon the circular piece in the top base plate one half cubit above, and also the same seating in the bottom circular base plate also of one half a cubit. The base itself was only three cubits high. The total height of the laver in its base then would be four cubits. Four is the number of the earth. We think of the four corners of the earth, the four seasons, the four directions of the compass. Four is the worldwide number. It is also the number of the God-Man. God came to earth in the Man Christ at the close of the fourth ''day of the Lord'' (2 Peter 3:8; Psalm 90:4). He ministered on earth.

He commanded His disciples to take the Gospel to all the world. They were to begin at Jerusalem, then Judea, then Samaria and then to the uttermost parts of the earth (Matthew 28:18-20; Acts 1:8). Cleansing through the Gospel is available for every kindred, tongue, tribe and nation.

4. Lavers for Sacrifices

The molten sea was for the priests to wash thereat. The ten lavers were for the sacrifices to be washed therein (2 Chronicles 4:6).

The sacrifices were washed first at the lavers, then offered on the brazen altar.

The apparent truth seen here again is that which pertains to "blood and water" mingled together continually. Blood and water were mingled here, but at the brazen altar the sacrifices were burnt, while at the brazen lavers they were washed with water.

Jesus Christ is both priest and sacrifice; priest as to His divinity and sacrifice as to His humanity. This is also true of the believer who is also a priest and a sacrifice (John 1:29,36).

At Calvary, when the soldier pierced His side, forthwith flowed blood and water (John 19:34-35; 1 John 5:7-8; 1 Peter 1:18-19; Hebrews 10:1-12).

Blood and water were distinctly seen in the ceremonials cleansings of the law. In the cleansing of the leper and in the consecration of the priests, blood and water mingled together in cleansing and consecration (Leviticus 14:1-32). With the leper, one living bird was dipped in the blood of the dead bird and then let loose to fly in the open field testifying that a leper had been cleansed.

The sacrifices of the law were thus washed in water, then presented on the altar of God. These lavers were brass, yet the blood and the water are there. So Jesus Christ was judged (brass) for us on Calvary, and the blood and water cleansings flowed from His wounded side.

The church, His priests, are also to be living sacrifices unto God. As such we have to be cleansed in the blood and the water (Romans 12:1; Ephesians 5:2; 1 Peter 2:1-10). Sin and self must be judged. We must be cleansed by the blood and washed by the water of the Word.

5. Forty Baths of Water

Each laver contained 40 baths of water. Here we have some symbolic significance in the number forty. Forty is the number of probation, testing and trial. It is also vitally linked with the number four (10×4), and also the number 120 (3×40).

There were ten lavers of 40 baths of water totalling 400 baths of water. Thus we have the number four in its multiples. We note some of the most prominent forties in the Scripture relative to Christ and to the saints of God.

Christ's mother, Mary, experienced the 40 days of ceremonial cleansing after His birth (Luke 2:21-24; Leviticus 12:1-4).

Jesus experienced 40 days temptation and testing of the Devil in the wilderness (Matthew 4:2; Luke 4:2).

Jesus witnessed of the kingdom to His disciples 40 days in resurrection (Acts 1:3).

The rain in Noah's time lasted for 40 days and 40 nights (Genesis 7:4).

It took 40 days for the flood waters to abate (Genesis 8:6).

Moses experienced several 40 day periods in his life time. Also Moses experienced 120 years of life which were broken up into 3×40 periods of time (Acts 7:22,23,30,36).

Israel wandered in the wilderness 40 years under times of trial and testing which ended in failure (Numbers 13-14).

Elijah journeyed 40 days in the strength of Divine food (1 Kings 19:8).

Jonah called Ninevah to repentance with a 40 day message (Jonah 3:4).

The 6000 years of time allotted to man equal 50×120 years.

There are many other forties mentioned in the Scripture. It is the number of probation, trial and testing that closes in either victory or defeat.

Then we have the number 400 in the total baths of water in the 10 lavers.

Four hundred is the number of affliction being 10×40.

The seed of Abraham would be afflicted 400 years and then would come deliverance (Genesis 15).

Abraham bought the burial ground from the Gentile for 400 shekels of silver (Genesis 23).

David's army distressed, indebted and discontented numbered 400 men (1 Samuel 22:2).

The prophet speaks of the "water of affliction" that comes to God's people at times (Isaiah 30:20).

A generation is forty years, thus ten generations would equal 400 years.

For other references read Genesis 32:6; Judges 21:11-12.

Thus the numbers ten, forty and four-hundred are seen in symbolic truth in the brazen lavers. The lavers speak of law and order, probation, testing, trial and affliction which will bring God's sacrifices and His priests to full cleansing.

D. The Bases of the Lavers

1. The Laver Bases

Each laver had its own base, stand or pedestal (1 Kings 7:27-38). The bases were responsible to uphold the lavers. All ten lavers had one casting, one measure, one size and thus all were according to God's pattern. Christ measured up to God's standard, so must the believers measure up to Christ. The bases were of brass and their number ten, so we have the same truths symbolically seen here again in judgment and law order.

2. The Measurements of the Bases

Each stand was 4 cubits long by 4 cubits wide and 3 cubits high. Again we see the number of the earth, the worldwide cleansing ministry of the water of God's word. The bases were foursquare pointing, as always, to the ultimate foursquare seen in the city of God, New Jerusalem.

Three is the number of the Godhead. Water baptism is in the name of the eternal Godhead; the Father, the Son and the Holy Spirit. It is into the triune name of the triune Godhead (Matthew 28:18-20; Acts 2:34-42). Cleansing by water symbolized in water baptism is to all four corners of the earth.

The cubical capacity of each base then would be $4\times4\times3=48$ cubical capacity of each stand. Here we have $4\times12=48$ in numbers. In the Tabernacle of Moses there were 48 boards on 96 (2×48) silver sockets. The spiritual truths of four and twelve may be seen here again. The Gospel of the twelve apostles of the Lamb goes forth into every kindred, tongue, tribe and nation (Acts 1:8; Isaiah 9:6).

3. The Ornamentation of the Bases

Altogether there were five particular ornamentations on the bases (1 Kings 7:28-36). Each of these also have their symbolic truths and set forth both for Christ and the church.

a) **Lions** — The symbol of strength, courage, kingship. Christ is the Lion of the tribe of Judah. The righteous are as bold as a lion (Genesis 49:9-10; Revelation 4:7; 5:5; Proverbs 28:1; Ezekiel 1:10). Christ the Lion is seen in the Gospel of Matthew.

b) **Oxen** — The symbol of servanthood, apostolic ministry. Think of the 12 oxen under the molten sea speaking of the twelve apostles of Christ (Read also 1 Kings 19:19-21; Numbers 7; Hebrews 3:1). Christ the oxen is seen in the Gospel of Mark.

c) **Cherubim** — The symbol of the Godhead, that which is Divine, Divine nature. The fulness of the Godhead dwelt bodily in Christ. Christ the Son of God is seen in the Gospel of John.

d) **Palm Trees** — The symbol of victory, peace and righteousness. The ornamentation of the palm trees was upon the Temple walls of cedar wood. Think of the 70 palm trees at Elim. The palm tree was used in the Feast of Tabernacles. Christ the righteous one is seen in the Gospel of Luke (Leviticus 23:40; 1 Kings 7:36; 2 Chronicles 3:5; Exodus 15:27; Psalm 92:12; Nehemiah 8:15; Numbers 33:9).

e) **Wreathen Work** — The symbol of victory. The wreathen work was as garlands, wreaths of victory which crown the victor's head. Christ is the victim and the victor over all things. He is crowned with many crowns, King of kings and Lord of lords.

The stands of the lavers then present the glories of the character of Christ to the whole wide world. He is the Lion of the tribe of Judah with the sceptre (Matthew's Gospel). He is the Oxen, the apostle and high priest of our confession, our sacrificial one (Mark's Gospel). He is the fulness of the Godhead bodily (John's Gospel). He is the righteous one (Luke's Gospel). And He is the victorious one (Revelation). All the ornamentation presents Christ in His glory. This same glory is to be revealed in the church. Christ is the laver. He is the cleanser from sin and self.

4. **The Wheels of the Bases**

"Each base had four bronze chariot (six-spoked) wheels, which turned on one piece with the trolley" (Moffatt's Trans. 1 Kings 7:32).

Underneath each base were placed four brazen wheels with their axles (1 Kings 7:30-34). The height of each wheel was 1½ cubits. They were as chariot wheels. By the wheels the lavers were able to transported to and fro in the court. Wheels speak of transport.

It speaks of the chariot of the Gospel being transported into the entire earth. Without these wheels the lavers would be stationary.

Each had four wheels, four speaking of the four directions of the earth. In Daniel 7:9 the Ancient of Days, white as snow, pure as wool sat on a throne of fiery flame and His wheels were as burning fire. Wheels on the throne of God speak of rapidity of transport. They speak of speed, swiftness. The chariot of fire transported Elijah to heaven (2 Kings 2:11-12; Psalm 68:17).

In Ezekiel's vision of the cherubim he saw the throne of God and "wheels within wheels" and the Spirit was in the wheels giving rapidity of transport.

This is in contrast to the transport of the furniture in the Tabernacle of Moses which was by staves on the shoulders of the Levites and priests. Transport was humanly slow. Here in the Temple chariot wheels are seen on the lavers in the court, and then on the two great olive cherubim in the holy oracle.

The height of the wheel being 1½ cubits may be linked in that which was in both Tabernacle and Temple. In Moses Tabernacle, the brazen grate on the brazen altar was 1½ cubits high, the table of shewbread was 1½ cubits high, the mercyseat of the ark was 1½ cubits high as well as the ark itself, and the 48 boards of the Tabernacle were 1½ cubits wide. All are linked together by the same measurements and therefore the same truth. The wheels of the lavers here were 1½ cubits high also.

On the basis of the cleansing water we may enter the holy place and take the shewbread and come to the mercyseat of God.

There are 48 wheels in all, each 1½ cubits high. Such is linked in measurements with the 48 boards of Moses Tabernacle, each 1½ cubits wide. Though fuller revelation is in the Temple, God would not let them forget the truths of the Tabernacle.

Jesus Christ is the fulfilment of all that is symbolized in the lavers, their bases and wheels. He was transported from heaven to earth, then moved in this earth in His ministry and then was transported back to heaven by the power of the Spirit (Hebrews 1:3; Mark 16:15-20).

Now the church has "the Gospel chariot" to take the message of "blood and water" cleansings to the whole earth, bringing conviction of sin, of righteousness and judgment by the power of the Holy Spirit (John 16:8-10). The Gospel Word needs wheels!

D. The Position of the Lavers and Bases

In 1 Kings 7:39 we have the Divinely ordained position of these lavers. There were five set on the right side of the house, and five lavers with their bases on the left side of the house. Therefore we have two sets of five on the north and south sides of the altar.

The number ten has been mentioned as the number of law, order and responsibility. We may think of the number five pertaining to man's hands and feet with five fingers on each hand and five toes on each foot. The hands are responsible for service and the feet responsible for transport. The hands and feet of the priests had to be clean as they ministered in the Tabernacle or Temple of the Lord. This was the purpose of the laver back there. Here it is for the sacrifices. The molten sea was for the priests.

E. Purpose of the Lavers

One does not need to repeat the basic truth of the purpose of the lavers. The purpose of both lavers and molten sea was for washing by water. The water in the sea was for the priests to wash, and the water in the lavers were for the sacrifices to be washed.

The whole truth pertains to washing (Ephesians 5:26-27; Titus 3:5).

The believer is both priest and sacrifice and must always know the washing of water by the Word in his ministry before the Father and His blessed Son.

F. The Lavers and God's Throne

It is worthy of consideration to compare that which pertains to the lavers and bases and that which pertains to the throne of God in Ezekiel.

The Lavers and Bases in the Temple	—	The Throne of God in Vision
Ornamentation of the lion	—	The living creature-face of a lion
The cherubim	—	The face of an eagle
The oxen	—	The face of an ox
The palm trees	—	The face of a man
The wreathen work	—	The rainbow round the throne
The foursquare shape	—	The four living cherubim with four faces
The four brazen wheels	—	The wheels within wheels
Of molten brass	—	Feet as burnished brass
For cleansing water	—	Voice as sound of great waters
Chariot wheels	—	The throne of God

Who can fail to see that there is connection between that in the lavers and bases and the throne of God? The truth is that we can only come to the throne of God through the cleansing of the Word of God in its fulness. The cleansing in the court brings us to the throne in the holy oracle.

G. Laver Bases Desecrated

Again, as seen in the chapters on the brazen altar and the molten sea, we see wicked king Ahaz bringing damage to these Divinely appointed lavers and bases.

In 2 Kings 2:17 king Ahaz cut off the borders of the bases and moved the lavers from them. Ungodly leadership always attack the foundational work of redemption. Godly leadership will restore these foundations, for "if the foundations be destroyed, what can the righteous do?" (Psalm 11:3).

Wicked king Ahaz made a counterfeit altar, took the foundation oxen from the molten sea and now cuts off the borders of the lavers. He touches that which pertains to cleansings by blood and water! God judged him in due time for these wicked deeds, and so will He do to all other leadership that follows his wicked steps.

IN SUMMARY:

The molten sea and the brazen lavers basically teach the same major truths, the need of both priest and sacrifice to be washed before the Lord. The priest must be washed for ministry. The sacrifice must be washed for the altar.

So as Christ is both priest and sacrifice, the believer is both priest and sacrifice. Christ needed no cleansing as He was perfect and sinless. The believer needs continual cleansing until he is made perfect and sinless. Therefore, let us always have our hearts and minds cleansed by the blood of Jesus and the washing of water by the Word in order to be pure priests and sacrifices unto the Lord and His Christ.

FRONT ELEVATION OF TEMPLE AND TWO PILLARS

CHAPTER TWENTYFOUR

THE TEMPLE PORCH

In 1 Chronicles 28:11,19 we are told that David was given the pattern of the porch in writing by the Spirit of the Lord upon him.

This porch was just immediately before the entrance to the Temple itself, or into the holy place. The Temple was entered from the east through this porch. It was like a vestibule, portico or entrance hall, not as a room with doors. It was a roofed porch, protecting the entrance to the Temple having two pillars standing on each side of the Temple doorway.

There has been some disagreement over the excessive height of the porch as in the Authorized Version for, if this 120 cubits was its height, then it would be more of a tower than a porch. The Amplified Bible says, ''The length of the vestibule in front of the Temple was 20 cubits, equal to the width of the house, and its depth in front of the house was 10 cubits'' (1 Kings 6:3).

A. **The Temple Porch** — 1 Kings 6:3; 2 Chronicles 3:4

The length of the porch was 20 cubits, which was the width of the Temple and the breadth thereof was 10 cubits, and the height thereof probably 20 cubits, 10 cubits lower than the walls.

As noted, the Chronicles record says the height was 120 cubits. If this was correct then the porch would have been a lofty tower, four times as high as the rest of the Temple.

However, some ancient versions omit the ''hundred'' and read ''the height was 20 cubits''. This would be more in keeping with a porch and with the Temple itself.

Taking the measurements of the porch as $20 \times 20 \times 10$ cubits, this would be the same cubic capacity as the brazen altar in the court, and also the upper room over the holy oracle. Thus we would have 4000 cubical capacity. In its symbolic measurements it would be linked with the altar and the upper room. Man must first touch the redemptive truth of the altar of blood before he can enter the Temple of God through the porch and have access to the upper rooms of the Lord.

The prophetic measurements again speak of the 4 days from Adam to Christ, or 4000 years when He the true Temple was manifested in the earth (2 Peter 3:8; Psalm 90:4; John 2:20-21). He also shed His blood as the consummation of blood sacrifice. No blood was shed in the Temple. Christ's blood sacrifice was once and for all time.

1. **Made of Cedar Beams** — 1 Kings 7:12

Cedar speaks of incorruptibility, royalty. It is like the porch of the king's house. Christ is the incorruptible Son of God raised from the grave. He is the King of kings. He is the only way into the Temple or Church of God. He is God's access. He is God's porch, God's way of entrance into His holy house (Psalm 16:10; John 14:1,6).

2. **Overlaid with Gold** — 2 Chronicles 3:4

The porch was overlaid with pure gold. Gold, as always, speaks of Deity. The cedar speaks of Christ's sinless and incorruptible humanity. The gold speaks of His absolute Deity. Thus two materials, always distinguishable but united as one, speaking of His two natures, the human and Divine natures, always distinguishable but indivisible.

Gold relative to the believer also speaks of being partaker of the Divine nature (2 Peter 1:3-4).

B. **Ascent to the House of the Lord**

It seems that there were steps of ascent to the porch and through the porch into the house of the Lord by the folding doors (Ezekiel 40:38-39).

The queen of Sheba was overcome in spirit when she saw Solomon's ascent to the house of the Lord (1 Kings 10:4-5).

Hezekiah went up the Lord's house after his miraculous healing (Isaiah 38:22).

The language of the prophets always speak of going up to the house of the Lord (Isaiah 2:1-4). Spiritually speaking one always go up in direction to God's house, but descends when going down and away from it (Proverbs 7:27).

The steps of a good man are ordered by the Lord (Psalm 37:23). Righteousness sets us in the way of His steps (Psalm 85:13). Our walk is in the steps of that faith of Abraham (Romans 4:12).

C. The Porch and the Altar

The place between the porch and the altar was generally a place of seeking the Lord in prayer, weeping, fasting, or rejoicing in worship according to the spiritual condition of the nation.

The prophet calls on God's people at times to ''weep between the porch and the altar'' especially the priests of the Lord (Joel 2:17; 2 Chronicles 8:12; 15:8; 29:7,17).

Christ ministered in Solomon's porch, as it later came to be called (John 10:23). The man was healed at the Gate called Beautiful and the testimony of it was seen in Solomon's porch (Acts 3:11; 5:12).

Solomon's house also had a porch and in it was the throne of judgment (1 Kings 7:6-14). So the Holy Spirit comes as the Spirit of Burning and Judgment, the Spirit of conviction (Isaiah 4:4; John 16:8-11). Other Scriptures may be read in Ezekiel 40:7-15,39-49; 41:15,25-26; 44:3; 46:2,8 where the gates of the court had their special porches also.

The porch therefore speaks of a vestibule, an entrance in the Temple of the Lord and its daily ministrations. Christ is the only entrance into priestly ministrations in the new covenant priesthood of all believers.

THE PILLARS OF THE TEMPLE

JACHIN AND BOAZ

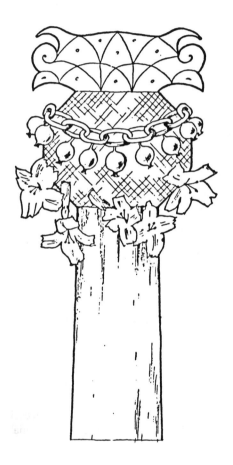
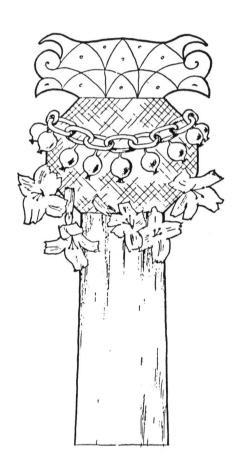

CHAPTER TWENTYFIVE

THE TWO BRAZEN PILLARS

Closely connected with and inseparable from the porch were the two brazen pillars. These pillars were before the Temple and probably upheld the porch. However, they deserve a special chapter as to their revelation and design.
The account of the details are provided for us in 1 Kings 7:13-22,41-42 and 2 Chronicles 3:15-17. These two were also part of the revelation and pattern given to king David which was then given to Solomon.

A. The Two Brazen Pillars

1. Made of Brass

The pillars were made of bright or scoured brass (1 Kings 7:45; 1 Chronicles 18:8). Brass speaks of Divine judgment on sin. Scouring speaks of the sufferings and chastisement that believers experience as the Lord deals with sin and selfishness (Hebrews 12:11).

2. Two Pillars

The number two is significant of witness. The testimony of two was required both by Old and New Testaments (Deuteronomy 17:6; 2 Corinthians 13:1). These two pillars stand like two witnesses in the porch at the entrance of the Temple.
The Law and the Prophets can be represented here, the Hebrew Bible being divided simply into these two sections in the Old Testament. Note these Scriptures on the ministry of the Law and the Prophets (Luke 16:16,29; 24:27; Acts 24:14; 28:23; Romans 3:21). The Law and the Prophets witnessed of the righteousness of God.

3. Hollow Pillars

Jeremiah 52:20-21 shows that these brazen pillars were hollow, and the thickness of a hand, or four fingers.

B. Measurements of the Pillars

1. Their Height

The height of the pillars was 18 cubits, together being 36 cubits, but allowed a cubit on each pillar for the chapter that fitted on each (2 Chronicles 3:15; 2 Kings 25:17; Jeremiah 52:20-21).

Eighteen is a multiple of nine, nine being the number of completeness and finality. It is also the number of the Holy Spirit.
There are nine fruit of the Spirit, nine gifts of the Spirit, nine beautitudes. Thus the pillars speak of that which is completed, that which is final as to the outer court ministry and the final step before entering into the Lord's house.

2. Their Circumference

The compass of the pillars was 12 cubits. The number twelve, as already seen, is the number of Divine government, apostolic government. The number ten is an end-time number as is the number eleven and thirteen. Eleven is one short of twelve while thirteen is one beyond twelve. Eleven is the number of lawlessness, of the antichrist spirit, while thirteen is the number of rebellion. Twelve is the number of God's government being seen in the city of God, the new Jerusalem (Revelation 21-22). There everything is according to God's order, God's law and His government.

C. Chapiters of the Pillars

1. Chapiters

The pillars had chapiters or crowns or caps on them. The pillars in the outer court of Moses Tabernacle also had crowns of silver on them, as did the five pillars of the Tabernacle door (Exodus 36:37-38). The crowns speak of that which is kingly. Christ is crowned with honour and glory. The saints will receive their crowns when earthly ministry is completed (Hebrews 2:9; Ephesians 6:17; James 1:12; Revelation 2:10; 3:11; 1 Peter 5:4).

2. Five Cubits High

These crowns were five cubits high, according to 1 Kings 7:16 but three cubits according to 2 Kings 25:17. The discrepancy seems to be in the fact that the chapiter was three cubits and the bowls that these were set in would make up the other two cubits, making the total five cubits. Five is the number of God's grace, the number of life, the number of the atonement. These pillars symbolically spoke of such to all who entered the house of the Lord.

3. The Pommels

In 2 Chronicles 4:12 and 1 Kings 7:41-42 it speaks of the two pillars and the two bowls of the chapiters that were on the top of these two pillars. They are also called pommels. These were simply a round bowl for the chapiters.

D. Ornamentation of the Pillars

The ornamentation of the pillars is especially significant as is seen here.

1. Nets of Checker Work

In 1 Kings 7:17,41-42 it speaks of the nets of checker work. It seems that the two bowl-like chapiters on top of the pillars were set, then these nets of checker work were on top of these bowls.

The net in Scriptures reminds us of Christ's call to His disciples to become fishers of men and catch men in the Gospel net (Matthew 4:19; Mark 1:17; Matthew 13:47-50; Ezekiel 47:10-14).

Christ is the master fisherman. He knows the right bait to catch fish out of the sea of humanity. The parable of the kingdom shows the Gospel net bringing in all kinds of fish. The Lord said He would send for many fishers and fish for His people (Jeremiah 16:16).

2. Wreaths of Chain Work

Wreathen chain work is generally the symbol of exaltation. Chains are made of numerous links. Both Joseph and Daniel were adorned in exaltation with chains of gold and set next to the king (Genesis 41:42; Daniel 5:29).

The high priest had chains of gold on his breastplate of judgment (Exodus 28). The holy oracle in the Temple had golden chains across its doors also (2 Chronicles 3:16).

Here the pillars have wreathen chains of brass. Justice and judgment are exalted before the Lord.

3. Seven Wreathen Chains

According to 1 Kings 7:17 each chapiter had seven wreathen chains. Seven, as has been seen, is the number of perfection, completeness. So these two pillars have the numbers five, three, twelve and seven stamped upon them in the Divine pattern.

Seven is the number of the end-times, the number of the Book of Revelation.

4. Pomegranates on the Chains

In 2 Chronicles 3:16; 1 Kings 7:18-20,42 along with 2 Chronicles 4:12-13 we note that there were pomegranates on the chain work apparently entwined with the network on top of the pillars and their wreathen chains.

A study of these Scriptures show that there were altogether 400 pomegranates, 200 on each pillár in two rows of 100 each round about. These no doubt hung from the wreathen chain work and network. One chain work of pomegranates was over against the belly of the pillar with its 100 pomegranates and the other exactly the same. Each pillar had 200 pomegranates.

The pomegranate was a fruit of the promised land. It was a fruit with blood-red encased seed in it. On the garments of glory on the high priest were the golden bells and pomegranates of blue, purple and scarlet (Exodus 28). These were down low on the hem and here the woman with the issue of blood touched the hem of Christ's garment and received the fruit of His healing ministry. (Matthew 9:20-22).

Here on the pillars the fruit is up high. The pomegranates speak of fruitfulness, the fruit of the Spirit on the two pillars (Numbers 13:23; Deuteronomy 8:8; Song of Solomon 4:3,13; 6:7,11; 7:12; 8:2; Exodus 28:33-34).

The number 400 has already been mentioned in connection with the 400 baths of water in the ten lavers. It is the number of affliction and suffering. The fruit of the Spirit is often borne out of affliction and suffering. It is the manifestation of the life of the tree (John 15:1-16).

5. **Lily Work on the Chapiters**

On the chapiters also was seen beautiful lily work in a total of 5 cubits. The lily is used in the Temple in ornamentation. (1 Kings 7:19,22; Song 2:16; 4:5; 5:13; 6:3; 2:1,2; Matthew 6:28). It speaks of the loveliness, purity and fragrance of Christ.

Jesus said, Solomon in all his glory was not arrayed as one of the beautiful lilies of the field (Luke 12:27). The Hebrew meaning of "lily" is "whiteness"; also a trumpet, from its tubular shape. So Christ is absolute whiteness, perfect purity within and without. His saints are to be lily white also! They also lift their voice like a trumpet and warn people (Isaiah 58:1; Ezekiel 33).

E. **Position of the Pillars**

These two pillars were before the Temple and placed in the porch of the temple, one on the right hand and the other on the left hand. They looked toward the brazen sea and the brazen altar, and the priests and worshippers in the courts of the Lord.

We think of Christ speaking of the positions on His right hand and left hand being reserved for two whom the Father had chosen. They would be like these two pillars of the porch. They stood there as sentinels, as two guards to the house of the Lord.

F. **Names of the Pillars**

The names of the pillars are specified in 1 Kings 7:21 with 2 Chronicles 3:17 as Jachin and Boaz. Jachin means "He shall establish", while Boaz means "In Him is strength". As with everything, all points first of all to the Lord Jesus Christ. Christ is the One who established His people, and in Him is their strength. Eternal stability and strength for Israel would be found in the Lord God. He is the saving strength of His anointed (Psalm 28:8; 18:1; Deuteronomy 33:25). God will also establish His Word for it is for ever settled in heaven. He said in both Testaments that "in the mouth of two or three witnesses every word would be established" (Deuteronomy 17:7; 2 Corinthians 13:1). As we believe His prophets so we are established and strengthed (2 Chronicles 20:20; Isaiah 9:6-7; Psalm 99:4; 1 Samuel 2:10).

G. **Destroyed by Babylon**

The final mention of these pillars is when the king of Babylon came against Jerusalem and the Temple of God and destroyed these beautiful pillars, taking them as scrap metal to Babylon (2 Kings 25:13-17; 2 Chronicles 18:8; Jeremiah 52:17; 27:19-22). All had been foretold by the Lord through His prophets.

Babylon will always destroy the pillars of the Lord's house if the priests of the Lord fail to keep His house holy unto the Lord. Babylon counts all these things as scrap metal.

H. Significance of Pillars

The Bible shows the significance of pillars. A pillar speaks of stability, uprightness and solidarity in the work of the Lord, in the position which God sets it. A pillar speaks of faithfulness.

1.   There were 60 pillars in the outer court of Moses Tabernacle. These upheld the fine linen cloth as the wall around the Lord's Tabernacle. These pillars stood in sockets of brass, crowned with a silver cap and joined together with silver rods and the fine linen curtains hanging on them (Exodus 27:10-17). Four of these pillars were specially chosen for the court gate with its special colours of blue, purple and scarlet.

2.   The Lord Jesus is pictured as having legs as pillars of marble (Song of Solomon 5:15; Revelation 10:1).

3.   Jeremiah the prophet was made an iron pillar and a brazen wall in the midst of the people he was sent to (Jeremiah 1:18).

4.   Peter, James and John were pillars in the church at Jerusalem (Galatians 2:9).

5.   The church is the pillar and support of the truth (1 Timothy 3:15).

6.   The promise to the overcomer is that he would be a pillar in the Temple of the Lord (Revelation 3:12).

7.   Solomon's sixty valiant men were likened to pillars (Song of Solomon 3:6-7).

Heathen and idolatrous temples had their various pillars dedicated to men or their gods, often inscribed with the names upon them. All were counterfeit of the Temple of the Lord, these two pillars with the Divinely appointed names in them.

Jacob set up the stone for a pillar and anointed it with oil calling it Bethel, the house of God (Genesis 28:18-22; 31:13,45).

Moses set up 12 pillars at Mt Sinai representing the 12 tribes of the nation of Israel (Exodus 24:4).

God Himself led Israel as a pillar of cloud by day and a pillar of fire by night (Exodus 13:21-22; 14:19-24).

Thus pillars speak of position, security, strength, stability and responsibility. Things are upheld by them. Ezekiel's vision of the Temple mentions two pillars also (Ezekiel 40:49).

Christ is THE pillar. Apostolic ministries are pillars. Believers who are overcomers are also pillars.

I. Prophetic Significance of the Pillars

There is that pertaining to these two brazen pillars which seems to have some prophetic significance, especially when it comes to the Book of Revelation.

The number two, as noted, is the number of testimony, the number of witness. In the mouth of two or three witnesses shall every word be established. The testimony of two men was strength in the case.

Jesus sent out His twelve apostles two by two. He also sent out the 70 disciples two by two into every city whither He Himself would come (Mark 6:7; Luke 10:1). In Revelation we see Christ speaking of His TWO Witnesses (Revelation 11). There is that in the two pillars of brass in Solomon's Temple which has much that would correspond to the ministry of the two witnesses in Revelation.

Solomon's Two Pillars	—	Christ's Two Witnesses
The pillars are two	—	The witnesses are two
Two pillars of brass	—	The Law and the Prophets
In the outer court of the Temple	—	Measure not the court
The Temple is measured	—	The Temple and altar are measured
One on the right hand and one on the left hand	—	Two who stand at Christ's right hand and left hand (Matthew 20:20-28).
Brass speaks of judgment	—	Two witnesses bring judgments on the earth with plagues and no rain
The pillars were stamped with the numbers five, twelve, seven and nine	—	The two witnesses are the grace of God, God's government, in the end-time, the fulness of this age
Jachin and Boaz were their names	—	The Lord will establish and He will strengthen His two witnesses
The pillars were ornamented with Divine beauty	—	The witnesses are ornamented with Divine power, anointing and gifting
Babylon destroyed the pillars	—	Antichrist overcomes the two witnesses but God raises them from death
All pertaining to them is brass	—	The witnesses minister judgments of the Lord

As we consider the pillars, their number, size, material, ornamentation, crowns, chains, nets, pomegranates and lily work, many lessons are learnt as they point to Christ and His church and believers in the house of the Lord.

THE GOLDEN CANDLESTICK

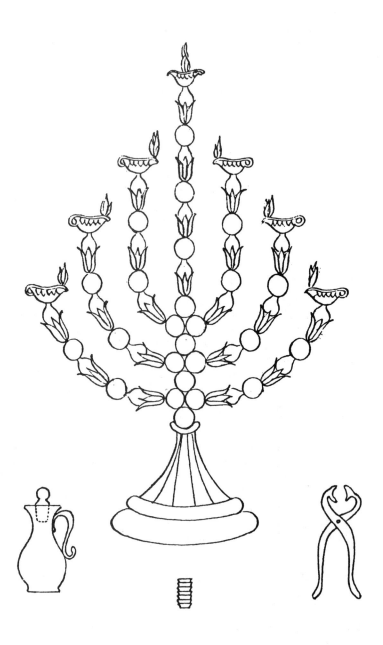

Diagram — R.S. Jackson (Snr)

CHAPTER TWENTYSIX

THE GOLDEN CANDLESTICKS

Having considered the furniture in the outer court, namely, the brazen altar, the molten sea and the lavers with their bases, we proceed in these next several chapters to a consideration of the furniture in the holy place.

The furniture in the holy place consisted of the golden candlesticks (or more properly, lampstands), the golden tables of shewbread and the golden altar of incense. As all was brass in the outer court, the court of the priests, so all is gold in the holy place, the sanctuary of the Lord.

A. The Golden Lampstands

The brief details of the golden candlesticks, or lampstands (as they were not lamps burning candles, but oil lights) are to be found in 1 Kings 7:49-50 with 2 Chronicles 4:7,19-22.

These lampstands, as that of the Tabernacle of Moses, must have been after the same fashion as that given to Moses. In contrast, there was but one lampstand in Moses Tabernacle but ten lampstands here in the Temple of Solomon.

By a study of the lampstand in the Tabernacle we see the general description and design of these light-bearers (Exodus 25:31-40; Leviticus 24:1-4).

1. Made of Pure Gold — 1 Chronicles 28:15

The marginal reading of 2 Chronicles 4:19-22 speaks of "perfect" gold, that is, pure gold. Gold, as always in relation to Divine things speaks of the perfections of the Divine nature in Christ, who is the light of the world. His life was the light of men (Hebrews 1:1-4; John 1:1-4; 1 John 1:1-9). Jesus Christ is the light of God. Light is pure, light is perfect, even as perfect and pure gold. No impurity was ever found in Him.

The one candlestick in Moses Tabernacle spoke first of Christ, then of the church which is His body, and the light of the world.

2. Made According to the Pattern

In 2 Chronicles 4:7,20 we are told that the lampstands were made "according to their form", and "after their manner". God only had one pattern in mind. The Temple and all of its furnishings was "according to the pattern" given to David by the Spirit. This was true also of the pattern given to Moses by the Spirit. Both Moses and David wrote these things under the inspiration of the Holy Spirit.

For this pattern we consider the Scriptures above from Exodus and Leviticus. We give but a brief outline of the ornamentation of the golden candlestick as fuller details are covered in the author's textbook on the Tabernacle of Moses. The golden lampstand speaks of both Christ and His church.

a) **Made of beaten work** — speaking of the sufferings of Christ and His church.

b) **Made of one piece of gold** — speaking of the unity of Christ and His church.

c) **Made with seven branches** — that is, having a shaft and six branches out of the side of the shaft.
In the ornamentation we see the branches and shaft with their knops, flowers and buds. The impress of the number nine is seen in the ornamentation of the branches with its three groups of knops, flowers and buds. The impress of the number twelve is seen in the shaft itself, having four groups of knops, flowers and buds.
In the total we have the number 66, pointing to the 66 books of the Bible which are our

Divine light and truth from the inspiration of the Spirit of God.

In the twelve we see the foundation twelve apostles of the Lamb. In the number nine we think of the nine fruit, nine gifts of the Spirit, and the nine beatitudes. There are other nines in the Scripture also.

It seems, by a consideration of Numbers 17:8 and the ornamentation of Aaron's rod that budded, with its bud, flower and almond fruit that the golden candlestick was made after this ornamentation.

The significance of this points to the truth that the church, God's lampstand, must have the same beauty and pattern in it that Christ, God's rod and high priest has in Himself. The church must be like Christ.

d)   **Made with three foundational knops** — speaking of the foundation of the church in the revelation of the Godhead, the Father, Son and Holy Spirit. These three knops were the support of the six branches which proceeded out of the side of the lampstand shaft.

e)   **Made with Seven Lamps** — speaking of the perfections of the sevenfold Spirit of God (Isaiah 11:1-4). The Lord Jesus, as God's lampstand, manifested the sevenfold perfections of the Holy Spirit in His perfect life. His life was indeed the light of man.

Such was the beauty and pattern of the lampstand in Moses Tabernacle and undoubtedly the same was in the lampstands in Solomon's Temple.

3.   **Ten Golden Lampstands**

The significance of the number ten is seen here also. In the Tabernacle of Moses there was one lampstand. In the Temple of Solomon there were ten lampstands.

The Temple is prominent in its tens. We think of the ten lavers, the ten tables of shewbread, and the ten lampstands.

This is in contrast to the Tabernacle with its one altar, one laver, one table, one lampstand, one gate, one door, one incense altar. All of this speaks of the one Christ, the one way to the Father, the one mediator between God and man. There was only ever one ark of the covenant for both Tabernacle and Temple. There is ever and only one throne of God and the Lamb.

The Temple, however, speaks first of Christ, but also of the church, His body, and the fulness of Him who fills all in all. Hence the emphasis on the number ten.

One is the number of beginning, the number of unity, the origin, the source of things and from which all other numbers proceed. So Christ in His Godhead is one and He is the beginning, the source of all things.

Ten is the number of law and order, the number of Divine law. So there must be Divine law and order in the church, the body of Christ.

These ten golden lampstands would illuminate the Temple holy place and all the furnishings therein. All would be in darkness without their light. The priests could walk in the light of the lamps, enjoying the table of shewbread, burning the incense on the altar, and walking in the beauty of the ornamented walls of the Temple, and golden floor.

All other furniture would be seen in the light of the lampstands.

So it is only "in Christ" by the Spirit that His beauty may be seen, as also the beauty of the church, which is His house.

4.   **The Golden Lamps**

Upon the ten lampstands were the golden lamps burning oil, shining light. The significance is seen also in the numbers seven and seventy.

a)   **The Lamps**

The lamp in Scripture is used in a threefold application as seen in the following Scriptures.

* The Psalmist says that God's Word is a lamp unto our feet and a light unto our pathway (Psalm 119:105).

* The spirit of man is also the lamp of the Lord (Proverbs 20:27 with Proverbs 6:23; 13:9).

* The Holy Spirit is likened unto seven lamps burning before the throne of God (Revelation 4:5; 2:1).

Other examples of God's use of lamps are seen in the following.

Gideon's army of 300 had lamps burning within their pitchers and at the given signal the light shined forth as the pitchers were broken (Judges 7).

God confirmed the Abrahamic covenant with the burning lamp of promise (Genesis 15:17).

The eyes of Christ are likened to lamps of fire burning with light (Ezekiel 1:13; Daniel 10:6).

The salvation of the Lord is like a burning lamp going forth (Isaiah 62:1).

Read also (Isaiah 2:5; 60:1-3,19,20; Habakkuk 3:4; Job 12:5; 41:19).

The lamps of the golden candlestick were always to be burning, never to go out so that there would always be light shining before the Lord (Exodus 25:31-40; 27:20; 35:14; 37:23; 39:37; Exodus 40:4,25; Numbers 4:9; 8:2-3; Leviticus 24:2-4).

The virgins had to have oil in their lamps as they waited for the bridegroom at the midnight hour (Matthew 25:1-13). Ten virgins are like the ten lampstands.

The lamps in the Temple of the Lord had to be continually burning before the Lord (1 Chronicles 28:15; 2 Chronicles 13:11; 29:7; 1 Samuel 3:3; 1 Kings 15:4; 2 Samuel 22:29). So the believer is to let his light shine before men (John 8:12; 12:35-36).

b) **The Seventy Lamps**

In all there were ten lampstands each with their seven lamps making a total of seventy lamps in all.

Here we would note the significance of the numbers seven and seventy.

1) **Seven**

There are various sevens in Scripture many of which may be used to illustrate the seven lamps of fire in the holy place. We list a few of these sevens by way of illustration.

* The seven principles of the doctrine of Christ (Hebrews 6:1-2).

* The seven Spirits of God on Messiah (Isaiah 11:1-4; Zechariah 3:9;4:10).

* The seven kingdom of heaven parables in Matthew 13.

* The seven churches in Asia (Revelation 1,2,3).

* The seven Spirits of God as seven lamps before the throne (Revelation 1:4; 3:1; 5:6; 4:5).

* The sevens "ones" of unity in Ephesians 4:4-6.

* The seven times a day of praise to the Lord (Psalm 119:164).

* The seven special feast days in the feasts of the Lord (Leviticus 23).

2) **Seventy**

There are various seventies in Scripture also of which we list a few.

* Seventy elders of the Sanhedrin in Jewish Courts (Ezekiel 8:11).

* The seventy sons of Jacob who went to Egypt (Genesis 46:27; Exodus 1:5).

* The seventy elders of Israel who saw God (Exodus 24:1; Numbers 11:16-25).

* The seventy palm trees at Elim (Exodus 15:27; Numbers 33:9).

* The seventy years of Babylonish captivity (Jeremiah 25:11-12; 29:10).

* The seventy years allotted to man (Psalm 90:10).

* The seventy bullock offerings at the feast of tabernacles (Numbers 29:12-40). The seventieth bullock was offered on the seventh day.

* The seventy disciples Jesus sent out (Luke 10:1,17).
Seventy is the number prior to increase among the people of God. Here we have increased light, yet light is also one.

God never leaves Himself without witness, without a lamp of light.

The seven churches of seven lamps equal 49 lamps (Revelation 1:12).
The two witnesses are likened to two lampstands shining in the darkness of the great tribulation period (Revelation 11:1-3; Zechariah 4).

With Christ having the seven lamps, and the church having fortynine lamps, and the two witnesses having fourteen lamps, we have seventy lamps in all.

One of the greatest prophecies in the Bible is that pertaining to the Seventy Weeks given to Daniel (Daniel 9:24-27). This also concerned the holy place and the cleansing of the sanctuary of the Lord.

B. Purpose of Existence

The whole purpose of the existence of the lampstand was for light, not for the beauty of its ornamentation. It was a light-bearer. So Christ is the light of the world. The church also is the light of the world, to shine forth His light in the midst of the crooked and perversed generation (John 7:12; 1 John 1:5; John 1:4,9; Ephesians 5:8).
The candlestick illumined the holy place. The candlestick was to give light before the Lord. The candlestick gave light upon the tables of shewbread and the incense altar. The priests could walk and minister in the light of the candlestick. The candlestick illumined itself also.

We are to let our light shine before men (Matthew 5:15-16; Luke 8:16; 11:33; 12:35; Revelation 21:23). No man lights a lamp and puts in under cover but lights it to give light to all in the house. The believer's life, like Christ, should be the light of men who walk in darkness.

C. Daily Ministry

The Scriptures show that there had to be a daily ministration to the seven lamps and this at the time of the burning of incense (Leviticus 24:2; 1 Kings 7:49-50).
Daily the lamps had to be trimmed. Daily the ashes had to be taken away. Daily the oil was supplied so that the lamps could shine forth light. This took place in the morning and evening. This was the purpose of the tongs of gold, the bowls of oil and snuffers in the lamp-trimming time.

1 The Snuffers of Gold

The snuffers were used to trim the lamps to cause them to shine brighter. In Revelation chapters 1-2-3 we see Christ using the snuffers to deal with and trim the lamps of the seven churches. His purpose is to deal with snuff, not extinguish the light (Revelation 2:3; 3:19). The snuffers took away that which was superfluous. They were used wisely by the priest.
The Lord, our great high priest, uses reproofs, rebukes, exhortations and admonitions to deal with our lamps (Titus 2:12, 1 Corinthians 5:4-5; 2 Corinthians 13:10).

2 The Snuff Dishes

These were used with the snuffers of gold. The ashes were put in them. It kept the gold covered floor of the house of the Lord clean as well as the hands of the priest who trimmed the lamps (Exodus 25:38; 37:23; Numbers 4:9). The Lord does not want the ashes of past burnt out experiences to defile the floor of His house.

3 **The Tongs of Gold**

There were various tongs of brass and gold used in the Tabernacle and Temple services. Tongs were used about the altar of brass to order the fire. Tongs were used to take fire from the altar to light the golden candlesticks. In Moses Tabernacle, the original fire came to the altar, lit from heaven, but when kindled had to be maintained by a daily supply of oil by the priests on earth (Leviticus 9:24; 2 Chronicles 7:1; Exodus 40:24-25; Levitucus 24:2,3; Numbers 8:3).

Tongs were used for the altar of incense.

4 **The Bowls of Oil**

The bowls, or basins, contained the daily supply of oil for the lamps. This was poured into the lamps morning and evening to cause the lamps to burn always before the Lord.

All of this speaks of the fact that believers need daily trimming of their spiritual lives by the instruments of the Lord. All need a daily supply of the Holy Spirit, the oil of the Lord, in order to let their lamps manifest the light of Christ's life.

D. **Position in the Holy Place**

As in the Tabernacle, so in the Temple, the lampstands were placed in the holy place. In the Tabernacle of Moses, the lampstand was placed on the south side. In the Temple the lampstands were placed on the north and south sides, five lampstands on each side.

This was very similar to the ten brazen lavers in the court of the priests, these also being five on the north and south sides of the Temple.

Ten, as already seen, is also the number of responsibility. We think of the ten virgins, five wise and five foolish. All were responsible to have oil in their lamps, to trim them to burn brighter. However, five allowed their lamps to go out and realized the need of oil — too late!

F. **Lampstands in Scripture**

An overview of lampstands in Scripture give some progressive revelation of the Lord's truth concerning this beautiful article of furniture and its distinctive truths.

* In the Tabernacle of Moses there was one golden candlestick (Exodus 25:31-40).

* In the Temple of Solomon there were ten golden candlesticks (1 Chronicles 28:15; 1 Kings 7:49,50).

* In Babylon God used the golden candlestick to bring about the fall of Babylon relative to the tongues and interpretation by the writing on the wall (Daniel 5:1-5). The church will be used by the Lord in the last days to bring about the fall of last day Babylon (1 Peter 5:13).

* The golden candlestick is seen in relation to the restoration of Judah from Babylon in connection with the golden bowl of oil supply (Zechariah 4).

* The two witnesses are likened to two olive trees and two golden candlesticks (Revelation 11:1-4 with Zechariah 4:1-14).

* The seven local churches are likened to golden candlesticks (Revelation 1:12-20). Christ warns the church of the danger of its candlestick being removed after the fall from first love. Each local church is responsible before the Lord to be a light in the city in which it has been set.

* In 1 Chronicles 28:15 there is mention of silver candlesticks in relation to Solomon's Temple. As will be seen it seems that these were used in the chambers of the priests.

Thus the golden lampstand is a beautiful picture of Christ and His church as the light of the world. Paul wrote to the Philippian believers encouraging them to be "harmless and blameless, the sons of God without rebuke, in the midst of a crooked and perverse generation, among whom ye shine as lights in the world" (Philippians 2:15).

THE GOLDEN TABLE OF SHEWBREAD

Diagram — Flannelgraph

CHAPTER TWENTYSEVEN

THE TABLES OF SHEWBREAD

In our chapter we come to the second grouping of furniture in the holy place, these being the golden tables of shewbread.
In the Temple studies we have seen the ten brazen lavers in the outer court, then the ten golden lampstands in the holy place and now we have ten golden tables of the shewbread before the Lord.

The Scriptures which speak of these are found in 1 Kings 7:48; 1 Chronicles 28:16 and 2 Chronicles 4:8,19.

Again we see that the Tabernacle of Moses had but one table of shewbread which spoke of Christ and the 12 tribes of Israel in the Old Testament and the 12 apostles of the Lamb in the New Testament (Exodus 25:30).

The Temple of Solomon has ten tables of shewbread which speak of the fulness of Christ in His church as the bread of life.
We look further at the significant truths in the brief details provided. Undoubtedly the reason for brevity on these tables is the same as that concerning the lampstands, for all follow the pattern gives to Moses in Mt Sinai.

A. The Gold Tables of Shewbread

These tables could only be seen in the light of the golden lampstands. So the truth of God's Word, the bread of life, can only be seen by the light and the illumination of the Spirit of God.

1. **Made of Pure Gold** — 1 Kings 7:48

   Gold, as always, speaks of that which is Divine, that which is wholly of God, the Divine nature.
   The revelation of the table originated in the heart of God. Pure gold speaks of pure Divinity. Jesus Christ is God incarnate. He becomes our table of communion.

2. **Ten Tables of Gold**

   Ten again is the number of law, order and responsibility before God. All in the house of the Lord is according to Divine order. There must be order at the table of the Lord by the priests of the Lord.

3. **Made According to Pattern**

   Though not specifically mentioned, we may safely assume that these tables, as the golden lampstands, were ''after the pattern'' of that in the Tabernacle of Moses.
   The table in the Tabernacle of Moses was made of acacia wood overlaid with gold. The table here in the Temple may have been made of cedar wood and overlaid with gold, even as was the altar of incence (1 Kings 6:20). Or, it may have been made of gold itself.
   If it was of cedar wood, then we have Christ as the royal Man, the King of kings and the Lord of lords. It speaks of incorruptibility, of royalty. Christ's incorruptible nature and character is seen in the four Gospels in His earthly walk as the bread of life.
   Gold, of course, speaks of His Divine nature, His deity. Jesus Christ is the God-Man, deity and humanity come together in one person.

   Other things related to the pattern of the table as seen in Moses Tabernacle would be as follows:

   a) **Measurements of the Table** — Two cubits long, by one cubit wide, and one and a half cubits high. All must measure up to the Divine standard. Jesus Christ measured up to God's standard.

b) **Table had four legs** — speaks of the four Gospels which present Christ as the bread of life and present Christ in His earthly ministry, His earth-walk.

As the four legs upheld the bread on the table, so the four Gospels uphold Christ as the bread of God.

The four legs also speak of the fact that the Gospel was to go into the four corners of the world, taking the bread of life to all nations (Matthew 28:18-20; Mark 15:15-20; Acts 1:8; Revelation 5:8-10).

4. **Names of the Tables**

* The table of acacia wood in Moses Tabernacle (Exodus 25:23).

* The pure table (Leviticus 24:6).

* The table (Exodus 39:36).

* The table of gold (1 Kings 7:48).

* The table of shewbread (Exodus 25:30).

In 1 Chronicles 28:16 it speaks of tables of silver, possibly for use in the priests chambers as also the silver lampstands.

The table points to the New Covenant table of the Lord around which believer priests gather for communion and fellowship (1 Corinthians 11:23-34; Matthew 26:26-28).

Here at the table there is life, health, healing, sharing, communication, communion, participation for all priests of the Lord.

B. **The Shewbread**

Assuming that the tables of shewbread were after the order of that in the Tabernacle of Moses, we would see the 12 loaves of shewbread on each table.

The bread in Scripture speaks invariably of (1) Christ Himself, John 6; or (2) The 12 apostles of the Lamb as representing the people of God, breaking the bread of Christ to them, or (3) The church, the body of Christ, being many, yet one bread (1 Corinthians 10:16-17).

Christ was born in Bethlehem, which means "The House of Bread". The meal offering was of fine flour (Levitucus 2). Christ has promised the believer "hidden manna" which speaks of the bread of heaven, the bread of God also (Revelation 2:17).

We consider some of the details pertaining to the bread of the Lord.

1. **Names of the Bread**

* Shewbread — The Bread of His Presence (Exodus 25:30; 35:13; 39:36). David ate of this bread (Matthew 12:4; Mark 2:20; Luke 6:4).

* Presence Bread — Numbers 4:7.

* Loaves set before God — Luke 6:4; Matthew 12:4; Mark 2:26.

* A Setting forth of the Loaves — Hebrews 9:2.

* Bread of Arrangement — 1 Chronicles 9:32; 23:29; Nehemiah 10:33; 2 Chronicles 13:11.

* Arrangement Bread — 1 Chronicles 28:16; 2 Chronicles 2:4; 29:18.

* The Continual Shewbread — 2 Chronicles 2:4; Numbers 4:7.

* The Bread of God — Leviticus 21:21.

* The Bread of His Face — 2 Corinthians 4:6; Revelation 22:4.

All these speak of the various facets of truth connected with Christ as the bread of life, and also may be applied to the table of the Lord as believers gather together for communion. Paul says as often as we eat this bread and drink this cup we do shew (i.e., Shew-bread, declare, tell forth) the Lord's death till He come (1 Corinthians 11:26).

2. Bread of Fine Flour

Jesus was the corn of wheat who fell into the ground and died to bring the church to birth (John 12:24).

Jesus was bruised as corn is bruised to become the bread of life to us (Isaiah 53:2-5; 28:27-29).

Jesus experienced the suffering of the fire of Calvary's oven to become the bread of life. His whole life was of fine flour, nothing rough or coarse was ever seen in Him.

3. Unleavened Bread

Leaven speaks of sin, corruption and that which puffs up. There was no leaven of sin in Him. There was nothing of pride or puffed up areas in His life. He saw no corruption in life or death. None could convict Him of sin (Hebrews 4:15).

4. Frankincense on the Bread

Frankincense was placed on the bread. It spoke of the life of prayer, intercession and unbroken communion that Jesus experienced with His Father. The fragrance of this ascended continually to heaven pleasing the Father God.

5. Twelve Loaves of Bread

Twelve loaves of bread were placed on each table. In all there would be $10 \times 12 = 120$ loaves of shewbread. The significance of the numbers 12 and 120 are noted here again in brief.

a) Twelve

As mentioned previously, twelve is the number of government, apostolic government. The student is referred to the 12 brazen oxen in the chapter of the molten sea.

Here again the 12 loaves speak firstly of the 12 tribes of Old Testament Israel, and then of the New Testament Israel of God, the church. They also speak of the 12 apostles of the Lamb. Then ultimately they would point to the bride city of God and the Lamb with it numerous twelves (Luke 6:13; Revelation 21-22 chapters).

b) One Hundred and Twenty

One hundred and twenty is the number of the end of all flesh and the beginning of life in the Spirit. Examples of this number may be seen in these Scripture references.

* The Spirit of God convicted men during the 120 years of Noah's preaching before all ungodly flesh was brought to an end (Genesis 6:1-13; 1 Peter 3:21).

* Moses lived 120 years in the flesh life and at the close was taken to glory after his bodily resurrection (Deuteronomy 34:7; Jude 9; Luke 9:30; Acts 7:23,30,36,42).

* At the dedication of the Temple 120 priests sounded with 120 trumpets consummating in the Spirit of God descending as the glory-fire of God (2 Chronicles 5:11-14).

* On the day of Pentecost 120 disciples of Jesus in one accord in one place were filled with the Holy Spirit and began to speak in a new tongue and live the new life in the Spirit as never known before (Acts 1:15; 2:1-4; Zechariah 4:6).

* In dispensational sense the 120 loaves could be linked with the 120 Jubilees ($120 \times 50 = 6000$ years) in which the bread of life is available to believing mankind. The manna fell for 6 days. There was none on the seventh day. In Canaan land they partook of the fruit (Joshua 5:12; Exodus 16).

Therefore the 120 loaves of bread symbolized the feeding on the life of the bread of God in His presence and before His face in priestly communion and fellowship. The early church continued stedfastly in the apostles doctrine, and in fellowship and in the breaking of bread and in prayers (Acts 2:42).

C. Table for the Priests

The table was strictly for the priests in the house of the Lord. Two major truths may be seen here.

1. New Testament Priests

As only Old Testament priests could eat of the table of shewbread, so only New Testament priests may partake of the table of the Lord. All must eat for themselves. None could eat for another.

Believers are kings and priests after the order of Melchisedek and as such may eat of the table of the Lord (Revelation 1:6; 5:9-10; 1 Peter 2:5-9; Leviticus 24:9).

The bread could only be eaten in the holy place, the sanctuary of the Lord.

2. Bread Partaken Weekly

The bread was placed on the table weekly, that is, every seventh day. It was eaten weekly by the priests of the Lord (Leviticus 24:6-9).

So it seems that the New Testament priests partook weekly of the Lord's table, on the first day of the week of the New Covenant, not the seventh or last day of the week as under Old Covenant times (Acts 20:7).

3. The Drink Offering Cup

In Numbers 28:7; Exodus 25:29; 29:40 and Leviticus 23:13,18,27 we have mention of the drink offering of wine. The drink offering was also associated with the table of the Lord. However, this was poured out before the Lord. The priests did not partake of it.

The vessels associated with the table were "covers" and "bowls" (or "flagons" and "chalices"). Numbers 4:7; Exodus 25:29. These covers and bowls were for the wine, or so it seems.

The fact that the wine was poured probably symbolized the fact that life could not be given under the Law Covenant. Jesus changed that and told the disciples to take the cup and drink of it, for His body and His blood bring life (John 6; Matthew 26:26-28; Luke 22:14-20).

4. The Communion of Bread and Wine

Melchisedek ministered bread and wine to Abraham, the father of all who believe, as he received tithes from him (Genesis 14:18). The table and the giving of tithes is connected here, along with faith and priesthood order.

Believers are to eat bread in the kingdom of God with their risen Lord (Luke 14:15).

The bread of God provides healing, health, life, nourishment, strength, fellowship, and communion. As we partake of the bread and the one cup we receive the life of Christ, the head of the church.

D. Position of the Tables

These ten tables, as also the ten lampstands, were placed in the holy place, five on each side (2 Chronicles 4:8). The priests would eat the shewbread in the light of the lamps.

E. The Singers and The Table

The singers in Solomon's Temple had the joy of preparing the table of shewbread (1 Chronicles 9:27, 32-33). Songs and singing have always been connected with the table of the Lord. This is true in the New Testament church also (Matthew 26:26; Mark 14:26).

Bread is spoken of as being "the staff of life". Throughout Israel's history we see many prophetic pictures of the bread of life. All point to Christ as the staff of life in the church which is spiritual Israel.

* Unleavened bread was used in the Feast of Passover (Exodus 12:14-20,34).

* Israel had the bread of manna for 40 years in the wilderness (Exodus 16).

* The meal offering was the bread on God's altar (Leviticus 2).

* The ark of the Covenant had the hidden manna in it over the wilderness wanderings (Hebrews 9:4; Revelation 2:17).

* David the king received strength from the shewbread the priest gave him to eat (1 Samuel 21:6; Matthew 12:1-4).

* Jesus fed the 5000 people and the 4000 people with miracle bread in the wilderness. It pointed to Himself as being the very bread and sustainer of life (Matthew 14:14-21; 15:32-38; John 6).

In Christ we have spiritual meat and spiritual drink, as shadowed forth in the miracle manna and the miracle supply of water from the rock (1 Corinthians 10:1-4,15-21).

THE GOLDEN ALTAR OF INCENSE

CHAPTER TWENTYEIGHT

THE ALTAR OF INCENSE

In contrast to and comparison with the golden altar of incense in the Tabernacle of Moses, which has about fourteen verses given to its description, the golden altar of incense in the Temple of Solomon has only about four verses given to it.

These references are found in 1 Kings 6:20,22; 7:48 and 2 Chronicles 4:19. No doubt this is because the details of this altar follow the same pattern as given to Moses at Mt Sinai even as for the other furniture in the holy place.

We note some of the spiritual significances relative to this golden altar before the Lord.

A. The Golden Altar of Incense

1. Names of the Altar

The Temple altar was called:

* The whole altar (1 Kings 6:22).

* The altar of gold (1 Kings 7:48).

* The golden altar (2 Chronicles 4:19).

* The altar of incense (1 Chronicles 28:18).

* The altar (1 Kings 6:20).

* The altar of cedar (1 Kings 6:20).

Note also the names of this altar in Moses Tabernacle (Exodus 30:27, 31:8; 35:15; Leviticus 4:7; Revelation 8:3).

2. Pattern Given by the Spirit

As Moses was given the pattern of the altar of incense for the Tabernacle in the wilderness, so king David received the pattern for the golden altar for the Temple. He received it by the Spirit. He wrote it down under inspiration of the Spirit (1 Chronicles 28:11-12,19).

The measurements would possibly be the same as those of the golden altar in Moses Tabernacle, that being the tallest article of furniture in the holy place.

The pattern given to Moses is found in Exodus 30:1-10 from which we briefly note the following, as this has been dealt with more fully in the textbook on the Tabernacle of Moses. We note that which pertains to the Temple incense altar also.

a) Made of acacia wood

It speaks of the incorruptible humanity of the Lord Jesus Christ as our intercessor.

In contrast to this, the altar of incense in the Temple was made of cedar wood (1 Kings 6:20).

The acacia wood spoke of Christ in His wilderness journey, His earth-walk and His prayers and intercessions on earth. The cedar wood in the incense altar speaks of Christ in His heavenly ministry, and His ministry as king-priest, even as the Temple was a house of cedars, all speaking of royalty.

In the two kinds of wood we would see the earthly and heavenly viewpoint of ministry.

b) Overlaid with gold

The altar in Moses Tabernacle and Solomon's Temple was overlaid with gold (1 Kings 6:22).

Gold again speaks of Christ's Divine nature, His perfect deity. Thus we have with the wood and the gold, two materials, distinguishable yet indivisible. Such speaks of the

two natures of the one Christ, His deity and humanity, distinguishable yet indivisible in
the one mediator between God and man, the man Christ Jesus. The wood never became
the gold, nor the gold the wood. So the two natures in Christ are distinguishable yet in
absolute union in His united person, the God-Man. God took on Himself perfect
manhood. He was and ever will be the God-Man, the heavenly priest and intercessor.
The altar of incense in Moses Tabernacle stood on the earth floor. The altar of incense
in Solomon's Temple stood on the gold floor. One speaks of Christ's earthly prayers
and intercessory ministry, the other of His heavenly prayers and intercessions for the
church, His body.

c) **Measurements of Altar**

Its measurements were a cubit in length and breadth and two cubits the height (Exodus
30:2). In relation to the other articles of furniture it was the highest article. This speaks
of the fact that Christ's ministry of intercession is the highest ministry now in behalf of
His people. He ever lives to make intercession (Hebrews 7:26).

d) **A Foursquare Altar**

The altar was foursquare, just as the brazen altar and the most holy place were. Four is
the number of the earth. Christ's intercessions are for the whole wide world, for the
redeemed.
And again, all the foursquares in both Tabernacle and Temple point ultimately to the
foursquare city of God, the bride city, the New Jerusalem (Revelation 21-22 chapters).
All who enter will enter basically upon the mediatorial and intercessory ministry of
Christ our great high priest.
The Gospel goes into all the world, to the four corners of the earth (Matthew 28:18-20;
Mark 16:15-20; Acts 1:8; Revelation 5:9-10).
The prayers of the saints arise from the four corners of the earth into the heavenly
sanctuary acceptable to God as they pass through Christ.

e) **The Four Horns**

The altar also had four horns on its four corners. Horns in Scripture are always
significant of power, authority and kingship. This has been noted relative to the horns
on the great altar of brass in the court in a previous chapter.
Horns coming out of His hand speak of the hiding of His power (Habakkuk 3:4; Genesis
22:13). All power is given to Him both in heaven and earth.

f) **The Crown of Gold**

Assuming that this altar was after the fashion of Moses Tabernacle it also had a crown
on it. The crown speaks of Christ as king, and because it is the altar of incense, it speaks
of Christ as the king and priest, ruler and intercessor (Psalm 2:1-6; 110:1-2; 45:1-2;
Hebrews 7:1-4; 2:9).

3. **One Golden Altar**

In contrast to the other vessels in the outer court and the holy place, there was only ever one
altar of incense. There was one brazen altar, one molten sea, one golden altar of incense and
one ark of the Covenant.
Surely the truth is evident. These "ones" speak of the Lord Jesus Christ, the one and only
way to the Father God, the one and only Saviour from sin, the one and only mediator
between God and man (John 14:1,6; 2 Timothy 2:5; Hebrews 7:26-27).

The "tens" in the golden lampstands, the tables of shewbread and the brazen lavers point to
the fulness of Christ in His church and the Divine order brought into the house of the Lord by
reason of cleansing, light and fellowship as symbolized in these vessels.

But the one altar speaks that there is only one place of prayer, one person through whom all prayer must ascend to the Father and that is through Christ Jesus, the eternal God-Man.

4. Position of the Golden Altar

The golden altar was placed in the holy place immediately before the veil of the holy oracle. The fragrance of the incense ascended within the veil into the very presence of the Lord.

So it speaks of the fact that the prayers of the saints also ascend within the veil of the heavenly sanctuary where Christ our great high priest intercedes before the Father for His redeemed people.

5. The Golden Censer

In Hebrews 8:1-4 and Revelation 8:1-6 along with Leviticus 16:1-12 we have the mention of the golden censer.

The censer was of gold, not of brass as was the rebel censer of Korah and his company in Numbers 16. They rose up against Aaron, God's anointed and appointed high priest and were smitten by the Lord in judgment by being swallowed down into the pit. This becomes prophetic of all rebellious religions who by-pass Christ, God's anointed and appointed high priest.

The censer was used especially on the great Day of Atonement when the high priest went within the veil into the holiest of all with the blood. So Christ has entered within the veil as the forerunner, taking His own blood to the throne of the Father, and on the basis of His sacrificial blood He now makes intercession for all His people (John 17).

B. The Sweet Incense

Although there is no mention of the incense ingredients in the Temple we know that God has but one pattern. The incense would be after the order given to Moses. There was never to be any substitute, or imitation of the incense and its ingredients as given to Moses.

The ingredients for the incense are written in Exodus 30:34-38. Again we briefly note the significance of these ingredients and the spiritual truth in the church of Jesus Christ.

The ingredients that compounded the incense were:

1. **Stacte** — a fragrant sap or gum from a tree. It had to be crushed fine.

2. **Onycha** — a shell-fish which was taken from the Red Sea and ground in order for its fragrance to come forth.

3. **Galbanum** — this also was a gum from a tree or plant-like shrub. It was a bitter gum used to drive away insects. It also had to be crushed fine.

4. **Frankincense** — this is white in colour and comes from the sap of a tree. It speaks of purity and righteousness.

5. **Salt** — salt acts as a seasoning and preservative. It speaks of purity of speech that is full of grace and truth. Salt has an enduring quality. It speaks of covenant (2 Chronicles 13:5; Matthew 5:13).

Each of these ingredients had to be crushed fine and then blended together to make the holy incense.

There were other things mentioned about this incense that speak of Christ's perfect intercessions and also point to that kind of prayer that should arise from the hearts of the believers.

The incense was to be:

1. **Sweet** — Christ's ministry was filled with sweetness and fragrance.

2. **Pure** — Christ was absolutely pure and holy.

3. **Holy** — Christ ministered in absolute holiness and sinlessness (Hebrews 7:26).

4. **Perpetual** — Christ ministers in the power of an endless life. He ever lives to make intercession for us (Hebrews 7:25-26).

5. **Perfume** — Christ's whole life was a fragrance to the Father (Ephesians 5:2).

As the cloud of incense ascended within the veil, the Lord promised that He would appear in the cloud, both the glory-cloud and the cloud of incense that was formed out of the prayers of His people (Leviticus 16:1-12).

From 1 Timothy 2:1 and Psalm 104:34 we may liken the five ingredients of the incense to the five ingredients of true prayer, Biblical prayer.

The ingredients of Biblical prayer are:

1. Supplications — entreaty to the Lord.

2. Prayers — making known our requests.

3. Intercessions — born out of the heart of God and taken back to God.

4. Thanksgivings — appreciation, gratefulness, thanks, praise.

5. Meditations — contemplation, worship, musings.

A proper blending of these ingredients make a cloud of incense to the Father God as it passes to Him through His Christ, and our mediator.

C. **The Daily Ministrations**

There were certain things in the sanctuary services that were known as the daily ministrations.

There was "the daily sacrifice", "the daily lamplighting" and here "the daily incense". These ministrations took place in the morning and evening. There was a continual ascent to the Lord in His heavenly sanctuary as well as His earthly sanctuary of sacrifice, light and incense.

Believer-priests are to fulfil these daily services by presenting themselves to God as a daily sacrifice, daily trimming their lamps and a daily supply of the oil of the Spirit, and a daily ascent of prayer and its ingredients before the Lord. Our prayer life should be revealed in thought, word and deed. There should be the spirit of prayer and the life of prayer continually before the Lord.

D. **The Incense of Prayer**

There is no mistaking the interpretation of the symbol of incense. Incense, with its ingredients always speaks of the prayer of the saints and the ingredients of prayer.

Prayer is set forth before the Lord as incense (Psalm 141:1-2). The Jehovah Angel is given much incense that He should offer it with the prayers of all saints before the golden altar and before God's throne (Revelation 8:1-5).

The multitude of the people were standing, praying without, in the court at the time of Zacharias offering of the incense (Luke 1:5-11).

The 24 elders, as king-priests, have bowls full of incense which are the prayers of the saints (Revelation 5:8).

E. **Strange Incense**

A number of Scriptures speak of Israel, as also other nations, offering "strange incense" to God.

The Lord, through Moses, forbade any imitation or substitute or making of the ingredients of the incense (Exodus 30:9).

"Strange incense" is that incense which is foreign to God and contrary to His Word. It speaks of substitution and imitation of Divine things. Nadab and Abihu offered strange fire before the Lord and were struck dead for such presumption (Leviticus 10:1-3. Note also Numbers 16 and the brazen censers of Korah and his company as "sinners against their own souls"). They brought judgment on themselves and their families for such presumption through pride and self-will.

Strange incense and all kinds of incense are an abomination to God since the rending of the veil of the Temple at Calvary's finished work (Isaiah 1:13; 66:3). It speaks of false worship, worship excited by sensuality as in heathen religions and cults, both inside and outside Christendom (Deuteronomy 18:9-14).

So today it speaks of the fact that all prayers, intercessions and meditation that are contrary to God's Word, that bypass Jesus Christ and endeavours to go to God direct apart from His Son is "strange incense". Such prayers are totally unacceptable to God and are an abomination to God. Such persons will be "cut off" by the judgments of the Lord (Psalm 66:18-19; Proverbs 28:9; Isaiah 66:3).

F. Presumption at the Golden Altar

It seemed as if a spirit of pride, self-will and presumption would come upon some of the kings of Judah at times. No doubt this would be instigated by Satan, the personification of pride, self-will and presumption.

Ahaz presumed to remove God's brazen altar from its rightful position and place his substitute and Assyrian-like altar beside it and act in priestly presumption, trying to be a king-priest.

He also removed the foundational twelve oxen off the great molten sea and set it on a pavement of stones.

He also took the brazen lavers off their bases, all in acts of pride, self-will and presumption. These were outer court vessels.

But in 2 Chronicles 26 we have the godly king Uzziah, in a moment of pride, moving in presumption and self-will from the outer court into the holy place. Here he dares to bypass God's appointed and anointed high priest, along with 84 other priests and presumes to offer incense before the Lord. He tried to unite the offices of king and priest. He was smitten with leprosy in the forehead while enraged at the priests who endeavoured to withstand his presumptuous act. It was at this time that the prophet Isaiah "saw the Lord sitting on His throne" in the heavenly Temple. While earthly kings may be deprived and disposed from their thrones, there is the eternal throne of God which will never be vacated. God and the Lamb are in that eternal throne.

This whole scene becomes prophetic of all leaders who rise in priestly presumption seeking to bypass God's Christ and His mediatorial work. Such will be smitten by Divine judgment. What a contrast to Uzziah's leprous forehead and the linen mitre with "Holiness to the Lord" on the forehead of the high priest.

G. The Golden Altar in Revelation

The final significance of the golden altar of incense is seen in the Book of Revelation.
In Revelation 8:1-5 we see the Jehovah Angel at the golden altar of incense and then, after receiving the incense — prayers of the saints, turning the golden censer upside down with God coming into activity in the affairs of earth.

In Revelation 9:13 there is a voice from the golden altar before the throne.

In Revelation 11:1 the altar of incense is measured, along with the temple of God, while the outer court is left unmeasured, to be trodden under foot for 3½ years of judgment.

In Revelation 14:18 and 16:7 it is possible that the voice comes from the altar of gold here also, in the midst of great judgments in the earth.

It is evident that the prayers and intercessions of the saints will come to their fulness in the final days prior to and unto the coming of Christ. The fragrance will fill heaven's Temple. His house shall be called the house of prayer for all nations (Matthew 21:13; Mark 11:17; Isaiah 52:6-8).

The sweetness of the incense could not be known until the action of fire caused it to ascend to God (Philippians 4:18).

The spirit of prayer and intercession will increase in the house of the Lord and His people in the final days.

The early church continued stedfastly in the apostles doctrine, in fellowship, breaking of bread and prayers (Acts 2:42).

We are to pray always with all prayer and supplication in the Sprit (Ephesians 6:18). We are to continue in prayer (Colossians 4:2; Romans 12:12). Christ is our supreme example of prayer.

In conclusion we see today that the golden censer is the believer's heart; the incense is the prayer-life and its ingredients, and the fire is the power of the Holy Spirit causing prayer to ascend to the heavenly sanctuary, to God through Christ.

Such is the beauty of the golden altar of incense in the Temple of the Lord.

CHAPTER TWENTYNINE

THE WINDOWS OF THE HOUSE

In 1 Kings 6:4 we have reference to the windows of the house of the Lord.

"For the house he made windows of narrow lights" (A.V.).

"For the house he made windows broad within, and narrow without" (A.V. Marginal reference).

It seems that these windows were probably at the top of the house in the walls which were 30 cubits high.

The Scripture tells us that at least 15 cubits of the height of the walls outside the house was taken up by the priestly chambers which surrounded the Temple, thus leaving 15 cubits above them which could be for these windows.

Then we note that the holy of holies was 20 cubits high (and perhaps even the holy place), so these windows could be at the top of the house as well as in the upper chambers. However, the purpose of these windows seemed to be for some Divine purpose which we consider here.

These windows were made of lattice work.

Windows in Scripture have their significance, even as they do in our day in our houses.

Noah's ark had a window in the third story. Noah could not see out and down but he could look to that which was heavenly. He would not see the desolation of ungodly flesh by the flood (Genesis 6:16; 8:6).

The windows of heaven were opened when the flood of judgment came on the earth and the rains descended (Genesis 7:11).

The Scripture speak of "the windows of heaven" being opened or closed according to man's obedience or disobedience (2 Kings 7:2,19; Isaiah 24:18; 60:8; Malachi 3:10). God told Israel to prove Him with tithes and offerings and He would open the windows of heaven and pour out blessing they could not contain.

It was a window with a scarlet thread in it that was the sign of salvation to Rahab and her household (Joshua 2:15-21). The sign of three days and the sign of the scarlet thread was deliverance to her whole house. It was in the window.

Daniel prayed with his window open towards Jerusalem three times daily while he was in Babylonish captivity (Daniel 6:10). As the smoke of the incense would arise from the altar through the windows to the heavens, so Daniel's prayers would arise out of his window unto heaven's sanctuary.

The bridegroom showed himself through the lattice and the windows in order to draw the bride after himself (Song of Solomon 2:9). The temple windows were latticed.

Solomon built a house in Lebanon with windows in three rows, and light was over against light in three ranks (2 Kings 7:2-5).

Other Scriptures relative to windows are 2 Kings 13:17; Ezekiel 40:16-26; Zephaniah 2:14; Isaiah 54:12; 1 Chronicles 15:29; 2 Samuel 6:16; Acts 20:9.

The language used of the windows is significant also. They were "broad within" and "narrow without". Jesus said, "Broad is the way to destruction . . . narrow is the way to life" (Matthew 7:13,14). To the world, Christ is "narrow" but to the believer Christ is "broad". In Christ the believer knows the truth.

Undoubtedly the main purpose of the windows was to allow the fragrance of the incense as it ascended and filled the holy place to escape heavenward.

Symbolically it pointed to the prayers of Israel ascending from the golden altar to God's throne in heaven. As the incense ascended from the windows in the earthly sanctuary of the Lord, so the Lord would open the windows of heaven and pour out His blessings on His people.

Also there would be the thought of latticed windows which would regulate the light in the height of the Temple. However, the fulness of light in the holy place was seen in the ten golden lampstands. In the holy oracle it was the very Shekinah-Glory light and presence of God that illumined that place which would have been in absolute darkness without that light of God.

God regulates the light to His people. God receives the prayers of the saints. It has been said that the ''eyes are the window of the soul'' of man.

The Lord Jesus Christ, our beloved bridegroom, shows Himself to His people as He stands behind the wall (like the Temple wall), looking forth through the windows (like the Temple windows), showing Himself through the lattice (like the Temple latticed windows) as He draws our hearts after Himself.

Truly every bit of the Temple speaks of His glory (Psalm 29:9).

THE HIGH PRIEST WITH GOLDEN CENSER

HIGH PRIEST WITH GOLDEN CENSER

A GOLDEN CENSER

FRANKINCENSE

CHAPTER THIRTY

THE HOLY ORACLE

A very rich truth is seen in the expression used much of the most holy place of the Temple, or the holiest of all.

We note some of the distinctive names of the most holy place of the house of the Lord.

A. **Names of the Holiest of All**

  1. The most holy house (2 Chronicles 3:10).

  2. The inner house (1 Kings 6:27).

  3. The holy place (Hebrews 9:12).

  4. The holiest of all (Hebrews 9:3).

  5. The holy of holinesses (Marginal).

  6. The holy oracle.

  7. The most holy place (1 Kings 6:16).

  8. The oracle (1 Kings 6:16,19,20,21,22,23).

B. **The Oracle**

The interpretation of the oracle is most significant. "The Oracle" literally means "The speaking place".

The most holy place was the oracle, the very place of the voice of God, speaking to the high priest from off the blood-stained mercy seat of the ark of the Covenant (Numbers 7:89). This voice spoke from between the Cherubim, through the blood to the high priest, and then he communicated to the people of God. There God communicated His mind to His people.

Once a year the high priest entered on the Day of Atonement and saw this blazing glory amidst the cloud of incense.

Note also Exodus 25:22; Numbers 7:89 again.

The same truth is manifested in the breastplate of the high priest. There God spoke and communicated His mind by means of the mysterious Urim and Thummin, the two precious stones in the breastplate of the high priest (Exodus 28; 2 Samuel 16:23).

Enquiring of the Urim and Thummin would be as a man enquiring at the oracle (Hebrew "dabar", or "word"). All other Scriptures in the Old Testament which are translated "oracle" come from the Hebrew word "debir", or "speaking place". The New Testament equivalent is the Greek word "logion" meaning "word", from which Logos, THE WORD is seen (John 1:1-3,14-18).

We note some of the beautiful references to the oracle and see how God has fulfilled all in Christ. Christ is God's speaking place to man. God has nothing to say to man apart from Christ.

  * The holiest of all was God's oracle, God's speaking place to Israel in the Temple (1 Kings 6:5-31; 7:49; 8:6-8; 2 Chronicles 3:16; 4:20; 5:7-9).

  * The Psalmist says, I will lift up my hands towards thy holy oracle (Marginal reference, "toward the oracle of thy sanctuary") (Psalm 28:2).

  * The ten commandments received from the Lord by Moses are spoken of as being "the lively oracles", given to the church in the wilderness by the mediator Moses (Acts 7:38).

  * To Israel was committed the oracles of God, their chief blessing. This consisted of the sacred Scriptures (Romans 3:2).

* The first principles of the doctrine of Christ are also referred to as the oracles of God (Hebrews 5:12).

* Peter exhorted any one who spoke to speak as the oracles of God (1 Peter 4:11).

All of this truth is fulfilled in the Lord Jesus Christ. He is God's "holiest of all". He is God's "oracle" — God's speaking place. God's speaking place is in the person of His Son now, THE TEMPLE of God.

He is God's Temple (John 2:19-21). God spoke to Him, through Him, and by Him. God has spoken to us in the person of His Son (Hebrews 1:1-3). Christ is also God's mercy seat, blood stained. God has nothing to say to man outside of Christ, only judgment.
The student should read these Scriptures (Deuteronomy 18:15-21; John 1:1-4,14-18; 3:31-36; 5:7-17; 8:43,47; 10:37-38; 12:44-50; 14:10). The words that Jesus spoke were not His words. They were His Father's words. He spoke as the Father gave Him commandment what to speak. He spoke what His Father spoke. To hear Him is to hear the Father.

It is this word, the Father's word, that will be our judge in "that day".

The church now is to be God's oracle. God speaks to man today through His church, His house and through His people (Jeremiah 15:19). If we take forth the precious from the vile, then we can be as His mouthpiece.

We speak for Christ as Christ spoke for God. This is the richness of truth as seen in the holy oracle of Solomon's Temple.

THE ARK OF THE COVENANT

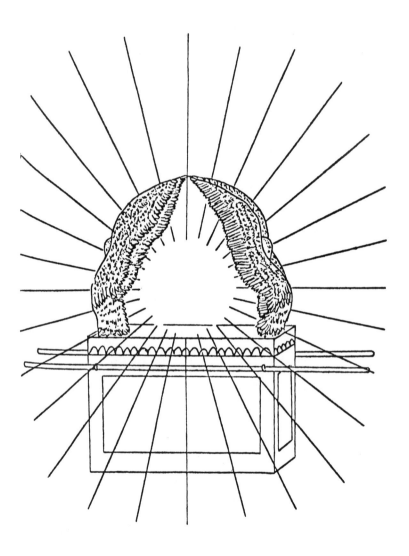

Diagram — Ray S. Jackson (Snr)

CHAPTER THIRTYONE

THE ARK OF THE COVENANT

In our previous chapters we have dealt with the furniture in the outer court, the furniture in the holy place. Now we come to the furniture in the holiest of all, the holy oracle. This article is the magnificent ark of Covenant.

The ark of the Covenant was the most important article of furniture. All other articles became meaningful in the light of this piece. The ark gave spiritual character and significance to all other articles. It was upon the ark that the visible manifestation of God's glory and presence dwelt and it was from between the Cherubim and the mercy seat that the audible voice of God spoke and was heard by the high priest.

We move on in our study to the fuller significance of the marvellously designed ark of the Lord, the very throne of God in the earth, in the midst of Israel, His chosen people.

It is significant that there were three arks in Scripture, each of them having to do with waters of judgment and deliverance for the people of God.
These arks were the following:

1. Noah's ark carried Noah over the judgment waters of the Flood and witnessed the death of all ungodly flesh (Genesis 6:24).

2. Moses ark carried him through the waters of death in the river Nile while other children suffered death (Exodus 2:3-5).

3. God's ark opened the waters of Jordan for Israel to pass into the promised land (Exodus 25:22 with Joshua 3-4 chapters).

A. **The Ark of the Covenant**

There was only ever one ark of the Covenant. David was not given revelation to make another or a new ark. This was the one and only ark, given by revelation to Moses at Mt Sinai, placed in the Tabernacle of Moses, then transferred in time to the Tabernacle of David, and finally here transferred into the Temple of Solomon, its ultimate resting place. The ark was the only article of furniture brought from the Tabernacle of Moses into Solomon's Temple.
Again, it speaks of the fact that there is but one Christ of God, one mediator between God and man. He will eternally be the one and the same Saviour and sacrifice for sin (John 14:1,6; 1 Timothy 2:5; Hebrews 10:12-14).

One brazen altar, one brazen laver, one lampstand, one table, one altar of incense was seen in Moses Tabernacle. One brazen altar, one molten, one altar of incense was seen in the Temple. Ten brazen lavers, ten lampstands, ten tables of shewbread are in the Temple. But there is only ever ONE ARK OF THE COVENANT in either Tabernacle or Temple. There is only ever and eternally ONE THRONE of God and the Lamb (Revelation 22:1-2).

From "*The Tabernacle of Moses*" we note the brief design of the ark and its symbolic details, as well as weaving throughout further truths as seen in the ark in Solomon's Temple.

1. **Its Revelation** — Exodus 25:1-22

   The ark was given by revelation to Moses in Mt Sinai. It was not of human imagination of origin. It originated out of the heart of God and His desire to have a place to dwell among His redeemed people.

2. **Its Construction** — Exodus 37:1-9

   It was made by the wisdom and the ability of the Spirit of God according to the Divine pattern given to Moses in the mount.

3. **Its Measurements**

In shape it was like an oblong box or chest with a lid on the top of it. Its measurements were 2½ cubits long, 1½ cubits wide and 1½ cubits high.

Its significance is that the grate of the brazen altar in Moses Tabernacle (blood sacrifice), and the table of shewbread (communion) and the blood-sprinkled mercy seat on the ark of the Covenant (atonement, propitiation, reconciliation) were the same height.

So Christ is our sacrificial Saviour, our Bread of communion and our blood-sprinkled mercy seat. All these are connected in His one person. Only as we are redeemed by blood sacrifice can we have communion in the light of His presence and His mercy.

4. **Its Materials**

The ark was made of acacia wood overlaid with gold within and without. Wood speaks of His incorruptible humanity, and gold His Divinity. Two materials, yet one ark; two natures yet one person, the God-Man.

This was the only article from the Tabernacle of Moses placed within the Temple. The acacia wood would remind Israel of their wanderings in the wilderness over the 40 years and their entrance to the land of promise where the kingdom was established, symbolized in the Temple by the cedar wood.

5. **Its Contents**

There were four articles relative to the ark, three of which were placed inside, and one in the side of the ark although not specifically stated how it was placed. These articles were:

* **The Tables of the Law** — Exodus 25:16-17; Deuteronomy 10:5; 31:26.
  Such was symbolic of the Father's law, the source of all order, authority and government. By these laws the nation was governed and protected morally, socially and spiritually, as long as they kept them. It also points to the fact that the Father's law was in the heart of Christ who is the only man who kept these laws perfectly (Psalm 40:8; Hebrews 10:7). The Father is the Law-giver.

* **The Golden Pot of Manna** — Exodus 16; Hebrews 9:4; John 6; Revelation 2:17.
  The manna was symbolic of the blessed Son of God, the heavenly bread of God without which all men will die.

* **The Rod of Aaron that Budded** — Numbers 17:10; Hebrews 9:4
  This speaks of the Holy Spirit, who is the life-giving one, sealing the priesthood of the Lord Jesus Christ by resurrection life and power. Even as the budding rod confirmed Aaron's anointed and appointed priesthood by the manifestation of life, so does the resurrection for Christ Jesus.

* **The Book of the Covenant** — Deuteronomy 31:26; 1 Kings 22
  The Book of the Covenant was placed in the side of the ark, though how is not specifically stated. However, it speaks of the Bible, the Book of God's covenantal dealings are written in His covenant book.

Thus we have four particular articles relative to the ark of the covenant. In another aspect we may see how all these articles in the ark speak of that which is fulfilled ''in Christ''.

Christ is THE WAY (God's Law), THE TRUTH (God's Bread), and THE LIFE (God's Rod). John 14:1,6. All find fulfilment in Him personally.

Christ is also God's NEW Covenant (The Living Word, The Living Bible) personified (Isaiah 42:1-8; 49:6-8).

The ark involved the three aspects of the law of God, these being, the moral law in the ten commandments, the civil law in the book of the law, and then the ceremonial law involved in the sacrificial blood on the mercy seat. The law was given by Moses but grace and truth came by Jesus Christ (John 1:17; Isaiah 42:21).

6. **Its Names**

The ark was known by various names and designations each of them having some distinctive aspect of truth the Lord wanted to impress upon Israel, His people. It was called:

* The Ark of the Testimony (Exodus 25:22)

* The Ark of the Covenant of the Lord (Numbers 10:33)

* The Ark of the Lord God (1 Kings 2:26)

* The Ark of the Lord, the Lord of all the earth (Joshua 3:13)

* The Ark of God (1 Samuel 3:3)

* The Holy Ark (2 Chronicles 35:3)

* The Ark of Thy Strength (Psalm 132:8)

* The Ark of the Covenant of God (Judges 20:27)

* The Ark of the Covenant (Joshua 3:6)

* The Ark of the Lord (Joshua 4:11)

* The Ark of the God of Israel (1 Samuel 5:7)

* The Ark of Acacia Wood (Exodus 25:10)

7. **Its Crown**

The ark had a crown of gold round about on the top of it. No doubt this also acted as a seat for the lid of the ark called the mercy seat. The crown speaks of Christ's kingship. The holiest of all was actually God's throne-room for the nation of Israel. He is the King of kings and Lord of lords. He is the King of the Jews. The Gospel of Matthew reveals Him as the king of His kingdom (Matthew 2:2). He is also king-priest eternally (Psalm 110:1-2; Hebrews 7:1-12; Psalm 2:6).

8. **Its Transport**

For transport the ark had four rings of gold in the four corners. These were to have staves of acacia wood overlaid with gold placed in them and were used for the transport of the ark in the wilderness journeyings to the promised land.

These staves were never to be taken from the ark until it entered the Temple. The ark was borne on the shoulders of the priests during the wilderness days.

However, once the ark was taken into the Temple of the Lord, the staves were taken out. Its journeyings were over. The staves were placed in such a position that the priests could see the ends of them, thus reminding them of their past pilgrimages and the promises of God now fulfilled in the land of rest (1 Kings 8:8; 1 Chronicles 15:15).

9. **Its Coverings**

In transport in the wilderness and pilgrimage days the ark was always covered from human eyes with the vail, the badgers skins and a cloth of blue. Symbolically we may view these coverings:

* **The Vail** — symbolic of the Son's humanity, the vail of His flesh rent at Calvary (Numbers 4:5-6; Hebrews 10:19-21).

* **The Badgers Skins** — symbolic of the Father God, who is over all and above all.

* **The Cloth of Blue** — symbolic of the Holy Spirit and heavenly authority.

Relating to Christ Himself, we would say that these three coverings speak of the Son's humanity (the vail), the Son's submission to authority (the blue), and as to Calvary, there was no beauty that we should desire Him (the badgers skins). Only those who had revelation of who He was really saw the beauty in Christ as God's covenant, but the unregenerate eyes never saw anything but the man after the flesh and thus missed the Christ of God in His earthly walk.

10. **Its Mercy Seat**

The covering or lid of the ark was the mercy seat with its magnificence in the cherub on each end and the mercy seat between, all beaten out of one piece of pure gold. It acted as a lid fitting within the crown on the box-like ark of the Covenant.

The mercy seat and the Cherubim overlooking the blood-stained mercy seat was fashioned out of one piece of gold. This triunity becomes a magnificent symbolic representation of the Godhead as Father, Son and Holy Spirit.

* **One Cherub** — symbolic of the Father.

* **The Mercy Seat** — symbolic of the Son, blood-stained, our propitiation (Greek "hilasterion". Mercy seat. Romans 3:25).

* **One Cherub** — symbolic of the Holy Spirit.

As the faces of the Cherubim gazed one toward another and yet toward the mercy seat and the blood, so the Father and the Holy Spirit gaze toward each other and yet look with satisfaction upon the sacrificial blood of Jesus Christ at Calvary. When I see the blood, I will pass over you (Exodus 12).

In the Temple there were an additional two great Cherubim made of olive wood overlaid with gold and placed within the holy oracle, overshadowing the ark of the Covenant. Therefore, treatment of the theme of the Cherubim will be covered more fully in the succeeding chapter.

B. **The Name of the Lord**

A study of these Scriptures reveal that the ark of the Covenant was the article of furniture upon which THE NAME OF THE LORD dwelt. This was the place where the redemptive name dwelt. Here between the Cherubim the glory-presence of God was manifested (2 Samuel 6:1-2; 2 Chronicles 5:14; 13:6).

From an earlier chapter we remember that the purpose of the building of the Temple was that God may have a place where His name could dwell, where His name could be made known to all nations. The name of the Lord in redemptive revelation is seen in the Old Testament compound redemptive names of Jehovah. All find their ultimate fulfilment in the New Testament compound redemptive name of the Lord Jesus Christ.

This is the greatest compound redemptive name ever to be revealed in this age or the ages to come, for it comprehends in a triune name all the redemptive names of God in the Old Testament (Acts 2:34-37; Ephesians 1:19-23).

C. **The History of the Ark of God**

There is absolutely no doubt that the history of the ark foreshadowed the history of the Lord Jesus Christ. Its history is "His Story" indeed! All that the ark was to Israel is what Christ is to His church.

The reader will bear with some repetition as we outline as briefly as possible the history of the ark of the Lord. However, it should be remembered that there are more details concerning the history of the ark of the Covenant than any of the other articles of furniture. This is rightly so. For, the ark of God, to Israel, represents His throne, His presence, His glory among His people.

In our brief outline we will endeavour to relate all to Christ who is God's ark of the Covenant personified.

1. The ark was made according to the pattern by the enablement of the Spirit of God in wisdom (Exodus 35:31-36:2; 25:10-22). This was prophetic of Christ's incarnation.

2. The ark was made by the wisdom and Spirit of God. So Christ was conceived of the Holy Spirit in the wisdom of God (Matthew 1:18-21; Luke 1:30-33).

3. It was the ark of the testimony (Exodus 26:33-34; 30:6). Christ is God's testimony to mankind.

4. The ark was anointed with holy oil (Exodus 30:26). Christ is God's anointed.

5. The ark was never exposed to human eyes in wilderness wanderings (Numbers 4:44-45). Christ was never seen in the fulness of His glory by unregenerate human eyes in His earthly walk.

6. The voice of God spoke from the ark of the Covenant (Exodus 25:22; Numbers 7:89). God spoke through Christ Jesus, who is God's mercy seat (Leviticus 16:2).

7. The ark was the Israelites ark of strength (Psalm 132:6-8). Christ is God's strength to His people.

8. The ark was set in the holiest of all. God has set Christ in heaven's holiest of all, within the veil (Exodus 40:3-5,20-21; 39:35; Hebrews 6:18-20).

9. The ark had the law, the manna, the budding rod within it (Hebrews 9:4). So Christ kept God's law, He was the bread of heaven, and He was raised from death to life as God's eternal high priest.

10. The ark had the book of the law in the side of it (Deuteronomy 31:9,25-26). So Christ is God's new covenant available for all repentant and believing mankind.

11. The cloud overshadowed the ark of the Covenant in the Tabernacle (Exodus 40:34-38). So the glory overshadowed Christ on the Mt of Transfiguration (Matthew 17:1-5). The voice spoke out of the cloud.

12. There was shouting and joy as the ark entered the city, so there was when Christ entered the city of Jerusalem on the donkey (Matthew 21:1-11; 2 Samuel 6:12-18).

13. Those who despised the ark of God and expressions of joy were smitten with barrenness physically (2 Samuel 6:20-23; 1 Chronicles 15:29). Spiritual barrenness comes to churches which despise the manifestations of the Spirit of God on His people because of His presence.

14. The ark was in the Tabernacle of David for many years amidst continual music, singing and instruments with sacrifices of praise (1 Chronicles 16:4,37,42). So there is singing in the midst of the church (Hebrews 2:12).

15. The ark was taken into captivity by the Gentile Philistines. They wanted to know what to do TO the ark, and what to do WITH the ark (1 Samuel 6:2; 5:8). When the ark was taken Israel fled (1 Samuel 4:10).
    So the disciples fled when Christ was taken to the Gentiles for crucifixion. They all wanted to know what to do TO Christ and WITH Christ (Matthew 27:22; Luke 6:11).

16. The ark was carried across the brook Kidron with the rejected king David at one time (2 Samuel 15:23-24). So Christ came across the brook Kidron (John 18:1). He was about to be despised and rejected of men.

17. The ark experienced 3 days journey seeking rest for the people of God. In this time the Tabernacle was taken down, the glory removed as it went to find rest for Israel. The glory returned when the Tabernacle was set up again (Numbers 10:33-36). So Christ was taken down from the cross, and then 3 days later resurrected in a glorified body as He brought rest from sin and Satan to the church, the New Testament people of God (Matthew 12:38-40).

18. The ark led the way into the Jordan, the river of judgment, 2000 cubits ahead of the people, and then held the waters back for Israel to pass through (Joshua 3:3-15). So Christ has conquered the waters of death about 2000 years ago, making way for the church to follow.

19. The ark was sprinkled with blood on the great Day of Atonement when the priest went within the veil (Leviticus 16). So Christ is both our high priest and is blood-sprinkled by Calvary and has gone within the veil of the heavenly sanctuary (Hebrews 9-10 chapters; Romans 5:11).

20. The position of the ark was "in the midst" of the camp of Israel when in the wanderings period, and also as they marched (Numbers 2:17; 10:14-28). Christ is always "in the midst" of His people when they gather together in His name (Matthew 18:18-20).

21. Presuming to fight without the ark of God meant defeat (Numbers 14:44-45). Without Christ there is defeat in battles against Satan's kingdom.

22. The ark meant blessing to Israel but judgment to the enemies (1 Samuel 4:1-22; 1 Samuel 5; 2 Samuel 6:11). So the Gospel of Christ is life to those who believe and death to those who reject (2 Corinthians 2:15-16).

23. The ark was the place where the high priest and people enquired for the mind of God (Joshua 21:1-2). Christ is God's oracle, the person we seek in order to find the mind of God the Father (1 Timothy 2:5; Hebrews 7:26-27).

24. No false god could stand before the ark of the true God if Israel (1 Samuel 5:1-4). So all false gods of men and devils will fall before His glory (John 18:6; Philippians 2:1-10).

25. Seven priests with seven trumpets preceded the ark when Jericho city fell. At the seventh time, on the seventh day, at the sound of the seventh trumpet there was a great shout and the city collapsed. The kingdom was possessed by the Israel of God (Joshua 6; Hebrews 11:30). In Revelation we see seven angels with seven trumpets. At the sounding of the seventh (the last) trumpet the kingdoms of this world become the kingdoms of our God and His Christ. He comes with a great shout at the last trump (1 Thessalonians 4:16).

26. The ark was placed "in the midst" of two companies of the tribes Israel, one on Mt Ebal, the mount of cursing, and the other on Mt Gerizim, the mount of blessing (Joshua 8:30-35 and Deuteronomy 11:29). The day will come when all nations will stand before Christ. The ones on the right hand come into blessing, and the ones on the left hand come into cursing and judgment (Matthew 25:32-46).

27. The ark eventually is taken from the Tabernacle of David and set in the Temple of Solomon, its final resting place (1 Kings 8). However, this brings us to our final thoughts in this chapter.

In our overview of the history of the ark, we see the truths of Christ's incarnation, His anointing, His rejection, His humiliation at the hands of the Gentiles and Israel, His resurrection, ascension, exaltation, glorification and enthronement at the Father's right hand. The history of the ark also shows Christ's position in the midst of His people, and brings us to His second coming and the final judgments on all nations.

What tremendous truth is seen in the Biblical revelation and history of the ark of the Covenant. It is truly "His Story", the Christ of history!

The Tabernacle of Moses sets forth more of Christ's humiliation, while the Temple of Solomon sets forth more of Christ's exaltation, yet both complete each other is symbolic revelation.

D. The Ark of God into the Temple of God

Having traced in brief outline the history of the ark from its revelation and construction and its journeys through the wilderness into Canaan land, we come now to the ark's final resting place — in the Temple of the Lord.

The Temple was actually built to house the ark of God. King David expressed his burden when he dwelt in a house of cedars while the ark of God was in a tent. It was this concern for God's throne in earth that precipitated his desire to build a house for the Lord. This desire of David was fulfilled through his son Solomon who built the Temple according to the pattern given to David (1 Chronicles 28:1-2; 17:1-27; 2 Chronicles 6:41; 2 Samuel 7:1-29).

The Lord had dwelt in a tent up to this time. The Temple would be God's rest.

Solomon, at the completion of the Temple, went to Mt Zion, to the Tabernacle of David where the ark of God had been for about 30 years or more to bring it into its resting place (1 Kings 8:1-11). From Mt Zion it was brought to Mt Moriah, or, from the Tabernacle of David to the Temple of Solomon.

In the Temple it was placed in the most holy place which was called "the holy oracle", or "the speaking place". The holy oracle was "His place" (2 Chronicles 6:7).

It is significant that the ark was the first article made for the Tabernacle but it was the last piece to enter the Temple. Christ is also "the first and the last", the beginning and the ending, THE Alpha and Omega (Genesis 1:1; Revelation 22:21). In the volume of the book it is written of Him (Psalm 40:7-8; Hebrews 10:5-8).

1. The Contents of the Ark — 1 Kings 8:9; 2 Chronicles 5:10

When the ark was placed in the Temple the only contents in the ark were the two tables of the law of God. The golden pot of manna was removed. The budding rod of Aaron was gone. The law of God only remained.

Perhaps the significance of these may be seen in the following thoughts. The manna was a result of the murmurings of Israel in the wilderness days. The manna was also a wilderness food. When Israel entered Canaan land they partook of the fruit of the land (Joshua 5:12). It seems also to have prophetic significance in the Book of Revelation. There the overcomer is given the promise of eating the hidden manna (Revelation 2:17). The hidden manna speaks of eternal life. It corresponds with the tree of eternal life which will be restored to those who are redeemed (Revelation 22:1-4).

The budding rod of Aaron also was the result of the murmurings of Israel in the wilderness. God confirmed Aaron's priesthood by the sign of the budding rod. Aaron was the high priest of the wilderness days. Since Israel entered Canaan Eleazer was the high priest of this first period. In New Covenant times Christ is our eternal and great high priest, having no successor to His ministry. He lives in the power of an endless life after the order of Melchisedek. So there is no need of the budding rod for all who enter the eternal kingdom of God. Christ's priesthood is for ever settled by the fact of His resurrection and ascension to heaven.

The law remains. God's law is eternal, spiritual, holy, just and good. The law of the Lord is perfect. It is the eternal law of love and loving obedience. Angelic beings or redeemed mankind will live eternally according to God's holy law. All will keep the law of love; love to God and love to one another. All other laws are fulfilled in the law of love. Self-will is lawlessness. In that day all will know the law of the Lord and keep in the heart, perfectly, even as Christ did (Hebrews 8:10-12; Psalm 40:8; Hebrews 10:7; Deuteronomy 10:5; 31:26).

2.   **The Removal of the Staves** — 1 Kings 8:1-11; 2 Chronicles 5:1-10

The staves were never taken out while the ark was in the Tabernacle in the wilderness, or in the journeying period (Exodus 25:15). It spoke of the fact that there was no permanent rest while travelling in the wilderness. It was the period of wandering. Christ, as the Son of Man had nowhere to lay His head while in His earthly walk. The Temple would be the place of rest. So Christ has entered into heaven's sanctuary, the heavenly Temple, and has found rest in the finished work of atonement. This rest is for the believer, not now in a land but in a person (Matthew 11:28-30).

The Psalmist speaks of the ark coming into rest in the Temple of God (Psalms 132:8. Read also these Scriptures pertaining to the ark of God in the holy Temple. 1 Kings 3:15; 6:19; 1 Chronicles 6:31; 13:3-14; 15:1-29; 16:1-6,37; 17:1; 22:19; 28:2,18; 2 Chronicles 1:4; 5:1-10; 6:11,41; 8:11; 35:3; Hebrews 9:4).

The tent stage was significant of the pilgrimage character of God's people. They lived in tents in the wilderness days. Now in Canaan land houses replace tents. Permanency is taking precedence over wanderings.

The Temple stage speaks of rest, permanence and victory over all enemies. The Temple is God's place of rest, His dwelling place amongst the redeemed Israel of God. Such is the truth symbolized in the removal of the staves from the ark of the Lord.

E.   **The Throne Room of the Lord**

It has already been noted that the holiest of all in both Tabernacle and Temple was foursquare as to its measurements. This foursquare room symbolized the very throne room of God amongst His people.

It points, as do all foursquares in both Tabernacle and Temple to the ultimate foursquare in the Book of Revelation, the foursquare city of God. John saw the holy city, the New Jerusalem, coming down out of heaven as a bride adorned for her husband. The city was foursquare, it's streets of gold. In it was the throne of God and the Lamb (Revelation 21-22).

In that city there will no veil between. All the redeemed as kings and priests unto God will have access.

CONCLUSION

In bringing this chapter to a close it worthy to note the very final mention of the ark of God in both Old and New Testaments.

In the Old Testament the final mention of the ark is found in Jeremiah 3:16. There the Lord told Israel that the time was coming when they would no more remember the ark, or talk about the ark of the Lord, nor would it even come into their mind. This is a remarkable prophecy when the ark was the most important article of furniture in the whole history of nation, for Tabernacle of Moses, Tabernacle of David and Temple of Solomon.

At that time they would seek the Lord and His throne at Jerusalem. That is, the eternal throne and the eternal Jerusalem, not the earthly thing which would pass away.

The final mention of the ark in the New Testament is found in Revelation 11:19. There John sees the heavenly Temple opened and the ark of God sending forth flashings of Divine activity into the earth. This is the eternal ark or throne of God. The ark on earth was but the passing shadow of the eternal. This is the ark or throne of God that believers will gather around in the ages to come, for all eternity to worship God the Father and the redeeming Lamb, His Son.

The contrast between the Tabernacle of Moses, of David and Solomon's Temple is significant also.

Tabernacle of Moses →	Tabernacle of David →	Temple of Solomon
Outer Court	No Outer Court	Inner and Outer Courts
Brazen Altar	No Brazen Altar	The Great Brazen Altar
Brazen Laver	No Brazen Laver	Ten Brazen Lavers
Holy Place	No Holy Place	Holy Place
One Golden Lampstand	No Golden Lampstand	Ten Golden Lampstands
One Table of Shewbread	No Table of Shewbread	Ten Tables of Shewbread
One Altar of Incense	No Altar of Incense	One Altar of Incense
Most Holy Place	Most Holy Place	The Holy Oracle
The Veil	No Veil	The Doors and The Veil
Ark of the Covenant	Ark of the Covenant	Ark of the Covenant
		Two Olive Cherubim
Silent Worship	Singers and Musicians	Singers and Musicians

God moves ever onwards in His revelation to His people. This was so in Israel's history and it is so in the history of the church. Eternal life is to know God and Jesus Christ whom He sent. For all eternity God will be unveiling and revealing Himself to His redeemed, as we move from "glory to glory".

CHAPTER THIRTYTWO

THE TWO GREAT OLIVE CHERUBIM

One of the most marvellous glories in the Temple were the two great cherubim placed in the holy oracle, or the most holy place, overshadowing the ark of the Covenant. The details given by revelation to king David are to be found in 1 Chronicles 28:18; 1 Kings 6:23-28 and 2 Chronicles 3:10-13; 5:7-8.

Expositors vary in their interpretation of who the cherubim represent. There are three ways in which the cherubim are viewed.

1. Some suggest the cherubim represent the angels who are ministering spirits sent to them who are the heirs of salvation (Hebrews 1:13-14).
    Ezekiel speaks of the covering cherub of the throne of God. He is also called the anointed cherub. There the mystery of iniquity began and he was cast out of the immediate presence of God (Ezekiel 28:12-19). Most expositors interpret this to be also speaking of Satan, the fallen prince and arch-angel of the throne of God until his fall. Hence they interpret the cherubim to be representative of angelic beings.

2. Some suggest that the cherubim represent the redeemed of mankind, especially the cherubim and the living creatures spoken of in Ezekiel 1 and Revelation 4.

3. Others suggest the cherubim to represent the Divine persons in the Godhead.

To the author, there seems to be facets of truth in each of these views. However, the emphasis in this chapter follows the interpretation that the majority of references to the cherubim speak of and more especially relate to the Godhead.

The great Bible theme of *"The Cherubim"* and its progressive revelation seems to confirm this thought as will be developed here.

First we will consider the details given concerning the two great olive cherubim and the truths symbolized therein.

A. The Two Great Olive Cherubim

1. Made of Olive Wood

The two great cherubim were made of olive wood. The olive wood is the oil tree, the source of the anointing oil. The two witnesses in Zechariah and Revelation are likened to olive trees. In them is the fulness of the anointing of the Holy Spirit, the holy oil. These two olive trees are called "the sons of oil" (Zechariah 4: Revelation 11:4).

The Father and the Holy Spirit are together associated in the anointing of the Son of the living God. The Father anointed His Son with the oil of the Holy Spirit who is the anointing (Luke 4:18; Acts 10:38; Isaiah 61:1-3; 1 John 2:20,27).

The anointing oil is the Divine chrisma.

2. Two Great Cherubim

The two great olive cherubim speak of the Father and the Holy Spirit. Together they overshadowed the ark of the covenant. How beautiful to see these two great olive cherubim overshadowing the small ark of the covenant as it was placed in the holy oracle after the wilderness wanderings were over.

So the Father and the Holy Spirit overshadowed the blessed Son of God in His whole earthly pilgrimage unto the entrance into the heavenly Temple of God. Two is also the number of witness. The Father and the Holy Spirit witnessed to all that the Son was, to all He said, to all He did.

Jesus Himself recognized and received the witness of the Father and the Holy Spirit in His life and ministry.

3. **Ten Cubits High**

   The two great olive cherubim were each ten cubits high. Ten is the number of law, of Divine order and responsibility. All was perfect law and order in the holy oracle. Father, Son and Holy Spirit demonstrate Divine order in nature and being.

4. **The Wings of the Cherubim**

   The breadth and height were the same for the two cherubim, that is, ten cubits high and ten cubits broad. The wings of the cherubim equalled twenty cubits across. The tips of their wings touched the walls of the oracle, and touched one another in the midst. Each wing was five cubits wide.

   The ark of the covenant was "in the midst" of these wings of the two great cherubim. Jesus Christ is the one "in the midst" of the eternal Godhead (Matthew 18:20).

   The cherubim in Ezekiel chapters 1 and 10 also have wings. The living creatures in Revelation chapters 4 and 5 also have wings. In Ezekiel they have four wings each. In Revelation they each have six wings.

   Wings in Scripture speak of flight, security and protection of the bird; so the wings of the Almighty God to His own people. The Lord brought Israel out of Egypt unto Himself on eagle's wings (Exodus 19:1-6). The Lord likens Himself to a great eagle stirring His nest for His own (Deuteronomy 32:11).

   Ruth the Gentile came to trust under the shadow of the wings of the Lord (Ruth 2:12). The Psalmist cries to the Lord for the protection of His wings (Psalm 17:8; 36:7; 57:1; 61:4; 63:7; 91:4).

   Jesus called to His people to come and trust under His wings but they would not (Matthew 23:37; Luke 13:34).

   The church is given two wings of a great eagle to fly into her place of safety before the Lord in the time of tribulation and persecution from the great red dragon (Revelation 12:14).

   In the Tabernacle of Moses the priests walked and ministered under the shadow of the wings of the cherubim interwoven in the linen ceiling curtains. In the Temple of Solomon the priests also walked and ministered under the shadow of the wings of the cherubim engraved and ornamented into the Temple walls. All spoke of security, safety, protection from the Lord their God. The prophet Malachi said that the Sun of Righteousness would rise with healing in His wings (Malachi 4:2).

5. **One Measure and One Size**

   The two great olive cherubim were of one measure and one size. This speaks symbolically of the unity of the Father and the Holy Spirit. Father and Spirit are co-equal, co-eternal, working together in the one plan, with one mind, one will, distinguishable yet indivisible as persons in the eternal Godhead.

6. **Overlaid with Gold**

   The two great olive cherubim here were overlaid with gold. This is in contrast to the two cherubim on the mercy seat of the ark of the Covenant. There they were fashioned out of one piece of pure gold. Here the two cherubim are of olive wood overlaid with pure gold.

   In the ark of the Covenant, the truth of triunity is seen because the two cherubim and the mercy seat were fashioned out of one piece of pure gold. Here the distinction of the Father and the Spirit and the Son are seen in the two olive cherubim and the humble ark of the Covenant.

   The two cherubim speak of the two persons of the Godhead, the Father and the Spirit. The olive speaks of the ministry of the Father and Spirit in relation to the anointing; the anointer and the anointing revealed in the Father and the Spirit. The gold speaks of Deity, the Divine nature, the character and righteousness of the Father and the Spirit.

The ark of the Covenant, in this symbolic scene, speaks of the fulness of the Godhead manifested in the Son of God in His humanity (Colossians 1:19; 2:9; Romans 1:20).

7. The Feet of the Cherubim

The cherubim stood upon their feet. It speaks of the fact that God walks and talks with His own. He has promised to walk with us and walk in us as well as walk before us (2 Corinthians 6:16-18).

8. Made of Moveable Work

In 2 Chronicles 3:10 and 1 Chronicles 28:18 we are told that the cherubim were of image work, that is, of moveable work. The Hebrew word "*tsaatsuim*" means moveable work in 2 Chronicles 3:10, marginal reference.

In 1 Chronicles 28:18 it speaks of the "chariot of the cherubim". The Hebrew word "*merkabah*" means "riding chariot".

The thought is linked here then of the chariot of the cherubim with the chariot wheels on the ten brazen lavers in the court of the priests (1 Kings 7:33).

David said, "He rode upon a cherub, and did fly" (2 Samuel 22:11).

Elijah was translated supernaturally to heaven in chariots of the Lord, chariots of fire (2 Kings 2:11,12; 6:17).

The Psalmist speaks of the chariots of God which are in the thousands (Psalm 68:17). The cherubim in Ezekiel's version are seen to be involved in Divine transport of the throne of God. There are "wheels within wheels" and wherever the Spirit went the spirit of the living creatures went. There was such unity of movement and direction there. These "wheels within wheels" seemed to be the chariot of the throne of the Lord in Ezekiel's vision (Ezekiel 1).

The Lord walks and moves with His people and will ultimately translate them to glory.

9. The Faces of the Cherubim

The faces of the cherubim were inward. That is, their faces were toward the house (2 Chronicles 3:13). The house faced the east.

In Ezekiel the living creatures also have wings, feet, faces and chariot wheels.

In the ark of the Covenant the cherubim faces looked one toward another and yet toward the blood-stained mercy seat. They gaze with satisfaction upon redemptive blood, and yet on mercy.

Here the cherubim looked toward the house, toward the east. They would behold the priests in ministry in the holy place and the daily ministrations. They would behold the doors, and the inwrought veil. Yet together they overshadowed the humble ark of the Covenant.

So the Father and the Holy Spirit look toward the house, "whose house are we" (Hebrews 3:1-6). The Godhead behold as the believing priests minister the daily ministrations; fellowship at the table, walking in the light of the lampstands and offering the daily incense at the golden altar.

The Scripture speaks of Cain being driven out from the face of the Lord because he was a liar, and murderer and rejected the blood of the Lamb (Genesis 4). For those redeemed by the blood of the Lamb they shall eternally "see His face" and His name shall be in their forehead (Revelation 22:4).

The bread on the table of the Lord was known as "the bread of His face", or "bread of the faces". In the coming of Christ we shall see Him face to face and not through a dark glass.

10. The Most Holy Place

The two great olive cherubim were placed within the holy oracle, the most holy place. This place, as noted, was foursquare. The floor was overlaid with gold and the very shekinah glory filled this place.

Ultimately it speaks of the foursquare city of God, where the streets are of gold and the city is filled with the glory-light and presence of the eternal Godhead (Revelation 21-22).

B. The Progressive Revelation of the Cherubim

A study of the Bible theme of the cherubim reveals the Divinely progressive revelation. It seems to confirm the cherubim are related more especially to the persons in the Godhead, more than redeemed mankind or angelic hosts. However, these views are not invalidated by this statement.

We pursue the theme in Scripture from the Godhead aspect; i.e., that the two great cherubim represent the Father and the Holy Spirit in connection with the redemptive work of the Son, our Lord Jesus Christ. They can only be touched upon in brief.

1. The Cherubim and the Flaming Sword (Genesis 3:21-24)

In the garden of Eden, after the fall of man, we see the cherubim and the flaming sword placed (Lit. tabernacle, dwell) at the gate of Eden toward the east. The cherubim and the flaming sword guarded the way to the tree of eternal life.

The cherubim represent the Father and the Spirit. The flaming sword represents the Word of God. The Tabernacle of Moses and the Temple of Solomon are shadowed forth in seed form here.

It meant death to go through the sword to make the way open to the tree of life. Jesus has gone through death on Calvary and He offers the tree of life to him who overcomes and keeps the commandments of the Lord (Revelation 2:1-6; 22:14).

2. The Cherubim and the Veil (Exodus 26:31; 36:35; Hebrews 10:19-20)

As seen in the veil in both Tabernacle and Temple the cherubim are inwrought into the very material of fine linen with its respective colours. The veil was a divider and kept man separated from God, hiding the glory of God within. Again the cherubim of the Father and the Spirit inwrought and involved in the redemptive plan with the Son is seen. When Jesus died on the cross, and the veil of His flesh was rent, so the earthly temple was rent from top to bottom. The way into the holiest of all is now open for all who would enter by the body and blood of Jesus.

The shekinah-glory shone through the veil of His flesh on the Mt of Transfiguration (Matthew 17:1-9).

3. The Cherubim and the Mercy Seat (Exodus 25:18-22; 37:7-9; Hebrews 9:5)

Here in the ark of the Covenant we see the two cherubim, one cherub on each end of the mercy seat, yet fashioned out of the same piece of gold. The blood is sprinkled upon the mercy seat.

The Father and the Spirit alone are one with the Son in the redemptive work. The angels cannot have any part in redemption's work. They are but ministering spirits. The Father and the Spirit gaze with satisfaction upon the blood of Jesus shed for our redemption.

Here we have that magnificent revelation of the triunity of the Godhead, the Father, the Son and the Holy Spirit, as seen in the chapter on the ark of the Covenant.

4. The Cherubim and The Voice (Numbers 7:89)

From between the cherubim and the blood-stained mercy seat the high priest heard the audible voice of God. God spoke to Israel through His high priest on the basis of blood atonement.

So all of God's communications to mankind today can only come through blood atonement, through the blood of Jesus. Otherwise there is Divine judgment, not mercy. God speaks through the glory of His Son's redemptive work.

5. **The Cherubim and the Curtains** (Exodus 26:1; 36:8)

In the Tabernacle of Moses, the linen ceiling curtains were interwoven with the cherubims and their wings. The priests walked and ministered under the shadow of those wings. This was their covering, their protection, under the wings of the almighty (Psalm 91:1-2; Exodus 19:1-6; Revelation 12:6).

So, as already seen, the believer is under the shadow and protection of the wings of the Lord God. Under His wings we can safely abide.

6. **The Cherubim and Indwelling** (1 Samuel 4:4; 2 Samuel 6:2; Psalm 80:1)

The very presence of the Lord, His very glory dwelt between the two cherubim on the ark of the Covenant. This was the secret place of the most high (Psalm 91:1-2). So the fulness of the Godhead indwelt Christ. The fulness of the Godhead bodily was manifested in Him (Colossians 1:19; 2:9).

7. **The Cherubim and The Shepherd** (Psalm 80:1; John 10; Hebrews 13:20-21; 1 Peter 5:1-5)

The Psalmist prays that the Shepherd of Israel who dwelt between the cherubim would shine forth. He prays that there would be a manifestation of His glory and that He would visit the vine brought out of Egypt.

Surely we see here the Lord Jesus Christ as the Shepherd of Israel. He shone forth in the incarnation to the vine of Israel. He is the one who leads His flock like a shepherd. He is the good shepherd, the great shepherd and the chief shepherd. He dwells in the eternal Godhead having given His life for His sheep.

We note that the central revelation always connects with the central person in the Godhead, the eternal Son of God.

He is the Shepherd. He went through the sword of Calvary. He shed His blood. His fleshly-veil was rent to make the way open into the presence of God. He laid down His life for the sheep. His blood is the evidence of death, that He went through the sword. It is His blood of the everlasting covenant.

8. **The Cherubim and The Redemptive Name** (2 Samuel 6:2; Isaiah 37:16)

Upon the ark of the Covenant was the very name of the Lord. It was the redemptive name. The Lord Jehovah of Hosts, the Elohim (God) of Israel dwelt between the cherubims. This is the redemptive name of God. His name was called or invoked upon the ark of the Covenant. It is a redemptive covenant name.

So in the name of the Lord Jesus Christ we have the most comprehensive redemptive and covenant name ever to be revealed. It is the name of the eternal Godhead. It is the triune name for the triune God (Acts 2:36).

The name of the Father, and of the Son, and of the Holy Spirit is comprehended in the name of the Lord Jesus Christ. Interpret the name, we interpret the persons behind that glorious name. It is the greatest name ever to be revealed, both in this world and the world to come.

9. **The Cherubim and The King** (Psalm 99:1)

The Psalmist says, The Lord reigneth, He sitteth between the cherubim. In Psalm 80:1 we saw the Shepherd. Here we see the King. Christ is both shepherd and king, but first the shepherd then the king. In His rejection and humiliation He is the shepherd. In His exaltation and enthronement He is the king. We think of many of the kingly Psalms (Psalms 72,24,110 with Zechariah 6:12-13).

He is a king-priest upon His throne for both offices are now united in His one person. He does not sit enthroned between the angels, but He sits in the throne of the eternal Godhead (Revelation 22:1-2).

10. **The Cherubim and The Throne** (Ezekiel chapters 1; 9:3; 10; 11:22).)

    In the vision we see the four faces of the cherubim. They represent the four standards under which the twelve tribes of Israel gathered. There was the face of the man, the lion, the ox and the eagle. The man is the king of creation. The lion is the king of the beasts. The ox is the king of domestic animals. The eagle is the king of the birds of the air.
    All first symbolize Christ, then the believers.
    In the midst of the four cherubim was THE MAN in the throne. This speaks to us of Christ, the God-Man in the throne of the Lord, dwelling between the Father and the Holy Spirit.

11. **The Cherubim and Transport** (Psalm 18:10; 2 Samuel 22:11)

    The Lord rode upon the cherub and did fly. It symbolizes Divine transport, as noted previously. The Lord likens Himself to the great eagle. He stirred Israel's nest in Goshen, fluttering His wings over them and as an eagle brought them forth unto Himself (Exodus 19:1-6). Elijah experienced this "eagle wing" transport to heaven, as also did Philip in Acts. So will the saints be supernaturally transported from this earth to the new heavens and new earth in due time.

12. **The Cherubim and The Temple Oracle**

    The mention of the cherubim in the Temple is quite prominent. The Scriptures are noted here. (1 Kings 6:23-25; 7:29,36; 8:6-9; 2 Chronicles 3:10-13; 5:7-8; 1 Chronicles 13:6; Hebrews 9:5).

    Here we see the final revelation of the cherubim in the Old Testament. The two great olive cherubim were set in the holiest of all, overshadowing the ark of the Covenant.

    Cherubim are engraven in the Temple walls, upon the brazen lavers as well as the two great cherubim.
    In Ezekiel's Temple we see the cherubim engraven in the walls, along with the face of the man, the face of the lion and the palm trees (Ezekiel 41:18-25).
    The revelation of the Godhead is given clearly to us in John's Gospel, chapters 14,15,16,17.
    In the two olive cherubim and the ark we have one of the richest symbolizations of the work of the Godhead.

    In the Tabernacle of Moses we see the cherubimed ark of the Covenant as symbolic of the Lord Jesus Christ, in whom the fulness of the Godhead dwelt bodily (John 3:33-34; John 14:1-10; Colossians 1:19; 2:9). This spoke of Christ's earth walk.

    In the Temple we see the two olive cherubim representing the Father and the Spirit overshadowing the ark, the Son of God in His perfect humanity. This speaks of Christ's heavenly ministry.
    Both present different aspects of truth concerning the Godhead and the Lord Jesus Christ. One is the earthly; the other is the heavenly. One is Christ's ministry in earth; the other is Christ's ministry in heaven.
    The glory of God is seen upon the ark even as the glory of God is seen in the face of Jesus Christ. He is our high priest, our sacrifice, our redeemer, our covenant, our God-Man. He lives in the power of an endless life making intercession for His own.

SUMMARY:—

Truly the unfolding revelation of the cherubim reveals the glory of the Godhead in the plan of redemption. The Father and the Spirit work with the Son in the redemptive work and the Son is seen in His lowliness, His humiliation and then in His final exaltation.
He is the ark of God. He is the Shepherd who dwells between the cherubim. He is the King seated on the throne of God. In Him the fulness of the Godhead name is seen. He dwells in His glorified humanity in the Godhead, between the Father and the Spirit. He is the one who is worshipped by angels and redeemed mankind. He is the eternal God-Man.

CHAPTER THIRTYTHREE

THE UPPER CHAMBERS AND TREASURIES

A. The Pattern of the Chambers and Treasuries

In 1 Chronicles 28:11-12 and 2 Chronicles 3:9 we have references to the "upper chambers". They are also referred to as "the treasuries" and "the inner parlours" of the house of the Lord. These are sometimes translated as "lofts" or "rooms" and these rooms had their inner parlours.

There are no specific details or instructions recorded in Scripture concerning these treasure chambers except what we have in these verses. However, the measurements of the Temple suggest where these upper chambers would be. The word "chambers" is in the plural so there would be at least two major chambers and, undoubtedly, these would have smaller rooms. These chambers became the treasure chambers of the king, of the Lord and of the nation.

The house of the Lord, as already seen, was 60 cubits in length, 20 cubits in width and 30 cubits in height (2 Chronicles 3:3; 1 Kings 6:1-2). Concerning the holiest of all, or the oracle, we have specific measurements given. This was a perfect cube, 20 cubits by 20 cubits by 20 cubits (2 Chronicles 3:8; 1 Kings 6:16-20).

This leaves an unaccounted for area above the holy oracle measuring 10 cubits high, 20 cubits wide and 20 cubits long. Though not specifically mentioned, it is this fact of Scripture measurements which suggest the only place for such "upper chambers" and "treasuries" would be above the holiest of all. It could also be that there were chambers even above the holy place, as all other areas are accounted for.

Comparing 1 Kings 6:2 and verse 20 we find there is ample room for a large chamber above the oracle having its various inner parlours for the various treasures of the Lord. The upper chambers were also overlaid with gold (2 Chronicles 3:9).

B. The Treasure Chambers

Scattered throughout the Scriptures we have some indication of the various treasures that were placed in these chambers. The Lord Jesus seems to allude to these in His teaching as will be seen in the appropriate place. We consider some of the Scriptures will speak of the various treasures in the chambers of the house of the Lord, His holy Temple.

1. Treasures of the Kings

The treasures of the kings which were dedicated to the Lord were placed in these temple chambers (1 Kings 7:51; 1 Chronicles 22:14; 2 Samuel 8:9-15). These treasures consisted of gold and silver, and were the spoils from the victories of war won by David and other kings.

The law of the spoils from war involved the cleansing by the waters of purification and then they could be dedicated to the service of the Lord (Numbers 31:21-54; Ecclesiastes 2:8).

David mentioned the various materials he had won in battles. These had been through the fire or the water and presented to the Lord as treasures. The godly king Asa also brought dedicated things into the house of the Lord and placed them in these upper chambers. Various other treasures were brought from time to time (1 Kings 15:15).

2. The Spoils of Battles

The spoils of battles has already been mentioned relative to the treasures of the kings. But other Scriptures speak of these spoils also. When Israel came out of Egyptian bondage the Lord allowed them to "spoil" the Egyptians. They took of their silver and gold, and precious stones. These "spoils" were dedicated to the Lord for the service of the Tabernacle (Exodus 12:36). The same is true for the building of the Temple. The enemies of Israel were spoilt and the dedicated things were used for the house of the Lord (1 Chronicles 26:20-28; 2 Samuel 8:9-14).

Christ has spoilt Satan, principalities and powers and we enter into His victory and use all things for the dedication of His spiritual house, the church (Colossians 2:14-15).

3. **Purified by Fire and Water** (Numbers 31:21-24)

    Again we note the fact that the law of the Lord commanded that all spoils from war were to be purified either by fire or water according to the material. After this they could be dedicated to the service of the Lord. It seems that Paul alludes to this purification by fire (at least) in 1 Corinthians 3:9-15 where he told the believers that all a believer's works will go through the fire. The gold, silver and precious stones would abide the fire, but the wood, hay and stubble would be reduced to ashes by the fire. Gold, silver and precious stones — all materials used in the Temple — speak of those works done according to the Word of God, inspired by the Spirit of God and motivated by the love of God. All else is wood, hay and stubble and will be reduced to ashes in a moment of His time.

    The believer's works before the Lord, the victories won in battle, will be amongst the treasures of the Lord in His heavenly city. All our lives must be dedicated to the Lord and must abide the purification by fire or water to be acceptable to Him.

4. **The Musical Instruments of David**

    David made about 4000 musical instruments with which to praise the Lord. These were for the Temple orchestra. It seems as if these musical instruments were kept in the treasure chambers of the house of the Lord (2 Chronicles 7:6; 1 Chronicles 23:5; 2 Chronicles 29:25-30).

    The New Testament fulfilment is in the church, God's holy Temple. There the believers become the instruments of the Lord to make melody in their hearts unto the Lord. There they sings Psalms, and hymns and spiritual songs (Ephesians 5:18-19; Colossians 3:16).

    We also see the musical instruments in the heavenly worship in Revelation 5:8; 14:2-3; 15:2. In heaven there will be music unto perfection. No discordant note will mar the perfect harmony of heaven.

5. **The Tabernacle of the Wilderness**

    By reading 2 Chronicles 5:1,5 it seems that there were still some remnants of the Tabernacle of Moses with Israel. The Tabernacle and vessels were placed in the temple treasure chambers.

    The only article of furniture that went into the Temple itself was the ark of the Covenant. The other remnants were apparently placed in these treasure chambers. These things would remind them of the Lord's preservation through the wilderness years.

    The Tabernacle of Moses provides spiritual treasures for the believer in the New Testament church also, treasures of Divine redemptive truths. Israel's clothes and shoes were miraculously preserved through the 40 years wilderness journeyings (Deuteronomy 8). So the Lord preserved some things of the Tabernacle which were placed in the treasure chambers, whatever these may have been.

C. **Temple Treasuries Plundered**

    One of the tragic things of Israel's history is seen in the fact that oftentimes the enemies of God plundered the Temple treasure chambers.

    Because of their sin and idolatry, the glory of God left the Temple, and therefore the treasure chambers were plundered. They were robbed by the enemy over various times and brought shame and disgrace to the people of God.

    *   The king of Syria was appeased by treasures taken from the Temple (2 Kings 12:18).

    *   The wicked son of Athaliah broke into the house of the Lord and took treasures from the Temple (2 Chronicles 24:7).

* Wicked king Nebuchadnezzar also plundered the Temple treasures and took them to Babylon (2 Chronicles 36:18-19; 2 Kings 24:8-17; 2 Chronicles 25:23-24). In due time judgment from God came upon Babylon for these things (Daniel 5:1-5,23).

Proverbs says that riches take their wings and fly away (Proverbs 23:5).
Israel found this to true in times of idolatry and apostasy from the Lord and in their forsaking of His house.

All this speaks of the fact that the enemy of the church will rob and plunder the treasures of God from God's people if they fall into idolatry or turn from the Lord and forsake His house.
Spiritual Babylon has done this but will be judged by the Lord in the last days (Revelation 17-18).

These Scriptures intimate the vast amount of wealth that was stored in the treasure chambers of the Temple. There was untold wealth and riches there in the house of the Lord. It speaks of the need to guard the treasure chambers of God's house (Proverbs 25:3-5).

D. **Lay up Treasure in Heaven**

Undoubtedly the Lord Jesus was referring to these treasure chambers (Matthew 6:19-21; 19:21).
He exhorted His disciples to lay up treasures in heaven where no thief could break in and steal, and where neither moth nor rust could corrupt. Such could happen, and did happen, to Israel's earthly Temple and earthly treasure chambers. Heaven's treasure chambers are safe and secure from any enemy who would come to rob, to kill, steal and destroy.
Heaven's treasures are incorruptible. Where our treasure is there will be our heart (Mark 10:21; Matthew 13:44).

The treasures of Israel were above the holy oracle of God, that foursquare place. So shall the treasures of the saints be in the foursquare city of God.

The word ''treasure'' means ''a thing laid up''. The Lord promised Israel He would open up His good treasure (Deuteronomy 28:12).

Jesus wanted us to lay down earthly treasures in preference for the heavenly and eternal treasures.

We note some of the precious Scriptures concerning riches in the chambers of the Lord.

* The king has brought into His chamber and His banner over me is love (Song of Solomon 2:4).

* Enter into your chambers and hide until the indignation be past (Isaiah 26:20).

* Jesus had communion of the new covenant in an upper chamber with His disciples (Mark 14:15; Luke 22:12).

* The day of Pentecost took place in an upper chamber (Acts 1:13; 2:1-4).

* The teaching of Jesus concerning the ministry of the Holy Spirit also took place in an upper chamber, where He also washed the disciples feet (John 14,15,16,17).

Read also Isaiah 33:6; 45:3; Proverbs 15:6; 2:4; 10:2; Matthew 2:11; 12:35; 13:52; Luke 12:33,34; Colossians 2:3; Hebrews 11:26; Mark 12:41-42).

The believer is given the riches of His grace and the riches of glory (Ephesians 1:7,18; 2:4,7; 3:16).

The believer learns from the Temple treasuries and chambers that he is to lay up spiritual riches, spiritual and eternal treasures in heaven. There is that which is eternal wealth, eternal and incorruptible riches. The Lord has given His name, His word, His love, His grace, His glory, His all as the true riches both in this life and in the life to come (1 Timothy 6:6-11,17-19).

THE CHAMBERS OF THE TEMPLE

THE THIRTY CHAMBERS

The Chambers Resting upon the Walls of the Temple

THE PRIESTLY SIDE CHAMBERS

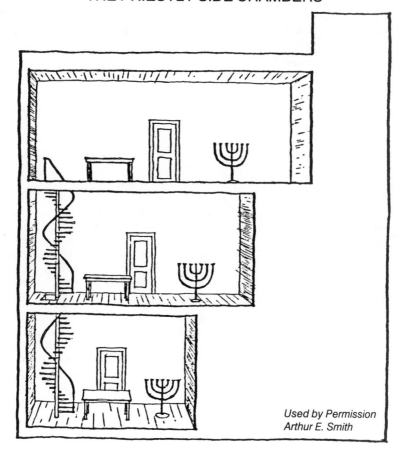

CHAPTER THIRTYFOUR

THE CHAMBERS OF THE PRIESTS

The Tabernacle in the wilderness was a tent for the Lord. There He dwelt in the midst of His people Israel, who also lived in tents. The wilderness spoke of the wanderings of Israel and God with them, leading them in these wanderings. There the priests of the Lord lived in tents, and fulfilled their daily services in pilgrim character.

In contrast, *the Temple* spoke of rest, promised rest, both for God and for His people. The wanderings and the journeyings were over. Here the priests would fulfil their daily ministrations in the Temple. Here in the Temple they would also find rest. It is this that brings us to the chambers of the priests that were built and surrounded the Temple, especially the north and south sides of the Temple building.

A. **The Chambers for the Priests** (1 Kings 6:5-10)

Surrounding the walls of the Temple, that is of the holy place and the oracle, were built chambers for the priests. These chambers must be distinguished from the upper chambers where the treasures of the Lord and of the nation were kept, as dealt with in our previous chapter.

1. **Thirty Chambers**

Scripture does not specifically state how many chambers there were, but according to the measurements given and their respective sizes, there would be approximately 30 chambers altogether in each of the three stories. Josephus, the Jewish historian suggests 30 in *"Antiquities of the Jews"*, Book 7, Chapter 3.
The Temple mentioned in Ezekiel also speaks of 30 chambers of the priests (Ezekiel 41:5-6; 40:7). These were on the north and south sides of the Temple.

Thirty is the number of consecration to ministry, as we have already seen. Joseph was 30 years of age when he came to the throne. David was 30 years of age when he came to the throne. Priests were thirty years of age when they were consecrated to priestly office and ministry. Jesus Himself was about 30 years of age when baptized in water in Jordan and anointed with the Holy Spirit for ministry. And here the priestly chambers number 30, for the priests were consecrated to the work of the house of the Lord.

2. **Three Stories High**

In 1 Kings 6:6-8 we are told that the priests chambers were three stories high. The first story was five cubits broad, the middle story was six cubits broad and the third story was seven cubits broad.
These three stories varied in their measurements, some smaller, some larger, and some higher.
These chambers rested against the walls of the Temple (1 Kings 6:5-7). They were built to lean on the Temple, not actually joined or fastened to it (1 Kings 6:10).

There is no doubt there is some significant link up with the ark of Noah. In Genesis 6:14-16 we are given the details of the measurements of the ark of Noah. It also had three stories as to its height. It was built of gopher wood, pitched within and without. The central story had the one and only door of entrance. All had to enter through this door or perish. The third story had the window in it. The measurements of the ark were as follows; 300 cubits in length by 50 cubits in breadth and 30 cubits in height. These three stories had "rooms" (or, "nests", Margin), or chambers in them for the animals that were saved through the flood of waters.

The prophet Amos speaks of "the stories in the heavens" (Amos 9:6). The margin speaks of these as "spheres" or "ascensions". The Scripture reveals that there are three heavens, these being, the atmospheric, planetary and the third heaven, which is the very Paradise of God.

Thus the 3 stories in the ark of Noah, the 3 divisions of the Tabernacle of Moses, and the 3 stories of the priests chambers relative to the Temple are seen to be linked in the same Divine truths.

Jesus is "the way, the truth and the life" (John 14:1,6).

Noah's name means "rest". The ark brought rest and safety and security for Noah and his family and the animals in the ark. The earth was cleansed of all ungodly and corrupted flesh through the judgment by water, as the windows of heaven were opened in this deluge.

The sinful and ungodly flesh was also dealt with in the outer court of the Temple by the brazen altar and the molten sea, by blood and water. Now the priests could enter into Temple ministry and in their respective courses find rest in the priest's chambers around the Temple.

Three is the number of God or the Godhead, as Father, Son and Holy Spirit. It was one ark, yet three stories. The chambers were for the one Temple, yet in three stories. Such speak of the rest that is found in the Godhead and in the redemptive plan wrought by the Father, Son and Holy Spirit.

Other numbers in the priest's chambers were the numbers five, six and seven. Five is the number of the grace of God, the number of atonement, the number of life. Six is the number of man. Seven is the number of completion, fulness and perfection.

For the priests in the Temple services, through the significance of these numbers, they would find the grace of God, as redeemed man, and enjoy the completion of rest that comes through redemption.

3. **The Door**

Also there was but one door for the ark of Noah, and there was one door into the priests chambers.

As always, the one door speaks of Christ (John 10:9). Only through Him can we find access into rest as a priest unto God (Revelation 1:6; 5:9-10).

Christ is the door of access to all the fulness of the Godhead. He is the door into the Temple of the Lord, into His house, which house we are.

4. **The Winding Stairs**

In 1 Kings 6:8 we find that these three stories were made accessible first by the door, and then inside by winding stairs. These stairs began in the lowest story, spiralling up through and into the middle story, and then on out of the middle story into the third story. Note also (Ezekiel 41:7).

The thought of "winding stairs" is "that by which to ascend". In Genesis 28:12 we are told about Jacob's dream where he saw "a ladder" or more literally "a stairway" leading from earth to heaven. The Lord was at the top of that stairway. This was Jacob's experience at Bethel, the house of God, founded upon the anointed rock.

The bridegroom and bride speaks of being "in the clefts of the rock, in the secret places of the stairs" also (Song of Solomon 2:14).

The stairway speaks of the believers walk. We go from "faith to faith", and "glory to glory" and from "grace to grace" in the things of the Lord.

The Lord has steps and stairs in the spiritual walk of His priests. Hebrews 6:1-2 lists a basic outline of the steps unto perfection and full maturity. The believer priest is to go from repentance from dead works on to faith in God, and then water baptism and Holy Spirit baptism, on through the laying on of hands, resurrection from the dead, eternal judgment and on to perfection. We begin at His feet and ascend in these spiritual steps unto the Lord.

5.   **Made of Cedar**

The Temple chambers for the priests were also made of cedar wood as to boards and beams. As always, cedar speaks of incorruptibility, and of royalty, both of Christ and the saints. Christ was incorruptible in His human nature, and royalty in His office as King of kings and Lord of lords. The saints are called unto an incorruptible life-style and to be kings and priests unto God and His Christ.

It is worthy to note, by way of comparison, the definite connection between the ark of Noah and the Temple of Solomon. The wonderful truth here, as noted in the beginning of this textbook, is that the Temple includes in itself, symbolically, not only the Tabernacle of Moses, the Tabernacle of David, but also the ark of Noah.

The Ark of Noah	—	**The Temple of Solomon**
One Ark	—	One Temple
Given by Divine revelation	—	Given by Divine revelation
Made of gopher wood	—	Made of cedar wood mainly
Three stories high	—	Priests chambers 3 stories high
Thirty cubits high	—	Thirty priestly chambers
Rooms for the occupants	—	Rooms for the priests
One door	—	One door and winding stairs
A window above	—	Windows above in the Temple

B.   **The Furniture of the Priests Chambers**

In 1 Chronicles 28:11-12 the "upper chambers" of the Temple are distinguished from "the chambers round about", or the house and chambers of the priests.

Also in 1 Chronicles 28:11-21 we have various vessels spoken of by David which were for use in the Temple services. Among these things we have candlesticks of gold, and candlesticks of silver, and tables of gold and tables of silver.

Reference has already been made concerning the vast amount of silver that was given for use in the Temple. This was about ten times the amount of gold that was given. Of the silver given, the only use we have of it was in the possible overlaying of the stones of the Temple as plaister, or silver encased stones. There is absolutely no other reference of silver in the Temple itself. All in the Temple is gold, which speaks of glory. All in the courts is of brass, which speaks of judgment. But here we have silver, which speaks of redemption, which is for the priests.

Therefore, the thought that we have here is that these candlesticks of SILVER and the tables of SILVER were the furniture for the priests chambers.

It is very clear that the candlesticks of GOLD, and the tables of GOLD were placed in the holy place itself. For what purpose then would the candlesticks of silver, and the tables of silver be except for the priests chambers?

In 2 Kings 4:8-17 we have an evident allusion to the priests chambers by the chamber built by the great woman on the wall of her house for the man of God. A comparison shows that the woman built this chamber after the apparent pattern of the chambers of the priests in Temple services. Let us note the comparison.

The Chamber for the Man of God	—	**The Chamber for the Priests**
She built a little chamber	—	The Temple had their chambers
On the wall of the house	—	Against the wall of God's house
A bed for rest and relaxation	—	Possibly the same here
A table and stool, for sitting and eating	—	Table of silver
A candlestick, for light	—	Candlestick of silver

This comparison surely lends weight to the fact that the priestly chambers had these articles of furniture for the priests to use. Silver in use in the chambers of the priests spoke of redemptive ministry. What a privilege to be a priest in the Temple of the Lord, to touch the spiritual realities of these material things.

We note the furniture further as to spiritual significances for the priests.

1. A Silver Table

Silver speaks of the atonement, of redemption, the price of a soul. The priest must touch the truth of silver before he can touch the truth of the gold. Redemption precedes glory.

The table speaks of communion, of spiritual nourishment. The silver table speaks of the Lord's table also, as to redemption. All priests may eat and drink with the Lord, communing with Him day by day and through their priestly ministrations.

The priests could also partake of the shewbread on the golden table in the holy place week by week. But here they could feed on the holy things of the Lord, partaking of the priests food in the sacrifices. Here they became partakers of the altar of the Lord (1 Corinthians 10:1-17; 11:23-34; Matthew 26:26-28; Psalm 23). The Lord prepared a table for them. All spoke of their redemption.

2. A Silver Candlestick

The silver candlestick (or lampstand) spoke of light and illumination. Perhaps the same ornamentation was on these as on the golden lampstands in the holy place. There is no mention of other light in the priests chambers. God gave them light through the oil of the candlestick. God has provided the light of His Word for priests to meditate on day and night in their service to Him. Again, the light has been provided through the price of redemption, as symbolized in the silver.

3. A Bed and Stool

Although not specifically mentioned in the record of the Temple, it is understood by the chamber built for Elisha by the great woman, and also by implication, that the table and lampstand were both in the chambers of the priests.

A table needs a stool to sit on. The lampstand would stand on the table also to provide light.

In 1 Chronicles 9:26-34 we are told of the priests in their courses where they were before the Lord "day and night".

This would imply that the bed for rest, and the stool for the table would be required in the priestly chambers as they served in their respective courses.

In all of these articles we have the thought of communion, illumination, relaxation and position. These are the things the Lord provides for His New Testament priests in their sevice to Him in His house also.

C. The Chambers of Rest from Service

A study of 1 Chronicles 9:26-34 (R.V.) along with Ezekiel 42:13-14 provides us with thoughts of the service of the priests in their courses, after which they would find rest in the priestly chambers. We note some of the services of these priests and Levites relative to the Temple.

* Some prepared the anointing oil with the spices (vs 30).

* Some looked after the vessels of ministry (vs 28).

* Some had the preparation of the bread for the table every Sabbath (vs 32).

* Some were the singers who dwelt in the chambers and were free from other duties (vs 33).

* Some were over the treasuries of the house of God (vs 26).

* Here they would change their priestly apparel.

* Here they would feast upon the holy sacrifices and portions for the priests (Ezekiel 42:13-14).

* It is possible that young king Joash was hidden for 6 years from the wicked queen Athaliah when she slew the royal seed (2 Kings 11).

* Nehemiah chased wicked Tobiah out of the chamber that belonged to the priests, along with his stuff (Nehemiah 13:4-9). No stranger should be in the chambers of the priests.

So the various priests had their respective duties to fulfil. 'Some of the priests remaining in the chambers were free from service. The Scripture says they lodged round about the house of the Lord.

It seems that David longed to dwell in the house of the Lord and alluded to the vision of the house (Psalm 27:4; 65:4).

A consideration of the chambers for the priests seems to indicate more clearly what the Lord Jesus meant when He spoke of ''His Father's house'' and ''many mansions''.

The Father's house spoke of the Temple (John 2:16-21). It also spoke of the Father's heavenly house (John 14:2). The ''mansions'' means ''resting places'' and undoubtedly referred to the chambers of the priests who rested from service in their courses. Jesus would prepare a place for His disciples in the Father's house. Solomon prepared places for the priests in the house of the Lord.

So the various rooms or chambers in the three stories became places of rest, the lodging places as they ministered to the Lord in their particular courses of the 24,000's of Israel's courses.
God had rest in the holy oracle. The priests had rest in the chambers. Jesus called all who would come to Him and He would give them rest, and they would also find rest as they learnt of Him (Matthew 11:28-30).

Viewing the Temple in its heavenly aspect, the Lord Jesus is preparing the ''many mansions'' or ''lodging places'' of rest for believer priests in the city of God. All points to that eternal rest in heaven's city; rest from sin, from sickness, from Satan and death and sorrow — eternal rest in God and His Christ (Revelation 21-22).

In the church, the believer finds his place as a priest unto God and serves in the house of the Lord, finding spiritual rest in Christ. All have a function to fulfil as members of the priestly body of Christ (1 Corinthians 11).

IN SUMMARY:—

* There are chambers of rest (Matthew 11:28-30; Hebrews 4:3).

* There are chambers of safety (2 Kings 11:1-3; 2 Chronicles 31:11-12; Isaiah 26:20).

* There are chambers of love and communion (Song of Solomon 1:4; 3:4).

* There are treasure chambers — dedicated to the Lord (Refer Chapter 33 of the text).

* There are chambers for the vessels of the Lord (Ezra 8:24-30).

* There are chambers of Divine teaching and revelation of the work and ministry of the Holy Spirit. Jesus gave the teaching of John 13-14-15-16-17 in an upper chamber. There was the communion, the washing of the disciples feet, and the teaching of the person and work of the Spirit.

* In an upper chamber the Holy Spirit fell on the disciples on the day of Pentecost (Acts 1-2).

* In Hezekiah's time of reformation, chambers were prepared for the tithes and offerings of the people. These were under the hands of priests and Levites (2 Chronicles 31:11-21). These chambers were the storehouse in the house of the Lord to which Malachi refers (Malachi 3:8-12).

CHAPTER THIRTYFIVE

THE DEDICATION OF THE TEMPLE

The dedication of the Temple was a day to be remembered in Israel's national history. Significant things took place on this great day and such became the seal of God's favour on the house built for His name. The house was crowned with His glory and presence.

We consider in our present chapter some of the most significant things that took place on this dedication day, for all point to and become prophetic of something that finds its fulfilment in Christ and His church.

A. **The Feast of Tabernacles** — 1 Kings 8:1-2; 2 Chronicles 5:2-3

The dedication of the Temple took place in the Feast of the seventh month, the Feast of Tabernacles. This is the first most significant thing to consider. Solomon could have dedicated the Temple in the Feast of Passover and Unleavened Bread in the first month of this twelfth year of his reign. Or he could have dedicated the Temple in the third month which was the Feast of Pentecost month. But he was undoubtedly directed by the Lord to dedicate it in the Feast of the seventh month, the great Feast of Tabernacles.

The revelation of the Tabernacle of Moses was given relative to the Feast of Pentecost. But it is the Feast of Tabernacles that seals the dedication of the Temple of Solomon.

1. PASSOVER, or Unleavened Bread and Sheaf of Firstfruits took place in the first month of the sacred year (Exodus 12). It commemorated Israel's deliverance from the bondage of Egypt by the power of God. It was the beginning of months, the foundational month of their experiences with the Lord their God.

2. PENTECOST took place in the third month of the sacred year. This day commemorated Israel's reception of the Law of God; moral, civil and ceremonial law, at Mt Sinai (Exodus 19-40; Leviticus 1-27).

3. TABERNACLES took place in the seventh month of the sacred year. It commemorated their deliverance from Egypt, their journey through the wilderness into the land of promise. It was the consummation of months. In this was the Feast Day of Trumpets, the first day of the month, the great national Day of Atonement on the tenth day; then it concluded with the Feast of Tabernacles proper from the 15th to the 21st day, with the 22nd solemn day to crown it all.

Exodus chapter 12, Leviticus chapters 16 and 23 along with Deuteronomy chapters 12 and 16 should be studied in connection with the details of these festival occasions. (Note — The student is referred to the author's textbook on *"The Feasts of Israel"* for a full exposition of this glorious subject.)

The Feast of Tabernacles was the ultimate of these three feasts and we find more about this feast than any other. It seems the most significant things took place in this feast of the seventh month.

* Israel kept the Feast of Tabernacles only in Canaan land, not in Egypt or the wilderness.

* Solomon dedicated the Temple in this festival month.

* The restored Temple also was dedicated in the Feast of Tabernacles (Haggai 2:9; Nehemiah 8:17; Ezra 3).

* Christ taught significant truths in the month also (John 7:37-39).

B. **The Number Seven**

In considering the dedication of the Temple in this month we discover that the feast of the seventh month is stamped with the number seven. A study of these Scriptures here confirm this fact (2 Chronicles 7:8-10; 1 Kings 8:65-66).

* Solomon was seven years in the building of the Temple. He began to build the Temple in the second day of the second month in the fourth year of his reign (1 Kings 6:1; 2 Chronicles 3:1-2).

 The Temple was finished in the eighth month of the eleventh year of his reign (1 Kings 6:37-38).

 The Scripture says the house was "finished" and "perfected" (2 Chronicles 8:16; 1 Kings 6:37-38). This points to the church, God's house, which will one day be a finished work and brought to perfection (John 17:1-3; 19:30; Hebrews 6:1-2; Ephesians 4:9-16).

* The Temple was dedicated in the seventh month, the Feast of Tabernacles, in the twelfth year of Solomon's reign after an interim period of about 11 months (2 Chronicles 5:3; 1 Kings 8:2).

1. **Seven Days Preparation of the People**

 The first day of the seventh month was the day of blowing of trumpets (Leviticus 23:23-25; Numbers 29:1-6). This was a time of preparation of the people over the seven days.

2. **Seven Days Dedication of the Altar**

 In this seven days dedication of the altar, the tenth day was the great Day of Atonement (Leviticus 23:27-32; Numbers 29:7-11). A study of the offerings in this period, according to the law, reveals the number seven stamped upon all of the Levitical sacrifices (Numbers 29:12-34; Leviticus 23:23-39). Sin had to be cleansed by blood atonement over these seven days.

3. **Seven Days Dedication of the Temple**

 In this seven days the Temple was dedicated to the Lord God of Israel. All was sealed by the descent of the glory-fire and presence of God.

Thus we have 21 days, or 3 × 7 days in all.

This Feast, both in Moses time and Solomon's dedicatory month, was consummated with an extra Sabbath, a day of rejoicing as the people returned to their own habitations (Leviticus 23:39-44; Numbers 29:35-40; 1 Kings 8:65-66; 2 Chronicles 7:10-11).

The number seven is the number of completeness, of fulness and perfection. It points to the end-times relative to the plan of redemption. It is prophetic of the fact that God's people, His church, will come to completeness, to fulness of maturity and perfection as the church enters in and experiences all that was prophetically symbolized in the Feast of Tabernacles.

C. **The Ark of God in the Holy of Holiest** — 1 Kings 8:1-9; 2 Chronicles 5:1-10

Fuller details of this have been dealt with in a previous chapter. Sufficient for here is to remember that, after the dedication of the great altar by blood sacrifices, the ark of God could be then taken into the most holy place, the holy oracle.

In the procession, the lowly ark was taken from Mt Zion, from the Tabernacle of David and brought into the Temple on Mt Moriah and placed in "His place" in the holiest of all. The king led the way, with the priests following, then the singers and musicians. It is possible that Psalm 24:9-10 was sung. The call came clearly. "Lift up your heads, O ye gates, and be ye lifted up, ye everlasting doors", even the doors of the Temple. The priests would receive the ark from the Levites at these Temple doors and then take the ark into the most holy place. There the ark was set between the two great olive cherubim, overshadowing it by their outspread wings. The staves were taken out. Its journeyings were over. Only the law of God on the tables of stone from Mt Horeb remained in the ark of the Lord. Thus the order of Moses and David are united in the Temple order with the ark and worship. All was now ready for the glory of the Lord to descend and dwell among His people. As the priests retired from the holy oracle, the glory cloud would descend and fill the house.

D. **The Singers and Musicians** — 2 Chronicles 5:11-14

At the dedication of the Temple, we find the Davidic order of singers and musicians functioning. Glorious lessons are seen in practical operation for the New Testament believers in the church.

1. **Davidic Order**

    In the Tabernacle of David, approximately 30 years beforehand, the order of singers and musicians was established. Here in the dedication of the Temple that order is seen and heard at its best under the anointing of the Spirit of God.

2. **White Linen**

    The singers and musicians were arrayed in white linen. These were of the Levites and of the three chief singers of Asaph, Heman and Jeduthun. They had instruments of cymbals, psalteries and harps as well as trumpets, all spoken of as the musical instruments of David (2 Chronicles 7:6). White linen is always the symbol of righteousness and purity. The worshipping priests of the Lord should be clothed in the righteousness of Christ (Revelation 19:8).

3. **The East end of the Altar**

    It was at the east end of the altar that the ashes were kept and then carried outside the camp in time. Ashes always spoke of a finished work, a completed sacrifice (Leviticus 1:16; 6:11; Hebrews 13:11-13). So these priests were presenting themselves a living sacrifice and this truth was symbolized in their standing at the east end of the sacrificial altar.

4. **The 120 Trumpeters**

    There were 120 trumpeters at this dedication. The number 120 is significant of the end of all flesh and the beginning of life in the Spirit.
    In the days of Noah the Spirit strove with man for 120 years (Genesis 6:1-13; 1 Peter 3:20-21). Moses lived 120 years in this world and then was taken to glory after His burial and resurrection (Deuteronomy 34:7; Jude 9; Luke 9:30; Acts 7:23-42).
    There were 120 disciples in the upper room for the day of Pentecost when the Holy Spirit fell. This was the dedication of the New Testament church, the house of the Lord (Acts 1:15).
    Saul, David and Solomon reigned 120 years in total over a united kingdom of Israel, each having 40 years reign (Acts 13:21; 1 Kings 2:11; 11:42).
    There were 120 loaves of shewbread on the golden tables in Solomon's Temple.

    And here we have 120 trumpeters making one sound and of one accord when the glory of the Lord fell on the house.

    Significantly also we have 120 Jubilees (120 × 50) which equal 6000 years of time given to man in the flesh in redemptive design. The seventh day of the Lord brings all in Christ to total life in the Spirit, even eternal life.

5. **One Accord**

    Unnaturally, almost supernaturally, the singers and trumpeters became as one, making one sound in praising and thanking the Lord, along with the other instruments of music.
    Their choir number was ''For the Lord is good, for His mercy endureth for ever.'' With such unity, the Lord commanded the blessing of His glory cloud.

The Scriptures speak much of the unity of God's people in order that God can command His blessing, even life for ever more (Psalm 133).

The 120 disciples were of one accord in one place in prayer before Pentecost and also on the day of Pentecost (Acts 1:15; 2:1-4). There the Holy Spirit fell in that unity and they all spoke with tongues. The end result of Peter's preaching was seen when 3000 souls turned to the Lord and were added to the church (Acts 2).

E. **The Cloud of Glory** — 1 Kings 8:10-11; 2 Chronicles 5:14; 7:1-3

It seems that, after the dedication of the altar of sacrifice, the placing of the ark of the Lord in the holy oracle amidst the unity of singers and musicians, that the glory cloud of the Lord descended and filled the house of the Lord.

The priests could not stand to minister by reason of the glory of the Lord. It was the cessation of man's ministry and the revelation of the glory of God. The Spirit reigned supreme in that period of time.

*   It was this glory cloud which led Israel as the church in the wilderness for 40 years (Exodus 13:21-22; Acts 7:38).

*   It was this cloud that gave Israel light and fire by night and provided a cloud of covering in the day time from the heat.

*   The cloud was darkness to the Egyptians but light to Israel as the people of God (Exodus 14:19-31).

*   Paul says that Israel was baptized in the Red Sea and in the cloud (1 Corinthians 10:1-4).

*   That cloud was upon Mt Sinai in the giving of the revelation of the law, the priesthood and the Tabernacle of Moses (Exodus 24:15-18; 34:5-7).

*   The Lord left Mt Sinai and appeared in this cloud over the blood-stained mercy seat in the Tabernacle of Moses (Exodus 40:34-38; Numbers 7:89; Leviticus 16:1-2).

*   Israel's life was governed by the movements of the cloud in connection with the silver trumpets (Numbers 9:15-23; 10:1-36; Deuteronomy 1:33; Nehemiah 9:19; Psalm 78:14). All had to follow the cloud.

That cloud had lifted over the years because of Israel's idolatry in Canaan land. But now in the dedication of the Temple of the Lord, that cloud returns in glory and fills the house of God. Here it takes its place once again on the mercy seat of the ark of the Covenant, the throne of God in the earth, between the two great olive cherubim.

The ultimate fulfilment of the cloud of God is seen on the Mt of Transfiguration when the true Tabernacle and Temple was revealed. There the Lord Jesus Christ was overshadowed by the bright cloud and the Father's voice spoke out of the cloud, ''This is My beloved Son, hear Him'' (Matthew 17:1-9; Luke 9:28-36; Mark 9:1-7).

A cloud received Jesus back into heaven and He will come with the clouds again (Acts 1:9; Revelation 10:1; Luke 21:27).

F. **Solomon's Brazen Scaffold** — 2 Chronicles 6:12-13

Another significant thing in the dedication of the Temple is Solomon's symbolic personal dedication to the Lord.

Solomon set a brazen scaffold in the middle of the great court, stood upon it, and then knelt before the Lord and the people as he made the dedicatory prayer to the Lord. Here was the king of Israel praying to the King of kings and Lord of lords. Significant truths are seen here.

1. **A Brazen Scaffold**

    Brass, as always, is the symbol of judgment against sin and self. Here Solomon allows sin and self to be dealt with in symbolic manner. If only he had maintained the truth of this over his years, then his reign would not have ended in tragedy as it did.

2. Measurements of Scaffold

The measurements of the scaffold were 5 cubits long by 5 cubits broad, or foursquare, and also 3 cubits high.
The significance of these measurements is seen in Exodus 27:1-8, for there the brazen altar in the Tabernacle of Moses measured exactly the same.

The brazen altar was the altar of sacrifice and cleansing from sin. So Solomon is presenting himself "a living sacrifice" to the Lord on this dedicatory scaffold. Again, if only he had maintained this attitude over all his reign, the end of his life would not have been so tragic.

3. Position of Scaffold

The scaffold was positioned in the middle of the court which had been hallowed for the numerous animal sacrifices (1 Kings 8:64; 2 Chronicles 7:7). While the sacrifices of unwilling animals were being offered to the Lord, yet voluntarily offered by the priests, Solomon was presenting himself as a living sacrifice, willingly and humbly before the Lord. Truly the sacrifices of the Lord are a broken and contrite heart. Then will the Lord be pleased with the sacrifice of animals. The external must symbolize the internal or else all is but formal ceremonialism.

4. Solomon's Position

Solomon stood on this scaffold, first of all, and then, with outstretched hands knelt before the Lord and Israel as he made his great prayer (1 Kings 8:54-55; 2 Chronicles 6:12-13).
Standing, kneeling, and the lifting up of the hands speak of absolute and total surrender to the Lord in prayer.

G. Solomon's Dedicatory Prayer — 1 Kings 8:12-61; 2 Chronicles 6:1-42

Solomon begins his prayer by a recognition of the fact that the Lord said He would dwell in "thick darkness". It seems contradictory because God Himself is light (2 Chronicles 6:1; Exodus 20:21; 1 John 1:7; John 1:5-8; 1 Thessalonians 5:5; Ephesians 5:8).

It spoke of the "thick darkness" of the most holy place, but God would light it with His glory-presence. Without His presence there, then it would be thick darkness, for, the holy oracle was foursquare, and locked in with the folding doors and the veil from human eyes.

Spiritually speaking, believers see the Lord "through a glass darkly" but one day we will see Him "face to face" (1 Corinthians 13).

The key words to be noted in these Scriptures have to do with "prayer", "His Name", "this place", "confession of sins" and "this house". The prayer is too vast to deal with in full detail. Following is an outline for the student to study.

* Solomon asks God's constant care — 1 Kings 8:22-30; 2 Chronicles 6:12-21.
* Oaths may be made at God's altar — 1 Kings 8:31-32; 2 Chronicles 6:22-23.
* Prayer in defeat — 1 Kings 8:33-34; 2 Chronicles 6:24-25.
* Prayer in drought — 1 Kings 8:35-36; 2 Chronicles 6:26-27.
* Prayer in famine and pestilence — 1 Kings 8:37-40; 2 Chronicles 6:28-31.
* Prayer of the stranger — 1 Kings 8:41-43; 2 Chronicles 6:32-33.
* Prayer in warfare — 1 Kings 8:44-45; 2 Chronicles 6:34-35.
* Prayer in captivity — 1 Kings 8:46-53; 2 Chronicles 6:36-39.
* Close of Prayer   2 Chronicles 6:40-42.

The prayer covers every area of personal and national life. This house was to be a house of prayer for all nations, not just for Israel.

Godly kings were always men of prayer.

We think of Jehoshaphat's prayer in time of battle (2 Chronicles 20).

Hezekiah prayed against the Assyrian invasion of Judah (Isaiah 37:15).

Hezekiah prayed at the cleansing of the Temple and the restoration of the Davidic worship (2 Chronicles 29-30).

Solomon's prayer is a powerful prayer, having all the ingredients of true prayer unto the Lord. The king was a man of dedicatory prayer. So all leadership should be.

H. The Glory-Fire of the Lord — 2 Chronicles 7:1-3

The passage here indicates that when Solomon had made an end of praying, fire came down from heaven and consumed the offerings on the great altar. The glory of the Lord filled the house and no priest could stand to minister by reason of that glory. When Israel saw the glory and fire on the house, they prostrated themselves with their faces to the ground, worshipping and praising the Lord for His goodness and mercy.

It seems that the order of God's descent was probably as follows:

1. The descent of the cloud of God's presence over the house.

2. The glory of the Lord settling upon the ark of the Covenant in the holy oracle between the cherubim.

3. The dedicatory personal offering and prayer of king Solomon.

4. The fire coming out from the glory cloud to consume the sacrifice on the great altar in the court.

5. The prostration of the congregation in worship and praise in the courts of the Lord's house.

This seemed to be similar to the order of the Lord's descent at the dedication of the Tabernacle of Moses at Mt Sinai (Exodus 40:34-38; Leviticus 9:22-24; 10:1-3).

The Tabernacle was finished according to Divine pattern. The dedicatory sacrifices had been offered on the altar, which had been dedicated over 12 days (Numbers 7).

The glory cloud of the Lord came from Mt Sinai and filled the Tabernacle of the Lord. Fire came out from the glory and consumed the sacrifices. The people fell on their faces before the Lord.

So it seems that this followed the same order in the dedication of Solomon's Temple and the descent of the cloud of glory and fire.

"*Glory*" and "*fire*" are generally associated in Israel's history.

*   The cloudy pillar of glory and fire led Israel in the wilderness (Exodus 13).
    The fire of God falling on the sacrifice was the seal of God's acceptance.

*   Fire possibly sealed Abel's sacrifice and acceptance (Genesis 4; Hebrews 11:4).

*   Fire sealed the sacrifices in the dedication of the Tabernacle of Moses (Leviticus 9:22-24).

*   Fire sealed David's sacrifice at Ornan's threshing floor (1 Chronicles 21:26).

*   Fire sealed the sacrifice of Elijah on the renewed altar of Israel at Mt Carmel (1 Kings 19).

*   Fire sealed Solomon's sacrifices at the dedication of the Temple (2 Chronicles 7:1-3).

So it was on the day of Pentecost, "tongues like as of fire" sealed the 120 disciples as they presented themselves living sacrifices to the Lord Jesus Christ on the dedication day of the New Covenant church and house of the Lord (Acts 2:1-4).

I. The Dedicatory Sacrifices — 1 Kings 8:62-64; 2 Chronicles 7:4-5

With the glory of the Lord filling the house, the fire of God burning on the altar, Solomon and Israel offered to the Lord numerous sacrifices on this same day.

There were   22,000 oxen

                       120,000 sheep

Total =   142,000 offerings.

These were burnt offerings and peace offerings with their meal offerings. These were voluntary offerings.

The compulsory sin and trespass offerings are not mentioned. These would have been offered by the priests, not by king Solomon.

So Christ as our priest offered Himself as our sin and trespass offering at Calvary. In the building of the house of the Lord, believers offer themselves as voluntary offerings (Psalm 110). God's people are free-will or voluntary offerings in the day of Messiah's power.

Solomon presented himself as a "living sacrifice".

Solomon and all Israel presented thousands of animal sacrifices.

All point to the fact, first of all, that Christ would give Himself a living sacrifice and a voluntary once-for-all sacrifice for sin (Daniel 9:24-27; Hebrews 9-10). But what were all the Old Testament sacrifices compared to the glory of Christ's sinless and perfect sacrifice? (Ephesians 5:2; Isaiah 53). No animal offering could compare with His Divine-human offering.

Believers also are to present themselves "living sacrifices", wholly and holy, and acceptable unto God which is their reasonable and priestly service (Romans 12:1-2).

Believers also present "spiritual sacrifices" unto the Lord as a royal priesthood. Solomon officiated as a king-priest in this day. Believers are, under the New Covenant, kings and priests and called to offer sacrifices to the Lord acceptable to God through Christ Jesus (1 Peter 2:5-9; Revelation 1:6; 5:9-10).

J.   The Benediction Blessing

King Solomon blessed the people at the conclusion of the whole day of dedication (2 Chronicles 6:4-11).

Melchisedek, as king-priest, blessed father Abraham (Genesis 14:19).

King David, as king-priest, blessed the nation also (2 Samuel 6:18).

King Solomon, as king-priest (in typical sense) blessed the nation also here.

It is significant that the high priest is not mentioned at all in the whole of this Temple dedication. The emphasis is on THE KING, king Solomon.

So all points to Christ who sacrificed as PRIEST but who is now in heaven as THE KING, the king-priest, the King of kings, and Lord of lords and now blesses His church (Zechariah 6:13).

IN SUMMARY:—

We note the major comparisons between the dedication of the Tabernacle of Moses and the Temple of Solomon.

Dedication of Moses Tabernacle	—	Dedication of Solomon's Temple
Mt Sinai	—	Mt Moriah
Priest Moses	—	King Solomon
Built to Divine revelation	—	Built to Divine revelation
Preparation of materials	—	Preparation of materials
No music or singers	—	Singers and musicians
Quiet worship and fear	—	Davidic worship and joy
Feast of Pentecost	—	Feast of Tabernacles
Priests in white linen	—	Priests in white linen
Glory cloud descends	—	Glory cloud descends
Fire from the glory on altar	—	Fire from the glory on altar
Brazen altar, 5 × 5 × 3 cubits	—	Brazen scafold 5 × 5 × 3 cubits
Animal sacrifices	—	Animal sacrifices on great altar
Sealed by fire	—	Sealed by fire
Moses and Aaron before God	—	Solomon presents himself
Blessing of Moses	—	Blessing of Solomon

The dedicatory service is replete with lessons for the church. The church, God's people are now God's Temple. The Holy Spirit is the shekinah glory in the midst of His people. In His church, the name, the law, the presence and glory of the Lord abide. There believers make spiritual sacrifices to the Lord in new covenant priesthood, a royal priesthood. The Lord desires to have us maintain a pure and holy Temple for His dwelling place (1 Corinthians 3:16; 1 Timothy 3:15-16; 1 Peter 2:5-9).

DRESS OF HIGH PRIEST AND LEVITE PRIEST

CHAPTER THIRTYSIX

THE TWENTY-FOUR COURSES AND TEMPLE ORDERS

With the dedication of the Temple completed and sealed by the descent of the glory presence of the Lord, now the Divine order of the priestly courses in their ministry could begin to function as revealed to David.

The details of these various courses are set out in several chapters of Chronicles, namely, 1 Chronicles 23,24,25,26,27. These chapters are devoted to the basic details of the courses pertaining to the Temple services, and the service of the king. (Note also 2 Chronicles 8:14.)
The predominant truth is to be found in the significant use of the number twenty-four as stamped on these courses, or the number twelve. The number twelve, as already seen, is the number of apostolic government. The number twenty-four is the number of priestly courses and ministration. Combined we have the thought of Divine and apostolic government in the priestly ministrations of the house of the Lord.
It was in their service to the Lord, in their courses, that the priests could function in Divine order and behold the beauty of the Lord and enquire in His Temple.

A. **The Courses of the Levites in Outline** — 1 Chronicles 23:1-32

An outline of the chapter provides the following information as to the service of the Levites.

Vs 1-2   The Levites from the age of 30 years and upwards numbered 38,000 in all. The law of Moses forbade the Levites to be numbered with Israel, for the whole tribe was given as a gift to Aaron and his sons, the house of the high priest, as a service to them. The Levites were given for the work of the Tabernacle, the Sanctuary and now here for the Temple services. Thirty was the age for service in the priesthood, the age of consecration (Note Numbers 1,2,3,4 chapters; also Luke 2:23; Hebrews 7:28).
Jesus our high priest was 30 years of age when anointed for service unto the Father.

Vs 3   In all we have 38,000 Levites who were set apart for Temple service.

Vs 4-5   These verses tell how these were divided for the Temple service. Twenty-four thousand were to oversee the work of the house of the Lord.
Six thousand were officers (scribes) and judges (magistrates).
Four thousand were porters (Note 1 Chronicles 26:1).
Four thousand were musicians to praise the Lord with David's instruments (Note 1 Chronicles 25:1; Amos 6:5).

Vs 6   These were divided into courses according to the three sons of Levi and were rotated in their service in God's house.

Vs 7-23   Here the three divisions are outlined according to the house of their fathers.

1. **The Course of Gershon** (vs 7-11. Note Luke 1:5. The course of Abia)
These were in their divisions according to the house of their fathers. In all we have 18 houses mentioned.

2. **The Course of Kohath** (vs 12-20 with 24:20-31)
Again these are grouped in the house of their fathers. Moses family was generally counted among the Levites as of the same tribe. In chapter 24:20-31 we have further details of the lots cast before king David, Zadok and Ahimelech for their service in God's house.

3. **The Course of Merari** (vs 21-23)
Here six are named after the house of their fathers.

Thus the courses are named after the three sons of Levi (1 Chronicles 6:1-3). In all we have 9 + 9 + 6 = 24 courses. These were all 30 years of age and above who served in priesthood duties.

Vs 24-27   It is significant to note that, while Moses had the age for ministry of the Levites as 30 years, David lowered the age for service to 20 years old and upwards (Numbers 1:3; 4:3; 8:24).

With the nation at the height of its glory under David and Solomon, there was need to increase workers for the house of the Lord. So David lowered the age for service of the Levites from 30 years to 20 years of age.

Vs 28-32   In these verses we have the ministry of the Levites. Their office was to wait on the sons of Aaron for the service of the house of the Lord. Here they were to serve:

1.   In the courts, outer and inner courts,
2.   In the chambers, both priests and treasure chambers,
3.   In the purification of holy things,
4.   In the service of the house of God,
    a)   For the shewbread
    b)   For the meal offerings
    c)   For the unleavened cakes of all kinds
5.   In the morning and evening thanks and praise to the Lord,
6.   In the sacrifices for:
    a)   The sabbaths,
    b)   The new moons,
    c)   The feast days.
7.   In keeping the charge of the Lord's house, the holy place, and the charge of the sons of Aaron in the house of the Lord.

All had their particular function and responsibility as priests in the Lord's house. The priesthood was a functioning body and each member of the priesthood worked as a member to fulfil the service to the Lord and the Israel of God. All find fulfilment in the new covenant priesthood of all believers functioning as the many membered body of Christ (1 Corinthians 12).

B.   **The Division of the Sons of Aaron** — 1 Chronicles 24:1-19

In this section we have the courses outlined for the house of Aaron, the household of the high priest.

Vs 1   Aaron and his sons are named here.

Vs 2   Nadab and Abihu died before the Lord and had no offspring, so Eleazar and Ithamar executed the priests office.

Vs 3-4   Of the sons of Eleazar and Ithamar we have 16 chief men and 8 chief men respectively, making 24 in all.

Vs 5-19   Lots were cast before the Lord, the king, the princes and chief priests as to the order in which the courses served and all was written in a book by the scribe.

The Scripture makes it clear that, in the casting of lots under Old Testament times, Divine sovereignty was evidenced. "The lot is cast into the lap but the disposing (choice) thereof is of the Lord" (Proverbs 16:33; Leviticus 16:8-10; Matthew 27:35; Acts 1:26; Joshua 18-19).

Thus we have 24 lots cast for the 24 courses of Aaron's house, the priestly house of the tribe of Levi, who were the governors of God's house (vs 5). The Levites, it should be remembered, served as the "diakonate" the priests.

It is God's choice where, when and how His redeemed will serve in His Temple. The casting of lots would remove all jealousy, fears of favouritism, or deceit, as all would recognize the choice of the Lord as to service. So it is in the body of Christ in New Testament times. God sets in the body the members, gifts and ministries and functions as it pleases Him.

C. **The Courses of the Singers and Musicians** — 1 Chronicles 25:1-31

We noted in 1 Chronicles 23:4-5 that 4,000 were chosen to praise the Lord with the instruments which David had made.

In this chapter David outlines the 24 courses of the singers and musicians. The ministry of music and song played a very important part in the Temple services, even as music and song find an important place in the new covenant temple, the church.

There are spiritual lessons for the church to learn from the courses of the singers and musicians some of which we note here.

Vs 1-5   The sons of Asaph, Heman and Jeduthan were separated to the service of music and song.

1. Of Asaph, four sons (vs 12). Asaph means "gatherer".
2. Of Jeduthan, six sons (vs 3). Jeduthan means "praising".
3. Of Heman, 14 sons (vs 4,5). Heman means "trusty" or "faithful".
   In all we have 24 sons.

Vs 6   All were under the hands of their father for song and music in the house of the Lord according to king David's order.
Note the significant expressions relative to this ministry.

1. They prophesied with instruments (vs 1,2,3 with 2 Kings 3:15).
2. They gave thanks and praise to the Lord (vs 3).
3. They lifted up the horn with the words of God (vs 5).
4. They were separated to this service (vs 1).
5. They were under the hands of the instructor (vs 2,3,6).
6. They were skilled or cunning in this ministry (vs 7).
7. They ministered in their respective courses (vs 8).
8. There were teachers (music teachers) and scholars (pupils) (vs 8).
9. They were instructed in the songs of the Lord (vs 7).
10. They had musical instruments of harps, psalteries and cymbals (vs 1 with Amos 6:5 and 1 Chronicles 23:5).

Vs 7   They numbered 288 (or $12 \times 24 = 288$, or 2×144) in all.

Vs 8-31 These verses set forth the 24 lots of 12 who would minister in their respective courses.

In the author's textbook *"The Tabernacle of David"* these things have been dealt with more fully. The order of music and song in Israel established in David's Tabernacle is now incorporated into the Temple order in the Temple choir and orchestra (Amos 8:3).

Songs and music have always played an important part in Israel's history, as also in church history. The spiritual rise and fall of the nation was reflected in its music as it is today in the life of a believer personally and a church corporately.

* The song of Moses is the first recorded song in the Bible after the great deliverance from Egyptian bondage (Exodus 15).

* The song of Deborah also arose out of victory over Israel's enemies (Judges 5).

* The songs of David cover a wide range of subjects as seen in the book of Psalms (2 Samuel 23:1-2).

* The songs of Zion could not be sung in Babylonian Captivity (Psalm 137 with Psalm 126; Isaiah 44:23; 42:11).

* There were new songs continually through Israel's history (Psalm 33:3; 40:3; 96:1).

As the ultimate of that which pertains to the Temple finds its fulfilment in the Book of Revelation, so it is with the ministry of music and song. That which is seen in both David's Tabernacle and Solomon's Temple is combined in revelation's order of worship as our contrast and comparison shows.

Tabernacle and Temple	—	Revelation
David and 3 Chief Singers	—	Four Living Creatures
Twenty-four Courses	—	Twenty-four Elders
The 288 (2×144) Singers	—	The 144,000 Singers
New Songs	—	New Song
Harps of God	—	Harps of God
Clothed in white linen	—	Clothed in white linen
Temple choir	—	Heavenly Choir
Songs of Creation and Redemption	—	Songs of Creation and Redemption
The thousands of Israel	—	The thousands of the redeemed
The one chosen nation	—	Out of every kindred, tongue, nation

The student should consider these Scriptures relative to these things. 1 Chronicles 15:22,27; 16:37-43; 25:1-7; 2 Chronicles 29:26-28; Psalm 47:6,7; 68:25; 134:1-2; Colossians 3:16; Ephesians 5:18,19; Matthew 26:30; Revelation 4:1-11; 5:1-14; 7:1-4; 14:1-11.

The ministry of music and song will find its perfect and richest expression in the city of God around the throne of God and the Lamb for all eternity. That which was in Solomon's Temple was the prophetic foreshadowing of eternal music and song from the heart of the redeemed of earth, out of every kindred, tongue, tribe and nation, the spiritual Israel of God.

D. **The Courses of the Porters** — 1 Chronicles 26:1-32

In 1 Chronicles 23:5 we are told that 4000 of the Levites were also set aside to be porters in the service of the house of the Lord. These were of Gershom, Kohath and Merari (1 Chronicles 23:6 with 26:1,10,21).

In this chapter we seem to have those porters who are over the gates of the Temple and those who are over the treasure chambers.

1. **The Porters of the gates** — vs 1-19

   a) Of Meshelemiah — vs 1-3,9
   Seven sons, plus 18 descendants, or 25 in all.

   b) Of Obededom — vs 4-8
   Seventy-two descendants listed here. God blessed Obededom's household because of his faithful care of the ark of God (2 Samuel 6:11-12; Psalm 127:5).
   All were strong men, mighty men of valour, able men for the service in the house of God. Such would be needed to guard the Temple court gates.

The keeping of the gates was also assigned by lot. In all we have 24 gate-keepers, watching the gates north, south, east and west (vs 10-19; 1 Chronicles 9:18;25; 2 Chronicles 8:14).

It would seem that these were responsible for the divisions of the 4000 porters, superintending the Temple watches both day and night.

The charge laid on these porters involved various services pertaining to the Lord's house. The charge laid on them was similar to that laid on the Levites by Moses for the service of the Tabernacle (Numbers 3).

* They were to watch at the gates of the house of the Lord, at the gates of the outer and inner court, and at the doors of the Temple of God (2 Chronicles 35:15).

* They were to watch that no unqualified person would enter these gates, so that no one unclean would defile the Lord's habitation (2 Chronicles 23:19).

* They were to resist any presumptuous act such as king Uzziah's as he presumed to enter the house of the Lord to burn incense. He sinned himself out of God's house (2 Chronicles 26:20-21).

So God has in His church today those who are "gate-keepers", to guard the gate and keep those out who would presume to touch Divine things in their unholy state.

2.   **The Porters of the Dedicated Treasures** — vs 20-32

Certain of the Levites were over the treasures of the house of God and the treasures of the dedicated things. Note the use of the word "treasure" in verses 20,22,24,26, and the use of the word "dedicated" in verses 20,26,27,28.

The treasures of the Lord are those things dedicated by His people to maintain His house. Various worthies are mentioned by name who dedicated things to the Lord.

* David the king dedicated things to the Lord's house (vs 26).

* The chief fathers and captains did the same (vs 26).

* Samuel the prophet had dedicated things (vs 28).

* Even king Saul had dedicated things (vs 28).

* Abner also (vs 28).

* Joab also (vs 28).

* Others in the nation of Israel (vs 28).

These things were dedicated out of the spoils of war and used to maintain the Lord's house (vs 27).

So members of the body of Christ today dedicate themselves and all things to the Lord for His service and these are the Lord's treasures in His house.

Together the gate-keepers and treasure keepers were the porters to guard the Temple and its treasury stores day and night.

3.   **The Porters of the Holy Things** — 1 Chronicles 9:18-34

The student is referred to the chapter on the Temple Chambers for it seems that some of the porters had charge of other things in the Lord's house. In the portion of Scripture here we see the following:

* Porters over the king's gate

* Porters over the gates of the Tabernacle (i.e. Lord's habitation)

* Porters in the gates numbered 212 in all

* Porters over the chambers and treasures of the house of God

* Porters whose charge involved:

    a)   The storehouses of the Lord's house

    b)   The treasures of God's house

    c)   The vessels of the house

    d)   The ingredients of the meal offerings

e) The spices for the anointing oil

f) The preparation of the shewbread

g) The singers employed in this ministry

h) The offerings of finance for the Lord's house (2 Chronicles 34:9; 31:14; 2 Kings 12:9-11; 22:4).

All had their particular ministry to fulfil pertaining to the house of the Lord.

E. The Significance of the Porters

The porters were like watchman, the Lord's ministers, in their various places of responsibility and accountability in the house of the Lord. They were consecrated to this ministry (Nehemiah 13:22).
So ministers today are the Lord's watchmen (Ezekiel 3:17; 33:7; Isaiah 21:11).
The porter opens the door to the true shepherd (John 10:3). Watchmen need to watch against defiling persons and things entering into the house of the Lord (Acts 20:27-31; 2 Timothy 4:5; Revelation 3:2-3).

Porters need to be watchful, diligent, and persons of valour to resist any who should enter into the gates of the Lord presumptuously.
Watchman need to guard the treasures of the Lord, the things that have been prepared in the Lord's house (1 Corinthians 4:1; 2 Corinthians 4:7; 1 Peter 4:10; Ephesians 4:11-13).
Wicked king Ahaz took the treasures from the Lord's house and sent it to Assyria (2 Kings 16:8). It is the responsibility of true leadership to watch over the Lord's house, His people, His treasures. In doing so they will be true porters.

Again we are brought to the 24 "porters" in the city of God in Revelation. There are the 12 apostles of the Lamb having their names in the foundation of the city. There are the 12 unnamed messengers (angels) in the gates of the city. Together two lots of twelve, making twenty-four. And all who enter into the gates of that city will enter through them and who and what they represent. Nothing that defiles may enter the holy city of God (Revelation 21-22).

E. The Officers and Judges — 1 Chronicles 26:29-32

In 1 Chronicles 23:4 David also set aside 6000 officers and judges for the work of the Lord.
In the passage under consideration the work of these is specified. These were for the outward business over Israel, the business of the Lord and the service of the king.
There was a chief man with 1,700 officers this side of Jordan for the Lord's business (vs 30), and a chief man with 2,700 rulers for the things of the Lord and the king (vs 32). Perhaps the remaining 1,600 served in other areas of the king's business though not specified here.

The lesson to be learnt is that the Lord's business requires leadership; responsible and capable leadership both in the Old Testament church and the New Testament church.

F. The Twelve Princes of Israel — 1 Chronicles 27:1-34

In our final chapter dealing with the courses of Israel, David sets forth the 12 captains or princes of Israel who served for 12 months of the year in their particular course.
Each prince had a course of 24,000 men. These were the standing army of Israel, all enlisted in the king's service. Probably there were regiments of 1000 each, making 24 regiments of 24,000 in all, the companies each of 100 men having 240 centurians. This would make 12 legions according to the number of the 12 tribes of Israel.

Each legion consisting of 24,000 men served each month by rotation, stationed at Jerusalem or other places as the king desired. Their will was to do the king's will.
An outline of the chapter provides the following:

Vs 1   The chief fathers, captains and officers of the thousands and hundreds of Israel served
           the king month by month each having their course of 24,000 men.

Vs 2-15   The 12 captains are named with their courses of 24,000 each.

Vs 16-22   The tribes are named here with their 12 princes also (Asher is not mentioned but is
           probably represented in another tribe).

Vs 23-24   Those 20 years and under were not numbered in Israel for war (Note Numbers 1:1-4).

Vs 25-34   In these verses we have those who were over the portion of the king's possessions.
           Note Solomon's 12 princes who provided for his kingdom affairs (1 Kings 4:7, 1-19).

Thus all Israel is looked upon by the Lord in their 24 courses, or 24,000's with the 12 leaders
over them representing all before the Lord. So the high priest would have the 12 names of the 12
tribes of Israel on his breastplate and represented all before the Lord in His mediatorial
ministrations.

G. Spiritual Significance in the Church

We bring our chapter to its conclusion by noting the most significant truths in Israel's order.
The numbers or multiples of the same are the 12 princes, the 24 courses, the 24,000 in their
courses and the number 144 also.

1. In the Tabernacle

These same numbers have been mentioned previously as seen in the Tabernacle of Moses.
Think of the 12 loaves of shewbread, the number 12 in the shaft of the golden lampstand, the
12 princes and their gifts at the dedication of the altar of brass, with the 12 oxen and the 6
wagons.
Think of the 24,000 souls represented in the 4 silver sockets of the pillars of the inner veil.
Think of the $4 \times 144,000 = 576,000$ redeemed souls represented in the 96 silver sockets
of the sanctuary boards. And again, think of the goat's hair curtains especially the six over
the holy place and the 5×144 cubital goats hair curtains area.

2. In the Temple

Many twelves and its multiples have been mentioned already in the Temple itself.
There were the 12 loaves of shewbread on the tables. Then we have the 12 princes,
the 24 priests on duty, the 24 porters for the gates, representing the 24,000's and the
thousands of Israel before the Lord. Then we have the $2 \times 144 = 288$ singers, and the
$12 \times 24,000 = 288,000$ in their courses.
The Temple measurements, especially the holy place measured in multiples of twelve also.

3. In the Revelation

The book of Revelation reveals the ultimate of the number twelve and its multiples.

Here we see the 12 stars on the crown of the bride of Christ (Revelation 12:1).

Here we see the 24 elders round about the throne of God and the Lamb. Then we have the 12
apostles in the foundation of the bride city, and the 12 messengers in the 12 gates, making 24
in all.

The wall of the city is 144 cubits hight. There are 12,000 chosen out of each of the 12 tribes
of Israel, making up the 144,000 who are the redeemed from the earth. These have harps
and sing a new song in Mt Zion.

Twelve manner of fruit comes from the tree of life for the 12 months of the year. The city of
God is 12,000 furlongs square (Revelation 4-5, 21-22).

The numbers twelve and twenty-four have been seen as the numbers of apostolic government
and priestly ministrations. Multiples of such only intensify the truth. God's complete and perfect

government will be manifested in His people who are an everlasting order of kings and priests, redeemed out of all ages from the earth.

The New Testament shows that all believers are kings and priests in the body of Christ. All have a place, all have a function to fulfil. All have their responsibility to serve the Lord in their distinctive ministry in His house.

These are the major lessons we learn from the Temple courses that David ordered by Divine revelation.

CHAPTER THIRTYSEVEN

THE VISIT OF THE QUEEN OF SHEBA

Solomon's Temple was one of the wonders of the then-known world. The Scripture tells how the kings and queens of all nations came to hear of the wisdom of Solomon and see the house he had built to the Lord, as well as the glory of his kingdom (1 Kings 4:29-34).

One of the more detailed accounts of such is given in Kings and Chronicles concerning the visit of a Gentile queen, the queen of Sheba. She came from the ends of the earth to see and hear the wisdom of Solomon. So great was this that the Lord Jesus Christ Himself spoke of it. He told His generation how the queen of Sheba came from the ends of the earth to hear the wisdom of Solomon and "behold, a greater than Solomon is here" (Matthew 12:38-42).

This visit, as well as other visits from Gentile kings and queens and their peoples, was prophetic of that coming in of the Gentiles, along with Israel, to see the wisdom of God in the church, the new covenant house of the Lord.

We outline some of the things which impressed the queen of Sheba relative to Solomon's reign, wisdom, and the house of the Lord and his kingdom. For, in the church is to be seen the manifold wisdom of God. There should be that excellence that glorifies God and not man. The strangers who know not the Lord should see in the church the wisdom of the Lord.

The student should study carefully the details found in 1 Kings 10:1-10 and 2 Chronicles 9:1-9. The queen of Sheba "saw" and "heard" the excellence of Solomon's kingdom.

1. **The Excellence of the Fame of the Name of the Lord**

    1 Kings 8:16-21,29-35,42-43. The Temple had been built for the name of the Lord. Heathen kings built temples for their deities, but the Temple was built for the true God.
    There was always to be a place for His name (Deuteronomy 12, 16).
    The church is the habitation for the name of the Lord, in the name of the Lord Jesus Christ (Matthew 28:18-20; 18:15-20; 2 Timothy 2:19).

2. **The Excellence of the House he had built**

    Solomon was a wise master-builder. Paul was a wise master-builder. The church is God's spiritual house to be filled with His glory. The Lord's house is to be established in the last days, hallowed for His name (1 Corinthians 3:9-10; 1 Peter 2:5-9; Hebrews 3:1-5; 1 Timothy 3:15; Psalm 127:1; Isaiah 2:1-5; Haggai 1:7-8).

3. **The Excellence of the Meat of his Table**

    The queen of Sheba saw the food of his table. The church should have good food on the table for the hungry (Hebrews 5:12-14; Malachi 3:8-10; 1 Corinthians 3:1-3; John 4:32-34).

4. **The Excellence of the Sitting of his Servants**

    The believer is seated with Christ in heavenly places in Christ, at the king's table (Ephesians 2:6; Revelation 3:21; 2 Samuel 9:1-13).

5. **The Excellence of the Attendance of his Ministers**

    The attendance speaks of their office, their place, their position and standing in the presence of the king (Psalm 134). The believer is to stand in the house of the Lord as befitting for a king.

6. **The Excellence of their Apparel**

    The queen of Sheba was impressed with their apparel. The church is to be clothed in the fine linen of righteousness, the only apparel that God accepts (Isaiah 52:1; 61:3,10; Revelation 19:7-8).

7. **The Excellence of the Cupbearers**

The cupbearers were the butlers. This was a responsible position before the king. They had to prove things before anything was given to the king. There are those in the house of the Lord who fulfil this function (Nehemiah 2:1; Genesis 40:9-13).

8. **The Excellence of Solomon's Ascent to the House of the Lord**

The queen of Sheba was impressed with Solomon's ascent to the house of the Lord. How much more should the unbeliever be impressed by our entrance to God's house (Psalm 100:4; 24:3-4; 122:1-2). We should be glad to go into the house of the Lord.

9. **The Excellence of his happy Servants**

Solomon's servants were happy in his service. They served him with joy, joy in the presence of their king. Joy is an infallible sign of the presence of the Lord. The joy of the Lord is our strength (Psalm 1:1-3; Matthew 5:1-12; Psalm 144:12-15; John 13:17).

10. **The Excellence of his Divine Wisdom**

Wisdom, knowledge and understanding characterized all that Solomon said and did. Through wisdom is a house builded. The principalities and powers in heavenly places are to behold the manifold wisdom of the Lord in the church and in the believer (Proverb 1:1-6; 24:3-4; Ephesians 3:10).

The queen of Sheba was overcome with all she saw and heard. There was no more spirit in her. She blessed the Lord and blessed Solomon for all she had seen and heard. A Gentile queen acknowledges the true God of Israel because of the wisdom she had seen. She gave gifts to Solomon and went back to her own country with a great testimony of the greatness of the God of Israel and Israel's king.

What great lessons may be found here for the individual believer and for the church as a whole. Instead of foolishness and ignorance, the unregenerate world should behold the glory and wisdom and knowledge of God in His church. They should be able to acknowledge that God is in the midst of his church and be convinced of Divine things.

A greater than Solomon is here, even the King of kings, and Lord of lords, even our Lord Jesus Christ. He reigns in His house, in His church, and He desires to manifest the fulness of the wisdom of God so that the Gentiles will come into the glory of His kingdom.

The Ethiopian under Candace, queen of Ethiopia, found the Lord Jesus Christ as his own personal Saviour under the ministry and wisdom of Philip, the evangelist. It foreshadowed the coming in of the Gentiles into the church, the house of God in these last days (Acts 8; Isaiah 2:1-4).

The church should aim for excellence without extravagance!

THE HIGH PRIEST IN HIS GARMENTS OF GLORY AND BEAUTY

Diagram — Flannelgraph

CHAPTER THIRTYEIGHT

ONE GREATER THAN THE TEMPLE

The Lord Jesus said that there was "one greater than the Temple" (Matthew 12:6). He also said "A greater than Solomon is here" (Matthew 12:42).

We know that this One is none other than the Lord Jesus Christ Himself. He is THE Tabernacle, THE Temple of God. All that was typified, symbolized and prophetic in the material temple pointed to and finds its fulfilment in Him personally.

The prophet Ezekiel told the people, in the time when they were bereft of all temple externals, "Thus says the Lord . . . I will be to them as *a little sanctuary* in the countries where they shall come" (Ezekiel 11:16). The sanctuary is no longer A PLACE but it is A PERSON!

It is absolutely significant that the glory of God never ever did return to the material rebuilt Temple under the restoration prophets.

However, on the Mt of Transfiguration, Jesus Christ is seen as THE TEMPLE of God, and the Shekinah-Glory-Light and cloud overshadowed Him as the Father's voice spoke out of the cloud, "This is My beloved son, HEAR HIM!" (Matthew 17:1-5; John 1:14-18; 2:20-21).

We worship Him who is God's Tabernacle and Temple, not as a place, but as a person. He is the fulfilment, personally of all that was symbolized and typified materially. He is God's pure and holy temple, undefiled and filled with the Father's glory, in whom the fulness of the name of God dwells. To worship in the Temple today is to worship God "in Christ" who is THE TEMPLE (John 2:19-21; Colossians 2:6,19).

In this place is ONE greater than the Temple. How or in what way is Christ greater than the Temple?

1. The Temple was built by the wisdom of God.
   Christ is the wisdom of God personified.

2. The Temple was built according to the pattern by the Spirit.
   Christ was made after the flesh according to Divine pattern by the Spirit.

3. The Temple was beautiful inside and outside.
   Christ is altogether lovely, both within and without.

4. The Temple was the attraction for all Israel's worship.
   Christ is the attraction to God the Father for all our worship.

5. The Temple veil was rent when the time was fully come.
   Christ died for all sin in the fulness of time.

6. The Temple was rich in glory and untold wealth.
   Christ is the riches of the glory and wealth of the Father God.

7. The Temple was defiled and destroyed by Babylon.
   Christ was holy, harmless and undefiled, and though crucified by man, He was raised from the dead by the Father.

8 The Temple was in a localized and geographical place.
   Christ is universally present by the Spirit with all His people.

9. The Temple was built by a king for priestly ministrations.
   Christ is both king and priest in the order of Melchisedek which consists of all believers as kings and priests unto God.

10. The Temple was God's temporal dwelling place, for sacrifices.
    Christ is God's eternal dwelling and once-for-all sacrifice.

CONCLUSION

Our study is at an end. The Temple study has been considered from a fourfold aspect; as a type of Christ, THE Temple of God, then of the believers, individually God's Temple, and then the Church, as God's corporate Temple and ultimately the city of God, the eternal dwelling place of the redeemed.

With all that has been written, where indeed "every bit of the Temple utters His glory" (Psalm 29:9), we can only bring our study to its conclusion with a word from the king and the prophets about this Temple.

King Solomon, who built the Temple, recognized that the material Temple he built could never contain God, that God was not limited to this house. Solomon himself said, "But who is able to build Him a house, seeing the heaven of heavens cannot contain Him?" (2 Chronicles 2:6; 1 Kings 8:27; 2 Chronicles 6:18; Acts 7:47-50).

The prophet Isaiah also said as he asked the Lord's question, "Where is the house that you build Me?", after stating the truth that the heavens are His throne and the earth is His footstool (Isaiah 66:1-2; Matthew 5:34; Acts 17:24).

The sad thing both in Jeremiah's day and Messiah's times, is seen in the fact that the Jews worshipped the Temple of God and missed the God of the Temple. In AD 70 God allowed the whole Temple system to be totally destroyed, never to be restored again either in this age or any age to come (Jeremiah 7:1-7; Matthew 23:37-38; 24:1-3).

Will God dwell with men? He did so in the person of Christ (John 1:14; 2:19-21). God dwells in Christ. Christ dwells in His people. We will eternally worship God and the Lamb in that eternal dwelling place, of which all earthly dwelling places were prophetic.
In that city of God there is no Temple for the Lord God and the Lamb are the Temple there and the light is the glory thereof (Revelation 21:22-23).

— AMEN & AMEN —

SUPPLEMENTAL CHAPTERS ON THE TEMPLE

The following chapters deal with other Temples in Scripture. However, it should be remembered that these subsequent Temples were all but restorations or additions of the foundation Temple, the Temple of Solomon.

The chapters presented here deal in brief with these Temples and draw some practical and concluding lessons from such for the believer and the church today. They seek to answer some valid questions relative to the restoration and rebuilding of material Temples either in this age or an age to come. This is especially true concerning the visionary Temple of Ezekiel's prophecy.

The believer, after studying these chapters, should rejoice eternally that he is now God's true Temple, of which all material Temples were temporal and transitory shadows.

Chapter   **Page**

CHAPTER ONE

THE TEMPLE OF SOLOMON — TEMPLE HISTORY

The history of Solomon's Temple reveals the spiritual condition of the nation, its kings, priests and rulers. Its glory rises and falls under godly or ungodly leadership.

Over the years the house of the Lord was plundered and desecrated by ungodly kings of Judah or Israel and Gentile kings. Under godly kings there were great cleansings and fresh dedications of the Temple services. The final days, however, reveal the glory of the Lord departing from its holy oracle because of the great abominations which had been brought into it. The final chapters give account of its destruction under the king of Babylon.

From the dedication of the Temple under king Solomon in Jerusalem to its destruction and desolation under king Nebuchadnezzar of Babylon we have a sad history.

The lesson to be learnt from this history is graphically summed up in Paul's writings to the Corinthian believers. "Know you not that you are the temple of God and that the Spirit of God dwells in you. If any man defile the temple of God, him will God destroy; for the temple of God is holy, which temple are you" (1 Corinthians 3:16-17).

Following we provide a brief outline and overview of Temple history from its dedication through to its desecration and final desolation and destruction.

1.   The Temple built and dedicated to the glory of the Lord under king Solomon in Jerusalem (1 Kings 3-10 with 2 Chronicles 1-9).

2.   The Temple plundered of gold, silver and treasures by Shishak, king of Egypt under king Rehoboam's evil reign (1 Kings 14:25-28).

3.   The Temple treasures taken by king Asa and sent to Benhadad, king of Syria to help in the war between Israel and Judah (1 Kings 15:16-24).

4.   The Temple had its outer court renewed under godly king Jehoshaphat and became a place of prayer and praise (2 Chronicles 20:5, 1-22).

5.   The Temple breaches repaired under godly king Jehoash under the priest Jehoiada's instruction (2 Chronicles 24:1-14; 2 Kings 12:1-16). However, Jehoash departed from the Lord and Temple treasures were given to Hazael, king of Syria, to appease him (2 Chronicles 24:15-22; 2 Kings 12:17-18).

6.   The Temple broken up by the wicked woman, queen Athaliah and the dedicated things bestowed on idols (2 Chronicles 24:7).

7.   The Temple treasuries broken into and plundered by Jehoash king of Israel and taken to Samaria (2 Kings 14:14).

8.   The higher gate of the house of the Lord built by godly king Jotham (2 Kings 15:35; 2 Chronicles 27:3).

9.   Wicked king Ahaz desecrated the temple vessels. He removed the 12 oxen from under the molten sea and set it on the pavement of brass. He also took the lavers from their bases. He moved the brazen altar to one side of the court and set his Assyrian altar next to it, acting presumptuously as a king-priest (2 Kings 16:10-17). He also plundered the Temple treasures to finance the king of Assyria agaisnt the king of Syria (2 Kings 16:8).

10.   King Hezekiah also gave the king of Assyria silver treasures out of the Lord's house to appease him at the time of invasion of Israel, and the northern kingdom's captivity. He also cut off the

gold from the doors of the Temple. This silver and gold were paid as a tribute to the enemies of the people of God (2 Kings 18:13-16).

11. Wicked king Manasseh, Hezekiah's son born to him in his 15 year life extension, desecrated the Temple order. Altars of all kinds were placed in the Temple courts to worship the host of heaven. All kinds of abominations were brought into the house of the Lord, even houses for the sodomites (2 Kings 21:1-16; 23:5-14).

12. Godly king Josiah purged the Temple of the corruptions and abominations of his fathers (2 Kings 22-23:1-25).

13. The desolation and destruction of the Temple took place under Nebuchadnezzar, king of Babylon. The Temple was destroyed. The vessels were broken or taken off to Babylon's treasuries because of the abominations of Israel and Judah (2 Kings 25; Jeremiah 52).

The sad history of the Temple is seen in this brief outline. Two of the greatest reasons for God allowing the destruction of the Temple are to be found in the writings of the prophets, Jeremiah and Ezekiel.

Jeremiah reproved the people of Judah because they idolized the Temple of God. They worshipped the Temple and missed the God of the Temple. This is idolatry. They believed that God would never allow the Temple He designed to be destroyed. Such was their blindness and false security. The Lord reminded them of what He did to His Tabernacle at Shiloh and said He would do the same to His Temple for their abominations. This He did by the hands of Babylon. His house had become a den of thieves.

The same evils occurred in Messiah's times. Jewry worshipped the Temple of God and crucified the Messiah of the Temple. God allowed the New Testament "Babylon" — Rome — to destroy the whole Temple system in AD 70 because of greater abominations (Matthew 23:38; 24:1-2).

Such had been Israel's history. They worshipped the symbol and missed the one the symbol pointed to. They worshipped the serpent of brass and missed the one who brought healing. They worshipped the ark of God and missed the God of the ark. They worshipped the gold of the Temple and missed the God of the Temple. They worshipped the symbol, the shadow and the type and missed the substance, the reality and the antitype (John 3:14-16; 2 Samuel 6:3).

Ezekiel, in Babylonian Captivity, gave the same reason as Jeremiah for the destruction of the Temple. In Ezekiel chapters 1-10 he visions the terrible abominations being brought into the house of the Lord. Gradually, reluctantly the glory of the Lord lifts from the ark of the Covenant. Step by step it leaves the house and finally ascends to heaven from Olivet. With the desolation of the Temple, it becomes "Ichabod", or "The Glory has departed". The Temple can only fall to destruction. A house without inhabitant is soon destroyed. So did the house of the Lord under the king of Babylon (Isaiah 66:1-4; Jeremiah 7:1-7; Ezekiel 9:3; 10:4,18; 11:23).

The Lord Jesus Christ, at the close of His ministry told Jewry, "Your house is left unto you desolate" (Matthew 23:38). When He departed from the Temple, He was the departing glory. Then He prophesied of its destruction under Rome (Matthew 24:1-2).

In conclusion, who can fail to see the lessons of Temple history, applicable personally and corporately? Believers constitute God's Temple (1 Corinthians 3:16-17; 6:16; Ephesians 2:19-22). We are God's house, dedicated to holiness. The Holy Spirit is the shekinah glory of God within us. Any believer — or church — that brings abominations into God's Temple to defile it will be destroyed. As sure as God's glory departed and the material Temple was left to destruction, so sure will the same happen to a believer or a church that defiles God's holy Temple. This is the whole burden of the apostle Paul when he speaks of the church as the Temple of God. This is the lesson of the dedication, desecration, desolation and destruction of Temple history.

CHAPTER TWO

THE TEMPLE OF ZERUBBABEL

The Temple of Zerubbabel deals with the Temple of the period of restoration after the Babylonian Captivity of the house of Judah.

The historical books of Ezra, Nehemiah and Esther cover this period of time, as well as the prophetical books of Haggai and Zechariah.

Many lessons may be learnt from these books relative to the Temple of the Lord. Here we outline in brief the important details of this restored Temple.

1. **The Decree of Cyrus**

    About B.C. 536-538 Cyrus gave the decree for the release of the captives of Judah and their return to Judah to rebuild the city of Jerusalem and the Temple of the Lord (2 Chronicles 36:23; Ezra 1:1-4).

    This decree had been foretold about 100 years previously by the word of the Lord through the prophet Isaiah (Isaiah 44-45 chapters). Cyrus not only issued this decree but also restored the sacred vessels of the Temple and provided a tax upon some of his provinces to provide materials for the restoration of the house of the Lord besides the freewill offerings of the people (Ezra 1:6-11).

    Only a small remnant of Judah returned to become involved in the work of restoration. The principal leaders of the restoration movement were Joshua, the high priest, and Zerubbabel, governor of the house of Judah. Together in these two leaders we have the union of Levi (priestly) and Judah (royalty) in the restoration of the Lord's house (Hagga 1:1).

2. **The Altar Restored**

    The first thing restored by Joshua and Zerubbabel was the altar of sacrifice on its original site (Ezra 3). This was done in the Feast of the Seventh month, the Feast of Tabernacles.

    Only upon sacrificial and atoning blood could God's house be restored.

3. **The Temple Foundation**

    The next thing to be laid was the foundation of the Temple. Stone masons and carpenters were engaged in the restoration of the Lord's house. In the second year the foundations were completed amidst the weeping and shouting of the people of Judah who remembered the glory of the former house.

4. **Opposition and Completion**

    However, the work suffered great opposition from the mixed population of the Samaritans. With pressure on the authorities, the work was caused to cease for some years unto the reign of Darius (B.C. 520). However, he re-confirmed and reissued the decree for the Temple to be finished (Ezra 4). The Temple was completed with much more speed than previous work under the inspiration of the prophets Haggai and Zechariah (Ezra 5,6).

5. **The Temple Structure**

    Very few details are provided concerning the restored Temple. Zerubbabel's Temple was 60 cubits high and 60 cubits broad and 100 cubits long (Ezra 6:3). It stood on its original site and seemed to follow as much of Solomon's Temple and some of Ezekiel's visionary Temple in parts.

    However, the Temple was far inferior to Solomon's as to interior and exterior beauty owing to lack of costly materials. The "greater glory" of the former Temple must speak to them of the adornment of the Temple and the particular articles of furniture absent from it (Ezra 3:12; Haggai 2:3).

The Temple was divided, like Solomon's, into a holy and most holy place. The Book of Maccabees speaks of "the veil" in this Temple (1 Maccabbees 1:21-22).

6. The "Absent Five"

Undoubtedly the saddest thing about the restored Temple, lamented by the leaders and the people of Judah, was the "absent five". The Talmud speaks of these five things that were missing from the restored Temple, which Solomon's Temple had. These things were:

* The Ark of the Covenant

The final mention of the ark of the Covenant is found in Jeremiah 3:16. There the prophet said that the ark would no more be remembered, nor come to mind, nor would they seek after it. The ark has never been seen since Jeremiah's time. A Temple without the ark is a house without inhabitant, as far as Jewry is concerned. No Temple since Solomon's has had the ark of God in it. This itself is most significant.

Instead, they placed a stone on which the high priest placed his censer on the great Day of Atonement, after the sprinkling of the blood of atonement.

* The Shekinah Glory

The next thing missing from the rebuilt Temple was the glory-presence of the Lord, or what the Hebrews called "the Shekinah". Without the ark of the Lord there could be no Shekinah, for the ark was the throne of God in Israel. He dwelt upon the blood-stained mercy seat. No throne, no blood-stained mercy seat meant no glory-presence of the Lord.

* The Sacred Fire

Again, the Divine fire was absent from the restored Temple. The fire came out from the glory of the Lord in the dedication of the Tabernacle of Moses and the Temple of Solomon. Here, however, there is no ark, no glory, no sacred fire on the sacrificial altar to seal it all. Surely Jewry must have realized some significance in this absent manifestation in a rebuilt material Temple.

* The Urim and Thummin

The fourth thing notable by its absence was the operation of the Lord through the mysterious stones in the breastplate of the high priest called "Urim and Thummin", or "Lights and Perfections". Through these mysterious stones the high priest received the mind of God for the people (Exodus 28-29; Ezra 2:63).

* The Holy Spirit Prophets

Haggai, Zechariah and then Malachi were the last of the Old Testament Holy Spirit inspired prophets. The nation of Jewry entered into what has been spoken of as "the 400 silent years" when there was no prophetic voice to be heard. We have the uninspired Apocryphal Books of this period, but no more Scriptural revelation.

If Jewry would not hear "Moses and the prophets" what need was there to send other prophets? John the Baptist would usher in the Messiah Himself of whom Moses and the prophets spoke. If Jewry would not hear them there was no hope of salvation or promised redemption for the nation.

However, the Divine purpose in allowing the Temple to be restored was to hold the nation in the land until the coming of John and the Messiah, even though these five things were missing from the nation's central religious point.

7. Temple Furnishings

There were other differences in the restored Temple as to its furnishings. According to the Maccabees they had an altar of stone, not of brass in the outer court (1 Maccabees 4:43-46).

Also there was but one golden candlestick, one table of shewbread, and, as always, one altar of incense (1 Maccabees 4:41-61).

8. **Temple History**

History shows that this Temple was plundered by Antiochus Epiphanes. He defiled it with idolatrous worship.
Judas Maccabees pulled down the defiled altar and built a new one. The sanctuary was cleansed and the Temple dedicated to the Lord afresh and the Feast of Dedication was kept yearly from then on (John 10:22; 1 Maccabees 4).

Later on the Temple was taken by Pompey on the Day of Atonement after a three months seige, and then later on by Herod the Great. Rome nominated Herod to be king of Judea about B.C. 39 and was in power when the Messiah of God "came to His Temple" suddenly!

The enigmatic prophecy of Haggai was fulfilled in Christ. "The glory of the latter house" was greater than the former (Haggai 2:9). Messiah, in whose face is the light of the glory of God said "In this place is One greater than the Temple" (Matthew 12:6). That One was Himself!

Many lessons are evident in the Temple of Zerubbabel, the Temple of the restoration period.
The church, as God's Temple, is being restored today, after a spiritual Babylonian Captivity. However, all restoration is incomplete without the throne of God, His presence, His glory-fire, His mind and His Spirit. Christ Himself must be in the Temple or all become formalism and ritualism and idolatry without Him, the Lord Jesus Christ!

RECONSTRUCTION OF HEROD'S TEMPLE

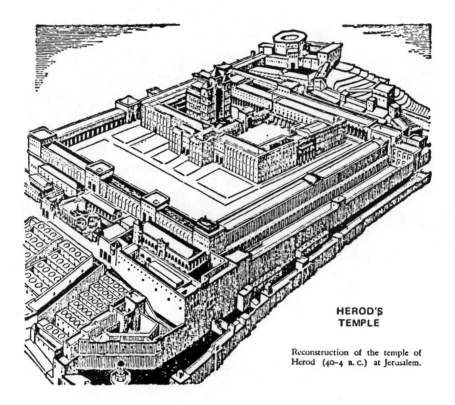

**HEROD'S
TEMPLE**

Reconstruction of the temple of
Herod (40–4 B.C.) at Jerusalem.

CHAPTER THREE

THE TEMPLE OF HEROD

The Temple of Herod or Herod's Temple, as it is referred to, was only a restoration and extension of the previously restored Temple.

Herod became de facto king of Judea by the capture of Jerusalem under Rome about B.C. 37. We are indebted to the Jewish Historian Josephus for most of the information we have about Herod's Temple.

Herod formed this project of rebuilding Zerubbabel's Temple on a grander scale and tried to make this the fulfilment of Haggai 2:9 concerning the glory of the latter house being greater than the former.

About 1000 priests were trained to be masons and carpenters for the work on the sanctuary, while about 10,000 skilled workmen were involved in the work altogether.

The building commenced about 20-19 B.C. The total erection took about 46 years (John 2:20). The work was entirely completed about A.D. 64 or about 6 years before its destruction by Rome.

The Temple was built of white marble, covered with heavy plates of gold in front, and rising high above its marble-cloistered courts the Temple was a dazzling conspicuous object from every direction.

It was a Temple larger than Solomon's and had additional courts surrounding it. Although there was much similarity between Solomon's and Herod's Temple, there were several important features having their own special significance, as will be noted. The Temple consisted of its house as its predecessor with the holiest of all and holy place. It had a porch immediately in front of it with the altar of burnt offering, a court for Israel, then in front of this a court for the women, and round the whole of the preceding, a court for and open to the Gentiles. Each court was ascended by steps. Each court had its dividing walls and their respective gates.

(The student is referred to the Diagram of the Temple at Jerusalem for some idea of these courts).

We note these particular courts and their distinctive message. We consider the approach outward to inward, according to the person's state before the Lord.

1. **The Court of the Gentiles**

    In the Court of the Gentiles any Gentile or stranger or proselyte could come and pray to the Lord God of Israel. His house was to be a house of prayer for all nations, according to Solomon's prayer years before. Note the publican's prayer which probably took place here (Luke 18:10-14). The Gentiles were "afar off" from God.

2. **The Sacred Enclosure**

    The Sacred Enclosure was a space between the Court of the Gentiles and other particular Courts. It told any Gentile, "thus far and no further". A stone was discovered with this Greek inscription written: "No stranger must enter within the balustrade round the temple and enclosure: whosoever is caught will be responsible for his own death" (Note — Acts 21:28).

    It is also said that this was a triple wall separating the Gentile Court from all other Courts. It had nine gates in this middle wall of partition. The message to the Gentile was clear.

3. **The Court of the Women**

    No doubt it was in the Court of the Women that the sinful woman was brought by the Jews to be stoned (John 8:1-12). Here she found mercy and truth in the Lord Jesus Christ, her Saviour.

    In the Court of the Women there were 13 trumpet-shaped chests for the reception of the money and offerings of the worshippers. Here the widow placed her mite and was blessed of the Lord (Mark 12:41-44; Luke 21:1-2). The Temple treasury began here.

4. The Court of Israel

This court was strinctly for Jewish males. No doubt the Pharisee prayed from this as he looked down upon the publican in the Court of the Gentiles (Luke 18:10-14). In Christ's earthly walk, this is as far as He could enter as a male Jew.

5. The Court of the Priests

This court was strictly for the priests of the Levitical tribe, the priestly tribe. None other dare enter this court. Here the priestly ministrations took place as the sacrifices were offered to God, which was to precede those priests who would enter the Temple ministrations.
A reference to the Temple and its altar may be seen in Matthew 23:35; 5:23,24.

6. The Temple of the Lord

This house was for the priests only. The Levitical priests could minister in the holy place but only the high priest could enter within the veil on the great Day of Atonement once a year. This veil was rent at the death of Christ on Calvary (Matthew 27:51; Mark 15:38).

7. Solomon's Porch

This was a remnant of Solomon's Temple and was the place where the money-changers and cattle dealers set up their stalls for pilgrims coming to the Temple to offer sacrifices in the yearly festival times (Matthew 21-12; John 2:14-16; 10:23; Mark 11:27; Luke 2:46; 19:47; Acts 3:11-12).

Our next chapter will deal with the Lord's ministry in Herod's Temple, for He still recognized it as "His Father's house" in principle.

The Temple of Herod was destroyed by the Roman armies under prince Titus in A.D. 70 as foretold by Jesus some 40 years previous (Matthew 24:1-2). Years later, the Roman Emperor, Hadrian, erected an altar to Jupiter on the site of the Temple (A.D. 130).
Years later the Mosque of Omar was erected on the Temple and is there unto this day.
What tragedy is seen in the history of this site. Instead of the Temple of God for Israel's God to dwell in, the Mosque of Omar of the flesh seed of Ishmael stands in its stead, an evidence of the judgment of God upon His own unbelieving people.

The most important lessons we can learn from Herod's Temple and its courts seem to be alluded to in the writings of the apostle Paul.
Undoubtedly he is alluding to the various courts which were the evidence of the distinctive divisions between both Jews and Gentiles when he speaks the following truths.
He writes to the Ephesian believers that "the middle wall of partition" that once existed between Jew and Gentile has been broken down at the cross and both ethnic groups are one body through the body and blood of Christ (Ephesians 2).
He writes to the Galatians also and tells them that "in Christ there is neither Jew nor Gentile, bond nor free, male or female, circumcision nor uncircumcision". All are one in Christ Jesus (Galatians 3:28).

Male and female are one in Christ. Jew and Gentile are one in Christ. All believers whether Jew or Gentile, male or female, are priests unto the Lord and all may enter within the veil. The veil has been rent in two. The middle walls of divisions and separations have been broken down. Together we are the habitation of God by His Spirit.

RESTORATION OF TEMPLE OF SOLOMON BY FRISBEE

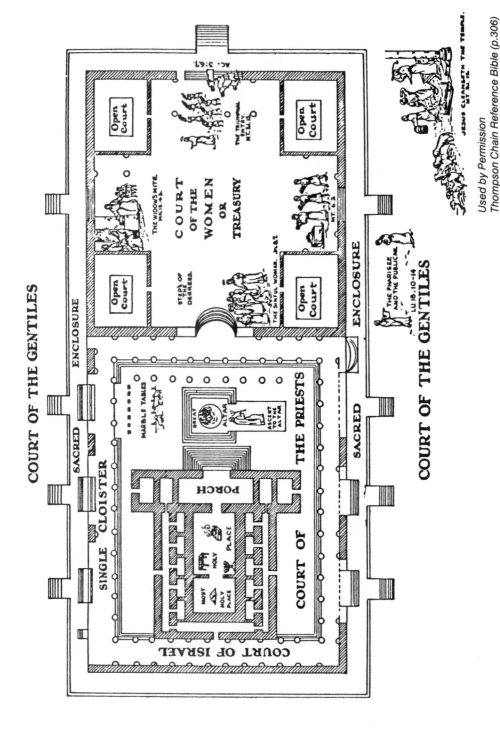

COURT OF THE GENTILES

COURT OF THE GENTILES

ENCLOSURE

ENCLOSURE

SACRED

SACRED

SINGLE CLOISTER

Open Court

Open Court

Open Court

Open Court

COURT OF THE WOMEN OR TREASURY

THE WIDOW'S MITE. MK.12.4.

THE SINFUL WOMAN. JN.8.2

THE TRIUMPHAL ENTRY. MT.21.10.

AC. 3.4?

STEPS OF THE DEGREES.

MT. 6.2

COURT OF THE PRIESTS

MARBLE TABLS

GREAT ALTAR

ASCENT TO THE ALTAR

PORCH

HOLY PLACE

MOST HOLY PLACE

COURT OF ISRAEL

THE PHARISEE AND THE PUBLICAN. LU.18.10-14

JESUS CLEANSETH THE TEMPLE. MT.21.12.

Used by Permission
Thompson Chain Reference Bible (p.306)

CHAPTER FOUR

THE TEMPLE MINISTRY OF CHRIST AND THE CHURCH

Linked with the previous chapter on Herod's Temple is the several years ministry of Christ and then the New Testament relative to this Temple at Jerusalem. Even though the Temple was referred to as Solomon's, Zerubbabel's or Herod's, the foundational truth of it all was that it still symbolized "My Father's house" according to Christ (John 2:16; Matthew 21:12,13). The original pattern was of the Lord.

We note in the Gospels and the Acts some of the outstanding ministry relative to this Temple. The prophet Malachi prophesied that the "messenger of the covenant" and "the Lord whom you seek" would come suddenly to His Temple (Malachi 3:1-6). It was this prophecy especially which held the Jews in Jerusalem for they looked for the Messiah to come suddenly to the material Temple. Messiah did come to His Temple but not the way they expected Him to come.

Consider the ministry in this Temple or its environs that took place in Christ's 3½ years ministry and in the Book of Acts in the probationary years unto its destruction.

A. **Temple Ministry and Messiah**

1. Messiah would come suddenly to His Temple in great cleansing power (Malachi 3:1-6). None would be able to stand this day of power.

2. The archangel Gabriel came to the Temple and foretold the birth of John the Baptist to Zacharias, as also the coming of the Messiah. This was at the time of the ascent of the incense and at the right side of the golden altar in the holy place as Zacharias served in his priestly course after the order of David (Luke 1). It was fitting that the archangel who gave to Daniel the notable Seventy Week Prophecy concerning Messiah's ministry bring this declaration.

3. Satan took Christ to the pinnacle of the Temple and tempted Him to cast Himself down in a presumptuous act in order for the angels to protect Him. Jewry expected the Messiah to come to His Temple. Satan's temptation was to by-pass the cross and do something spectacular for the Jews to accept Him as their long-promised Messiah (Matthew 4:5-6; Luke 4:9-11).
    But this was not the way the Father wanted the Son to come to His Temple.

4. Here in the Temple Court of the Women Mary presented Jesus for circumcision and naming. Here also the godly Simeon and the prophetess Anna gave their prophetic utterances (Luke 2).

5. At the age of 12 Jesus was found in the Temple confounding the learned Rabbis with His understanding of the Scriptures (Luke 2:46).

6. Christ came to the Temple "suddenly" in a way they did not expect and cleansed it of the corrupt money-changers and dealers. He said it was His Father's house and was meant to be a house of prayer, not a den of thieves (John 2:13-22).

7. Over His 3½ year period of ministry Christ taught much in the Temple court.

    * Here after the Temple cleansing He gave the sign of His death, the 3 days and 3 nights (John 2:19-20).

    * Jesus found the man in the Temple after He had healed him at the pool of Bethesda (John 5:14).

* Jesus gave the teaching in the Temple concerning the rivers of living water at the Feast of Tabernacles. He came to the Temple as it were in secret (John 7).

* Jesus taught in the Temple treasury area about being the light of the world in connection with the healing of the blind man at the Feast of Dedication (John 8:2,20; 10:23).

* Jesus taught about the true spirit of giving as He sat over against the Treasury (Mark 12:41-44).

* He told them that there was One greater than the Temple and a greater than Solomon was there, speaking of Himself (Matthew 12:6,42). Jewry failed to receive the message.

* Christ gave many parables of the kingdom in the Temple area (Matthew 21,22,23 chapters. Note also Luke 19:45-47; 20:1; 21:37-38).

8. At the close of His ministry He cleansed the Temple the second time of its corrupted services to the pilgrims (Matthew 21:1-12; Mark 11:15-17; Isaiah 56:7). Again He reminded them that His house was to be a house of prayer for all nations and not a den of thieves.

9. The final message of Christ to the nation relative to the Temple was its coming destruction under the Roman armies. As the disciples showed Him the glory of the Temple, Christ prophesied that the time was coming when not one stone would be left unturned upon another (Matthew 24:1-2; Luke 21:5).

10. The crowning act of God the Father was in the rending of the veil of this Temple as Jesus hung on the cross. It signified to Jewry that a new dispensation was opened and that access into the presence of the Father was available for all men through Christ, the perfect, sinless and once-for-all sacrifice (Matthew 27:51; Luke 23:45; Mark 15:38).

   The Jews had mocked Him at His trial about destroying and building the Temple in 3 days. However, they looked at the material Temple and did not understand that He spoke of the Temple of His body. The "destroying" and "building" in 3 days spoke of the time period of His death to His resurrection (Mark 14:58; Matthew 27:40; John 2:19-20).

Thus Christ ministered in the Temple environs over His years of ministry. He did come suddenly to His Temple. He sought to cleanse it and make it all it was meant to be. Jewry rejected His cleansing. They worshipped the Temple of God and missed the God of the Temple. When Jesus went out and departed from the Temple, He prophesied of its destruction.
No longer would the Father or the Son be concerned with material Temples. The New Covenant Temple would be the church, the body of Christ, made up of Jew and Gentile, living stones made into a habitation of God by the Spirit.

B. Temple Ministry and the Church

The early church continued to be associated with the Temple order in the period of transition from the Law Covenant to the Grace Covenant, from the old to the new.

1. After the ascension of Jesus the disciples were in the Temple praising and blessing God (Luke 24:53).

2. On the Day of Pentecost the Holy Spirit by-passed the letteristic keeping of this feast day and came to the disciples in an upper room and kept the spirit of Pentecost (Acts 1-2). However, the new converts were in the Temple daily and broke bread from house to house also (Acts 2:42-47).

3. The apostles, Peter and John, healed the lame man at the gate called Beautiful as they were going up to the Temple at the hour of prayer (Acts 3:1-10).

4. The apostles taught daily in the Temple area (Acts 4:1). Even after their arrest by the priests

and captain of the Temple and their release from prison by the Lord they were told to speak the words of "this life" in the Temple (Acts 5).

5. The apostle Paul still came to the Temple for rituals that he no longer believed in but with the hope of being able to testify of the Messiah. However, it brought him under arrest and endangered his life (Acts 21:20-30; 22:17; 24:1-18; 25:8; 26:21). They thought he had brought a Greek believer beyond the Court of the Gentiles which would profane the Temple area.

6. The Sanhedrin failed to hear Stephen's address and his quotation from Solomon who built the original Temple when he said, "The Most High dwells not in Temples made with hands" (Acts 7:48. Also read 17:24).

C. Temple Destruction

God in His grace and mercy gave the Jewish nation 40 years "space to repent", but they repented not.

They recognized not the miraculous signs given to them over Christ's ministry unto His death. The miraculous earthquake, the rent veil, the darkening of the sun, the opened graves, the resurrection of Jesus of Nazareth, the outpoured Spirit on the disciples, and signs and wonders of both Christ and the early church — all seemed to fall upon blinded eyes and deafened ears.

The priesthood carried on the Old Testament sacrificial system in the Temple. The veil was apparently sewn up again and the whole system became an abomination to God. Forty is the number of probation. Forty years grace was given to the nation but they heard and understood not. They did to the apostles and believers what they had done to their own prophets in previous generations.

In A.D. 70, according to the prophetic word of their own Messiah, the Roman armies came and destroyed the city and the Temple. Since then Jewry has been desolate, without a Temple, without a priesthood, without a sacrifice, without God, without their Messiah, without the Holy Spirit. Upon the Temple site stands the abominable Mosque of Omar.

The clear message is that the Godhead, as Father, Son and Holy Spirit has finished with material Temples. God will never ever return to dwell in a material building. The fact that His Shekinah-glory-presence never returned to Zerubbabel's rebuilt Temple is significant in itself.

The Father finished with the Temple when He rent the veil in two from top to bottom. The Son finished with the Temple when He sought to cleanse it at the beginning and close of His ministry, which cleansing they rejected. Also He prophesied of its total destruction under Rome.

The Holy Spirit finished with the material Temple when He by-passed it and came to dwell in the new covenant Temple, the church, which is the body of Christ. The Holy Spirit has always wanted to dwell in redeemed hearts, living stones of a living Temple. He will never go back to a material Temple even though Jewry would built one!

CHAPTER FIVE

THE TEMPLE OF EZEKIEL'S VISION

The Book of Ezekiel gives a number of chapters to a vision of a Temple. The first ten chapters of his prophecy concern the progressive departure of God's glory from the material Temple at Jerusalem because of the great abominations which had defiled it (Ezekiel 1-10).
Most Bible expositors are agreed on the interpretation of these chapters that they speak concerning the desecration, desolation and destruction of Solomon's Temple.

However, Ezekiel is given another vision concerning a new Temple in the closing chapters of his prophecy (Ezekiel 40-48). It is here that Bible expositors are divided in their interpretation of this Temple. Is it a literal and material Temple that is to be built in this age or some future age? Or is it symbolic of spiritual realities clothed in the symbolism of the former material Temple? These are the basic questions that need to be considered in any interpretative view of this vision of Ezekiel. Is it a material or a spiritual Temple? This is the issue.

A simple overview of Ezekiel's prophecy relative to the "old" and the "new" Temple is appropriate here.

BOOK OF EZEKIEL

The Old Temple	National Destiny Prophecies	The New Temple
Chapters 1-10	Chapters 11-39	Chapters 40-48
Material Temple Glory Departs Abominations		??? Temple Glory Returns Cleansings

With relation to the Temple of Ezekiel, there are four different schools of interpretation, these being as follows:

1. **The Literal Prophetic View**

    According to this view the Temple of Ezekiel is the pattern of a Temple which should have been built when the exiles of Judah returned to restore and build Jerusalem in fulfilment of Daniel's prophecy (Daniel 9:24-27).

2. **The Dispensational View**

    This view has been popularized through the Dispensational School of Biblical Interpreters. It is propagated through the Scofield Reference Bible in which these chapters are entitled "Israel in the Land during the Kingdom Age" (Ezekiel 40-48). This view is literal and futuristic. It holds that there will be a restoration of the Mosaic Covenant economy with a literal Temple, literal sacrifices, and Levitical priesthood, as well as other Law Covenant ceremonials. Some expositors in this field say these sacrifices are memorials of Christ's sacrifice.

3. **The Messianic Apocalyptic View**

    This view holds that Ezekiel's vision was Messianic and Apocalyptic. They believe it represents all that God would do for His people in an age that would soon dawn. It is idealistic rather than materialistic.

4. The Symbolic Christian View

This view holds that the vision is symbolic of the Christian era and finds fulfilment in Christ and His church. It holds out strong objections both materially and theologically as to why Ezekiel's Temple vision cannot be a literally rebuilt or restored Temple in this age, or any age to come.

The writer once believed that this Temple was a literal and materially built Temple for the Millennial Age.
After much study and research, the writer of this text now believes in the fourth view and holds that the Temple is visionary and symbolic and finds fulfilment in spiritual realities, especially now in this Christian dispensation.

The purpose of this final chapter is an endeavour to prove that this view and interpretation is sound and based on Biblical principles of interpretation. It will be found that the principle of Jeremiah's twofold ministry has to be followed in dealing with this subject.
The Lord commanded Jeremiah to "root out, pull down, destroy and throw down" before he could "build and plant" (Jeremiah 1:10).

So it is that traditions of men and false interpretations of Scripture have to be "rooted out, pulled down, destroyed and thrown down" before one can "build and plant" what is believed to be the truth. This is the approach taken here.

Questions under consideration here will deal with such things as the following. Is it a literal and material Temple? Is it a Temple to be built by Jewry in a future Millennial Age? Or was it meant to be an actual Temple in the restoration of Jewry from Babylon and they failed to follow the vision through to actuality and have for ever missed the opportunity to build?
Why are there so many chapters and details given if it is not a material Temple? Or is the vision simply symbolical finding fulfilment in the church?

A detailed interpretation and exposition of Ezekiel's Temple cannot be undertaken here as this would be a small text in itself. However, because Ezekiel's Temple follows basically the same design as Solomon's Temple, the truths brought out there are also applicable truths here, along with other additional truths.

In seeking to answer the above questions we present the two major schools of thought concerning Ezekiel's prophecies, especially pertaining to the Temple.
In the second school of thought we consider the two major objections to a material Temple and then seek to draw some spiritual lessons from the same in our conclusions. For the sake of distinction we speak of these two schools as (A) The Literal/Material School and (B) The Symbolic/Spiritual School.

A. The Literal/Material School

It is evident that Ezekiel's temple is not a formerly built Temple. Nor does it refer to Zerubbabel's or Herod's Temple. The Jews have had no Temple since A.D. 70. Therefore, Ezekiel's Temple must refer to a future Temple, either material or symbolical, in this age or an age to come. By process of elimination it cannot be in the eternal age, for there is no Temple in the New Jerusalem, for "the Lord God and the Lamb are the Temple thereof" (Revelation 21:22).

Clarence Larkin in *"Dispensational Truth"* (pp.93-94) in dealing with the subject of the Millennium has this to say concerning Ezekiel's prophecies (Ezekiel 40-48), from which we note as briefly as possible the following.
He writes that the seat of government will be at Jerusalem. The present Jerusalem is to be trodden down until the Times of the Gentiles are fulfilled (Luke 21:24). Then it will be rebuilt. He writes that the prophet Ezekiel gives a detailed description of the restored Land and City (Ezekiel 48:1-35). From his comments we note six things in the literal/material school of thought.

1. The Land

Concerning the land he writes: The "Royal Grant" of land that God gave to Abraham and his descendants extended from the "River of Egypt" unto the "Great River", Euphrates

(Genesis 15:18). Ezekiel fixes the Northern boundary at Hamath, about 100 miles north of Damascus (Ezekiel 48:1), and the Southern boundary at Kadesh, about 100 miles south of Jerusalem (Ezekiel 48:28). This "Royal Grant" was not conditional and was never revoked. It is eight times as large as that formerly occupied by the Twelve Tribes.

This "Royal Grant" is to be divided among the restored Twelve Tribes in parallel horizontal sections, beginning at Hamath on the north with a section for Dan, next comes Asher, then Naphtali, Manasseh, Ephraim, Reuben and Judah. Then come the "Holy Oblation". South of the holy oblation will be the tribes of Benjamin, Simeon, Isaachar, Zebulun and Gad.

2. **The Holy Oblation**

    Concerning the holy oblation, C. Larkin writes: The "Holy Oblation" is a square tract on the west of Jordan, 25,000 reeds, or 50 miles on a side. A "reed" according to Ezekiel 40:5 is 6 cubits long (approx. 21 inches a cubit, these 6 cubits equal approx. 10½ feet). The Holy Oblation is divided into three horizontal sections. The Northern section is 25,000 reeds long, from east to west, and 10,000 reeds wide. It is called the "Levites portion". South of it is the "Priest's portion" of equal size. South of the "Priest's portion" is the section for the "City" with its suburbs and farming sections. This section is 25,000 reeds long, from east to west, and 5,000 reeds wide (Ezekiel 48:15-19).

3. **The Temple**

    Concerning the Temple he writes the following. The Temple or Sanctuary will not be rebuilt in the "New City" but in the middle of the "Holy Oblation" (Ezekiel 48:10,20,21). This will locate it at or near the ancient Shiloh, when the Tabernacle rested after Israel conquered the land, and where it remained until the Temple of Solomon was built. A highway, about 12 miles long, will connect Sanctuary and City (Isaiah 35:8). This "New Temple" will occupy a space of 500 reeds on a side, or nearly a mile square (Ezekiel 42:15-20). The old Temple was not a mile in circuit.

4. **The City**

    C. Larkin says that the City (Jerusalem) will be located in the centre of this third section and will be located on the site of the old. This "New City" will be much larger than the old. It will be 9 miles square and with its half mile suburbs on each will make 10 miles square. It will have a wall around it with 3 gates on each side like the New Jerusalem (Ezekiel 48:15-18,30-35). The gates will be named after the 12 sons of Jacob. The name of the city will be Jehobah-Shammah, the Lord is there (Ezekiel 48:35).

5. **The Living Waters**

    C. Larkin uses Zechariah 14:8 along with Ezekiel 47:8-12 and Revelation 22:1-2 to speak of the "Living Waters" flowing, not from Jerusalem, but the "Sanctuary". Ezekiel in vision saw these waters flow from the threshold of the door, past the altar of burnt offering, on the south side until the stream was deep enough to swim in.

    This author notes that, for such things to happen, great physical changes will have to take place in the land surface of Palestine and he quotes Zechariah 14:4,10,11 and Micah 1:3,4 as support for this. Such physical changes will level the land surface of Palestine and make room for the "New City" and raise the Dead Sea for the waters to flow into the Red and Mediterranean Seas.

6. **The Temple Worship**

    Finally the writer speaks of the Temple and its worship in this period of time.

    The Temple or Sanctuary will be located in the centre of the "Holy Oblation" and the full description of the Temple and its courts is given in 40:1-44:31. No Temple like Ezekiel's has ever been built. And it cannot refer to Zerubbabel's or Herod's Temples and there is no Temple in Jerusalem at present. It must refer to the Millennial Temple, according to C. Larkin. It cannot refer to the New Heavens and New Earth for there is no Temple there and no more sea. Clarence Larkin specifically mentions the following things as pertaining to this Temple.

* The Aaronic Priesthood will be re-established.

* The sons of Zadok shall officiate and offer sacrifices (Ezekiel 44:15-31).

* The new Temple will not have the following articles of furniture.

    There will be no:

    a) Ark of the Covenant

    b) Golden Pot of Manna

    c) Aaron's Rod that budded

    d) Tables of the Law

    e) Cherubim

    f) Mercy Seat

    g) Golden Candlestick

    h) Shewbread

    i) Altar of Incense

    j) Veil

    k) Holy of Holies for High Priest alone to enter

    l) High Priest to offer atonement for sins or make intercession
        (Unless Zechariah 6:12-13 speaks of Christ performing both offices of King and Priest).

* The Levites will perform Temple services but not priestly because of their past sins (Ezekiel 44:10-14).

* The daily "morning" sacrifice will be offered but not the "evening" sacrifice (Ezekiel 46:13-15).

* The Burnt, Meal, Drink, Sin, Peace and Trespass offerings will be offered (Ezekiel 45:17; 42:13).

* The Feasts of Passover and Tabernacles will be observed. No Passover Lamb will be offered, however, for Jesus fulfilled this (Ezekiel 45:21-24). Tabernacles is to be observed by all nations under penalty of drought and plague (Zechariah 14:16-19).

* The Feast of Pentecost is done away as it is already fulfilled (Acts 2:1-4).

* An outpouring of the Spirit, at least on Jewry, to fulfil Joel 2:28-32 will take place.

* One universal religion, and the knowledge of the Lord will be worldwide because of the Jews (Zechariah 8:22,23; Malachi 1:11).

* The "Shekinah Glory" that departed from the Temple at the time of the Babylonian Captivity will again take up its residence in the new temple (Ezekiel 10:18-20; 11:21-23; 43:1-5).

As noted earlier, this is the general Dispensationalist's view of Ezekiel's vision in chapters 40-48 inclusive.

From the *International Standard Bible Encyclopaedia* (pp. 2935-6, 1915 Edition) we quote — and sub-section — their description of Ezekiel's Temple should it be taken in its literalness as a material Temple.

TEMPLE DESCRIPTION

"The Temple itself is quite similar to the description of Solomon's Temple, yet in some respects it forecasts the plans of Zerubbabel's and Herod's Temples.
However, while there is this historical relation, Ezekiel's Temple is unique, presenting features not found in any of the Temples.

1. **The Courts**

   The Temple was enclosed in two courts — an outer and inner — quite different, however, in character and arrangement from those of the first Temple.

   The Outer Court was a large square of 500 cubits, bounded by a wall six cubits thick and six cubits high. The wall was pierced in the middle of its north, east and south sides by massive gateways, extending into the court by a distance of 50 cubits, with a width of 50 cubits (40:5,27).

   On either side of the passage in these gateways were three guardrooms, each six cubits square, and each gateway terminated in a porch eight cubits long and 20 cubits across (40:6,22,26).

   The ascent to the gateways was by seven steps, showing that the level of the court was to this extent higher than the ground outside. Round the courts, on the three sides named — its edge in line with the end of the gateways — was a "pavement", on which were built, against the wall, chambers, 30 in number. At the four corners were enclosures where the sacrifices were cooked — a fact which suggests that the cells were mainly for the purposes of feasting (46:21-24).

   The Inner Court was a square of 100 cubits, situated exactly in the centre of the larger court. It, too, was surrounded by a wall, and had gateways, with guardrooms, etc., similar to those of the outer court, saving that the gates projected outward, not inward (40:47,19,23,27). The gates of the outer and inner court were opposite each other on the north, east and south, a 100 cubits apart; the whole space, therefore, from wall to wall was 50 plus 100 plus 50 = 200 cubits.

   The ascent to the gates in this case was by 8 steps, indicating another rise in level for the inner court (40:37). There were two chambers at the sides of the north and south gates respectively; one for the Levites, the other for priests. At the gates also (perhaps only at the north gate) were stone tables for slaughtering (40:44-46,39-43).

2. **The Brazen Altar**

   In the centre of this inner court was the great altar of burnt offering, 18 cubits square at the base and rising in four stages (1,2,3 and 4 cubits high respectively) until it formed a square of 12 cubits at the top of hearth with four horns at the corners (43:14-17). Steps led up to it on the east.

3. **The Temple**

   The inner court was extended westward by a second square of 100 cubits, within which, a platform elevated another six cubits, stood the temple proper and its connected buildings (41:8).

   This platform or basement is shown by the measurements to be 60 cubits broad (north and south), and 105 cubits long (east and west) — five cubits projecting into the eastern square. The ascent to the temple porch was by ten steps (40:49).

   The temple itself was a building, like Solomon's, of three parts — a porch at the entrance, 20 cubits broad by 12 cubits deep; the holy place 40 cubits long by 20 cubits broad; the most holy place 20 cubits by 20 cubits; the measurements are internal (40:48-49; 41:1-4).

4. **The Pillars**

   At the sides of the porch stood two pillars, corresponding to the Jachin and Boaz of the older temple (40:49).

5. **The 'Veil'**

   The holy places were separated by a partition two cubits in thickness (41:3). The most holy place was empty.

6. **The Holy Place**

   Of the furniture of the holy place mention is only made of an altar of wood (41:22).
   The walls and doors were ornamented with cherubim and palm trees (41:18,25).

7. **The Chambers**

   The wall of the temple building was six cubits in thickness (41:5), and on the north, south and west sides, as in Solomon's temple there were side-chambers in three stories, 30 in number (41:6, perhaps in each story), with an outer wall five cubits in thickness (41:9).

   These chambers were, on the basement, four cubits broad; in the second and third stories, owing, as in the older temple, to rebatements in the wall, perhaps five or six cubits broad respectively (41:6,7; in Solomon's temple the side-chambers were 5,6 and 7 cubits. 1 Kings 6:6).

   These dimensions give a total external breadth to the house of 50 cubits (with a length of 100 cubits), leaving 5 cubits on either side and in the front as a passage round the edge of the platform on which the building stood (41:9-11).

   The western end, as far as the outer wall, was occupied, the whole width of the inner court, by a large building (41:12); all but a passage of 20 cubits between it and the temple belonging to what is called "the separate place" (41:12,13 etc.).

   The temple platform being only 60 cubits broad, there remained a space of 20 cubits on the north and south sides, running the entire length of the platform. This, continued round the back formed "the separate place" just named. Beyond this "separate place" for 50 cubits were other chambers, apparently, in two rows, the inner 100 cubits, the outer 50 cubits, long with a walk of 10 cubits between (42:1-14; the passage, however, is obscure; some place the "walk" outside the chambers). These chambers were assigned to the priests for the eating of "the most holy things" (42:13).

Such is the description of Ezekiel's Temple from I.S.B.E., and it helps us to, at least, understand what would be involved in the building of such a Temple, if of a material nature. (The student is referred to the Bibliography for other Dictionaries and descriptions of Ezekiel's Temple).

B. The Symbolic/Spiritual School

The Symbolic/Spiritual School hold the view that the vision of Ezekiel cannot be interpreted on a literal basis as speaking of a material Temple to be built in this age or any future ages.

Along with this author's comment, we note a major authority as representing this school of thought and interpretation, again recognizing that there will be some varying shades of interpretation and application.

J. Sidlow Baxter in *"Explore the Book"*, The Book of Ezekiel (pp.31-35) states some major objections to a literal/material interpretation of the Ezekiel chapters. The student should weigh carefully the arguments presented here as against those of the Dispensational School as they are set forth here following the general order as laid out there.

1. Geographical and Material Objections

a) The Land Area

The land area for the 12 tribes, distributed in equal portions, without respect of numbers, and these in parallel sections running from east to west presents great problems. The separate tribe portion limits all to about four to five miles of territory, seven of the tribes being north and five tribes to the south of the allotted area. This is certainly a very small land inheritance without respect of increase of numbers, if this be geographically so. If Israel is to be as numberless as the sand and the stars, then this is a very limited land area and so presents geographical objections.

b) The Holy Oblation Area

The holy oblation or threefold sacred land area for the Temple, the priests and the Levites covers a vast land area (42:15-20; 45:2; 48:20). It measures 25,000 by 25,000 reeds square, or about 47 square miles. About 19 square miles of this is a reserved portion for the priesthood, and again, about 19 square miles is a portion reserved for the Levites, again, without respect for numbers (45:3-5; 48:10,13). This is a lot of land just for one tribe, the priestly tribe of Levi, and again presents another geographical objection.

c) The Temple Area

The area allotted to the Temple itself covers all of the area allotted to the old city of Jerusalem, that is, about one mile square. In other words, the Temple is as large as the whole of the ancient city of Jerusalem (45:6; 48:15-19).

The outer court of the Temple is 500 reeds long by 500 reeds wide (42:15-20; 45:2). This Temple could not be contained on the Mt Zion or Mt Moriah area of Jerusalem.

J. Sidlow Baxter in *"Explore the Book"* (The Book of Ezekiel, pp.31-35) has this to say concerning the *temple* and the *sacred area* going with it.

"Take the size of the *temple* and of the *sacred area* going with it. The 'outer court' of the temple is 500 reeds long by 500 reeds wide (42:15-20; 45:2); and as the reed is about 10 feet, this court is one mile long by one mile wide, which means that the temple covers a space as large as the whole city enclosed by the walls of old Jerusalem. Certainly, *this* temple could not possibly be contained on Mount Zion, inside Jerusalem. But when we pass from the temple to the sacred area, or 'oblation' of land, going with it, we find this to be 25,000 reeds long by 25,000 reeds wide (48:20), that is, 47 miles north to south, and the same east to west, covering an area between six and seven times that of modern London! Of this an area 47 miles by 19 is reserved for the priesthood alone (45:3,4;

48:10), and an area the same size for the Levites (45:5; 48:13). There is also a third area, in which, although small compared with the whole 'oblation', is a 'city' with a circuit of 20,000 reeds, or nearly 38 miles (45:6; 48:15-19), whereas Josephus reckoned the circuit of Jerusalem in his day at only *four* miles! Now is it thinkable that there is to be a literal counterpart to this temple which itself is as large as the whole of Jerusalem, and in a sacred area of over two thousand two hundred square miles?

Moreover, this sacred area is *physically impossible* — unless the river Jordan be moved further east! The boundaries of the land are the Mediterranean on the west and the Jordan on the east (47:18), and this great square of 47 miles by 47 cannot be put between the two, for the distance between them in places is scarcely 40 miles. Even if we bend the great square to the slope of the coast we cannot get it in — the less so because on each side of the square, in Ezekiel's vision, is an *additional* area called 'the portion for the prince' (45:7; 48:21,22). Admittedly, God could move the Jordan; but is it thinkable that we are meant to infer this?''

d) The City Area

The third portion of the sacred area is reserved for the new city. The city has a circuit of 20,000 reeds, or approximately 38 miles (45:6; 48:15-19). The old city of Jerusalem had a circuit of approximately four miles. That means that this new city is as large as the whole frame of the land between Jordan and the Mediterranean Sea. The city area reaches to the Dead Sea.

Again we quote J.S. Baxter's remarks relative to the new city and the temple from the same reference pages.

"There is further difficulty that although this great area is 47 miles by 47, it *does not include the site of Jerusalem*; so that this 'city' which Ezekiel sees is not Jerusalem. If, then, we are to take this vision literally, what of all those other prophecies which speak of Jerusalem as the glorified centre of the coming new order?

Ezekiel's vision also places the new temple 500 reeds (some nine and a half miles) *away north from the 'city'*, in fact, fourteen and a quarter miles from the *centre* of it. Now the connection between the temple and Jerusalem is so deeply laid, both in the Scriptures and in the thought of the Jews, that to interpret literally a vision which separates them without giving the slightest reason seems again unthinkable. As C.J. Ellicott says, 'A temple in any other locality than Mount Moriah would hardly be the temple of Jewish hope.' Hard as we find it to picture Ezekiel's mile-square temple spread over the variety of hill and valley which the country presents, we find it even harder to think of the new city as miles away from Jerusalem, and the new temple still another fourteen miles north, and, in fact, well on the way to Samaria.''

e) The Living Waters

A further problem (and objection) has to do with the river which flows from the Temple threshold by way of the altar of sacrifice. An actual river flowing from a material Temple by way of a material altar of sacrifice in a great high mountain into the Dead Sea presents a problem also. This river parts into two main streams and becomes unfordable within 4,000 cubits of its source.

One final quotation from J.S. Baxter's comments concerning these waters from the Temple will suffice on this matter.

"Another problem in the way of a literal interpretation is found in the waters which Ezekiel saw flowing beneath the eastern threshold of the temple (47:1-12). To quote C.J. Ellicott again, 'These waters run to the ''east country'' and go down ''to the sea'', which can only be the Dead Sea': but such a course would be physically impossible without changes in the surface of the earth, since the temple of the vision is on the west of the watershed of the country. They had, moreover, the effect of 'healing' the waters of the sea, an effect which could not be produced naturally without providing an outlet from the sea: no supply of fresh water could remove the saltness while this water was all disposed of by evaporation; and Ezekiel (47:11) excludes the idea of an outlet. But above all, the character of the waters themselves is impossible without a perpetual miracle. Setting aside the difficulty of a spring of this magnitude upon the top of 'a very high mountain' (40:2) in this locality, at the distance of 1,000 cubits from their source the waters have greatly increased in volume; and so with each successive 1,000 cubits, until at the end of 4,000 cubits (about a mile and a half) they have become a river no longer fordable, or, in other words, comparable to the Jordan. Such an increase, without accessory streams, is clearly not natural. But, beyhond this, the description of the waters themselves clearly marks them as ideal. They are life-giving and healing; trees of perennial foliage and fruit grow upon their banks, the leaves being for 'medicine' and the fruit, although for food, never wasting.''

f) **The Temple Materials**

Another objection to be mentioned concerns the materials of this supposed new Temple.

In contrast to the Tabernacle of Moses and the Temple of Solomon, there is practically no mention concerning Temple materials. So many chapters and details are given for this Temple, yet there is almost total silence concerning materials for the Temple or the city. The only specific mentions of materials are in these several references.

The appearance of "the man" is as *brass* (40:3).
The four tables for the preparation of the burnt offerings are of hewn *stone* (40:42).
The doors, posts, windows and galleries were of *wood* (41:16).
The altar of incense was of *wood* (41:22).

There is no mention of gold, silver or brass or specified wood as in the Tabernacle of Moses and Temple of Solomon. One would have to assume that this new Temple is to be built of the same materials as Solomon's Temple. But the lack of mention of materials surely is in itself significant, for, the Temple of Ezekiel is predominantly visionary!

g) **The Temple Furniture**

One final objection, as to the material aspect, has to do with the lack of mention or the absence of so much Temple furniture.

If this Temple is a material Temple, and so important that it exceeds in glory and beauty Solomon's, Zerubbabel's and Herod's Temples, then why is there no mention of much of the furniture? It seems so much like a house without furniture. These discrepancies make it difficult to accept a material Temple because of their importance in the former, unless one again assumes that the same furniture will be rebuilt.

There is no mention of the following:

1. Ark of the Covenant (yet "The Glory" returns to fill the house).
2. Golden Pot of Manna.
3. Aaron's Rod that Budded (both 1 and 2 not in Solomon's Temple either).
4. Tables of the Law (Yet these were in Solomon's Temple).
5. Cherubim and Mercy Seat.
6. Golden Candlestick.
7. Table and Shewbread.
8. Golden Altar of Incense (Altar of wood is mentioned).
9. Veil on the Holy of Holies (Most Holy Place and partition mentioned).
10. High Priest (Zadok and Levitical Priesthood mentioned).
11. Evening Sacrifices (Burnt, Meal, Drink, Sin, Trespass and Morning Sacrifices are mentioned).
12. Feast of Pentecost (Passover and Tabernacles mentioned).

The student needs to remember that the Ark of God, upon which the glory of God dwelt, has not been seen since Jeremiah's time (Jeremiah 3:14-15), nor has the glory of God ever returned to any material Temple, whether Zerubbabel's or Herod's. Will it return to a Temple in the Millennium? We believe not!

These objections deal with the geographical and material problems if Ezekiel's Temple is an actual Temple to be built in a Millennium.

Of course, God can do anything He will do even if He changes the whole earth to do it. But is this the will of God and is this what the Bible teaches? We think not! Our reasons are more especially seen in the following section.

2. Covenantal and Theological Objections

In this final section we come to what we term the Covenantal and Theological Objections to a literal/material Temple in this age or an age to come.

If the previous Geographical and Material Objections have not convinced the student, or are rationalized away, then the Covenantal and Theological Objections should be considered and should convince one.

In an earlier chapter of this text we noted some of the major hermeneutical principles which would be used relative to interpreting Solomon's Temple. One of the most important principles is *The Covenantal Principle* in which it is vital that the believer understand the difference between the Covenants of Law and Grace, or, the Old and the New Covenants in particular.

Therefore, this section uses a very important hermeneutical principle of Biblical interpretation. That is, we do not use the Old Testament to interpret the New Testament but we use the New Testament to interpret the Old Testament *passing all through the cross*! The cross is the key. The cross becomes what may be called "the hermeneutical filter" of the Old Testament economy, especially those things which pertain to the Law or the Mosaic Covenant.

Again, it should be remembered that the New Testament *apostles* are the infallible interpreters of the Old Testament *prophets*. Ezekiel is one of these Old Testament prophets. The New Testament apostles, especially the apostle Paul, specifically deals with issues mentioned in Ezekiel's vision, as also other Old Testament prophets.

We proceed now to consider these issues which become the weightiest objections to a material Temple of Ezekiel's vision.

a) The Mosaic Covenant

As already intimated, the greatest difficulty of all concerning the vision of Ezekiel being interpreted actually or materially is in the fact that it would involve a restoration of the Mosaic economy, or the Law Covenant.

C. Larkin in *"Dispensational Truth"* (p.151) says, "The New Covenant has not yet been made. It is to be made with Israel after they get back to their own land. It is promised in Jeremiah 31:31-37. It is unconditional and will cover the Millennium and the New Heavens and New Earth. It is based on the finished work of Christ (Matthew 26:28). It has nothing to do with the Church and does not belong to this Dispensation."

In this author's understanding of the Bible and the Covenants, this is a sample of faulty hermeneutics. But it is this kind of interpretation that causes one to misinterpret the visions of Ezekiel. Faulty hermeneutics produce faulty exposition. This is a sample of covenantal confusion!

With C. Larkin's statement this writer must strongly disagree. Jesus established the New Covenant in Matthew 26:26-28. It was confirmed by other New Testament writers in 1 Corinthians 11:23-34 and Hebrews 8. Every time believers in the church partake of the Lord's table, they set forth in the bread and the cup the symbols of the New Covenant. If the New Covenant has not yet been made and it is nothing to do with the church, and it is only for Israel, then why has the church been commemorating the New Covenant table for about 2000 years? The work of the cross has been accomplished and the believer today is under the New Covenant "in Christ" whether believing Jew or Gentile.

We set out a number of things mentioned in Ezekiel's vision which, when passed through the cross, and considered in the light of the New Covenant, clearly show Ezekiel's Temple is not a material Temple but an idealistic vision of spiritual realities. Ezekiel, as most of the Old Testament prophets and writers, as well as the New Testament writers, use Old Covenant language to describe New Covenant realities, passing all through the cross!

1) **The Temple**

The New Testament writers all teach that the New Covenant Temple is now the believer individually and the church corporately is the true Temple. Ezekiel, as also Isaiah, pointed to Christ as "a little sanctuary" to His people where ever they are scattered (Ezekiel 11:16; Isaiah 8:14-18; Revelation 21:22). The Lord God and the Lamb are the eternal Temple. Father, Son and Holy Spirit set their seal to the rejection of a material Temple in the Gospels and Acts. The Godhead will never return to any material Temple when the reality is now in Christ in His church (Matthew 21:12-14; 23:38; 24:1; 27:51; Acts 2:1-4; Isaiah 66:1-4; Isaiah 66:1-4; 1 Corinthians 3:16).

2) **The Priesthood**

The Melchisedek priesthood for ever abolishes the Aaronic and Levitical priesthood. In the Old Covenant only one tribe was chosen to be the priestly tribe. In the New Covenant all believers are priests unto God, whether men or women (Revelation 1:6; 5:9-10; 1 Peter 2:5-9). God will never ever re-establish the Old Covenant priesthood in this age or any age to come.

3) **The Altars**

Ezekiel also mentions "altars" in his vision. The cross of Jesus for ever fulfilled and abolished all Old Covenant altars of sacrifice and incense. The Lord's table is the symbol of that eternally efficacious sacrifice. The only incense God accepts now is the prayers and intercessions from the heart of the believer.

4) **The Sacrifice and Oblation**

Ezekiel also mentions sacrifice and oblation. Daniel 9:24-27 with Hebrews 9-10 chapters show that Christ's one and once-for-all sacrifice and oblation on Calvary caused all animal sacrifice and oblation to cease. Neither will it suffice to say that sacrifices will not be offered for sin but only as a "memorial" of Christ's sacrifice. The bread and the cup of the Lord's table are our "memorial" now of His death and resurrection. Will God forsake the Lord's table and the bread and cup and go back to animal body and blood for a memorial? The body and blood of Jesus for ever repudiates animal body and blood. To have any other sacrifice is to deny the all-sufficiency of the sacrifice of Jesus. It has been said, "He who sacrificed before confessed Christ, but he who sacrifices now solemnly denies Him." Any return to animal sacrifices is an insult to the sacrifice of Jesus Christ.

5) **The Feasts of the Lord**

All feast days were fulfilled in Christ and then find fulfilment in the church. Christ is our Passover Lamb. The Holy Spirit came in fulfilment of Pentecost. The believers will enjoy the fulness of Tabernacles in Christ. The Book of Hebrews shows that Christ fulfilled the Day of Atonement ceremonies.
God will not re-establish the letterism and ceremonialism of these feasts when they have been abolished at the cross and find spiritual fulfilment in the experience of the true believer (Colossians 2:14-17).

6) **The Sabbaths and New Moons**

Ezekiel also mentions sabbaths and new moons. The sabbath was the sign and seal of the Mosaic Covenant. Sabbaths and new moons belonged to that covenant. All such were nailed to the cross, with other ordinances, so why should they be un-nailed to be re-established again in the future? (Colossians 2:14-17; Hebrews 8-9-10 chapters). We are not to go back to the beggarly elements of the Law Covenant again.

7) **The Rite of Circumcision**

Ezekiel also speaks of the rite of circumcision (Ezekiel 44:7-9). New Covenant circumcision is of the heart, and of the spirit, not of the flesh and of the letter (Romans 2:24-29; Colossians 2:12-17). Why then re-introduce this rite, which was the sign and seal of the Abrahamic Covenant, on people in a future age when such was also abolished at the cross?

8) **The Shekinah Glory**

Ezekiel also mentions the return of God's glory to this Temple even though the ark of God is not mentioned. As mentioned previously, the glory of God never ever did return to any materially rebuilt Temple. Why should it then return to one in a future age? Will God forsake the church, His Temple, to which all material habitations of God pointed, and return to a material building? Once this glory forsook Solomon's Temple it has not been seen since in a material one. The glory now is ''Christ in you, the hope of glory'', in the believer, in the church.

9) **The Worship**

In John 4:20-24 Jesus foretold the truth that worship would no longer be acceptable only in Jerusalem, as a place. True worship would be in spirit and in truth where ever true believers would be found. This statement of Jesus for ever repudiated external and formal worship at Jerusalem. How then can nations be forced to worship God and His Christ in a Millenniel age unless born of the Spirit? The final specific mention of Jerusalem is in Revelation 11:8 where it is that city which is ''spiritually Sodom and Egypt''.

b) **The New Covenant**

The New Testament writers abundantly confirm the fact that the Old or the Mosaic Covenant was fulfilled and abolished at the cross, as to its ritualism and ceremonialisms: It will never be re-instituted either in this age or another. God will never ''backslide'' to the other side of the cross to restore the Mosaic economy which He abolished.

The believer is eternally under the New Covenant in Christ (Jeremiah 31:31-34; Hebrews 8; 2 Corinthians 3).

To take these things mentioned in Ezekiel's Temple and see all restored in a material Temple is to do violence to the teaching and revelation of the New Testament writers and to give insult to the cross of Calvary.

The New Testament writers are the infallible interpreters of the Old Testament prophets. There is absolutely no mention by the New Testament writers of any return to the Mosaic economy. The things of the Old Covenant were temporal. The spiritual truths therein are eternal (2 Corinthians 3:18; 1 Corinthians 15:46-47).

To know the truth is to be set free from all covenantal confusion.

C. Spiritual Lessons from Temple Truths

This chapter would be incomplete without providing, at least, some brief spiritual lessons and guidelines in discovering Temple truths.

These spiritual lessons may be developed even as one develops lessons from the Tabernacle of Moses, Tabernacle of David and Temple of Solomon. The same principles of Biblical interpretation and exposition apply in interpreting Ezekiel's Temple as in previous structures.

Following is a brief outline of the major truths found in Ezekiel's Temple which the diligent student may develop.

1. **Measure the Temple**

   In Ezekiel 40-41 the key thought is in the much use of the word "measure". Everything in the Temple must measure up to the Divine standard. The spiritual lesson is confirmed in the New Testament for the Church, as God's habitation by the Spirit must also measure up to the man Christ Jesus (1 Corinthians 3:16; 6:16; 2 Corinthians 6:16; 10:12; Revelation 11:1-2; Ephesians 4:9-16).

2. **The Man with the Measuring Line**

   Throughout the chapters on the measuring of the Temple is seen "the man" with the measuring line (Ezekiel 40:1-4). The Lord Jesus Christ is God's Man, the standard Man, and His Word is the measuring rod to which all in His Temple must measure up.

3. **The Glory in the Temple**

   As the Shekinah Glory departed from the old and material Temple (Ezekiel 1-10 chapters) and returned to the new and spiritual Temple (Ezekiel 43:1-3), so it becomes prophetic of Christ leaving the old material, and Old Covenant Temple, and taking up His abode, by the Spirit, in the Church, the New Covenant Temple (Ephesians 2:19-22; 1 Peter 2:5-9).

4. **The Feasts of the Lord**

   Believers in Christ may enjoy spiritually all that was foreshadowed in the Feasts of the Lord in the Old Covenant. In Christ we have Passover. In the Holy Spirit we have Pentecost. In the Father we have the Tabernacles. In the fulness of the Godhead we enjoy true festival times (1 Corinthians 5; Acts 2; 2 Corinthians 3; Hebrews 8-9-10).

5. **The Rivers of God**

   In Ezekiel 47 we see the river of God. Where ever the river flowed there was life, health, healing and a great multitude of fish. Jesus stood in the Temple and spoke of the rivers in the Feast of Tabernacles (John 7:37-39). The rivers of the Spirit bring life, healing and health and multitudes of souls are saved when the river is flowing from the house of God by way of the altar of the cross of Jesus (Revelation 22:1-2; Psalm 46: Joel 3:18; Zechariah 14:8). This river replaces the waters of the molten sea and brazen lavers.

6. **The Priesthood of Ordinances**

   Ezekiel speaks of the priesthood of Zadok and Levi (Ezekiel 44). There are many spiritual lessons which can be learned from Old Testament priests even as from Old Testament kings. Believers are kings and priests unto God today after the order of Melchisedek. There are Divine ordinances established in the New Testament church for all to keep after the spirit (Revelation 1:6, 5:9-10; 1 Peter 2:5-9).

7. **Inheritances in the Land**

   The land inheritances spoken of by Ezekiel for the 12 tribes point us to our inheritance in Christ, the same as the inheritances of the tribes in the Book of Joshua (Ephesians 1:3). Ultimately the saints inherit the world and the kingdom of God (Romans 4:13). All believers find their place in the spiritual Israel of God (Romans 9:1-6).

8. **The Prince of the East Gate**

   The mysterious Prince of the East Gate points to Messiah the Prince (Daniel 9:24-27; Acts 5:31). He is our Prince and Saviour. He came to the east, died and rose in the east and will return to the east in blazing glory to establish His kingdom (Matthew 24:27; 2 Peter 3:11-14; Malachi 4:2).

9. **The Jehovah-Shammah City**

   Ezekiel 48 speaks of the city of God and it is called Jehovah-Shammah, The Lord is there.

All points ultimately to the city of God which John saw (Revelation 21-22). There the 12 tribes of spiritual Israel will enter through the gates of the city. The Lord God and the Lamb are there — eternally (Matthew 18:20). His eternal presence and glory abide there for ever.

These are some of the great lessons which find fulfilment spiritually in Christ and in His church, both here and now, and in the ages to come and for all eternity.

CHAPTER SIX

THE TEMPLE IN THESSALONIANS

Paul, in writing to the Thessalonians, spoke of the coming of the Man of Sin, who would "sit in the temple of God, shewing himself that he is God". This personified "mystery of iniquity" would seek the worship that only belongs to God. Paul warned them that this one would be revealed "in his time" and foretold the believers that he would be destroyed by the brightness of the coming of Christ (2 Thessalonians 2:1-12, especially vs 4).

Most expositors of Scripture believe that this passage speaks of the coming of a personal antichrist, the consummation of the mystery of iniquity that was already at work in Paul's day.

Differences of opinion do arise concerning this antichrist as to whether it refers to a spirit, or a system or a person. A study of the total Scriptures on this subject would imply that all three are involved in the manifestation of antichrist.

However, the issue at hand here is "the temple of God" in which this Man of Sin is revealed.

Paul says that the coming of Christ and the gathering of the saints unto Him will not come until two major events take place. The first is, there would come the great falling away from the faith, an apostasy of believers and professors of the faith. The second is, the Man of Sin would be revealed as the son of perdition. This Man of Sin would oppose the true God and exalt himself above all that is called God or worshipped as God. He would set himself up in THE TEMPLE OF GOD, showing himself that he is God. He would be destroyed by the brightness of Christ's second coming.

The question of course is: "What is the temple of God" here? Is it referring to a literally rebuilt Jewish Temple and a re-established Mosaic economy and covenant? Or is it referring to a spiritual Temple, and therefore used in symbolic sense?

There seems to be two options before us for our consideration.

Paul, as an apostle, and Jew, had been for years under the Jerusalem Temple and its system of things. Over these years he had been to Jerusalem for the various festival occasions. Without doubt, he was, by this time, knowledgeable of Christ's prophecy concerning the destruction of the Temple of Jerusalem.

At the crucifixion of Christ, the veil of the Temple had been rent in the midst and from top to bottom. This testified that God was finished with the material Temple and the whole of the Mosaic Covenant and economy.
However, the Temple was still functioning at the time when Paul wrote this Epistle. It would be about 15 years or so before God would permit Titus and the Roman armies to destroy what, since the cross of Jesus, had become an abominable system.

Paul's experience at the Jerusalem Temple in the Acts certainly had no appeal to him.

History shows that the Temple of Jerusalem was destroyed and that no "Man of Sin" set himself up as God in it or in that material Temple to be worshipped as God. Therefore it must point to another Temple than the then-present Temple at Jerusalem.

A study of Paul's writings, as also the other New Testament writers, show their use of the word "temple". Paul especially uses the word "temple" to speak of the church, the New Covenant Temple.

The word is used a number of times by Paul. And without exception (unless 2 Thessalonians 2:4 is such), it is always used of THE CHURCH as being THE TEMPLE of God.

Let us consider these major references.

1. The believer is the Temple of God, and the Spirit of God dwells in him. If any man defile the Temple of God, which is holy, he shall be destroyed (1 Corinthians 3:16-17). This would be more meaningful to the Corinthian believers in the light of the heathen Temples in their city,

especially on the hill of Acra-Corinth. It was a heathen Temple, filled with idolatry and immorality and its defiled and defiling priesthood.

2.   The believer's body is the Temple of the Holy Spirit. We are to glorify God in our spirit and body which are God's (1 Corinthians 6:19-20).

3.   The Church, composed of Jew and Gentile, is growing into a holy Temple in the Lord, for an habitation of God through the Spirit (Ephesians 2:19-22). This meant much to the Ephesians, for the city of Ephesus had the great Temple to the goddess Diana.

4.   The believers are also lively stones being built into a spiritual house, to offer up spiritual sacrifices acceptable to God by Jesus Christ, according to the apostle Peter (1 Peter 2:4-9).

Paul's writings turn the believer's eyes away from the earthly, material Temple, whether they be heathen, Gentile and idolatrous Temples, or the Jerusalem Temple of the Jews. He points them to the church as God's Temple. Believers, individually and corporately constitute the New Covenant Temple of God. The Holy Spirit is the "Shekinah-Glory" within. God will never leave the church, the Temple of the Holy Spirit to return back to any material Temple.

What then? Is the Temple of 2 Thessalonians 2:4 a material Temple to be built by and for the Jews in the end-times in which antichrist deifies himself? Of course, these things are possible, but the writer believes it is very doubtful. The Mosque of Omar stands on the past sacred Temple site, "The Dome of the Rock". This would possibly have to be destroyed if a Temple was to be built on its reasonably original site. Or else a Temple would have to be built elsewhere. But the site remains important.

There are numerous problems in the consideration of a literal Temple being built in the last days. The writer therefore believes that "the temple" in which the Man of Sin is revealed speaks of the church in which the great apostasy takes place. Following is a significant pattern revealed in Scripture concerning "*Antichrist and the Temple*".

1.   **Antichrist and The Heavenly Temple**

The Scriptures clearly reveal that there is a heavenly Temple or Tabernacle (Revelation 11:19; 15:5-8; 16:1,17; Hebrews 9). It is the original Temple and all earthly Temples are but shadows of the same.

In the past eternities, Satan (Lucifer) rose up as the original "Antichrist". He opposed God and His Word. He exalted himself to be God, and set himself up in the heavenly Temple to be worshipped as God.

Angels fell with him and in heaven we see the first falling way, the original apostasy. Satan and his angels together constitute "Antichrist, the apostasy in the heavenly Temple" (Isaiah 14:12-14; Ezekiel 28; 2 Peter 2:4; Jude 6).

2.   **Antichrist and The Earthly Temple**

This original spirit of antichrist and spirit of apostasy manifested in heaven is now manifested in the earth.

In heathen Temples of the nations, rulers often set themselves up as God, to be worshipped as God. Self-exaltation and self-deification was manifested. "I will be like God", and "you shall be as gods" was the expression of this Satanic spirit.

In the Jerusalem Temple, that antichrist spirit manifested itself also. Kings who plundered the Temple, defiled it, had that self-deification attitude. Pride led to presumption and presumption led to judgment.

The apostasy of priests, rulers and the Israelite nation was manifested. Various of the tribes apostacised, falling into evil idolatrous practices and all of this in the light and sight of God's holy Temple.

Solomon, Ahaz, and Uzziah's idolatrous and presumptuous acts illustrate these things. Antiochus Epiphanes desecrations of the Temple also shadow this. The apostacies and back-slidings of Israel and Judah reveal the great falling away that took place in the chosen nation, the people of God. A study of the Historical Books provide the evidence.

3. Antichrist and The Church-Temple

The pattern should be evident. The heavenly Temple had its revealed antichrist and apostacy. The earthly Temple, both Gentile and Jewish, follow the same pattern of antichrists and apostacy. It is therefore consistent to expect and see the apostacy and revealed antichrist in the New Testament Temple, the church.

Paul's writings foretell, even in his days, the departure from the faith, the defilement of God's Temple, and the coming of the Man of Sin, the spirit of lawlessness at work amongst the people of God (Read 1 Timothy 4:1-3; Hebrews 6:1-6; 10:26-31; 2 Timothy 3:1-5; 2 Thessalonians 2:1-4).

The apostle John confirms the fact that antichrist would come and also that there would be many antichrists. Where did they originate? Where did they come from? From the church! They went out from us that they might be manifest that they were not of us (1 John 2:18-22; 4:1-6; 2 John 7).

The unregenerate have nothing to fall from. He has already fallen "in Adam". The falling — the apostacy — takes place in the church, even as the antichrist is revealed in the church, the Temple of God.

Thus "the antichrist and the apostacy" theme proceeds from the heavenly Temple to the Old Testament earthly Temple into its final manifestation in the New Testament Temple, the spiritual house of the Lord, the Church. In it is revealed the spirit of antichrist, as well as the person and system of antichrist. It is the mystery of iniquity that is at work unto its destruction at Christ's second coming.

This is what the writer understands 2 Thessalonians 2:4 to be speaking about! However, this view does not rule out the possibility of a material Temple. Only time will tell!

236

CHAPTER SEVEN

THE TEMPLE IN REVELATION

In Revelation 11:1-2 John is given a vision. Here the Jehovah-Angel comes to him with a measuring reed in His hand and tells him to rise and ''measure the temple, and the altar, and them that worship therein''.

The Temple vision given to John here in this chapter has provoked the thinking of Bible students over the years.

Briefly, the interpretation of this temple arises out of two simple questions. Is it speaking of a literal rebuilt material Temple, or, Is it speaking of a spiritual and symbolical Temple (e.g., the Church)?

It will be remembered that the material Temple at Jerusalem had been destroyed about twentyfive or more years before John received the vision on the isle of Patmos. So we ask ourselves again, Is this Temple measured here, with its altar and worshippers, and its court unmeasured, referring to a material or symbolical Temple; is it literal or spiritual?

Before considering this vision of John in fuller detail, it will be profitable to note every specific use of the word ''temple'' in this prophetic and symbolic book. It will be profitable to note whether these references refer to a literal or spiritual Temple, for again these are the only two options before us.

1. The overcomer will be made a pillar in the Temple of God having the name of God upon him (Revelation 3:12). This certainly is not a literal or material Temple but it is spoken of concerning the believer in a spiritual and symbolic sense.

2. The tribulation saints are to be before the throne of God and serve Him day and night in His Temple (Revelation 7:14-17). This is certainly not referring to a material building either, but to the spiritual Temple in heaven.

3. At the sounding of the seventh trumpet, the Temple of God is opened in heaven, and there is seen in His Temple the Ark of the Covenant (Revelation 11:19). This undoubtedly refers to the heavenly Temple, to heaven's Holiest of All and God coming into activity for His people.

4. The antichristal beast blasphemes God, and His name, and His Tabernacle and them that dwell in heaven (Revelation 13:6). Again John is seeing the heavenly Tabernacle of which the earthly was only the passing shadow. He is seeing the prototype, the heavenly original of all earthly shadows.

5. In Revelation 15:5-8 the Temple of the Tabernacle of the Testimony in heaven is opened, and the smoke of God's glory filled the place. No man could enter into the Temple until the seven final plagues of the wrath of God had been poured out on the earth.
Once more we see it is the heavenly Temple in view of which the earthly Temple was but the shadow.

6. John heard the voice of God out of the Temple, from the throne of God, in the midst of great judgments, as seen in Revelation 16:1,17.

7. The final mention of a Temple is found in Revelation 21:22 where John saw no (material, earthly) Temple, ''for the Lord God Almighty (the Father), and the Lamb (the Son) are the Temple of it'' — the city of God. Certainly not a material Temple here.

Thus we have about sixteen references altogether in Revelation to this word ''Temple''. The word ''Tabernacle'' is also used several times.

Fourteen out of these sixteen usages speak of the heavenly Temple — NOT a material Temple, not to a earthly or literal Temple.

How comforting this was to the apostle John. He had been with Christ in His 3½ years ministry at the literal or actual Temple in Jerusalem. He had heard Christ's prediction concerning its destruction under Prince Titus and the Roman armies. He had lived to see its destruction in A.D. 70 in the seige of Jerusalem. And here he is on the isle of Patmos about 25 years or so later than the destruction of that Temple at Jerusalem.

Here in vision he saw the real Temple, the spiritual Temple, the heavenly Temple. Earthly Temples may be defiled, desecrated and destroyed, but there was a heavenly Temple that would never be destroyed. Earthly Temples may be seen and be temporal, but the heavenly Temple, unseen (except in the Spirit) is eternal (2 Corinthians 4:18).

We return once more now to the vision of the Temple in Revelation 11:1-2. Is it a literal/material Temple or is it a symbolic/spiritual Temple?

The question may well be asked: "Why when every other reference to 'temple' in Revelation is spiritual and heavenly is this one interpreted to be a material or literally rebuilt Temple at Jerusalem? Why when John's whole vision is of the spiritual Temple would he return to a material Temple which he knew had been destroyed in the past?

Nowhere do the New Testament writers ever speak of a rebuilt material Temple for the Jewish nation in the end-time before the coming of Christ.

The idea of Revelation 11:1-2 being a rebuilt Jewish Temple has arisen out of the misinterpretation of the notable "Seventy Weeks Prophecy" of Daniel 9:24-27. It is claimed that the antichrist is the one who makes a covenant with the Jews and then sets himself up as god in the middle of a seven year tribulation period. This setting up would be in "the temple of God", based on the 2 Thessalonians 2:1-4 passage, which has been dealt with in a previous chapter.

The whole concept of a rebuilt Temple is based upon this misunderstanding of the Seventy Weeks Prophecy, and the same misunderstanding of 2 Thessalonians 2:4 and Revelation 11:1-2.

There are only two verses in the whole of the New Testament that are purported to refer to a literal Temple to be rebuilt by the Jews.

However, did the New Testament writers, who had been under the whole of the Temple system and seen it destroyed ever speak of or look for a re-establishment of the Temple order again — in this end of the age or a future age? The writer thinks not!

What then is the interpretation of this Temple vision of Revelation 11:1-2?

Because of all that has been noted in this chapter, the writer believes that the Temple is symbolic and spiritual — that it speaks of the church, or the people of God.

(**Please note!** If the Jew does rebuild a Temple of some sort, whether on the site of the the Mosque of Omar, "The Dome of the Rock", or elsewhere, God will never ever again endorse such Old Covenant and Mosaic ritualism again. His glory-presence will never ever return to such.

The glory of God never has returned to any rebuilt material Temple since the destruction of Solomon's Temple under Babylon. Any rebuilt Temple will just be another Temple that the Lord will destroy at His second coming!)

John's vision, then, shows a threefold measuring taking place. John, representative of apostolic ministries, is given a measuring rod. The Jehovah-Angel told him to rise and measure three things:

* The Temple of God

* The Altar

* The Worshippers.

The outer court is left unmeasured and to be trodden under foot for 3½ years.

The spiritual truth — symbolized here may be understood, at least in measure, in the following manner.

The church, the people of God, will experience the measuring rod of God, the Scriptures, applied to them in these last days.

As all in the Old Testament measured up to the Divine standard, so will believers as living stones in God's church, His New Covenant Temple (Ephesians 4:9-16; 1 Corinthians 3:16; Ephesians 2:19-22). The church must come to the measure of the stature of the fulness of Christ, unto a perfect and mature man.

The altar of the prayer's and intercessions of the saints will also be measured, even as the golden altar in the Old Covenant Temple had Divine measurements upon it, as also the incense burnt thereon.

The people of God, as worshippers, will also be measured up, for the Father is seeking true worshippers, who shall worship Him in spirit and in truth (John 4:20-24).

However, sad to say, there will be those believers who are in the ''outer court'' relationship with the Lord. These fail to measure up to the Divine standard. Jesus said, if the salt had lost its savour, wherewith could it be salted. It was good for nothing but to be cast out, and to be trodden underfoot of men (Matthew 5:13).

So these believers are unmeasured, cast out, trodden under foot in that 3½ year period of time. They are ''outer court'' saints, who, though not losing their salvation, lose their life in the final period of tribulation in the end-times immediately prior to the coming of the Lord.

Whatever else may be the full significance of John's ''Temple-vision'', it is evident that some people are measured by the rod of God, and others are not measured, but trodden under foot.

Even if the vision was applied to Jewry, these truths are still truths!

Surely there is enough in this vision to challenge all believers to measure up to the Divine standard, the rod of God, Jesus Christ our Lord!

CHAPTER EIGHT

PROBLEMS OF A TRIBULATION TEMPLE

There hardly seems to be any need for this chapter to be written in the light of the previous several chapters. However, some additional points in the light of the present modern day situation confirm the difficulties in looking for a rebuilt material temple, especially that which some writers call "The Tribulation Temple".

As mentioned, some expositors hold that there will be a tribulation temple, as well as Ezekiel's in the Millennium. These expositors hold that the temple must be built for the Antichrist to enter into and declare himself as God. This he does by breaking a covenant he made with the Jews in the middle of the seventieth week of Daniel's notable prophecy.

However, in this view there are modern day serious problems and obstacles to the rebuilding of a temple of some sort for this tribulation period.

Thomas S. McCall in *Bibliotheca Sacra* (Jan. 1972, pp. 75-80), while holding that a temple will be rebuilt presents five major problems in the second of his series on the temple. We adapt and arrange these five obstacles in the following manner.

1. **Problem of the Dome of the Rock**

   Probably one of the most serious obstacles to the building or rebuilding of a temple is the Mohammedan Dome of the Rock. This is situated on the ancient temple site. The Dome would have to be removed before any temple could be built in its place.
   The Mohammedans built the Dome in A.D. 691 and the Dome has experienced reparations and restoration several times. During the Crusades, the Dome was used as a Christian shrine but then retaken. It is one of the most sacred places in the world to the Arabs. To remove it would create a holy war. Also the Israeli laws forbid the disturbance of any sacred or religious sites. Judaism would not permit a temple to be built elsewhere. The law of the Lord chose the place for His name to dwell (Deuteronomy 12:10-12). Some Jews suggest that an earthquake may be used to destroy the Dome of the Rock making way for the temple to be built.

2. **Problem of the Messiah-Builder**

   Theological attitudes of many in rabbinical Judaism also present further problems. Orthodox Jewish theology holds that the Messiah is the only one who can build the temple. They hold that the first temple was built by king Solomon and the second by the command of the prophets Haggai, Zechariah and Malachi. The third temple must be built by the king Messiah when he establishes the Kingdom again. They hold that the Urim and Thummin must be in use again and the Sanhedrin to confirm the temple sanctification. This is all done with the reunion of the twelve tribes of Israel.

   Jews even today will go to the wailing wall to pray and worship but not to the temple site. The rabbinical argument is that since the Messiah is the only one who can build the temple and the Messiah has not yet come, they cannot build the temple. Some Jewish leaders, however, believe the messianic age began with the creation of the new State of Israel and believe it is alright to build the temple.

3. **Problem of the Extinct Priesthood**

   Another problem presented by Thomas McCall has to do with the extinct Levitical priesthood. If a temple is built, then there must be a priesthood to minister in it. Where is that priesthood? It has been extinct for 1900 years. Where will it come from?
   Some Jews named Cohen (which means "priest" in Hebrew) claim to be the direct descendants of the high priestly house of Aaron. Those claiming to be in the priestly lineage do have certain

privileges and responsibilities in the Synagogues on the Sabbath. Some suggest a priesthood of some kind could arise out of such.

4. Problem of the Sacrificial System

Another obstacle to a rebuilt temple has to do with the animal sacrifices. Rabbis in the Reform movement believe the sacrifice of an animal and worshipping God through such is now unthinkable. Sacrifices are repudiated as "slaughter house religion".

Modern Jewry would not entertain the thought of re-instituting animal sacrifices as a system of approach to God. They see that God gradually educated Israel to see He did not want sacrifices and such meant nothing to Him. They teach that God wanted repentance, prayer, good deeds, justice and mercy. Jewry would certainly have to be greatly re-educated to even think of such a system, let alone the numerous sacrificial animals required to fulfil the law of offerings. This is certainly a great obstacle to a rebuilt temple.

5. Problem of Christian Theology

Besides the Mohammedan and Jewish obstacles to a rebuilt temple, Thomas McCall recognizes the problem of Christian Theology.

As seen in our previous chapters there are those schools of thought who believe that the temple will never be built, and should never be rebuilt. The sacrifices, feasts and ordinances of the Mosaic Covenant have been fulfilled by Christ and abolished at the cross, never to be restored in any temple any time.

Enough has been written without repeating the arguments again here.

Thus in these things we have Muslim, Jewish and Christian obstacles to consider in the rebuilding of a temple before or during the tribulation period. The writer's view has been expressed clearly in these Supplemental Chapters. Even if Jewry did rebuild a temple, God will never inhabit the same but will destroy it all even as previous temples.

God dwells not in temples made with hands, but He dwells in the high and lofty place and He also dwells in the humble heart.

CHAPTER NINE

THE TABERNACLE AND TEMPLE IN HEBREWS AND REVELATION

As in the Tabernacle of Moses, so in the Tabernacle of David and Temple of Solomon, the ultimate of all truth is seen in the Book of Revelation, "The Book of Ultimates". The Book of Hebrews interprets the Tabernacle of Moses, and the Tabernacle of David more particularly, while Revelation interprets both plus the Temple of the Lord.

Hebrews chapters 5-6-7-8-9-10 especially deal with the major details of the Tabernacle of the Lord, its covenant, its priesthood, its sacrifices and its sanctuary.

In Hebrews chapter 12:18-29 we have the final contrast and comparison of Moses on Mt Sinai relative to the Tabernacle of the Lord, and then the Tabernacle of David as pertaining to Mt Zion. One symbolized Law, the other Grace.

However, in Revelation both Tabernacles of Moses and David along with Solomon's Temple are seen in their related parts.

The emphasis in this chapter is upon the ultimate revelation as seen in the Book of Revelation, although the other Tabernacles are woven throughout.

Moses, David and John are all beholding the one and the same heavenly pattern of things, the original, heaven's prototype.

1. The Brazen Altar	Revelation 6:9-11
2. The Sea of Glass, or Molten Sea	Revelation 4:6; 15:2
3. The Outer Courts	Revelation 11:1-2
4. The Two Brazen Pillars	Revelation 3:12; 11:3
5. The Golden Candlesticks	Revelation 1-2-3
6. The High Priest in Garments of Glory & Beauty	Revelation 1
7. The Four Pillars of the Veil, or Four Doors	Revelation 4
8. The Priestly Courses of Twentyfour	Revelation 4-5. The 24 Elders
9. The Lamb of God	Revelation 5:6-8; 21:22
10. The Twelve Princes	Revelation 12:1
11. The 12,000 out of each Tribe, 144,000 Singers	Revelation 7:1-8; 14:1-5
12. Mt Zion, Harps, New Song, Tabernacle of David	Revelation 14:1-5
13. The Altar of Incense and High Priest	Revelation 8:1-4; 14:18
14. The Golden Censers of the 24 Priest Courses	Revelation 4-5
15. The Silver Trumpets	Revelation 8,9,10
16. The Twelve Loaves of Shewbread & Crowns	Revelation 4-5
17. The Ark of the Covenant	Revelation 11:19
18. The Cloud of Glory	Revelation 11:12
19. The Blood of Atonement	Revelation 12:11
20. The Cleansing of the Sanctuary — Atonement	Revelation 1-2-3
21. The Scapegoat into the Wilderness	Revelation 12
22. The Tabernacle and Temple in Heaven	Revelation 13:6; 15:1-4; 21:3
23. The Name or Seal of God	Revelation 14:1
24. The Temple Choir and Leaders	Revelation 5:8; 14:2
25. The Temple in Heaven	Revelation 14:15; 15:6,8
26. The King of Kings and Lord of Lords	Revelation 19:16
27. The Twelve Brazen Oxen holding the Sea	Revelation 21:14
28. The Two Thousand Baths	The Church Age
29. The One Thousand Baths — Millenium	Revelation 20:1-10
30. The Porch of Judgement	Revelation 20:11-15
31. The City of God, the Holy Oracle Foursquare	Revelation 21:22
32. The 12,000 Furlongs of the City	Revelation 21:16

33. The Wall 144 cubits   Revelation 21:17
34. The Floor of Gold, Streets of Gold   Revelation 21:18,21
35. The Precious Stones in the Walls   Revelation 21:19-21
36. Foundation in Mt Zion   Revelation 21. High Mountain
37. The Shekinah Glory and Light-Presence   Revelation 21:23; 22:5
38. The New Jerusalem City, Heavenly Zion   Revelation 21:2,10; 14:1
39. The Twelve Gates of the City   Revelation 21:21,25
40. The Ten Lavers of Brass, Judgment   Book of Judgments in Earth
41. The Throne of God — The Oracle   Revelation 22:1-3
42. The Name of God in the Forehead   Revelation 22:4
43. The Kings and Priests, Order of Melchisedek   Revelation 1:5,6; 5:9-10;20:6
44. The Glory in the Temple — none can minister   Revelation 15.

Truly the Bible is one progressive and unfolding drama of Divine revelation in God's plan of redemption for fallen man.

CHAPTER TEN

THE TABERNACLES OF MOSES AND DAVID, THE TEMPLE OF SOLOMON AND THE CHURCH

TABERNACLE, TEMPLE AND CHURCH

	OLD COVENANT DWELLINGS		NEW COVENANT DWELLINGS
Tabernacle of Moses	Tabernacle of David	Temple of Solomon	The Church & The City of God
1. Moses a Priest-King	David a King	Solomon a King	Believers Kings and Priests
2. Received pattern from the Lord Ex. 25:9,40; Heb. 8:5	Received revelation from the Lord 2 Sam. 6:17; 2 Chr. 1:4	Received pattern from David & the Lord. 1 Chr 28:11,12	Church is pattern from the Lord God's Temple. 1 Cor. 3:9,10; Heb. 8:2
3. Made by freewill offerings. Ex. 25:1-2	Dedicatory animal sacrifices. 1 Chr. 15:26	Made by freewill offerings. 1 Chr. 29:6,7	Sacrifice freely given. Rom. 12:1; 2 Cor. 9:7
4. Bezaleel given the wisdom for such by the Holy Spirit. Ex. 31:1-7	David a wise man	Solomon received wisdom for the work by the Holy Spirit. 1 Kings 5:12	Church built by wisdom of the Holy Spirit. 1 Cor. 12:1-12
5. Tabernacle of Lord Josh 22:19	Tabernacle of Praise 1 Chr. 16:1-6	Temple, House of the Lord 2 Chr. 5:14; Psa. 68:29	Church, Temple & House of God 1 Cor. 3:16
6. Boards fit together Ex. 26:15	A Tent woven together	Stones fit together 1 Kgs. 6:7	Members as lively stones together 1 Pet. 2:5; Eph. 2:20-22
7. Boards in silver sockets	Stone foundation Zion Isa. 28:16	Stones encased in silver	Members, redeemed, not with corruptible silver & gold. 1 Pet. 1:19-20
8. Boards overlaid with gold. Ex. 36:34	A Tent	Whole house overlaid with gold. 1 Kgs. 6:22	City pure gold. Rev. 21:18,21. Saints tried as gold. Job 23:10
9. Ark of Covenant and glory of God Staves in Ark	Ark of the Lord	Ark of God, Glory of God Staves taken out	God and Lamb are light and glory of city. Journeys over
10. Lord spoke from the mercy seat & cherubim. Ex. 25:17,22	Communion with the Lord Psa. 80:1; 99:1	Mercy seat in the Temple Cherubim & Olive Cherubim. 2 Chr. 5:5-10	Lord speaks by His Spirit through the Son. Eph. 2:13,18
11. The Vail. Ex. 26:33	No Vail — Within the Vail	The Vail. Matt. 27:51; 2 Chr. 3:14	Vail of the Body of Christ rent. Heb. 10:19,20. No vail now.
12. One Candlestick Ex. 25:31-37	Rod that Budded	Ten Candlesticks. 1 Kgs 6:49	The 7 Candlesticks — Local Churches Rev. 1:12,13,20
13. Table of Shewbread Lev. 24:5,6	Gold Pot of Manna	Ten Tables of Shewbread 1 Kgs. 7:10,48	Christ the Bread of Life John 6:35-48
14. Altar of Incense Ex. 37:25-28	Prayer & Praise. Harps, Singers 1 Chr. 15:27-28	Altar of Incense 2 Chr. 29:6,7	Prayers & Praises & Harps Rev. 5:8; 8:1-4
15. Tabernacle Door	Tent Door	Folding Doors	Outside the City of God
16. Outer Court Measured	No Court	Outer & Inner Courts No measurements recorded	Outer Court — Rev. 11:1-2 Unmeasured Court
17. Brazen Altar Brazen Laver	Cleansed by blood Washed in water	Brazen Altar — Blood Brazen Sea — Water	Blood and Water from His side John 19:33-34; 1 John 5:6-8
18. God dwells in the midst of His own. Ex. 25:8	Presence of the Lord Psa. 16	Glory Presence 1 Kgs. 6:12,13	Church God's dwelling place God & Lamb. Rev. 21-22
19. Where God puts His Name. Ex. 20:24; Dt. 12:5	Name in the Ark of God 2 Sam. 6:1,2.	Name of God in the Temple 1 Kgs 9:3	God's Name on His people Matt. 28:19-20; Rev. 3:12; Acts 2:34-36
20. Dedication of the Tabernacle Lev. 9:22-24; Ex. 40:33-35	Dedication of David's Tabernacle 1 Chr. 15-16	Dedication of the Temple 2 Chr. 7:1-3	Dedication of the Church Acts 2:1-4
21. Tabernacle of Witness Num. 1:50	Tabernacle of Praise & Worship	Testimony of Israel's Temple at Jerusalem. Psa. 122:4	Church believers His witnesses Acts 1:8
22. The Man-child of the Tabernacle, Moses. Heb. 11:23	The Man-child of the Tabernacle, David. 2 Sam. 7	The Man-child of the Temple, Jesus. Matt. 1:2-16	The Man-child of the Church Rev. 12:5
23. Holy Place $10 \times 10 \times 20 =$ 2000 cubits	No measurements	Contents of Molten Sea 2000 baths. 1 Kgs. 7:26	The Church Age, 2000 years
24. Most Holy Place = $10 \times 10 \times 10 = 1000$ cubits	No measurements	Contents of Molten Sea when full, 3000 baths. 2 Chr. 4:5	The Millennial Kingdom Rev. 20:2,4
25. Mt Sinai. Ex. 19:1-6	Mt Zion-. Isa. 28:16; 2 Sam. 5:4-7	Mt Moriah. Gen. 22; 2 Chr. 3:1	Mt Calvary, Mt of the Lord. Rev. 21:10

Kevin J. Conner/W.W. Patterson

CHAPTER ELEVEN

SIGNIFICANCE OF NUMBERS IN SCRIPTURE

Numbers or Figures, as used in the Word of God, are never used promiscuously, but take on Spiritual meaning and significance; and for the searcher after Truth there is to be found "the treasures of wisdom and knowledge" (Proverbs 25:2).

All creation is stamped with the "Seal of God" in numerics. God has made man himself a Creature of Time and therefore, a Creature of Number!

And it is consistent with the very Nature and Being of God that His Book, the Holy Bible, should be stamped with this same "Seal" — BIBLE NUMBERS!

God is consistent throughout His Book, and though the Bible was written by various men of God over different periods of time and generations, yet there is manifest throughout all the Book, the same marvellous meaning and harmony in the use of numbers. This begins in Genesis and flows through each book and consummates in Revelation. All this confirms the fact of Divine Inspiration (2 Timothy 3:16; 2 Peter 1:21).

Following are the basic principles of Interpretation of Numbers. If the student follows the same it will preserve from error or extremity.

1. The simple numbers of 1 through 13 have spiritual significance.

2. Multiples of these numbers, or doubling and tripling, carry basically the same meaning only intensifying the truth.

3. The first use of the number in Scripture generally conveys its spiritual meaning.

4. Consistence of interpretation. God is consistent, and what a number means in Genesis, it means through all to Revelation.

5. The spiritual significance is not always stated, but may be veiled, or hidden, or seen by comparison with other Scriptures.

6. Generally there is good and evil, true and counterfeit, God and Satanic, aspects in Numbers.

Not all of the following Numbers are to be found in the Tabernacle, but many of them are, or multiples of them are there. By constant reference to this section on the Spiritual Significance of Numbers, the reader will become familiar with the truth typified therein.

One: Number of God. Beginning, Source, Commencement, First.
(Genesis 1:1; Mark 6:33.)

Number of Compound Unity.
(Deuteronomy 6:4; "Echad," John 17:21-23; 1 Corinthians 12:1-14.)

Numerical One — "Yacheed." Only one.
(Genesis 22:2; Zechariah 12:10; John 3:16.)

Two: Number of Witness, Testimony. 1 with 1 = 2.
(John 8:17, 18; Deuteronomy 17:6; 19:15; Matthew 18:16; Revelation 11:2-4; Luke 9:30-32; 10:1.)

Number of Division, Separation. 1 against 1 = 2.
(Exodus 8:23; 31:18; Matthew 7; Genesis 19; Genesis 1:7-8; Matthew 24:40-41; Luke 17:34-36; Amos 3:3.)

Three:	Number of Godhead.
	(1 John 5:6-7; Deuteronomy. 17:6; Matthew 28:19; 12:40.)
	Number of Divine Completeness, Perfect Testimony.
	Tri-angle. (Ezekiel 14:14-18; Daniel 3:23-24; Leviticus 23.)
	Three Feasts. (Exodus 12:7; Exodus 3:6.)
Three & One-Half:	Number of Incompleteness. (James 5:17-18; Daniel 9:24-27.)
Four:	Number of Earth, Creation, World. Proceeds from three, dependent thereon.
	(Genesis 2:10; Leviticus 11:20-27; Mark 16:15; Jeremiah 49:36; Ezekiel 37:9; 1 Corinthians 15:39.)
	Four seasons, Four winds, Four corners of earth.
Five:	Number of Cross, Grace, Atonement, Life.
	(Genesis 1:20-23; John 10:10; Leviticus 1:5.)
	Five Offerings. Ephesians 4:11; Exodus 26:3,9,26,27,37; 27:1, 18; Exodus 13:18, Margin: Joshua 1:14, margin.)
	The 5 I wills of Satan.
	The 5 wounds of Jesus on the Cross.
	Note: five in the Tabernacle.
Six:	Number of Man, Beast, Satanic.
	(Genesis 1:26-31.)
	6th Creative Day. (Genesis 4:6.)
	Six generations, Cain.
	(1 Samuel 17:4-7; 2 Samuel 21:20; Numbers 35:15.)
	Time — 6000 years.
Seven:	Numbers of Perfection, Completeness. $3 + 4 = 7$.
	(Genesis 2:1-3.) 7th Day.
	(Hebrews 6:1-2; Jude 14; Joshua 6; Genesis 4:15; Leviticus 14:7,16,27,51.)
	Note the "Seven Times Prophecies."
	Number of Book of Revelation.
	(Revelation 1:4,12,20; 4:5; 5:1; 6; 8:2; 10:3; 12:3; 15:1-7; 17:9-10.)
	Seven is used about 600 times in the Bible.
Eight:	Number of Resurrection, New Beginning.
	Genesis 5. "And he died" 8 times.
	(Leviticus 14:10-11; Exodus 22:30.)
	(Genesis 17.) Circumcision, 8th day. Named.
	(1 Peter 3:20.) Noah, eighth person.
	(2 Peter 3:13.) New Heavens and New Earth, eighth day.
	Resurrection of Jesus. (Matthew 28:1-6; John 20:26.)
	Music — Octave.
	Numerical value of "Jesus", 888.
Nine:	Number of completeness, Finality, Fulness.
	Final of digits. $3 \times 3 = 9$.
	(Matthew 27:45.) Number of the Holy Spirit.

(Galatians 5:22; 1 Corinthians 12:1-12.) 9 Fruits, 9 Gifts.
(Genesis 7:1,2; Genesis 17:1.)
9 months for the "Fruit of the womb".

Ten: Number of Law, Order, Government, Restoration.
(Genesis 1.) "God said."
(Exodus 34:28; Daniel 2.) 10 Toes.
(Daniel 7.) 10 Horns. Ten Tables, Ten Lampstands, Ten
Lavers in Temple.

Number of Trial, Testing, Responsibility. $2 \times 5 = 10$.
(Matthew 25:1, 28; Luke 15:8; Luke 19:13-25; Numbers
14:22; Revelation 2:10; 12:3; Leviticus 27:32; Exodus 12:3.)

Eleven: Number of Incompleteness, Disorganization, Disintegration.
One beyond 10, yet one short of 12.
(Genesis 32:22. 11 sons. Genesis 37:9.)
(Matthew 20:6; Exodus 26:7.) Goat's hair, sin offerings.
(Deuteronomy 1:2.)
(Daniel 7.) The 11th "Little Horn".

Number of Lawlessness, Disorder. The Antichrist.

Twelve: Number of Divine Government, Apostolic Fulness.
(Genesis 49:28; Exodus 15:27; Exodus 28.)
The 12 Stones. (Exodus 24:4; 28:21; Matthew 19:28.)
(Revelation 12:1; Revelation 21:12,21; 22:2.)
12 Apostles, 12 oxen, 12 stones breastplate.
12 Loaves Shewbread.
Note: number 12 in "Holy City, Jerusalem".
(Revelation, chapters 21-22.)

Thirteen: Number of Rebellion, Backsliding, Apostacy.
(Genesis 14:4; Genesis 10:10) — Nimrod, 13th from Adam.
(Genesis 17:25; 1 Kings 11:6; Esther 9:1.)

Number of Double Portion.
(Genesis 48.) Ephraim, 13th Tribe.
Compare Judas and Paul.

Fourteen: Number of Passover. $2 \times 7 - 14$. Pauline Epistles equal 14.
(Exodus 12:6; Numbers 9:5; Genesis 31:41; Acts 27:27-33.)

Seventeen: Number of Spiritual Order. $10 + 7 = 17$.
(Genesis 1; Genesis 37:2; 1 Chronicles 25:5; Jeremiah 32:9;
Acts 2:9-11.)
"Walk with God." (Genesis 5:24; 6:9.) Enoch the 7th and
Noah the 10th.
(Genesis 7:11; 8:4.) Ark rested on the 17th Day.

Twenty-four: Number of Priestly Courses, Governmental Perfection.
$2 \times 12 = 24$. Numerous 24's in Solomon's Temple.
(Joshua 4:2-9; 4:20; 1 Kings 19:19; 1 Chronicles 24:3-5; 1
Chronicles 25.)
(Revelation 4:4-10.) 4 Living Ones (24 wings), 24 Elders.

Tabernacle boards 48, Silver Sockets 96.
Note in the "Holy City, Jerusalem" (Revelation, chapters 21, 22.)

Thirty: Number of Consecration, Maturity for Ministry.
(Numbers 4:3; Genesis 41:46; 2 Samuel 5:4; Luke 3:23; Matthew 26:15.)

Forty: Number of Probation, Testing. Closing in Victory or Judgment.
(Numbers 13:25; 14:33; Matthew 4:2; Acts 1:3; Exodus 34:27-28; Ezekiel 4:6; Acts 7:30; 1 Kings 19:4-8.)

Forty-two: Number of Tribulation. (Revelation 11:2,3; Daniel 7:23-25.)

Fifty: Number of Pentecost, Liberty, Freedom, Jubilee.
(Exodus 26:5,8; Leviticus 23:24-25; 25:10-11; Acts 2:1-4; 1 Kings 18:4,13; 2 Kings 2:7; Numbers 8:25.)

Seventy: Number prior to increase.
(Genesis 11:26; Exodus 1:5; Genesis 46:27; Numbers 11:25; Exodus 15:27; Luke 10:1; Exodus 24:1,9.)

Seventy-Five: Number of Separation, Cleansing, Purification.
(Genesis 12:4; 8:5-6; Daniel 12:5-13; Exodus 27:1.)

One-Hundred-Twenty: Number of End of all Flesh, Beginning Life in the Spirit.
$3 \times 4 = 120$.
(Genesis 6:3; Deuteronomy 34-7; Leviticus 25;)
$120 \times 50 = 6000$ years of time.
(2 Chronicles 3:4; 7:5; 5:12; Acts 1:5.)

One-Hundred-Forty-Four: Number of God's Ultimate in Creation $12 \times 12 = 144$.
(Revelation 21:17; 1 Chronicles 25:7; Revelation 7:1-6; 14:1-3.) 288 Singers in Temple, $12 \times 24,000 = 288,000$.
(1 Chronicles 24-27.)

One-Hundred-Fifty-Three: Number of Revival and the Elect. (John 21:11); $9 \times 17 = 153$.

Three-Hundred: Number of Faithful Remnant.
(Genesis 5:22; 6:15; Judges 8:4; 15:4.)
Note, Three Entrances to Tabernacle, 3×100 cubits.

Four-Hundred: Number of Affliction, Suffering. (Genesis 15:13.)
$400 \times 360 = 144,000$ days of suffering of the seed of Abraham.
400 baths in ten lavers. 400 promegranates on Pillars.

Six-Hundred-Sixty-Six: Number of Antichrist, Satan, the Damned.
Triplicate. 666. (Daniel 3; 1 Samuel 17; Daniel 7.)
(Revelation 13:18. Connected with Number 11.)
(Revelation 14:9-11.)

CHAPTER TWELVE

BIBLIOGRAPHY OF TEMPLE SCRIPTURES

Recommended Textbook *"Harmony of Samuel, Kings and Chronicles"*, William Day Crockett.

A. **The Three Days Pestilence**

1.	David's Sin in Numbering the People	2 Samuel 24:1-9	1 Chronicles 21:1-6
2.	The Choice of Punishments	2 Samuel 24:10-14	1 Chronicles 21:7-13
3.	The Pestilence	2 Samuel 24:15-17	1 Chronicles 21:14-17
4.	David Purchases Araunah's Threshing floor and Erects an Altar	2 Samuel 24:18-25	1 Chronicles 21:18-30

B. **Preparations for the Building of the Temple**

1.	The Temple Site Chosen	2 Chronicles 2:1
2.	David's Plan and Foresight	1 Chronicles 22:2-5
3.	David's Charge to Solomon	1 Chronicles 22:6-16
4.	David's Charge to the Princes	1 Chronicles 22:17-19

C. **The National Convention**

1.	The Convention Summoned	1 Chronicles 23:1-2
2.	Date Concerning the Officials Gathered	
	a. The Number and Distribution of the Levites	1 Chronicles 23:3-5
	b. The 24 Houses of the Levites	1 Chronicles 23:6-23 1 Chronicles 24:20-30
	c. The Duties of the Levites	1 Chronicles 23:24-32 1 Chronicles 24:30-31
	d. The 24 Courses of the Priests	1 Chronicles 24:1-19
	e. The 24 Courses of the Singers	1 Chronicles 25:1-31
	f. The Courses of the Doorkeepers	1 Chronicles 26:1-19
	g. The Officers of the Treasuries of God's House	1 Chronicles 26:20-28 1 Chronicles 26:20-28
	h. The Officers & Judges "For the Outward Business"	1 Chronicles 26:29-32
	i. The Twelve Captains of the Army	1 Chronicles 27:1-15
	k. The Overseers of the King's Treasuries & Possessions	1 Chronicles 27:25-31
	l. The Officers of State	1 Chronicles 27:32-34
3.	The Convening into an Assembly of the Secular Officials Gathered	1 Chronicles 28:1
4.	The Public Acts in National Convention	
	a. David Causes Solomon to be made King (First Time)	1 Chronicles 23:1
	b. David's Address	1 Chronicles 28:2-8
	c. David directs Solomon concerning the building of the Temple	1 Chronicles 28:9-21
	d. Contribution of David & the Officials for the Temple building	1 Chronicles 29:1-9
	e. David's Thanksgiving and Prayer	1 Chronicles 29:10-19
5.	Close of the Convention	1 Chronicles 29:20-33

D. Solomon's Building of the Temple

1. Solomon Anointed King the Second Time (After all rebellion & enemies subdued)		1 Chronicles 29:22-25
2. Spiritual Condition of Solomon & his Kingdom	1 Kings 3:1-2	
3. Solomon's Sacrifice at Gibeon	1 Kings 3:4	2 Chronicles 1:2-6
4. Solomon's Dream & Prayer for Wisdom	1 Kings 3:5-15	2 Chronicles 1:7-13
5. Judgment of the Harlots	1 Kings 3:16-28	

E. Solomon in all His Glory — Temple Building Preparations

1. The League with Hiram, King of Tyre	1 Kings 5:1-12 1 Kings 7:13-14	2 Chronicles 2:1,3-16
2. Solomon's Levy of Labourers	1 Kings 5:13-18	2 Chronicles 2:2,17,18

F. The Building of the Temple

1. Commencement of the Temple	1 Kings 6:1	2 Chronicles 3:1,2
2. God's Promise to Solomon	1 Kings 6:11-13	
3. Dimensions of the Temple	1 Kings 6:2	2 Chronicles 3:3
4. Materials of the Temple	1 Kings 6:7,9,22	2 Chronicles 3:5-7
5. The Porch	1 Kings 6:3	2 Chronicles 3:4
6. The Windows	1 Kings 6:4	
7. The Stories	1 Kings 6:5,6,3,10	2 Chronicles 3:9
8. The Most Holy Place	1 Kings 6:16-22	2 Chronicles 3:8,9
9. The Cherubim	1 Kings 6:23-28	2 Chronicles 3:10-13
10. The Veil		2 Chronicles 3:14
11. The Walls	1 Kings 6:15,29	2 Chronicles 3:7
12. The Floor	1 Kings 6:15.30	
13. The Doors	1 Kings 6:31-35	
14. Completion of the Temple	1 Kings 6:9,14,37, 38	

G. The Making of the Vessels Pertaining to the Temple

1. Hiram, The Artisan of Tyre	1 Kings 7:13,14	
2. The Two Pillars	1 Kings 7:15-22	2 Chronicles 3:15-17
3. The Altar of Brass		2 Chronicles 4:1
4. The Molten Sea	1 Kings 7:23-26,39	2 Chronicles 4:2-6,10
5. The Ten Bases	1 Kings 7:27-37	
6. The Ten Lavers	1 Kings 7:38,39	2 Chronicles 4:6
7. The Courts	1 Kings 6:36	2 Chronicles 4:9
8. Summary of Hiram's Work in Brass	1 Kings 7:40-47	2 Chronicles 4:11-18
9. Summary of the Golden Vessels	1 Kings 7:48-50	2 Chronicles 4:7,8, 19-22

    a. The Golden Incense Altar
    b. The Golden Tables of Shewbread
    c. The Golden Candlesticks
    d. Attendant Vessels

10. Completion of the Work	1 Kings 7:51	2 Chronicles 4:11

H. The Dedication of the Temple

1. Removal of the Tabernacle of David & its contents from Zion to the Temple	1 Kings 8:1-11	2 Chronicles 5:2-14

2.	Solomon's Opening Address & Blessing	1 Kings 8:12-21	2 Chronicles 6:1-11
3.	Solomon's Dedicatory Prayer		
	a. God's Constant Care Invoked	1 Kings 8:22-30	2 Chronicles 6:12-21
	b. When an Oath is made at the Altar	1 Kings 8:31,32	2 Chronicles 6:22,23
	c. In Defeat	1 Kings 8:33,34	2 Chronicles 6:24,25
	d. In Drought	1 Kings 8:35,36	2 Chronicles 6:26,27
	e. In Famine and Pestilence	1 Kings 8:37-40	2 Chronicles 6:28-31
	f. For the Stranger	1 Kings 8:41-43	2 Chronicles 6:32,33
	g. In Battle	1 Kings 8:44.45	2 Chronicles 6:34,35
	h. In Captivity	1 Kings 8:46-53	2 Chronicles 6:36-39
	i. Close of Prayer		2 Chronicles 6:40-42
4.	Solomon's Closing Benediction	1 Kings 8:54-61	
5.	The Divine Confirmation		2 Chronicles 7:1-3
6.	The Sacrifice & Public Festival (Feast of Tabernacles)	1 Kings 8:62-66	2 Chronicles 7:4-10
7.	God's Second Appearance to Solomon	1 Kings 9:1-9	2 Chronicles 7:11-22
8.	Solomon's Worship	1 Kings 9:25	2 Chronicles 8:12-16
9.	The Visit of the Queen of Sheba	1 Kings 10:1-13	2 Chronicles 9:1-12

BIBLIOGRAPHY

1. Baxter, J. Sidlow, (1972) *Explore the Book*, Michigan, Zondervan Publishing House.

2. Bunyan, John, (1969) *Solomon's Temple Spiritualized,* Swengal, Pa., Reinver Publications.

3. Conner, Kevin J, (1976) *The Tabernacle of David*, Blackburn, Victoria, Acacia Press.

4. Conner, Kevin J., (1980) *The Feasts of Israel*, Blackburn, Victoria, Acacia Press.

5. Conner, Kevin J., (1975) *The Tabernacle of Moses,* Blackburn, Victoria, Acacia Press.

6. Conner, Kevin J., (1980) *Interpreting the Symbols and Types*, Blackburn, Victoria, Acacia Press.

7. Crockett, William Day, (1971) *A Harmony of Samuel, Kings and Chronicles*, Michigan, Baker.

8. Fausett, A. R., (1963) *Bible Dictionary,* Michigan, Zondervan Publishing House.

9. Fereday, W. W., *Solomon and His Temple*, Kilmarnock, John Ritchie Ltd. Great Britain.

10. Larkin, Clarence, *Dispensational Truth*, Philadelphia, Clarence Larkin Est. 1920.

11. Orr, James, (1915) *The International Standard Bible Encyclopaedia*, Wilmington, Delaware, Associated Publishers and Authors, 1915 Edition.

12. Raymond, E., (1979) *King Solomon's Temple.* Thousand Oaks, California, Artisan Sales.

13. Smith, Arthur E., (1956) *The Temple & Its Teaching*, Chicago, Moody Press.

14. Unger, Merrill F., (1972) *Unger's Bible Dictionary*, Chicago, Moody Press.

15. Williams, George,, (1976) *The Student's Commentary*, Michigan, Kregel Publications.

Other Resources Available by Kevin J. Conner

Kevin J. Conner

The Epistle to The Romans

The Book of Acts

Church in the New Testament

Interpreting the Book of Revelation

Interpreting the Symbol & Types

Feast of Israel

Foundations of Christian Doctrine

Mystery Parables of the Kingdom

The Tabernacle of Moses

The Tabernacle of David

Table Talks

Kevin J. Conner & Ken Malmin

The Covenants

Interpreting the Scriptures

New Testament Survey

Old Testament Survey